Foxfire 6

Foxfire 6

shoemaking, gourd banjos and songbows,
one hundred toys and games,
wooden locks, a water-powered sawmill, and
other affairs of just plain living

edited with an introduction by
ELIOT WIGGINTON

Anchor Books
Anchor Press / Doubleday
Garden City, New York
1980

Eliot Wigginton, who started *Foxfire* magazine with his ninth- and tenth-grade English classes in 1966, still teaches high school in the Appalachian Mountains of North Georgia and, with his students, guides the activities of The Foxfire Fund, Inc. His students have now expanded their efforts to include not only the production of the *Foxfire* magazine and books, but also the creation of television shows for their community cable-TV station, a series of record albums of traditional music, and a series of investigations into the environmental and political affairs of their community.

Foxfire 6, like its predecessors, has been drawn from articles first published in *Foxfire* magazine. Subscriptions to the magazine are $8.00 per year and may be obtained by writing to The Foxfire Fund, Inc., Rabun Gap, Georgia 30568. The Anchor Press edition is the first publication of *Foxfire 6* in book form. It is published simultaneously in hard and paper covers.
Anchor Press edition: 1980

Library of Congress Cataloging in Publication Data
Main entry under title:

Foxfire 6.

Includes "Cumulative index for Foxfire 4, Foxfire 5, and Foxfire 6."
1. Georgia—Social life and customs.   2. Country life—Georgia.
3. Handicraft—Georgia.   4. Appalachian Mountains, Southern—Social life and customs.
5. Country life—Appalachian Mountains, Southern.
6. Handicraft—Appalachian Mountains, Southern.
I. Wigginton, Eliot.   II. Foxfire.
F291.2.F624   975

ISBN: 0-385-15272-8 Paperback

Library of Congress Catalog Card Number 79-6541

First Edition

CONTENTS

This book is dedicated to those people who, in many different ways, embrace and celebrate their own cultural inheritance, recognizing in it the real wealth and strength of this nation.

And to Suzy

INTRODUCTION

I constantly find myself in awkward situations. Among the most uncomfortable are those in which I have accepted an invitation to work as a consultant for a day or two in a public school. Suddenly there I am, standing in front of a group of teachers who have every reason to expect me to tell them either that they are doing something wrong, or that they should be doing something else in addition to the heavy load they're already carrying. Why else would I be there? And this, given the fact that I have never seen any of them at work with their students, have no idea how they operate, or what specific daily problems they face. You see why it's an awkward situation. . . .

Such visits have given me the chance, however, to see firsthand a number of other public schools besides the one in which I teach. They've helped me grow. Sometimes I've developed lasting friendships with colleagues in those schools. And always we trade notes—which of us has the better principal, lunchroom, or working conditions—and combat stories.

Sometimes, on these visits, I'm asked for advice. I usually refuse, simply because I don't know the situation well enough (and wouldn't if I stayed a month). But recently, over coffee, a new friend and I sat down and half in jest, half seriously, posed the following:

Accept for the moment the fact that because there are too many variables at work, public schools will never be perfect learning environments. Accept also the fact that despite all the voices raised against them, and despite all the financial chaos, they are here to stay.

Now draw up a list of observations or principles or truths—say, five or six—that could be used as yardsticks to measure how any given public school is doing, or how far it has to go, given the potentials and limitations that exist within that institutional framework.

We drew up a list.

Over the next few months, as I became more and more convinced that this idea of a checklist was a workable notion, I refined it, and I present it here, realizing with some embarrassment that most of these principles are old truths "rediscovered" again and again, but realizing also that most schools still have a long way to go toward implementing them, and so they bear repeating. The 950-pupil consolidated public high school in which I teach, for example, has not, and undoubtedly will not, move wholesale to translate a list like this into action. None of the schools in which I have visited will either. I guess that's to be expected. However, after fourteen years of continuous, daily trial-and-error and observation inside the public-school system, I know that these principles *can* be recognized in that system, and I believe that *the extent* to which they have been recognized and acted upon by any public school is the extent to which that institution is becoming truly and sensitively responsive to the needs of the students and the communities it serves.

First: Every detail in the physical environment of a school, no matter how small, matters and contributes in a cumulative way to the overall tone.

Some of these details are so minor as to be unnoticeable by the ordinary observer, but in their own small way, each makes a difference that can lead to a sense of, *"Something's* right (or wrong) here, even though I don't know what it is."

Recently I taught an experimental course of five students. Because there were no classrooms available during that period, we "floated" from day to day from one available space to another. One of the rooms we used from time to time was a small windowless conference room that was almost womblike in its isolation from the rest of the school environment. Every time those students and I were in that room, their behavior was significantly different from their norm. It was almost as though they were lobotomized. Only through great effort were we able to break through that listless, unemotional trance and carry on some form of discussion. In another environment— one with windows and space and air—they were completely different people. We all recognized the effect the conference room had on us, but none of us was able to pinpoint exactly what was happening there. Somehow the combination of colors, windowless walls, isolation, and the incessant buzzing of the fluorescent lighting transformed us in a noticeable way. Had I been assigned to that space for the entire quarter and not been able to observe those same five students in different environments, I might have assumed that both the course and the students were lost causes—an experiment not worth repeating. How many other teachers struggle with students daily and assume the problems they are having are due to the students, or themselves, and forget the impact of environment on behavior?

On a more obvious level, classrooms with desks (often covered with graffiti) bolted to the floor, bathrooms with doorless stalls, shared locker spaces, indifferent food served indifferently, raucous bell systems, intercoms used so inconsiderately that every activity in the school is shattered by full-volume announcements like, "Teachers, pardon the interruption, but Susan Jones' mother is here to take her to a dentist appointment," all in fortresslike institutional structures with endless cement block halls and bulldozed, paved surroundings devoted more to efficient crowd control and total lack of privacy (read "trouble") than anything else—all such elements conspire to create an atmosphere that is alien, dehumanizing, intimidating, and filled with an undercurrent of frustration.

In one high school I visited recently, the signal to change classes was a deafening air-raid siren. In our own school, it is a long, piercing whine that is impossible to talk above and that goes through one's head with an intensity that almost translates into physical pain. Why any manufacturer would be instructed—or allowed—to create such a device, and why any humane architect would patronize such a company, is beyond me, especially considering the fact that it's not really needed at all. (How many colleges or universities, for example, can you name that use a bell system?)

Sometimes the physical environment so conspires against certain kinds of activities that they are simply eliminated from the life of the school. Our organization has actively sponsored concerts and plays, but we are about to give up in despair, not because the students don't enjoy such events, but because such events must be held in a gym that doubles as an auditorium. The space itself is simply not a workable combination for more reasons than I could list here, foremost among them being impossible acoustics and demonic seating arrangements.

Despite the fact that such buildings are built, there are plenty of solutions available once the problems with them are realized. The possibility of solutions, however, must be seen as a series of priceless opportunities to bring the second principle into play.

Second: Students must be allowed a measure of control over that environment, and a degree of decision-making responsibility within it. If this is ignored, the natural and healthy tendency students have to exert some influence over their surroundings manifests itself in ways the teachers and administrators find unacceptable, and much of their energy is spent in pitched battles with students over "classroom management" and in sleuthing out those responsible for vandalism and litter. The amount of "antisocial" behavior in a school is often directly proportional to the amount of hostility students feel toward an institution that is not responding to their needs as human beings.

The most obvious place to begin is at the classroom level. In most high-school classrooms, the norm, except for the blackboard and bulletin board, is totally blank walls and bland colors. (Walk into the only environment a child can call his or her own—usually a bedroom at home—and compare. If a child of mine actually preferred an environment with no color, nothing on the walls, no piles of books and posters and baseball gloves, and projects in progress, I would view that as cause for some alarm.)

At this classroom level, confronted with a teacher who maintains a filing cabinet full of laminated and dated bulletin-board displays ("This one about commas goes up at Halloween each year"), we may have a problem. Such a teacher may already have settled into a psychological rut that has, for example, manifested itself in lecture notes used year after year, and it may be too late for change.

But if it's not, some wonderful and appropriate things can happen. In our classroom, when students wanted to fill the walls with photographs, letters, documents, county maps, and quilts—all items appropriate to our work—they were given permission by the principal as long as they did not stick anything to or mount anything on the walls that might damage the paint. Undaunted, they eased up several of the suspended ceiling's tiles, hung long wooden dowel rods from wires they attached to the steel girders above, replaced the tiles undamaged, and hung the quilts and display panels from the rods. The walls remain unscarred.

Later, needing additional work, storage, and display spaces, they designed and built other pieces of classroom furniture such as cabinets, shelves, and counters, and set them into place. The ones not used as work spaces are now covered with pieces of folk art, tools, items that contacts have made for us, and supplies.

Most recently, deciding that the microscopic darkroom the school's architect had designed was unworkable, they designed and built a new darkroom inside our classroom with the help of the school custodian, who jury-rigged the necessary plumbing. The only requirement placed on the students by the principal and school board was that the new room conform in every way to the existing fire codes, thus giving students an opportunity to deal with yet another challenge. The outside walls of the darkroom are covered, floor to ceiling, with four-by-eight-foot sheets of bulletin-board material, thus tripling our space for exhibits of students' photographs and the like. While some classrooms nearby have sustained heavy damage from random student vandalism, ours has not suffered at all. The room is ablaze with color and life and energy, and has become a *working environment* that accurately reflects the amount of energy and commitment that is expended there.

Outside the classroom, students in our school have gotten permission to create at least one new mural a year to paint onto the blank walls in the commons and entrance areas. The principal was a little dubious about the first mural until we talked a professional artist into helping out and promised the principal final approval of the design. Three are completed now, one measuring eighteen by twenty-two feet, and another is under way. This series of low-cost, creative efforts can go on for years, will involve hundreds of students over those years, and will totally change the tone of those bland, impersonal spaces.

In a large urban school I visited recently, students in the horticulture and biology classes had voted to "adopt" a large outdoor gathering area as part of their classroom work. There they created a jewel of a park with gravel walks, wooden benches, and huge planters, which they keep filled with potted flowering plants, rotating them in season. On the fall day I was there, thousands of chrysanthemums of all colors were just about to burst into bloom.

In another school, as part of the curriculum, students in the home-economics classes work with their teacher and the dietician to create the school's menus, and then rotate for a week at a time through the kitchen to help prepare and serve those meals and make them as attractive and palatable as possible, using their imaginations to find ways around the budget they have to work with, and other institutional restrictions.

Allowing students to have a constructive impact on their surroundings in ways like the above is important, but it is not nearly enough. They must also be entrusted with the power to make real decisions that affect far more than the physical environment.

For example, in the magazine classes Margie Bennett and I conduct (out of which this book came), the students decide individually all details concerning their own articles (for which they do all the interviews, take and print all the photographs, etc.), and collectively decide such items as what the magazine's cover design and colors will be—seemingly mundane decisions, but for students who have never had experience in making such choices, enormously important. These experiences become part of their normal English curriculum and part of their daily routine. The same pattern is followed in the other classes we sponsor where students produce record albums, radio shows, television shows, active and passive solar collectors, and public exhibitions of photography. Their decisions affect not only the final product, but also such things as the specific budgets those classes will operate under given the financial resources available to us at any given time.

On the organizational level, my staff and I meet early every Monday morning to look at our organization. Sometimes we talk about specific students and strategies for meeting their needs. We also outline all things that need to be decided that week. Students are encouraged to attend the meeting.

That same day, during each period, the various Foxfire classes come together in one room to discuss each issue and vote. The votes are carried forward, cumulatively, through the school day. At the end of the day, the votes determine the decision. Those students who want to be involved in carrying it out begin to do so.

In a recent week, for example, among other things, students discussed and voted on:

• The disposition of an automobile donated to our organization. (They voted to sell it through sealed bids and split the profits between the school's beautification fund and Foxfire's scholarship fund. Students split up into teams to draft the radio and newspaper announcements. The car was sold and the money deposited in the funds the students had dictated.)

• Our response to a weekly regional newspaper that had reprinted material and photographs from *The Foxfire Book* on its front page without our permission and without credit to the source in any form. (The students voted to draft a letter to the publisher demanding an apology in print in the next edition of the paper. The letter was drafted by one of the classes and sent, and the apology appeared on the paper's front page. A subscriber to our magazine who brought the matter to our attention was thanked by another team of students.)

• Our response to a T-shirt manufacturer who had taken photographs of some of our contacts directly from the pages of our books and reproduced them on a line of T-shirts he was distributing throughout our region. (The students voted to sue the manufacturer and are now involved in the suit.)

The rule of thumb we use, and one that will probably evolve in time as we get better at, and more self-confident with, this whole business, is to turn over to the students all decisions concerning our organization that they themselves can be responsible for and implement to completion. This they do in an atmosphere where they learn to weigh the possible consequences of such decisions for themselves and the organization, and where mistakes that are made are accepted as new opportunities to learn—not as opportunities to condemn the students who made them.

There are parallels here that can be extended to any school as a whole. Each day, in every school in the nation, scores of decisions are made by the principal and assistant principal that affect the movements and activities of students within. Often these decisions are made by adults *not* because they refuse to believe students could make them just as well, but because it is so much more expedient to make them themselves. And they're right. But one of our mandates is to help students learn to make responsible choices, and the fact is that schools, as microcosms of society, can be perfect learning laboratories for building these skills. It is somewhat less convenient, but schools built for the convenience of adults are often schools where little learning takes place.

I am not advocating—as in some alternative schools—that students make *all* decisions, including such things as whether or not a teacher should be fired. That would place an impossibly heavy load on students' shoulders. Nor am I advocating the situation where students are allowed to make token, sham decisions of no consequence as a means of tricking them into believing they have some "say" in order to help keep them under control. I am advocating real responsibility of the best type that *is possible* within a normal public school, which is, granted, a controlled situation where adults will always be "in charge," but where they can also be regarded by their students as allies and mentors and guides rather than the opposite.

How could the process work? Some schools have experimented

creatively and well with the idea of student councils. A problem, of course, is that many student councils are not regarded as truly representative of, or responsible to, their classmates, and so elections degenerate into popularity contests and, knowing this, schools respond by diluting the responsibilities the student councils have to the point where the whole situation becomes even more of a joke. The members are allowed to plan the junior-senior dance, but little else.

A better, and certainly more lively, instructive, and interesting system would be for each homeroom to elect, on a rotating basis, a representative who would attend the weekly teachers' meetings. Substitutes could take the place of representatives who could not make a given meeting due to illness or other such conflicts. At these meetings, in addition to normal business (and, frankly, I can't think of a meeting I've been to in recent memory where something was discussed that students should not be allowed to hear, but they could always be excused if such matters arose), the principal and assistant principal would outline those items that needed student-body action. The students in attendance would ask as many questions as necessary to make sure they could present all the facts and ramifications to their homerooms as accurately as possible. Then, during homeroom periods each morning, the student representatives would present the issues one by one, lead the discussions, and take the vote. The homeroom teachers would be there to help students over snags. Votes from the homerooms would all be tallied by student groups as they were reported, and decisions, as completed, would be carried to the front office for announcement and implementation. The student newspaper would regularly report all tallies, along with needed clarifications and explanations.

What decisions would be made? An enlightened principal could easily get an idea simply by listing all decisions made in the course of one week at the administrative level, and then looking at the list. Much of it would consist of business concerning pep rallies, club meetings, test schedules, lunch schedules, disciplinary restrictions, smoking-area regulations, and the like, all of which lend themselves easily to student input. That's where they'd start. And what about decisions such as whether to use a bell system at all? Or the extent to which classes could be interrupted by such intrusions as intercom announcements? Those, too, should be subject to student input. And as the process became established, students themselves would begin to identify other areas that would justify student choice. In fact, once a certain public-school mind set is overcome, it becomes increasingly difficult to identify issues and decisions in which the students should *not* be directly involved. Excuses for not involving them even in matters as serious as strategies for dealing with teen-age pregnancy or alcohol and drug abuse begin to sound hollow and defensive.

The fact is that students in possession of accurate information are far more skillful, responsible, creative, and moral in making and carrying out decisions than most adults are willing to admit. Schools trying this for the first time sometimes give up in frustration from a feeling that the students aren't being responsible enough— that the students are "playing with them." The schools give up too easily. Invariably, these are schools where, usually for good reason, the students refuse to believe that their collective voice is going to be taken seriously. They are playing with the school because they feel that the school is, once again, playing with them. It takes time and patience—a slow forging of atypical alliances between young people and adults—and it's worth every ounce of energy it takes.

Third: All courses, to the fullest extent possible, should be experiential—rooted in the real. (At this point, every teacher who's forgotten should review Dale's Cone of Experience in that dusty educational philosophy text.)

A friend of mine has a young son who just completed a ninth-grade unit in botany as part of his science requirement. Not once did the class go outdoors. Not once did the teacher bring plant materials in. The entire course was taught from a text, undoubtedly without passion or conviction. The fact that any teacher in 1980, given all we know about education, would be allowed to—or even choose to—teach a unit like *botany* in that fashion is grounds for parent/student revolt.

Teachers must constantly ask themselves how material they are covering can be brought to life and application in the real world for the benefit of the students involved and for the ultimate benefit of the larger society they will enter. If teachers cannot, or will not, make those linkages, the course should probably not be taught at all.

Let me give one example.

One of my favorite students brought along an American history text during a recent trip to speak at an educational conference. He was studying for a test. One of the sections he had to learn concerned Spanish monasteries that were established during an early period in our history for the purpose of converting Indians to Christianity and to the Spanish way of life and to loyalty to the Crown. Now, the course over, that student tells me that he remembers nothing of that section of the book; he only remembers the motel room in which he studied it. The teacher completely missed a priceless opportunity to open up that piece of history and bring it to life through numerous real-world linkages that the students could have researched firsthand: the implicit arrogance, for example, of the missionary's calling, and the moral dilemma that must be posed by the imposition of one value system on another; to say nothing of the work of all agents of cultural change at work on that student's family, community, and throughout the Appalachian region yesterday and today; and the real—sometimes positive, sometimes negative—effect such people and organizations have on any indigenous group of people anywhere. Weeks could easily have been spent following that aspect of our history, and the fact that many of the events of the past have resulted from the desire of individuals or groups to exert dominance or influence over others. It has gone on throughout the past, it is going on today (students can witness that process in any peer group and community in this nation, and by extension come to a more focused understanding even of national and world affairs), and it will continue through all the tomorrows we have left.

How will that student deal with that fact as an adult? When confronted by injustice, for example, where will he draw his lines? To what extent will he shrug his shoulders and rationalize events and turn away, or stand for what he knows is a more moral and humane course of action in the world? He came no closer to a decision of any sort in that history course—in fact, he never saw how the material his class was covering applied to him at all—but he should have. Why else take history?

It has been shown through projects all over this country that experiential components can be built into every subject area of the curriculum, not in place of the academic aspects of the course or the basic skills, but as one of the few ways through which students master those skills and internalize them by having the chance to put them to work. The preparation of this book as a part of the language-arts offering at our school is only one small illustration of the kinds of low-cost, experiential options available to public schools today.

Alarm at declining test scores and student competence is one of the reasons some alternative schools are founded. However, some with which I am familiar turn their backs on what we know about the potential of experience, and try to correct the situation (as do many public high schools) by "bearing down" and increasing the amount and the intensity of drill and memorization. Demanding academic rigor is justifiable, but reaching for it through numerous new kits, packages, drills, and tests usually defeats the purpose, creating, instead, students who simply respond more quickly to certain stimuli—like Pavlov's dogs—but who know not a whit more about that world outside the school, the use of those skills within the world, or learning as an independent and lifelong passion. What we too often get for our money is a better class of robots.

Think of the role of the school as being threefold (leaving aside the role of sports):

• To develop the basic skills and basic academic knowledge of students.

• To develop and nourish the more esoteric appreciations and understandings—the arts, the humanities, the areas of human artistic and moral sensitivity and concern for life on this globe—and the ways to express those appreciations and concerns through action.

• To develop and foster the qualities students must have for success in any career—curiosity, self-confidence and self-esteem, patience and persistence, vision, leadership, wisdom, and the ability to think creatively, to analyze and problem-solve, to make humane and wise decisions, and to act on them.

Now look at your school. If it's like most in this country, it pays only minimal attention to the last two (it can be argued, in fact, that many schools not only do not nourish these areas, but also somehow accomplish the *opposite* with the majority of their students) and reserves most of its energy for the first. The success ratio? Look at the fact that students have language arts for *twelve years* in most public-school systems. Now ask any college or university why it still requires its freshman remedial English courses.

"Bearing down" with increased drill and memorization has not and will not solve this problem satisfactorily, to say nothing of the fact that at least two other vital areas of a student's development go untouched. The best experiential courses, on the other hand, are not only consciously interdisciplinary, but also bring all three areas of development into complete concert.

Fourth: The school and the community should be as one. Far more than simply using the community as a laboratory, or allowing the school facilities to be used by the community in the evenings and during vacations, students and teachers must be engaged directly with the community-at-large, forging two-way relationships that not only educate, but also endure and make a difference in the quality of life. One of the most distressing facts I encounter in every school I work with is how ignorant teachers are of the community from which their students are drawn. The teachers can sometimes recite some basic historical facts and figures and the results of some government surveys, but they know few people on a first-name basis.

This fall, for example, one of my students and I worked for several days as consultants to an urban high school in a decaying city where a group of teachers was interested in talking about and perhaps implementing some of the things we have tried. After working with them and their classes for a day, their consensus was that nothing we had talked about would work in their setting. For one thing, they claimed, there wasn't anything good about the surrounding community to celebrate, and everyone who lived there was dreaming of the day when he or she could move away. In the second place, there was so much hostility, anger, and fear that adults would be afraid to talk with students, and the students would be too fearful of their own safety to explore the area.

Believing that in a situation of this nature there is more need than ever to attend to this particular principle, I suggested we try an interview anyway. None of the teachers or students could think of a soul who would be willing to come into the school, and so a school librarian who had lived there all her life was invited. Since none of the teachers could demonstrate interviewing techniques, I spent several hours training a volunteer group of about twenty students, stressing that if anything else were to be done along these lines, members of that group would have to be the teachers.

At the appointed time, the librarian arrived, apprehensive and a little stiff ("I can't stay long; I'm very busy"), and the students arranged themselves in a semicircle around her and went to work. The teachers stayed in the background and observed. After about fifteen minutes, I could feel the mood changing as the woman relaxed and the prearranged questions of the students began to drop away and be replaced by amazed, genuine inquiries. She talked about such things as the goats she had raised as a child in the pasture where the city-block-huge school now stood, and how the gradual influx of new racial and age populations had begun to polarize and fragment what had been a cohesive community. The students were fascinated as they began to see her as a completely different human being from the one they had known previously in her professional role only.

After forty-five minutes, the pace had not slowed a bit, but since the bell was about to ring, I interrupted to ask the librarian, with the students present, how she thought things had gone. She admitted honestly that she was amazed at the quality and obvious sincerity of the students' questions. She had expected something completely different, had come prepared to dislike the experience, and in fact had not had enough time to get into numerous other areas she would have enjoyed sharing. When I asked if she knew other people in the community who would be willing to undergo the same thing, she said there were many. The students and teachers who were listening were amazed and elated at how things had turned out, and if nothing else comes of that experience at that school, all of us together at least had an opportunity to share a very nice moment, one we won't soon forget.

And if nothing else comes of that experiment, I think that would be too bad. There may be other ways to deal with the kinds of hostilities and suspicions and hatreds that exist in that area, but offhand I don't know of a better way than getting people talking together face to face, beginning to know each other for the first time, beginning to correct misconceptions and prejudices about each other, and beginning to explore together the reasons why the community is now in a siege mentality, and the strategies available for turning that around. It's hard to think of a more perfect setting for what could be one of the most fascinating and valuable high-school courses ever, set up to explore what conditions must exist for people to be able to live and work productively and positively together. It would take patience and time to implement, but the alternative is to leave all the barricades standing.

Students are basically moral—quick to recognize injustice and prejudice, and, in the proper atmosphere, challenge them. With their peer group, they sometimes make a great show about hating this group or race or that, but for most young people, those statements have not yet hardened into adult convictions.

Better still, once moved, they are willing to take action for what they believe is right. A student and I worked as consultants in a midwestern high school, and we discovered, within easy walking distance of the school, a historic feed mill still in operation that was about to be torn down, as it was in the path of a new highway project. The local students I was working with had never done interviews in the community before (despite the fact that they were enrolled in a local history course), and so we started with the mill. One of the former owners told us its history while the students tape-recorded and took black-and-white photographs and color slides—all for the first time. Then the new owner described the battle he was waging with the highway department, told us why he had decided to take a stand against all odds, and showed us the petitions he was circulating in the city.

As we left, the students wanted to sign one of the petitions, but their local history teacher, who had been along as an observer, refused to let them. Her fear was that some school-board members might favor the highway project, and she was afraid of repercussions. We left, the students visibly disappointed, and the teacher, I believe, regretful and feeling a little guilty. Such are school politics.

The next day, on the way to the airport, I asked our driver to stop by the mill so that my student and I, at least, could sign one of the petitions. We went in and I asked for one, and the owner apologized saying that he hadn't had a chance to have new ones printed yet, but they were ordered. I asked what had happened to the stack of blank ones he had had the day before. "Well, you know those kids that were in here with you?" he asked. "When school let out, they came back with their friends and took every blank one I had. They said they were going to get them all signed and bring them back."

It is too much to expect that students will get the stimulation, self-confidence, training, and commitment they will need to get directly involved in community affairs as adults if their only contact with that sort of action is through a civics text. They must be immersed in the realities as students.

Last spring, Sherrod Reynolds, one of our staff members, and I taught an experimental course designed to test strategies for and reactions to this immersion. We tried it with five students, but it could have been a full class.

We decided to work with Mountain City, Georgia, a town in our county with a population of about 450, and a town that has done little discussion about or planning for the future. Incorporated in 1903, the residents had never had a town meeting. With the cooperation of the mayor and the city council, we began to work toward having one.

Each of the students chose a nearby town, out of our county, but of similar size. Alone, each made appointments to talk with their town's officials, conducted a series of taped interviews, and took a series of color slides of important features. Then they put together a slide show and script that illustrated how each of the towns had changed over the years, how each had dealt with that change in different ways, and how each had prepared—or failed to prepare—for the future. The question posed by the show to the residents of Mountain City was, "To what extent can and should we be involved now in planning and shaping the future according to what we, as a group, want for our town?"

The students also researched and drew two complete maps, one showing what the town looked like thirty years ago, and another showing each house and building in the town today. They then drew up an announcement of the scheduled town meeting, had it printed, and distributed copies door to door to every house and business in the city limits.

On the appointed evening, nearly a hundred residents showed up. The mayor made some announcements concerning a planned town sewer and water project for which he had been trying to get federal help, and opened the floor to questions. Then the students presented their slide show and the maps. A long discussion followed, culminating in the request for more such meetings. The students organized two more, one of them complete with packets that contained more maps, copies of town ordinances that had been referred to in previous meetings, etc.

By the end of the twelve-week quarter, twenty-four residents had formed a committee to sponsor a townwide cleanup as one small initial form of community action. The cleanup was announced by the students, again through a door-to-door campaign. When it was held, the residents turned out in force to clean up their own yards, clean and mow the sides of every town street, and haul off all the trash they could find. A chicken barbecue and a square dance followed that afternoon. The committee still exists today, and now has students involved in plans for a city park and fountain.

A small beginning, but a beginning nevertheless. And the students who were involved know far more now about town politics, the structure of the city council and its duties, and positive organized town action than they would ever have learned in a classroom. It will be fascinating to watch them as adults.

The school and the community must marry. We've only begun the courtship, but already students in our classes, through the creation of visible end products created within, about, and with the co-operation and involvement of the surrounding towns, keep the residents in our area constantly involved in their work. Television shows Mike Cook and his students create are broadcast daily over the county CATV network. In fact, students run the CATV studio as part of their academic work. Radio shows that students create are broadcast locally. *Foxfire* magazine is constantly visible as are the record albums that come out of George Reynolds' classroom. Bob Bennett's environmental class recently displayed the solar collectors they had designed and built in the parking lot of the local bank, and Paul Gillespie's photography classes mount regular exhibitions of their work in the lobby of the same bank. When a group of my students helped a class of sixth-graders design and build a low-cost playground at their elementary school, the local newspaper devoted three pages of text and photographs to that project. (The willingness and ability of students to get involved in such ways, and their passion for doing so, has been documented hundreds of times by the National Commission of Resources for Youth [36 West 44th Street, New York, N.Y. 10036]. You might want to receive their newsletter.)

Fifth: There should be an atmosphere inside the school, fostered by the principal, of fermentation, excitement, and anticipation—the feeling that something is *happening* that is good and worth being a part of—all laced with a generous dose of the unexpected. Much of this will result automatically from allowing the previous four principles to dominate the school's life, but in addition to this, principals should encourage experiments that involve the entire school population. Some of them will fail, many will not; and in the right environment of creative unpredictability, all will be applauded as attempts worth the trying.

One of the most vivid illustrations I can give of this sort of school-wide experimentation (or craziness, if you will) happened recently in our school for the first time when our organization, in association with the school librarian and her staff, and with the co-operation of the principal and all the teachers, sponsored a three-day celebration of community resources. With the exception of two-period blocks each day for activities that the entire student body witnessed (concerts, plays, etc.), every class on every day was visited by a person from the community who could bring what was being studied in that classroom to life. An American history class was studying the Depression at the time, and so the people who visited that class were ones who could add a human, here-in-Rabun-County orientation to the study of that subject. They were people who, for example, had worked in CCC camps and on WPA projects in the area, and even included the Under Secretary of Agriculture for Roosevelt who lives in our county and was able to give a fascinating, behind-the-scenes look at that period of time in a way a text never could. A chemistry class was visited by a chemist from the local Burlington carpet mill who demonstrated the mixing of chemical dyes and talked about the role of chemistry in his work. A biology class was visited by a beekeeper who came with all the tools of his trade; an English class studying poetry, by a local songwriter; a drafting class, by an architect; a business class, by a secretary; a government class, by our local state representative; a small engine repair class, by a man who makes his living in that field—and so on, in every class, for three days. Hundreds of community residents were involved in a co-ordinated assault that kept the students in a state of anticipation and excitement I had never seen before—an invasion of the fortress that people in this area are still talking about. During an evaluation period the following week, 953 students (out of 956) and every teacher said they would like to see the same thing happen again the following school year. Since then, teachers who had never before invited community residents to work with them have been doing so with regularity.

A problem in many schools is that principals allow themselves to become so buried in the day-to-day minutiae of maintaining the status quo that they despair of ever having time to do anything else. Perhaps asking more of them is asking too much, but in schools where principals dream in broad strokes and lead and inspire in such ways, breaking out of the day-to-day and forcing a sense of forward motion and experimentation, the school is transformed in a magical way.

Some of you—teachers, students, principals, parents, librarians, school-board members, custodians, grandparents, and the like—may be tempted to use the yardstick I have drafted primarily for myself in evaluating your own school. May I offer two cautions?

• Use my yardstick as exactly that—a measuring device, not a road map. The examples of specific activities I have given, *Foxfire* magazine included, grew naturally and organically out of, and were tailor-made to, the needs of their specific environments. Different kinds of activities that evolve from your own situation's soil *will* (and perhaps already do) serve you far better than carbon copies of those developed by others. In fact, sometimes the developing and the testing of a new idea becomes as much a solution as the final project itself.

• The principles I advocate are evolutionary and based on personal observation. I grow and change as a teacher, my ideas change over time, and this list of principles will change with me. In their present form, they represent what will probably seem to me a pinched and limited vision after my next fourteen years in the classroom. Don't accept them at face value. Change them. Challenge them. Add to them.

Above all, move. Refuse to accept the status quo. Refuse to allow yourself to believe that you have finally found "the way." *Know* that despite the fact that public schools are less than perfect learning environments, within them exciting and creative environments can be nourished where genuine learning does take place; with sensitive leadership those environments can spread within the system to infect the whole and to embrace the surrounding communities and the larger community of man to the ultimate benefit of all.

I have not seen even this limited vision happen yet within even one entire public school. I have seen enough pieces of it happen to various extents in my school and others, however, to be convinced that it is a workable and attainable, if limited, dream.

And I am positive that when that dream does come true, at last, in one school, somewhere, that that school will shine like a lighthouse beacon across this land.

BEW

JAKE WALDROOP

Jake Waldroop, a lively ninety-one-year-old man, and his wife, Bertha, still live in the house that Jake himself built thirty-five years ago. I met Jake after transcribing tapes of interviews with him. I don't really know what I expected him to be like, but I was surprised when I met him. As soon as I did, he made me feel at ease and like one of the family. He has a great sense of humor, strong opinions, and is straightforward with others.

Jake was born on December 12, 1889, in a logging camp on the Nantahala River where his father had a logging contract. As a young boy Jake fished and hunted a great deal, and is still well known for this. He also helped tend the crops and look after the cattle and hogs that they kept in the mountains. He went to school through the fourth grade, but then quit so he could work to help feed the family. "Back then when I went to school the teachers only went to the seventh grade. I'm just afraid that we put too much value on education today. There's a whole lot of hard labor to be done yet, and you take these [college] graduates, they're not going to fall for it."

Due to his great love for, and knowledge of, the mountains, Jake got a job as a hunting guide when he was sixteen years old. Since that time he has done a little bit of everything, from logging to collecting ginseng and hewing crossties. "You just can't hardly name nothing, any kind of work that went on but that I've done some of it." There is one particular tree that Jake didn't cut down while he was logging, known in his area as the Giant Poplar [see Foxfire 4, page 314]. It stands on land that Jake's grandfather, Jake Waldroop, once owned, then later sold to the federal government. Jake's father, Zeb, had contracted to log the area in which the tree stands, and Jake was in charge of cutting the trees. They couldn't cut it down because they didn't have a crosscut saw long enough. It would have been extremely difficult to snake it down to the sawmill because it was so big; and the sawmill was not equipped to handle such large logs. So the tree still stands today, and is listed by the American Forestry Association as the largest yellow poplar in the United States.

The things Jake enjoys doing most now are "being in these mountains, fishing and squirrel hunting, though I don't see as good as I used to," taking care of his yard, which takes about three or four hours every week, and working in his garden patch. "I enjoy raising my truck patches to have vegetables and everything to do us a whole year round. I guess people eat just too much grub, but I get out·and work and tramp these mountains ·and burn it up."

Jake is in great health and has only had to have one prescription in his life. "I'd never had a prescription until last September." He went to the doctor and found he had high blood pressure. So he began eating garlic and ramps and taking his pills, and in less than a year his blood pressure was back to normal.

A wonderful storyteller, Jake has such a good memory that he can recollect those little everyday things that most of us forget, a talent that makes the tales he tells so warm and vital. He is the type of person who makes you like him and want to come back and see him often.

BRENDA CARPENTER

Article by Brenda Carpenter and Lynnette Williams

My [paternal] grandfather came here from Ireland with three of his brothers. Four of them came. Ellis stopped off in Tennessee, Summiner stopped off near Hayesville in Clay County, North Carolina, and Jake, my granddaddy, and Joe come on here to Franklin, North Carolina, to Macon County. They were among the first settlers, and my granddad said that when he first come here he could buy land at ten to twenty-five cents an acre.

My father's name was Zeb Waldroop. He was raised here in Macon County. At the time he and my mother got married, he was a Singer Sewing Machine agent and was selling sewing machines. That was the old timey machines, about the first ones. He also farmed but he was mostly a logger; he did more logging than anything else. He did a lot of contracting himself, and he'd take contracts from companies and he'd work for other people or for other contractors like Earl Judson, the Gennetts, and the Reynolds brothers. My daddy died when he was fifty-two years old—he took pneumonia fever. They didn't have penicillin back then to doctor with.

My mother's name was Arie Cruse, and she always went by the name of Aunt Doc. That was her nickname. She was raised over in Cherokee County, and her family used to live across on the Nantahala side on what they called the Apple Tree Place for a while, then they lived in Choga, then they lived here on Dirty John—that's

PLATE 1

down from Wayah Gap. Mother, she lacked just a few days of being ninety-four years old when she died, and she was out of a family that all lived to be old.

My mother loved to fish and she fished all up Nantahala River, every bit of it, every creek. She loved the mountains and she loved to go and hunt ginseng. She could really find that stuff. She'd hunt ginseng for days and days and days.

Now my uncles, the old Cruses, and my mother had bear dogs and they bear hunted. They killed thirty-six bears in one season here on Choga, back on Nantahala. They'd take them bear dogs into where they thought the bear was. The men folk, the brothers, they'd leave before daylight an' go on and get the stands, and later she'd take them bear dogs and turn 'em loose. So they'd get this bear track and they'd pretty nearly fight 'em. When the bear came out, why, they'd shoot him down. They said that in the fall of the year when there was lots of chestnut mast, they'd go in the chestnut country. The dogs'd find a sign and they'd take the bear's trail and go roost 'im through and start fighting 'im. Sometimes they'd make the bear climb a tree and they'd have to go and shoot 'im out, but lots of times he'd keep fighting [the dogs].

My mother would go a' coon hunting with them. She got up many a time at five or six o'clock to go hunting. They'd fry some eggs, cook some meat, eat some bread, and make some coffee. Then they'd take the dogs, and if they treed a coon they'd cut the tree down. [The coons'd] always be in a hole because it was broad daylight and my mother would hold the dogs to keep them from under the tree. After the tree fell down, she'd turn them loose and they'd run in and catch the coons.

Mammy had her own hogs. In her later years, we got so that we didn't want her to go off by herself, but when she caught us gone off from home or anywhere, she'd get her some corn and slip off and go herself. She was about ninety-one years old when she last went. She had an old sow back in the mountains [with] pigs, and my mother wanted to go feed them. She went up across that mountain—and it was about two miles to the top of it, a rough, high mountain—and she came to a campground. There was a game warden out there, a feller called Coffee. Well, he come along (she was a-sittin' on the bank a'restin'), and he got acquainted with her. He told her to get in the car and he'd take her to eat dinner [with him] and then he'd take her home. And he did. We kept her guarded after that and wouldn't let her go alone to the mountains.

I was born about seven miles from here going out [Highway] 64, but at that time there wasn't a good road. You went down through Wallace Gap and a little old path went down and across Nantahala River and off into an old cleared-off field where Sam Valentine had built a log house. When my daddy went to logging after that house was vacated, he made a logging camp out of it. That's where I was born, right there in the Roan Bottom almost on the bank of the Nantahala River. I've spent most of my life through these mountains here.

Our old homeplace was about a couple of miles right up on the head of the creek. We would fasten up the house and leave it as long as we was in the logging camp. When Daddy would get through with that job, why, he'd come back till he'd get another, then we'd move to the camp. He logged practically all of his life, especially after he and my mother were married. I don't know how long it was after they got married that he kept this job of selling Singer sewing machines, but not too long. He just liked to log better [than anything else], he said.

My daddy would take a contract of logging and he would put up a camp. My mother would cook for the men. [Daddy] boarded the men, and he'd hire them to work. My mother kept us children and at that time she had Grover, Mary, and Ed. They were older than me. I was the fourth child. There were six of us all together, four boys and two girls.

We had it pretty tough coming up in the cabin where I was born. My father had a camp built out of logs and used poles for rafters. I don't think that cabin had any lumber in it at all. It had a big rock chimney and they'd get up a lot of big wood and keep a big fire in there. Daddy had the kitchen partitioned off, and all the rest of it was just a big living room where we all stayed. Daddy had a little place built for the men to sleep, but we'd all eat at the same table. The work hands that he hired had them a little shack to themselves.

There was one section he logged that was a pretty big territory and I guess it took him from two to three years to log that out. When he finished [logging] he just went off and left [the camp]. There was some old people that lived in that old camp for years and years after he'd left. There'd be [people who] had hogs and cattle back in the mountains and they'd use it for a camp. They'd go there and spend a night or two while they rounded up their sheep, hogs, and cattle, and salted and looked after them.

That was virgin timber [that we cut] then, and they wouldn't fool with anything under twenty-four inches; they'd want it to be two foot or better. He wouldn't fool with it back then if it wasn't very fine timber. He'd have some logs that would have as much as seven or eight hundred feet to the log.

The cattle would just drag them out to the mill. Daddy never did use anything but the cattle. He never would use none of them cars, carts, or nothing, but just let them cattle drag the logs straight through to the mill. He would use three yoke—two steers to the yoke—that was six oxen to a team. They would get them out by hooking together anywhere from two to five logs.

He logged all out here all up and down Nantahala River. They built a big splash dam out there. The way they built them back in them days was with logs and *rock*. They used some lumber in 'em, not a whole lot. See, they'd build them big pens an' fill 'em with rock an' sand an' dirt. They built 'em so they'd hold that water up. Then they had a splash gate at the apron of that dam that they could raise or lower. When they'd lower it, that shut the water off and that dam would fill up. If they got a big batch of logs in the river, they'd let the splash off and the water'd come down and pick the logs up and carry 'em down through Nantahala Gorge and on to Nantahala Station. They had a mill there and that's where they took the logs out and sawed 'em. They had a kind of a boom built out there where the river leveled off, and they had cables and things fixed to stop the logs.

My daddy put in a slide on the Big Branch. They had landings to land the logs on. The day they were going to open the splash gate of the dam, they'd grease the slide. And the crew of men'd go up and dump them logs, roll them logs off the landings into that slide. The logs'd hit that slide, and it was like a greased bullet, boys, they went sh-ploog into that river. They'd put thousands of logs in, and the splash would pick 'em right up and take 'em right on down to the station. And there they got 'em out and sawed 'em into lumber, and I imagine it was shipped out from there to different points.

They had crews that when they turned these splashes loose, would drive the river and hunt for log jams. There were several men that would ride them logs right down through there, and if there was a jam, why, they broke it loose. They'd just pick and prise 'em loose with them peaveys—them big hooks they'd have. They'd break them jams loose an' get 'em started on. It was dangerous work, but I never did know of any of 'em getting drowned or getting hurt. They was pretty skillful men, and they knew how to take care of themselves.

When the hired hands were working in the Roan Bottom where I was born, [my father] paid them fifty cents a day plus board. A day then was ten hours right out on the job. I remember hearing him say when they went to the Tate Cove, he got a little more money on the thousand for his logging, and he paid them seventy-five cents a day plus board. That was considered a good job. They was glad to get it. The loggers were good, honest, hard-working men, and they'd work hard all day long to get that seventy-five cents a day and board.

[My father didn't saw the logs], there was always another outfit who got the contract for doing the sawing. All my daddy done was to cut the timber in the woods and log it out to the sawmill, and he was done with it. He was paid so much a thousand [feet] on it then.

I can remember my mother cooking for the hands. Daddy had several timber cutters and everything, and there'd be about sixteen to eighteen men. Sometimes they'd get somebody to stay with her to help her cook. There was a man cook, Mark Smith, and he stayed there and helped her. He was a good cook. When they'd be too far out for the men to come in for dinner and I'd got up big enough so that I could go help, [my sister] Mary, Mark Smith, me, and my mammy would pack all the food in buckets and pails and get the plates and the knives and forks and spoons and everything, and we'd take dinner out there. We'd go way on the Tate Branch where they were working and eat dinner, and afterward we'd put up all of our eating plates, spoons, forks, and everything, and bring them home and we'd wash and clean them after we got back to camp.

When we were in them camps we just played around and messed about, and when we got big enough, we'd fish. When we got up bigger we'd squirrel hunt some. Later on when [Daddy] got a job and we were older, we'd stay at home with Mammy and we'd make a crop. We'd raise corn, beans, potatoes, and everything like that. We always kept a lot of hogs. You could raise hogs then, back in these mountains. I know one fall we got up our killing hogs and had some men come and kill them for us. Daddy was a'workin' on a job and they come and killed twenty-seven at one time. We cut them up and salted them down. We had a great big smokehouse and it didn't have no floor in it, it just had shelves. We would just salt that meat down on the shelves, and we'd have plenty to eat.

Daddy always kept a milk cow and would kill a big beef every fall. Then there was no such thing as processing meat and there wasn't no deep freeze to put it in. We had that smokehouse, and we'd kill a big steer and just hang it in that smokehouse, and the beef would hang there all winter until we ate it up. It was cold enough [in the wintertime] to keep, and we never put salt or nothing on it, and it would dry out. In the spring of the year, when it did begin to get a little warm in the middle of February or the first of March, if we had any [beef] left, we would get it down and help my mother cut it in thin slices. Then she'd put it on sticks and hang it up in the smokehouse and soon it would dry. She'd sack that up like dried fruit or beans, and when she wanted a mess— say, if she wanted some beef tomorrow—she'd take it down tonight and put it in a big dishpan and pour some warm water in it and let it soak overnight. The next morning it would be pliant, and it was the best-tasting beef, a whole lot better than this frozen beef. It was good. It was just plain dried beef, not jerky.

We would never sell no ham meat. We always ate on the shoulders and the middlin's on up until the spring of the year, then we'd eat our hams. That was our favorite meat. We kept plenty of chickens, we had plenty of ham meat, eggs, milk, and butter. We always kept bees; we had honey.

We'd make a big crop of cane, and we'd make syrup. Daddy had an eighty-gallon syrup barrel and we'd make enough cane to fill that syrup barrel, and that'd do us for a year. They'd start making syrup in the latter part of September or October. We'd get our barrelful made, and we'd just set it on the back porch, and when we wanted syrup we'd just go out and draw out a can- or a pailful.

Daddy would send some of the work hands or Grover and Ed, my two older brothers [to get food for the logging camp]. They would come over to the farm and they'd shell up a lot of corn and take it to the mill to get a lot of meal ground. We never raised too much wheat—we'd raise some—but we'd go down to this place in Franklin called the Roller Mill. They'd go there and get several hundred pounds of flour, enough to do maybe two or three weeks or a month at a time. Then we'd have all this meat salted down, and they would load up what they thought it would take to do them for a week or two, and they would also bring dried fruit, beans, potatoes, and onions, and everything that we raised. We raised most

PLATE 2   Jake and his bull, Tom, a twelve-year-old polled Hereford.

of the food that he fed those men. He'd buy some coffee and sugar and maybe a case of salmon fish, and he'd get them for ten cents a can.

We got to go to school some. We'd have a four-months' school and we'd get to go to that school. We'd start in and go till it came time to pull fodder, and then we'd have to stop out then and cut them tops and pull the fodder. That was the only way that we had of feeding the stock in the wintertime. We had to cut up feed with a pocket knife. The only way that we had to sort of keep the land built up was by sowing rye when we got through with the fodder-topping and everything. We had to take a plow and go over and dig that ground up and do what we called chopping that rye in and you just about hoed that whole field.

There was a whole lot to do when I was growing up. When I got up to where I could, I did a whole lot of the tending to the cattle in the summertime. We had to feed the hogs and things in the mountains and tend to 'em, and we'd take them a little corn and salt and stuff every week or two to keep 'em gentle. If we just

let the hogs go all year long, they just went wild, and you'd have
to dog 'em and tie 'em and drive 'em in, but the other way we
kept 'em gentle. I kept them so that I could keep bells on 'em. I'd
come along up through the trail up here and if they were on the
other mountain or back on this mountain, why, I could hear that
bell and call to them. They'd come running and a'squealing from
as far as they could hear me.

When I got old enough I got a job and worked. I've worked in
logging camps a sight. Helped my father do a lot of logging. I did
what they called swamping or roading; I'd go ahead and trim out
a road for him, and then Daddy'd come along with three yoke of
cattle. I'd trim out the bushes and everything before he would go
up a holler and get what logs that were up there. I worked many
a day with my daddy.

I love to fish and hunt. I'd squirrel hunt, coon hunt, and everything
like that. I can remember the first coon that I ever helped kill. Grady,
my brother, and me told my daddy that we wanted to go down to
McKenzie Cove and Swap Branch and possum hunt. "Well," Daddy
said, "you'd better take an ax, there might be a coon." We come
down there to what we called the Spruce Pine Branch, and we heard
our dogs, old Rock and Con, strike. They went to trailing right
up that branch way up toward the head of it, and they treed [a
coon]. We went up there and he was treed up a small, grubby oak.
The moon was a'shining, and we could tell that there was a hole
in that tree. There was an old boy with us, Theo Riddle, and we
cut the tree down and the dogs ran in and that coon stayed in the
hole. The dogs just kept a'bayin' and a'barkin' at it. We didn't know
what it was—that was the first coon that we'd ever caught. We shined
the lantern in there and we seen its head. Well, we'd seen our daddy
bring in coons, so we knew what it was then.

"Boy," we said, "we've got us a coon and we can't let him get
away." We cut the hole big enough so that one of the dogs could
stick his head in there, and here [the dog] come with it.

Theo Riddle, the big boy that was with us, said, "I'm a'goin' to
stomp it." He started to stomp it and it reached up and got him
right in the calf of the leg, just laid it's tushes right in there—the
dogs jerked it loose but it was a bad gash there.

And then he said, "Boys, is a damned coon's tooth poison?" We
all laughed about Theo's wantin' to know if a coon's tooth was
poison.

I've went by myself [coon hunting] and the coons'd go in a hole under a cliff. I'd get me some dry stuff, kindling and shavings, and build a fire there right in the mouth of that hole. I'd get it to burning good and get a bunch of dry leaves and stuff and push it back in the hole and shut the air off. He'd start snortin' and a'coughin' and here he'd come. I'd just knock that brush out of the way and when he come out, the dogs would grab him, and I'd have a coon fight. I have had as many as two or three come out of one hole. Coons were good meat and [they're] still pretty plentiful. A coon wants fresh meat—it won't eat anything that's been dead a long time, but an old possum, all he wants is dead meat. A ground hog is one of the cleanest wild meats there is 'cause all he eats is vegetation. They ate my squash last year with me a-trying to trap and kill them. Now a squirrel don't eat nothing but vegetation. He just eats the acorns, hickory nuts, the buds on the trees, and berries.

Sometimes after we'd get all the logging-camp chores done, we'd go fishing. We'd get out there and we'd fish in the river and go up the branches. One day we went out fishing up the Tate Branch and it come up a big windstorm, and it blowed a big hemlock tree down. This hemlock was forked and we was out on a slide that Daddy had built for them logs to come down. I was standing along on the slide and my mammy was fishing the creek, and that big hemlock fell and just come right down over me, one prong on one side of me and the other on the other side of me. If that limb had a'hit me, why, it would have just crushed me, but I just barely escaped. I got out of there and we really went to the house then!

I can tell you about [my mother] catching a big fish one time. We was a'camping there at the White Oak Bottom and there was a hole that we called The Footlog Hole there in the river, and the footlog crossed it. It come up a pretty good shower of rain and the river was a'coming down a little dingy. At that time there was some chubs in the river, that was these little horny heads. Some of us caught one and my mother said, "I want that chub's head to catch me a big rainbow trout." None of us had a knife, so she laid it down and got her a sharp-edged rock and cut it off back behind the head. She put that big chub's head on her hook and she throwed it. She had a long line and when she throwed it, it came a floating down there. We seen it stop and I seen it a'startin' to pull off, and she pulled him and here she come with him. She had a nineteen-inch rainbow trout and she drug him right out on the sandbar and landed him. That's the first one I've ever seen caught on a chub's head.

Then we was a'fishing again and we was out there camped out

and we'd caught some fish. It'd come up a rain and we knowed where there was a big fish on Kimsey Creek, and I'd been trying to catch him all summer. He'd get a hook in there and he wouldn't bite them. He wouldn't take a hold. There was a little branch there and we went there and found a spring lizard. We hooked that spring lizard on and went back out and throwed the hook in and it came out a little way and we seen it stop. I started down the bank with it, and I yanked and I had a nineteen-inch rainbow trout. He had [already eaten] a big chub and three crawfish—one big one and two small ones. You could see that big crawfish's tail a'sticking down here in his throat and he still bit that lizard. He was worse than greedy.

It is different fishing now from what it was [back then]. Why, then three or four or five of us would bunch up and we'd make up our rations and go camping. We'd take bread, meat, and potatoes, and onions, and stuff like that to cook. Then we'd get out there and catch them fish, and we'd clean them and bring them back to the camp and fry 'em and we'd have plenty of fish to eat. Sometimes after we'd do all the fishing that we wanted to do, we'd get out and salt our cattle and sheep or hunt up the hogs and give them some corn and salt. Sometimes we'd turn the dogs loose and have a cat race and kill a wildcat.

There used to be a hotel out here through the Wallace Gap. That was on old Highway 64, and old man Bob Porter built a summer house out there and he'd keep boarders. My mammy and me, we'd go and fish and we could catch 'em and take them down there and them boarders (we called them lowlanders), they'd pay us a cent apiece for 'em. I know one time we went and fished the Long Branch and Mammy caught a hundred and seventy-five. She'd catch them and just hold them out to me, and I'd take them off the hook and I'd string 'em. We took them down to the hotel and them boarders were glad to get 'em. They give us a dollar and seventy-five cents for our fish and then they wanted us to clean them, so we told them that we had to have the same amount to clean them for 'em. They give us a cent apiece to clean them and we made three dollars and a half that day. We thought we were really in the money then. Fishing was great back then.

You could just go around them little streams and look over in a little pool there in a hole where it would pour over [the rocks], and you could see them a'darting everywhere. You could put a little redworm on your hook and drop it over in there, and when it hit the water, a fish would grab it. Mammy would pull it out and hold it out to me and I'd take it off and rebait her hook. Why, she would catch from six to ten out of one of those little holes and then just move down to another hole. [They were] speckled trout. At that time that was all the fish that was there. The Nantahala River was just full of speckled trout.

When Porter had that hotel, three men came out of Athens, Georgia [to vacation here]. They were professors—Payne, McGruder, and DeBois—and they'd come there along up in June and July, generally. They'd hire me to go and stay with them. I was their guide. I'd take them over these mountains and we'd go to Standing Indian, to the Ridge Pole, Pickens Nose, Albert Mountain, up to Foster Top, to Rock Knob, to Buck Knob, Fern Mountain, Buzzard Knob, Dull Knob, and just different places. We'd plan out a different place every day and we'd fish two days out of every week. Just catch enough fish to fry for one meal. Most of the time, we would go from the hotel and back every night. I'd come on home and spend the night and then go back the next morning. They'd always fix a lunch, and sometimes they'd have Mrs. Porter—that was old man Bob Porter's wife—fix us up some grub and we'd go out and spend a night or two at a time back in them mountains. They paid me a dollar a day, and I had the best job of anybody in this whole section here at that time. That job would usually last about three months, and they'd give me a dollar a day for the guide to go with them. My father was tickled about my job. Sometimes he wouldn't have no logging job and money was hard to come by and I'd always give about my week's wages. I'd turn it over to them and let them use it to help feed the family.

There was lots of fruit then, lots of June apples and sweet apples, and I could take a half a bushel across the mountain and some of them people would buy them. They loved to get them apples. They'd give me fifty cents for a half bushel of apples. That was a load of money.

Lots of times when I wouldn't take those three professors, there'd be some boys and girls and I'd take them a'hunting. There'd be as many as four, five, or six of 'em and they'd bunch up and I'd take them to the Standing Indian, Yellow Mountain, Buck Knob, Rock Knob, or Pickens Nose. They'd get a big kick out of that. Sometimes they'd camp, but most of the time they'd just take lunch and eat dinner and come back in. Sometimes [the boys'] mammy and daddy would come to me and have me take them out a'huntin'; squirrel huntin' or a'pheasant huntin', turkey huntin', or something.

I'd take them and I'd let them do whatever they wanted to do. If they wanted to turkey hunt, we'd turkey hunt. If they wanted to pheasant hunt, we'd pheasant hunt. And if they wanted to squirrel hunt, we'd go. It wasn't no trouble then to kill six, eight, and ten squirrels in a little bit in the late evening or of an early morning.

When I come up, one way that we had of making money was getting a team and hauling telephone poles and crossties to the railroad. This was just an old dirt road down through here then, and in the wintertime it was just axle deep—you just had to drag a wagon to Franklin and back. We'd load on from ten to fifteen crossties and take them down to the railroad, and we'd sell them. Mark Dowdle was the one who bought them crossties. We'd get out telephone poles when the chestnut timber was here. We'd cut them telephone poles anywhere from twenty-two to forty-five foot long. We'd put them on a wagon and haul them to Franklin to the railroad.

The Tallulah Falls Railroad came into Franklin at that time. When they got a carload of poles they'd load them and ship them out. That was a year-round job, just anytime that you could get the poles or crossties. I cut lots of my own chestnut poles, but generally somebody would hew them crossties and get 'em out, and I would haul 'em. It was fifty or seventy-five cents apiece we'd get for them, and we'd generally go halvers on them.

You just can't hardly name nothing, any kind of work that went on, but that I've done some of it. There used to be a big boom for isinglass—we always called it mica—and lots of people would come in here from everywhere [to hunt for it]. You could find little outcroppings of it, and we'd dig down and it'd play out and there wouldn't be nothing. Down here on Iotla they found a mica mine and it really did pay off. They got thousands and thousands of dollars' worth of mica out of that. It finally got so deep and the water come in so bad—and they didn't have sufficient pumps at that time—[that] they just disbanded it. They say it's just about filled up now with everybody's trash that they dumped in there. It was just a shaft that went down in the earth.

That was one in a thousand that you'd get any mica that was worth anything. You'd find a little outcropping, and you'd go there and dig there a month or two thinking that there was going to be something there that you could sell, and directly it would pinch out to nothing. I done lots of that myself. There would be people come in (I knew where lots of these little prospects was), and they'd say, "You take me and show me the Thorn Mountain Mine, or the old Glass Mine, or the one on Sassafras Ridge, or the one on Forester Mountain," and I knew where all those old prospects was. They'd give me five dollars to go and show them and it generally would take a half day to a day. I'd go and show it to them and that was the last of that. They'd look around a little bit and say, "Well, we may be back and try to open it up and see if there's anything," but nine times out of ten I would never see them anymore. Then another crew would come through and it would be the same thing. Sometimes I'd get to show them four or five in a week. And every prospect that I showed them, I got five dollars for it.

This was in about 1930, '32, and '33, when there was a Great Panic [the Depression]. That was when that mica was a big boom and everybody was trying to find it to get some work, to get some money, for there wasn't nothing that they could get no money from. I found one little prospect, my mother and me. We'd fished a while in Long Branch, and then we'd turned and come up White Branch and fished up White Branch, and she said, "We'll just go right on up and get up on White Ridge and go up the White Gap, and there's a trail there and we'll take that trail to the Rock Gap and go home." We was a'coming up out of there and we found an outcropping of mica. There was great big pieces as big as your two hands just a'sticking out of the ground. We come in the next morning, my brother and me and another boy. We took our dinner and we went back and went to work and we got out about three or four o'clock. We'd took us some tow sacks and we had all that we could pack out. We all got a load and loaded it up and fetched it in and went back and worked the next day and went down. It was a'going straight down in the ground and it pinched out. The last thing was a big block, the best big block that we got. I guess it would have weighed ten or fifteen pounds, but there was some rough places in it and it wasn't all pure salable mica. We got that block out, fetched it in, and I sorta trimmed it up. I took it to town and sold it and that was the most I ever got out of mica. I got twenty-seven dollars for what we got out in two days.

We still wasn't satisfied, so when they was a'building [Highway 64] up here on the mountain, I told old man Frank Dakis about it. He was the contractor and I was a'workin' for him. "Well," he said, "I'll tell you, Jake, I'll furnish you the dynamite and let you have a churndrill and you and your brother go out there and churn-drill a hole down about fifteen or twenty feet." Two people would get ahold of that churndrill and it would just keep pounding down. We took a twenty-five-foot churndrill, and we drilled a hole down about eighteen feet. We put about twenty sticks of dynamite down in there and matched it off, and it just turned the ridge wrong side outward and there wasn't a thing in the world besides dirt—there wasn't a speck of mica down in there.

About all the amusement and entertainment that we had was, the first thing in the fall of the year we'd pick the beans and we'd have as many as ten to fifteen bushels. They'd carry them in and just pour them out right in the middle of the house, and a crowd would gather in and we'd have a bean stringing. We'd get the beans done and then we'd have somebody there with a banjo and fiddle, and we'd start that music up and dance the rest of the night. We danced big ring and straight old buck danced. We'd have a big time.

Then we'd have corn shuckings. I'd get my corn gathered and have it throwed up under my cribshed and we'd ask in ten or fifteen men to come, and we'd start in along late in the evening along toward night and shuck corn. The women would bunch in and help get supper. Lots of times we'd have mutton and pork, and they'd bake up a sight of stuff. They'd have chicken and dumplings, punkin' custards and apple pies, beans, and all kinds of sweet bread. We'd have plenty to eat. Sometimes we'd have a jug. We'd get a gallon jug or sometimes it would be a two-gallon jug of corn whiskey. We'd put it back against the wall about the middle of that pile of corn, and when we got [the corn] shucked out, why then, we'd pass it around until we'd all drunk all that we wanted. Then we'd start in and fiddle and dance the rest of the night.

Sometimes when one was going to have new ground cleared up, he'd call it a log rolling and ask in some hands, and we'd all gather in and bring our hooks and spikes and everything. We'd cut and roll them logs all together and burn 'em. I've seen as many as ten to fifteen men at a log rolling, rolling and burning logs. We'd clear that up, plow it, and plant it in corn and beans. Then in the fall of the year when that corn had tassled out, about the time it shedded its tassle, we'd sow it in turnips, and there would be a whole mountainside of big turnips sitting there just as fresh and tender, not a worm or nothing about them because of that new ground. When they burned [the timber] off of the land, it killed the germs. They still call it the good old days, and I guess it was. We had plenty of everything in the world but money. Money was hard to come by.

PLATE 3   A view from the Waldroops' yard.

If you don't know and understand these mountains, you can get lost in 'em and won't know how to go. I never [got lost] but one time. Me and some boys went off the head of Kimsey Creek and went down Little Buck Creek and went up on Big Buck Creek, and the dogs struck a cat I reckon or something. Anyway, they trailed out to the Yellow Mountain, and when we got on the top of Yellow Mountain, why it was a'sleeting, a'raining, and snowing, and the wind was a'blowing. It was the roughest time that I ever saw. The fog shut down and we couldn't tell nothing and couldn't see a thing in the world. We just wandered around and around and around there. Finally we found an old big hollow chestnut tree, and we got some dry stuff out of it and got a fire started. We just dragged up everything and we had a big roaring fire, and if you get one hot enough you can burn nearly anything. We stomped around there until daylight and when it come daylight, why, the fog was still down so bad that we had to feel for one another.

We was a'walking back and forth on the top of the mountain. There was a boy with us, Laurence Beck, and he said, "Right here is these three chestnut trees. If you'll look now there's five corncobs. Me and Uncle Charlie fed his old sows right here at these trees."

Well, we got to looking and a'raking around there and we found the five corncobs and we knew he was right.

"Now," I said, "Laurence, do you have any idea which a'way you went?"

"Now," he said, "let's see. There's a big oak. When we fed those sows, we went right out the top just a little piece and there was the biggest oak tree that you've ever seen a'standing on the top of the mountain."

"Well," I said, "you go back that way and I'll go this way." I said, "You said it wasn't too far."

And he said, "It's not over a hundred yards either way to that big oak tree. If we find the oak tree and keep to the top of the mountain, that'll take us into the Brush Gap."

So I turned out one way, the way that I thought maybe might be right, and sure enough, there was that big oak tree. I hollered and told them to come on back and said, "There's that big oak tree."

And [Laurence] said, "That's the tree and we want to go right on this way." We could sort of tell we was a'following the top of the mountain and we went on down and down and by the time we got into the Brush Gap, the fog had began to go up a little bit and we could tell where we was a'going. There was an old trail that cut back and went out to the head of Kimsey Creek and there was an old stock camp that we was a'staying in, and we went to that camp. Allen Dills was with us, but we left his daddy at the camp that night—said he was a'gettin' old and he'd not go a'coon huntin' with us. When we got back to the camp, we ate.

Allen had left us on the Yellow Mountain. [He'd] said, "Ya'll can go any way that you want," and said, "I'm a'going this a'way."

"Well," I said, "I'm a'going the way Laurence says."

He said, "It ain't right, but me and Pa will come and hunt you." So we got to the camp and we stayed in the camp. It was just a cold drizzle all day, but along about three or four o'clock it began to lighten up a little bit.

I told them, "Allen's never come. We'd better get out and holler and shoot guns and see what's happened to him. He'll freeze to death if he has to stay out in the mountains again and with nothing to eat."

Vance said, "You and Laurence wait here and give me and Harley time to go to the Deep Gap." That was at the head of Kimsey Creek. He said, "It'll take us about an hour to go to the Deep Gap. We'll go there and holler and yell, and see if we can't hear him or nothing.

If we're not back in an hour, you and Laurence go to the top of Yellow Mountain"—that's where we'd left Allen—"and see if you can hear anything." We waited just about an hour, and we looked and seen them a'coming. Allen was in front and they was a'coming just a'stepping right down the trail.

[Allen] said, "I went to one camp and I got there in the head of Big Buck Creek and every way that I started, I'd come back to that stock camp there. I walked around Little Knob there, I bet I walked around it a hundred times. I just looked up there and I seen this light place and I said to myself, 'I'm a'going to pull up there to that light place.' " He pulled up to that light place and he still didn't know where he was at, but he said to himself, "I'm just a'going to go through and cross right down the branch." He went through the Water Oak Gap and through the branch and it fetched him to what we called the Tallulah River at the Will Standby camps. When he came to them camps, he realized where he was and he knowed he had to turn back and go up. So he turned back and took the trail to what they call the Steeps. Vance and Harley said that when they got in the Deep Gap and hollered, he was up over the top and it just took him a few minutes to climb out to them in the Deep Gap, and they fetched him back to camp. That's about the only time that I can say I've ever got lost. I knew where I was, but I just couldn't see which way to go to get off of there.

I got a call one time from an old feller, Dave Guffey. He lived out there on Nantahala at Will McGuire's place, and they had some sheep up there on the Trough Branch and Moore Creek. In the spring of the year they'd turn the ewes and the lambs out up there. He sent me word to bring my cat dogs and come, that the cats was a'killing their lambs. We went and I stayed all night with him, and we come back up the next morning to the Wallace Gap and got in the Appalachian Trail and we walked around the trail and got right in there in front of the Barnard Cove. I had a little black hound and I called him Ross and he was an awful good cat dog. I saw him run straight down to the head of Barnard Cove. Them sheep was just all around him, and I seen him jump up on a big rock and he began to twitch his tail. I said, "Hold on, Dave, I believe Ross smells him." Old Ross throwed up his head and squawled a time or two and jumped down. The others began to fall in with him and they trailed that cat right down across Moore Creek and out through Rattlesnake Gap and in toward Thorn Mountain and come back and went through the Big Stomp and turned down Rough

Fork. Went down the Dry Stand Ridge right down into the forks of Rough Forks on Wayah.

I heard them jump him. I could tell because they really began to let the yell out. Dave was with me, and he said there was a den right out there, and I said, "Dave, they've got him jumped."

And he said, "I'm going to go out to the den. They always come and go in there under that cliff, and you couldn't get 'em out."

"Well," I said, "I'll stand right here, they seem to be a'coming." I could just barely hear them a'coming closer and they were a'coming straight toward me. There was a little old path that went down that ridge, and directly I looked down about a hundred feet and I seen that old cat a'coming. He was just a'loping and them dogs wasn't over fifty to seventy-five yards behind him. He was just a'keeping his distance from them. He run right up and I throwed my gun in his face when he got up to about forty or fifty yards, I waited until he came up about twenty steps of me and I said, "Where are you a'goin'?" and he just kind of rared back and I let him have a whole load of shot right in the face and killed him.

We skinned him. Them dogs'd eat the meat, every bite of that cat, if you cut it up and fed it to 'em. We cut into its stomach and there was just one piece of meat in it and he had just sucked the blood from them lambs. When they killed one, they would cover it up with leaves but you could always see where they had raked up that little pile of leaves. I don't know why they would do that but they would, for a cat when he killed anything he'd eat it right then or get the blood. He never would go back to the carcass.

It was a bobcat. Back then when there was plenty of lambs and pigs and things for them to eat, I've knowed them to get up as big as thirty-five pounds. That was about as big a one as I've ever killed. They'd put up a good race. You could get a big kick out of hearing a pack of hounds a'coming and a'yelling down on one of them.

I knowed of [a cat] one time killing twenty-four lambs in one night. I caught him the next day. My brother come after me and I turned the dogs in on him. He was in on the Pine Mountain. He must have heard the dogs on his trail 'cause he got up in the Slipping Head and he went out at the head of Pork Creek and went down Little Buck and in Big Buck Creek, and in a big laurel there they caught him. When they fetched him out we skinned him and cut him up; he didn't have a bite of meat in him. He just had blood, a pint or a pint and a half of blood in his stomach. They had great big old tushes and they were mean. They'd kill pigs. When they killed a pig, they just cut him into the middle.

I never was [afraid when I was cat hunting], it never did bother me a bit in this world. I hunted over every bit of Nantahala and [I'd] build me up a fire, and sit there till daylight till I could see how to shoot him out. In most of my hunting back then, we didn't have no such thing as a flashlight. We just had to cut [the tree] down or build a fire and mind him up there till daylight and shoot him out.

My wife was a Nicholson, Bertha Nicholson, and she was raised over on Tallulah River in Georgia, at Tate City. I got to going over there and got acquainted with her, and [her family] finally moved up here to Macon County. Pretty soon after they moved, I went to the state of Washington.

There was a bunch of us in nineteen and twelve that went to Washington State. There was ten of us from down here at Franklin and two or three from Clayton. That TF Railroad came in here then, so we went to Atlanta and all bought our tickets for Sedro Woolley, Washington. That's going up the Skagit River from Seattle going right on up north under Mountain Baker. You could look up there and see snow on Mountain Baker the year round—it stayed froze over. That timber line went up to that snow and it stopped there.

Now, I was the oldest one in the bunch [I was around twenty-five and] I was the only one that was of age. They wouldn't let the others go in the saloons, and they couldn't get no beer and whiskey. I'd have to go in and buy it and they'd let us take it on the train. We'd take her right on in the coach with us. We'd go back in the smoker somewheres, open us a bottle of beer, and drink all we wanted to. It was against the rules for them to get into the saloon. I had to do all the purchasing. We was on the road ten days and nights a'gettin' from Franklin to Seattle, Washington. Sometimes we'd set on the siding half a night or half a day at a time waiting for 'em to patch up a trestle to where we could get through.

We all got jobs and went to work and in the time of it, I'd contracted measles. Somebody at Franklin had the measles, so I come down with the measles. We was there for the Dempsy Lumber Company, workin'. I took sick on Saturday evening. I was sick Sunday, and Monday mornin' I was still sick. That old camp foreman, he cut loose, "Roll up or roll out." That meant if you had a pillow or any cover, you rolled that up and carried that with you. So Grady, my brother, and me, we rolled up [and left].

I knew a couple of old people that come from back home, Jim McConnell and Aunt Lizzie. They'd only been out there two or three weeks but they set up out there at Lynden. They wouldn't let me on the train and I was broke, didn't have no money. I just had enough to get a ticket for home, but when I went in to get the ticket, they wouldn't sell it to me. They said I had some kind of 'tagions or something catching and they wouldn't let me get on the train. And I set around there at the depot. Well, they had a little old hospital place down there. I went down and asked the old man [at the admittance desk] to take me in. Said, "I got a brother going to Alger and he'll be back with some money for me in the morning." No. He wouldn't hear to it. And wouldn't take me in. So I went back up to the depot. I was a'sittin' around up there, and I didn't know *what* in the dickens I was gonna do.

I went down to the *livery* stableman to take me to Lynden. I was gonna go down there to Jim McConnell's. So they wired ahead that I was a'coming, and at the city limits they stopped the liveryman, and he had to take me back. They wouldn't let me into town there at Lynden. So I went back on to Hamilton and sat there at the depot.

Sittin' around at the platform, and there's an old feller come on up talking to me. He said, "Do you drink any liquor?"

I said, "I would if I had some. I ain't got none, and nothing to buy none with." He got up and went off and was gone a little while, and come back with a couple quart bottles. *Full.*

He said, "You take this."

I said, "I ain't got nothing to pay."

He said, "I don't want nothing. Just take it and drink you some of it."

Well, I just uncorked it and took four or five big swallows right there. I began to get where I could talk pretty good. I went back down to the little old hospital, and I just outtalked the old doctor and got him to take me in. And I told him, "You've not got a thing to worry about. There'll be somebody here in the morning with some money." So he took me in.

So the next morning, soon as the train come through there, old man John Kell and Grover [were on it]. So by that time, I had them measles. Lord, I was just broke out from my toes to the top

PLATE 4   Bertha making biscuits for dinner.

PLATE 5   Jake and Foxfire student Lynnette Williams.

of my head. And after them measles broke out, I got to feeling better. Why, I think I stayed there three days, then the doctor released me. I got the liveryman to take me to Lynden to old man Jim McConnell's and Aunt Lizzie's, and they took me in and took care of me.

I hadn't been there but a little bit till there come Ellis Roan, another old boy from here. He'd been up at the camp and he'd caught the measles from me. And he'd just about give 'em to the whole thing up and down the Skagit River. We spread the measles. I mean we *spread* 'em. So I stayed up there and took care of Ellis Roan till he got well. Then I went into the camps and went to loggin' and made it just fine. I'd work at one camp a while and decide I wanted to move to another'n, a better place, and I'd switch jobs. One was just as good as the other'n, but we thought there's better picking across the ridge. There's about three crews there all the time, one a'coming, one a'going, and one a'working.

They'd be pretty rowdy. You could go into town on payday and they'd fight till midnight or after. Wasn't no problem to get in a big fight. There'd be one a'going all the time, all the time. Right up and down the Skagit River and through that section. On up there most of them loggers would meet up and they'd go to getting boozed up and fight. Why, they'd go to havin' them brawls. They'd put on some good ones. Fact is, I was into several of 'em myself.

I wasn't married then. That was in 1912, and I stayed in Washington one summer. I went there toward the last of March and stayed there till October. I come back and in 1915 we got married. We married in September and we stayed with my mammy a while, and then I rented a house a little way from where my mother lived.

The next spring, Irv Hudson and Marsh come up there in the Ash Flats. There was a logging job and I worked that summer for them. I worked there when our oldest baby was born. She was born the twenty-third day of May. I worked there until they finished up that job and went from Ash Flats to what they called the Carpenter Cove. We logged out the Carpenter Cove, and then we went to Sugar Cove and logged that out. It was just from one different job to another.

In the wintertime and the fall of the year I'd get out and hunt some. We'd have possum dogs and coon dogs and we'd catch coons, possums, and muskrats and skunks and everything like that and I'd buy the fur and ship it. I'd make a little money there. Back then everybody kept a pack of hounds. Every family nearly would have from two to three hunting dogs. I always had some good coon dogs and cat dogs, and I'd catch them wildcats. They'd pay a bounty on them, the county commissioners would. I could take [the wildcat] in and they'd cut the ear off and they'd give me a three dollar bounty on it. They paid it on them to protect the lambs and the pigs.

Finally I bought thirty-five acres of land up on the creek here, and I just had a little bit of money to pay down on it. There was some folks who lived up above us and they got out there, and there hadn't been anybody a'digging or hunting ginseng for several years ('cause there'd been a pretty plenty of jobs), and they found a whole lot of ginseng. Their daddy come down and asked me if I knowed where I could sell it. "Well," I said, "right at the present I don't, but I'll go to town, to Franklin, tomorrow and I know a feller down there and it might be that I can work up a deal."

So I went, and it was old man John Harrison and he dealt in ginseng. I told him what I had done and he said, "I tell you what I'll do, Jake, I'll put up the money and you buy it and dry it and we'll go halvers." I'd give five hundred fifty dollars for the land that I had bought, and I made enough off that buying ginseng and selling it that fall to pay the mortgage off on the land. We built us a little house. We'd catch up an old hen and I'd take her and swap her for nails. My brother, or whoever I could pick up, we built that house. I got an old feller, Russet, to come along and he built me a chimney.

PLATE 6   The Waldroops' house, which Jake built thirty-five years ago.

Then old man Will McGuire had a place out on Nantahala and he wanted me to go and raise sheep and hogs, so I went out there and stayed there a couple of years. The summer after we come back, my brother, Ed, was a'working on Wayah Bald in a mica mine, and I drove a team and would haul supplies up there to them. When I wasn't hauling supplies, people would make crossties and get out telephone poles and I'd haul them to Franklin for 'em. Whatever come around, I'd take on some of it.

I bought a hundred acres from old man Newt Moody in 1930, [and] I sold my little place up there. We've been a'livin' here right about thirty-five years. Five hundred and sixty acres come up for sale. Newt Moody had got the timber off the land and wanted to sell it. I come down here and bought a hundred acres of it, and I paid him a thousand dollars down on it. I got the one hundred acres here for thirty-two hundred dollars. It takes a lot of land to make a hundred acres.

Sometimes in the fall of the year when I'd get out of work, I'd get out over these mountains and hunt ginseng. Back then you could find pretty plenty of it. I could get out and travel five or six hours and I'd have a big washpan full. Now you can get out and when you come in you can hold it in your hands. Back then when I was

young and my mother and me would "sang," we'd get about three
to four or five dollars a pound for it dried and about a dollar a
pound green.

When I sold sang for other people I paid them ten cents an ounce
for green sang. Let them wash it and dry the water off. Well, they
put out the word that I was a'buying ginseng again and a'paying
cash for it, and they would come and lots of Friday and Saturday
evenings they would bake up rations and go back in these mountains
and camp out a whole week at a time and tramp and hunt ginseng.
They'd come by my place then and sell it to me. I'd always buy
from two to five of these big-sized washtubs full of that ginseng.
Lord, you'd get great big roots then! It's a sight then to what it is
now. I made enough that fall to pay up my note from Newt Moody.

We was a'livin' pretty close trying to get this paid for. We got
up the money and we wrote him to come and bring the notes. When
I paid him off, I still had about three years' time. [But] I just paid
and got the interest stopped. We had a lawyer draw up a deed.

Our son, Lloyd, lives down the road [from us], and he has the
flowerhouse. Dover was in a car wreck at Myrtle Creek, Oregon,
and got killed. The oldest child and the youngest one of our children
are dead. Iona, that's the next girl, she lives over in Waynesville,
where she works in a cafe.

We have six grandchildren, but none of them live around here
at the present time. One of them works in a radio station; one is
a social worker; one's unemployed right now and one of them is
in Alaska workin' on that pipeline, and he's making two thousand
dollars a week. That's a lot of money. (I always spent the biggest
part of my laboring days making nine dollars a week.) He's an electri-
cian. He took schooling there in Charlotte for four years. Lord,
what about it to compare with what I come up with. We worked
ten hours a day, six days a week, and you had to be on the job at
seven o'clock and you stayed there until six. In the wintertime you
had to carry a lantern with you to see how to get backward and
forward through these mountains.

We don't do much farming anymore. I used to raise and buy
cattle, sell and fool with them for years, but now I've turned the
cattle all over to my son, Lloyd. I still help him to look after them.
I salt them and feed 'em and tend to 'em a whole lot in the wintertime.
We used to raise a lot of corn. I used to tend a fourteen-acre field
all by myself for seven years. I'd turn it and plow it and fix it and
get it ready. I know the fall that Harry Truman was elected President,

I was a'gatherin' the corn, and that fall I made a thousand bushels of corn on that field, and I gathered it every bit by myself. But now I've got too old. I couldn't work it no more, so I just put up enough hay to feed the cattle in the wintertime and let them graze it. They'll just stay there and eat on it all winter.

We've still got enough stuff in the canhouse to do us two or three years. I guess we've got five or six hundred cans of beans, peaches, and jellies, pickles, and everthing in the canhouse, and then we have the deep freeze and we keep it packed full. I guess people eat just too much grub, but I get out and tramp these mountains and I burn it up. I just raise a little sweet corn, beans—I sell lots of beans, Irish potatoes, sweet potatoes, just garden patches.

I've helped some in the last year or two in the hay, not much but I can work a little in it. And I still get stovewood. I keep me a big lot of stovewood ahead. We have a wood and electric stove combined. And I have to put in about three to four hours a week a'mowing this yard. Sometimes I have to go over the pasture and cut this stuff they call bull nettles and Texas thistle, and then there's this old stuff that comes up called burdock and it has a great big burr on it. It will spread all over the place. If the cows get enough of them burrs in their tails [when they twitch them, they can] scatter the whole place with it in the winter, so I have to go over the place and keep that grubbed up. I take me a ditching shovel and get under it and chop it off with that. You can really get tired at that.

I still fish some, several days a week. About all the fish we have now though is when they take them and pour 'em out as stockers. You're allowed to catch seven fish. We would go and catch our seven, but in about three days all of 'em were caught. It's over then until they decide to stock again.

I still squirrel hunt some. My eyes have got bad, but I've got my squirrel dog and [I] take him. My glasses don't help my eyes. If I can get a squirrel to move, why, I can see him, but if he'll just stick on the side of a tree or limb somewhere, I can't find him. I killed several squirrels last fall. I like to eat them. You take that squirrel and make squirrel gravy—trouble is I eat too much and gain weight.

I've never had a prescription filled in my life until last September. I went to the doctor and he said I had high blood. He put me on some pills, and I went to taking them pills and he said I'd have to take them the rest of my life. Then I went to eating garlic, and I eat garlic until the ramps came up and I had what garlic I had eat

PLATE 7 The Waldroops' barn.

up. Then I went to eating ramps. I've still got plenty of ramps to eat now. I've got seventeen quarts of 'em canned. I went to the doctor a couple of weeks ago, and he checked me over and took me off the pills. I figure that the garlic and the ramps and what little the pills helped just about got [the high blood] whipped. I'd always heard that it was good for high blood, but I like to eat them, too. Even eating onions is good for high blood and I'll eat a great big onion and a bunch of lettuce. I eat very little bread. I've always loved vegetables and been a big meat eater, but I don't eat much sweets.

I built this house myself, and I cleared a whole lot of this land. I had to clear the pasture, the land back on this side of the mountain. I had to do a lot of ditching. I brought these shade trees in my yard now from off the mountain and set them out when we first come here. I'm going to hold onto my land; I don't need to sell it. I built this house here and I still work, might' near every day.

GOURD BANJOS AND SONGBOWS

Nearly a decade ago, Foxfire began a study of southern Appalachian homemade musical instruments. A series of articles on banjo and dulcimer makers first appeared in the Fall 1974 issue of *Foxfire* magazine, and was subsequently published in *Foxfire 3* (1975, pp. 120–207). That was followed by two articles on fiddle makers in *Foxfire 4* (1977, pp. 106–25). Since then we have turned up reports of various other homemade instruments, among them the gourd banjo and the musical bow.

In the spring of 1977 we had the good fortune to meet Ernest Hodges, an extraordinary man whose musical experiences have covered the gamut from folk to fine-arts music. Since Mr. Hodges is a concert violinist and violin maker, we were surprised to learn that his first musical instrument was a gourd banjo made for him when he was a small boy in the mountains of North Carolina by his grandfather. He related the details of how his grandfather constructed the instrument out of a long-neck gourd, a tomcat's hide, and a hank of horsehair. We've asked a lot of people since then about gourd instruments and found that they were not uncommon at one time in our region's history.

Leonard Webb, whose instructions appear in this chapter, told us that his father and uncle had made gourd instruments. Leonard remembered a photograph of them holding two such instruments, a fiddle and a banjo, but, unfortunately, the photograph has been lost. We're not exactly certain what kind of gourd those instruments were made of, but Leonard's instrument is a close approximation of one his father would have made.

In addition to the gourd instrument, we have been aware of the musical bow, which is played by musicians scattered throughout the region. We have one musical bow (called "mouth bow," "tune bow," "song bow," and various other names) in our collection, which was made for us several years ago by Mr. Alex Stewart of Sneedville, Tennessee. One day a student named Mark Pruitt came through the office and remarked, "Hey, that's a song bow. My granny can make one of them." This summer we went to see Mark's granny and put together the story, "Babe Makes a Songbow."

We have been encouraged in recent years to include additional documentation in our publications. As you will see, we are making an effort to respond to this in annotative passages that follow each of the next two selections.

We have been building a small research library over the years, but, the tools of scholarly research are expensive and hard to come by. We are indebted to many people who offered information and direction either in person or over the phone. Some, like David Evans at Memphis State University, dug up useful information and sent it to us in the mail. Others, like Joe Hickerson at the Library of Congress and Helen Hollis at the Smithsonian Institution, made a high-school teacher and two teen-age kids feel at home in the big-city library.

LEONARD WEBB'S GOURD BANJO

As you come up the little dirt-and-gravel road leading to the house, two dogs, Spike and Tucker, come running, jumping, and barking to meet you. The house is in the center of a small clearing surrounded by an apple orchard on one side and woods on the other; a lawn is in front and a wooden shed that sometimes houses chickens is in the back. The wooden house is white and green with a bay window sticking out in front over the lawn. Then, as you are getting out of the car and trying to avoid the dogs jumping playfully but forcefully all over you, a warm and friendly man comes out of the house, waving and smiling. His name is Leonard Webb and he immediately invites you back inside to visit with his wife, Rittie, and him. The house is comfortably furnished and many genuine antiques are to be found. The old clock ticks regularly and the big wood stove puts out welcome heat on a bitter-cold day. While you are talking, Leonard may get out his banjo and play a tune—if you ask him nicely and are lucky. He plays and sings extremely well and his banjo has a neck that he made himself out of wild cherry. If your curiosity and luck continue, he may ask you downstairs to his shop beneath the house. It has a dirt floor, and almost every tool imaginable hangs upon the walls, windowsills, and workbenches. He uses all hand tools, except for an electric saw and drill. He even has a homemade vise, which he says works better than the one he bought.

Leonard Webb and his wife, Rittie, have been married for fifty-three years and they have raised eleven children. Leonard came from a large family himself, having three brothers and seven sisters. Except for a few months in other

PLATE 8

parts of the country, Leonard was born, raised, and still lives in Macon County, North Carolina. Leonard started playing the banjo when he was thirteen years old and played regularly in his home and at dances. He has done many things in his life but worked mostly at farming and carpentry. After we met Leonard, we were pleased to learn that he is the brother of Mrs. Magaline Zoellner and the late Mr. Andy Webb, both of whom have contributed greatly to Foxfire magazine. All of this information, however, was unknown to us until late last November, when we headed up the mountain to find, meet, and talk to Leonard Webb.

We wanted desperately to talk with Mr. Webb, since someone told us that he could make a banjo out of a long-necked gourd. We felt something like this would be extremely interesting and noteworthy, and demonstrate a skill that had not been described previously in our publications—or anywhere else, for that matter. And, sure enough, Mr. Webb could indeed make a banjo out of a gourd. He told us that his father had made banjos and that he had learned the art from him. Sensing that we wanted to ask him to make us a gourd banjo but were afraid to ask outright, he gently offered by telling us if we could find a good gourd, he would do it for us. The story of finding the right gourd will be told later in this section, but that first meeting marked the beginning of a long and pleasant series of interviews and visits with Leonard

PLATE 9

PLATE 10

PLATE 11

PLATE 12   PLATE 13

Webb and his wife. Not only did we eventually learn how to make and record the process for making a gourd banjo, we also established a tremendous, lasting, and solid friendship with a wonderful couple. This friendship is something one can never measure in rolls of film, miles traveled, or visits made. Simply, we had good times and good experiences doing this piece, and we hope you enjoy it.

WESLEY TAYLOR AND MITCH WHITMIRE

For more extensive information on banjos in general, please refer to *Foxfire 3* (pp. 121–87), which includes a partial history of the banjo and gives instructions for making other, different styles of the instrument. Included, among others, are banjo makers and well-known Foxfire contacts Tedra Harmon and Stanley Hicks.

PLATE 14 Leonard inspects the gourd and formulates plans on how it will be used.

PLATE 15 After cutting a hole in the dried gourd and getting out the seeds, Leonard proceeds to cut off that side as shown. He uses no tool to measure or draw lines to do this cutting—it is done completely from experience and with a keen eye.

Finding the Right Gourd

When we first went to see Leonard, he told us that we needed to find a dried gourd with a straight neck and as close to a perfect sphere on the "head end" as possible. We hunted and hunted but couldn't find a good gourd. We put out the word concerning our plight to student and staff, and the right gourd showed up as we were about to give up hope. We took it up the mountain and this story was on its way.

Cutting the Gourd

PLATE 16 Leonard was careful to cut the gourd approximately ½″ above the level of the neck as shown in Plate 17. This will allow the fingerboard to fit properly.

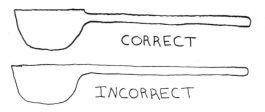

CORRECT

INCORRECT

PLATE 17

PLATE 18 The gourd with one side completely cut off.

PLATE 19 After completing the cutting process, Leonard explains to Foxfire adviser Paul Gillespie how the fingerboard will fit on the gourd neck. Arrow points out that the gourd was cut on a line slightly above the level of the neck.

Making the Fingerboard

It is important to point out at this time that the process of making the fingerboard was delicate, tedious, and time-consuming. The fingerboard was cut to fit this particular gourd, and measurements given will not apply to all gourds.

PLATE 20   Leonard told us to find a good slab of dry walnut approximately 3' long, 5" wide, and 2 to 3" thick. From this he cut out the heart or best part to be used for the fingerboard. Before he started chiseling this piece, it measured 26" x 2 ½" x 1 ¾"

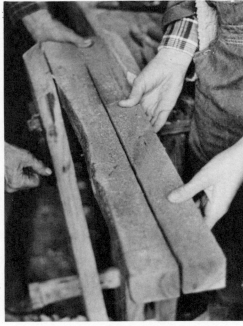

PLATE 21

PLATE 22 Leonard planes the piece of walnut to be used for the fingerboard.

PLATE 23 With a home-made chisel, Leonard starts to chisel out the area where the fingerboard will fit on the neck of the gourd.

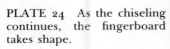

PLATE 24 As the chiseling continues, the fingerboard takes shape.

PLATE 25

PLATE 26 The fingerboard is rasped.

PLATE 27 Leonard rasps the fingerboard for precision fitting. Special attention is given to areas where the fingerboard meets the banjo head and on the sides where the fingerboard meets the neck.

PLATE 28 Top view of location for fifth string-tuning peg.

PLATE 29   Side view of location for fifth string-tuning peg. Plate 30 gives dimensions for the fingerboard of Leonard's banjo.

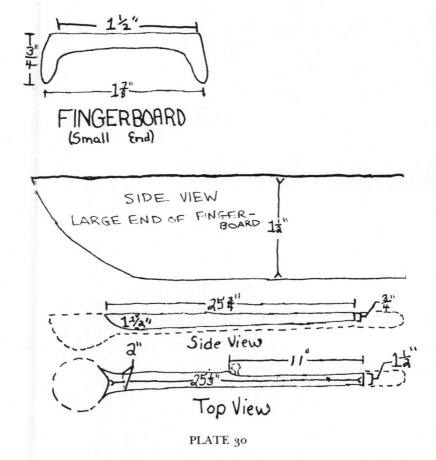

PLATE 30

PLATE 31   Leonard rests the unattached fingerboard on the neck of the gourd, showing how it will fit. The fingerboard is set aside for now and the next step is taken up.

Reinforcement and Apron Tail

PLATE 32   With brass tacks, Leonard attaches a thin strip of hickory ½″ wide inside the head to make it stronger.

PLATE 33   The apron tail, an anchor for the apron through which the strings are threaded, is attached 1″ below the top rim of the gourd with a ¼″ screw that is 1 ½″ long. Plate 34 gives specific dimensions.

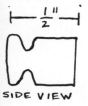

SIDE VIEW

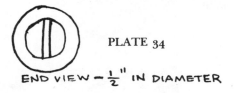

PLATE 34

END VIEW — ½″ IN DIAMETER

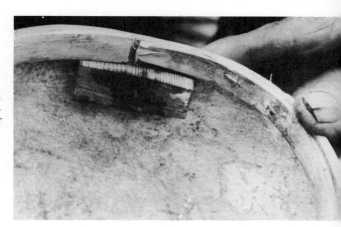

PLATE 35   The apron tail is anchored on the inside of the gourd with a small block of wood.

The Banjo Head

PLATE 36   The head for this banjo is made from a ground-hog hide. The hair had been removed and the skin had been allowed to dry out for several months. Here it is being stretched over the cut side of the gourd to insure that it will fit properly.

PLATE 37   Leonard trims the ground-hog hide to the proper shape. Enough of the hide is left to allow a 1″ overhang all the way around the gourd.

PLATE 38 Leonard applies glue around the top edge of the gourd. A modern glue is shown in the photograph, but Leonard remembers using old-time glues.

PLATE 39 Using a very small bit, Leonard begins drilling one hole at a time around the top edge of the gourd and into the reinforcement. Each time a hole is drilled, a ⅝" brass nail is driven lightly through the hide and into that hole. Leonard remembers using a hand drill in this step.

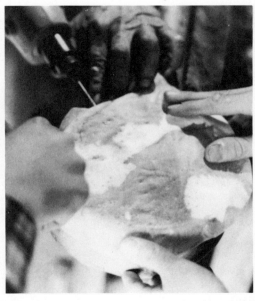

PLATE 40 The gourd with one side of the head tacked on.

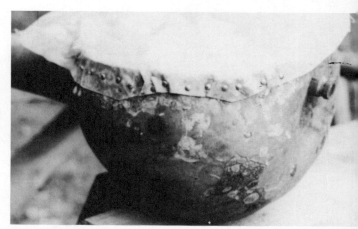

PLATE 41   While constantly pulling and keeping the head stretched as tightly as possible, it is then tacked around the gourd.

PLATE 42   The head is secured and the fingerboard is ready to be attached.

Attaching the Fingerboard

When finished, the fingerboard that was constructed earlier should fit snugly along the neck and up against the head of the gourd. The fingerboard is then ready to be anchored. To anchor the fingerboard, a hole is drilled through one side of the fingerboard near the middle of its length. This hole is made with a 1/4″ bit and should continue on through the neck of the gourd and the other side of the fingerboard. A walnut peg is driven through the hole and one "anchor" is finished. This process is repeated four more times, and all five holes with pegs should be evenly spaced along the length of the fingerboard.

PLATE 43   Leonard points to the last hole drilled.

PLATE 44   Leonard carves and rasps anchor pegs.

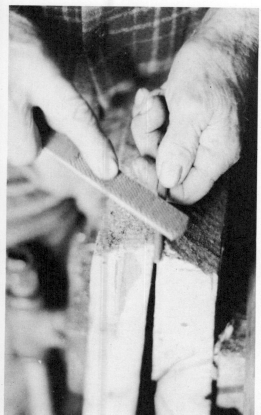

PLATE 45

PLATE 46 Leonard gently taps the
peg to start it into the hole.
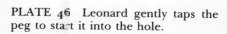

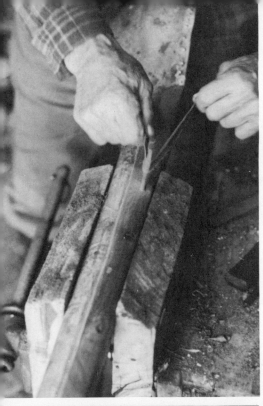

PLATE 47   Sanding and hammering are done alternately until the peg goes completely through the assembly.

PLATE 50   Glue and walnut dust are mixed and packed under the edges of the fingerboard on the sides.

PLATE 48

PLATE 49   The peg is sawed off flush with the side of the fingerboard.

The Fingerbridge, Bridge, and Apron

PLATE 51   A walnut fingerbridge (nut) is attached with ⅝″ brass nails to the upper end of the fingerboard. Four small notches for the strings are cut, as shown in Plate 52.

PLATE 52   *Note:* The diagrams for the fingerbridge, bridge, and apron may be used as patterns since they represent actual sizes.

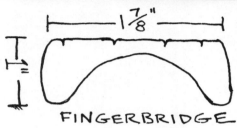

FINGERBRIDGE

PLATE 53   A close-up view of the apron (tailpiece) attached to the apron tail with a thin, twisted copper wire. A movable bridge with five small notches is cut for the banjo head. The movable bridge has one notch more than the fingerbridge to accommodate the fifth string. These parts are also made from walnut. See Plate 54 for specifications.

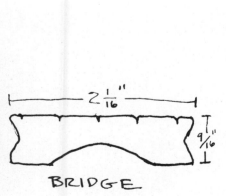

BRIDGE

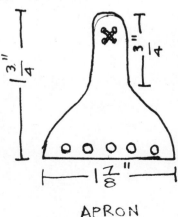

APRON

PLATE 54

The Tuning Pegs

PLATE 55 Leonard begins shaping one of four large tuning pegs from walnut. The tuning pegs are roughly 3 ½ " long overall, and the heads are about ⅞ " across and ¼ " thick. The stems are round with a diameter of about ¼ " (see Plate 56).

PLATE 56

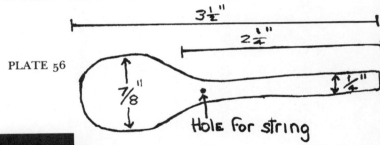

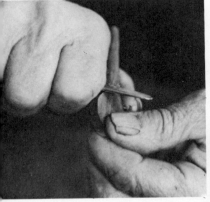

PLATE 57 Leonard carefully carves out the tuning pegs.

PLATE 58 The four pegs are carved almost exactly alike (not shown is the fifth string-tuning peg, which has the same dimensions as the others, except that its overall length is 2 ⅝ ").

The Strings

PLATE 59   Close-up showing the top of the gourd and the arrangement of the strings. The pegs are snugly fitted through holes roughly ¼ " in diameter. (During this step, extreme care must be taken so as not to make the holes too large.) The pegs are approximately ¾ " apart and the first one is placed ¾ " from the fingerbridge. Each peg has a small hole in it (as shown in Plate 56), and the banjo strings are run through these holes and twisted on the pegs to tune the banjo.

PLATE 60   Close-up showing strings and fifth tuning-peg position. Note that a small wood screw is used to position the G (fifth) string properly. (*Note:* Banjo strings can be purchased in hardware and music stores.)

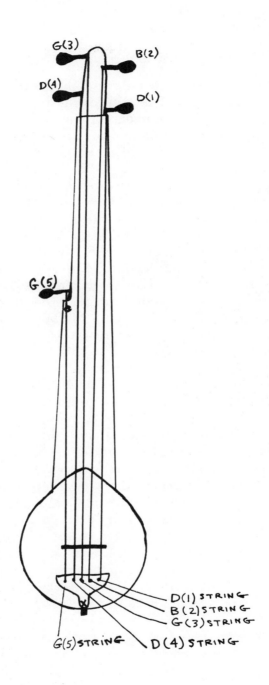

PLATE 61

The Finished Product

Little if anything has been written about the use of gourd instruments in Appalachia. The bulk of the documentation lies in oral accounts and in what remains of the instruments themselves. So far we have interviewed three contacts in different communities who remember seeing gourd banjos and fiddles as children. Additional inquiries may add to the list. As far as tangible evidence of their existence, we know of at least three Appalachian gourd fiddles. All are privately owned, but all have been shown in museums. The oldest documented example is shown in the Museum of Appalachia in Norris, Tennessee, a fiddle made by Frank Couch of Hancock County, Tennessee, in about 1840. Another gourd fiddle, probably old, belonging to Roderick Moore, is displayed in the Blue Ridge Folklife Museum in Ferrum, Virginia. Both pieces have a wooden fingerboard. A more recent example, one without a wooden fingerboard, made by Dewey Shepherd of David, Kentucky, was shown in the Renwick Gallery in Washington, D.C., in the summer of 1979. A gourd banjo made around Franklin, North Carolina, about fifty years ago hung in an antique shop in Franklin for several years but was sold to a museum in New Orleans, and we have not, as yet, been able to track down the gourd banjo.

Gourd instrument construction is widespread, ancient, and persistent. Gourd resonators are found on traditional instruments throughout several continents, including southern Asia, Africa, and the Americas. The Indian *sitar* is perhaps the most well-known example, but there are a host of others. A variety of African instruments, such as the *banza*, the *rankie*, and the *gurmi*, are thought to be possible antecedents of the American banjo. In fact, the most intriguing aspect of the Leonard Webb banjo is that it is so remarkably similar to the earliest forms of banjos found in this country.

It is generally accepted that the banjo is derived from African tradition and was first fashioned by African slaves in the New World colonies. Dena Epstein's exhaustive research into the history of Afro-American music has yielded a number of early reports describing banjolike instruments, and they consistently refer to gourd construction. The earliest report is one by Sir Hans Sloane, a visitor to Jamaica in the late 1680s, who described "Instruments in imitation of lutes, made of small Gourds fitted with Necks, strung with Horse hairs, or the peeled stalks of climbing Plants or Withs" (Sir Hans

PLATES 62–63 Two views of the completed gourd banjo.

TOP VIEW

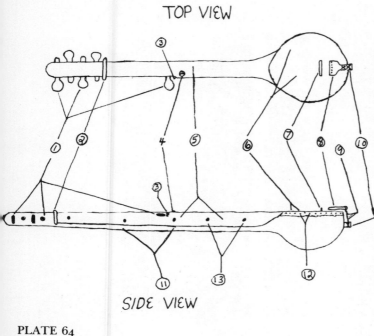

① Tuning Pegs
② Finger Bridge
③ 5th String Indention
④ Screw (wood) to hold
   5th String in Place
⑤ Fingerboard
⑥ Banjo head (covered
   with groundhog hide)
⑦ Bridge
⑧ Apron
⑨ Wire holding Apron
   in place
⑩ Apron Tail
⑪ Neck of Gourd
⑫ Tacks holding on head
⑬ Pegs holding the
   fingerboard to neck
   of gourd.

SIDE VIEW

PLATE 64

PLATE 65   Leonard, Wesley Taylor, and Mitch Whitmire test the new gourd banjo that took roughly twenty hours to complete.

Sloane, *A Voyage to the Islands of Madera, Barbados, Nieves, S. Christopher and Jamaica, with the Natural History of the . . . last of these Islands . . .* [London: print by B.M. for the author, 1707], Vol. I, p. lix, cited in Dena Epstein, "African Music in British and French America," *Musical Quarterly,* Vol. 59, No. 1 [Jan. 1973], pp. 74–75, Plate II).

Among the many sources that document the history of the folk banjo, a common reference is *The Old Plantation,* a painting in the

PLATE 66   "The Old Plantation." (Photo courtesy of the Abby Aldrich Rockefeller Folk Art Center.)

Abby Aldrich Rockefeller Folk Art Center, Williamsburg, Virginia. The anonymous watercolor (Plate 66) depicts slaves on a late eighteenth-century South Carolina plantation dancing to the music of a banjolike instrument identified by some ethnomusicologists as an African *molo.* One cannot help but notice the striking similarity of this instrument to the one made by Leonard Webb.

The course by which the banjo migrated from the southern plantation into the Appalachians is not entirely clear, but a rough historical outline has emerged. The banjo began as the exclusive property of southern blacks until sometime in the early nineteenth century, when minstrel-show musicians began using it in derisive caricatures of the Negro. Eventually, the instrument was disowned by blacks and embraced by whites, who began refining and factory-producing the instrument for use by popular and even classical musicians. Meanwhile, the instrument was gradually carried into the Appalachians, possibly by black migrant workers, possibly by way of minstrel shows or medicine shows, perhaps in some other way; no one knows for sure. It is generally agreed, though, that the banjo had taken a foothold in the Appalachian white tradition by the late nineteenth century.

One might argue that homemade southern-mountain banjos were copied after factory-made instruments apart from black influence. On the other hand, instruments like the gourd banjo suggest a possible carryover from the earlier black tradition.

The gourd banjo offers no definitive proof of direct transition—banjos have been made out of cheese hoops, lard cans, and automatic transmissions. Still, Leonard Webb's gourd banjo stands as an intriguing link in the chain of tradition.

GEORGE REYNOLDS WITH WESLEY TAYLOR

Bibliography

FOR FURTHER READING SEE:

Adler, Tom. "The Physical Development of the Banjo," *New York Folklore Quarterly*, Vol. 28, No. 3, Sept. 1972, pp. 187–208.

Bailey, Jay. "Historical Origin and Stylistic Developments of the Five-string Banjo," *Journal of American Folklore*, Vol. 85, No. 335, Jan.–Mar. 1972, pp. 58–65.

Epstein, Dena. *Sinful Tunes and Spirituals: Black Folk Music to the Civil War.* Urbana, Ill.: University of Illinois Press, 1977.

———. "Slave Music in the United States Before 1860: A Survey of Sources," in two parts, *Notes* (Music Library Association) Vol. 20, No. 2, Spring 1963, pp. 195–212; Vol. 20, No. 3, Summer 1963, pp. 377–90.

———. "The Folk Banjo: A Documentary History," *Ethnomusicology*, Vol. 19, No. 3, Sept. 1975, pp. 347–71.

Glassie, Henry. *Pattern in the Material Folk Culture of the Eastern United States.* Philadelphia, Pa.: University of Pennsylvania Press, 1968.

Irwin, John. *Instruments of the Southern Appalachian Mountains.* Norris, Tenn.: Museum of Appalachia Press, 1979.

Odell, Scott. "Folk Instruments," *Arts in Virginia* (Virginia Museum), Vol. 12, No. 1, Fall 1971, pp. 31–37.

Vlach, John Michael. *The Afro-American Tradition in Decorative Arts.* Cleveland, O.: Cleveland Museum of Art, 1978, Chap. 2, "Musical Instruments," pp. 20–26.

See also: *A Bibliography of the History and Playing Styles of the Five-string Banjo,* compiled by the Archive of Folk Song in the Library of Congress.

BABE HENSON'S SONGBOW

We had heard people mention songbows before, but we didn't know anybody who could make one or play one. One day we were talking about it and one of the Foxfire students, Mark Pruitt, said his grandmother could make one and play it, too. Mark set up the interview and we headed for Coweeta Mountain in North Carolina. When we got there we received a very friendly welcome from Babe and her husband, Mutt Henson. We sat on the porch and played music with Babe, Babe's sister, Mutt; and some of her neighbors. Besides playing the songbow, Babe can also play the banjo and sing.

A few days later we went back and Babe agreed to show us how to make a songbow. She explained how her momma showed her how: "Momma helped me and I made one and I played 'Chickens Crowing on Sourwood Mountain.' That's what Mommy learned me to play, the first thing. It's kinda hard to play 'cause you have to keep your finger moving and you have to work your mouth, too, so it takes your breath and it keeps your hand working at the same time. But anyway I love my songbow.

"One day I was kinda nervous and I didn't know what I wanted to do. I said, 'Mommy, I'm going to the woods and cut me a sourwood stick and make me a songbow.'

"Momma said, 'All right, go ahead.'

"Well, I went up there and I went and cut me a stick and I made that songbow and come back and said, 'Mommy, looky here.'

"Boy, you know Mommy was surprised. She didn't think her little old girl twelve-years-old could do it. But, boys, I did. Momma just died laughing. That pleased her, and you know, that made me feel awful good. So that's how I made my songbow."

Article and photographs by Boyd Queen with Mark Pruitt and Doug Young

Babe Henson's "songbow" is among the most primitive and perhaps obscure of the homemade instruments played in the southern Appalachians. As illustrated in the photos, the bow is placed against the mouth and plucked with the finger or a small pick. The string produces a fundamental tone providing a constant drone using the oral cavity as a resonator. A melody is produced by increasing or decreasing the size of the oral cavity in much the same way as whistling or playing a Jew's harp or jaw harp.

PLATE 67 "My mother took me up on the mountain and she said she was going to let me make a songbow and I said, 'A songbow? Mommy, what in the world is a songbow?'"

PLATE 68 "She said, 'Well, you go to a sourwood tree not very high . . .

The "songbow" is one of several similar instruments known by different names and referred to generically as musical bows. They are found in a variety of forms and are played with different techniques. Curt Sachs in *The History of Musical Instruments* (New York: W. W. Norton & Company, 1940), pp. 56–57, separates musical bows into three types: bows with separate resonators; bows with attached resonators; and bows that resonate in the player's mouth, such as Babe's "songbow," more commonly referred to as mouthbows. Sources indicate that the musical bow can be plucked, hammered with small sticks or paddles, or vibrated by force of the player's breath. It can also be bowed with yet another bow. Sometimes the string is stopped by touching it with the finger, a gourd neck, bottle, or pocket knife. In "Afro-American One-stringed Instruments" (*Western Folklore*, Vol. 29, No. 4, 1970), p. 236, David Evans cites a report of the "bottleneck" technique used by musical bow players in Kenya. He suggests a connection between this and the slide guitar technique used by American blues musicians.

The musical bow appears to have originated in prehistoric times and has diffused across several continents. Curt Sachs (*The History of Musical Instruments,* pp. 62–64) developed a historical framework that dates it as far back as the Neolithic period. Since the musical bow is identical to the shooting bow in shape, many people assume that it derived from the hunter's bow. References often cite the work of Percival R. Kirby, *The Musical Instruments of the Native Races of South Africa* (Oxford: Oxford University Press, 1934; Johannesburg: Witwatersrand University Press, 1953), who observed the Bushmen of South Africa convert the shooting bow to a musical instrument. Sachs, on the other hand, contends that "forms of the musical bow which we have good reason to believe as the oldest have nothing to do with the hunter's bow. They are ten feet long and therefore useless for shooting" (*History of Musical Instruments,* p. 56). (For a comparison of these theories see Sybil Marcuse, "Musical Bows," *A Survey of Musical Instruments* [New York: Harper & Row, 1975], p. 178.) Distribution of the instrument was documented as early as 1897 by Otis T. Mason, "Geographical Distribution of the Musical Bow," *American Anthropologist,* Vol. 10, pp. 377–80, and in 1899 by Henry Balfour, *The Natural History of the Musical Bow* (Oxford: Oxford University Press, 1899), pp. 38–47. The most recent source we've found is Musical Instruments of the World: An Illustrated Encyclopedia (New York: Paddington Press Ltd., 1976), p. 166, which describes musical bows as "commonly found in Africa, America, and Asia," and shows a number of examples.

PLATE 69 " '. . . and you get a limb off of it about 2' long and about 1" thick [the one we used was about ½"] . . .

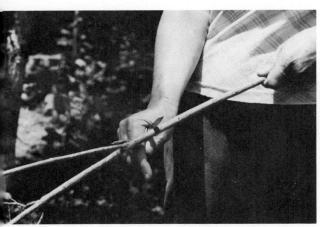

PLATE 70 " '. . . then cut it off and trim it.

PLATE 71 " 'You take and cut a notch around the little end . . .

PLATE 72 "'. . . and then at the big end you take the bark off two sides of it and make you a split down through it.

PLATE 73 " 'Then you take a thread [the one Babe used was about No. 10 weight cotton twine thread, which measured about twice the length of the stick]. Then you double it and you twist that.' Doug, you twist to the south and I'll twist to the north. That holds the thread together. That's what makes the thread make a racket more.

PLATE 74 "Then you tie a knot in each end and you tie the string around the ring in the small end.

PLATE 75 "Put the other knotted end through the split in the other end of the stick.

PLATE 76 "Bend the stick and wrap the string around it several times to increase the tension. You see, that makes it come up tighter.

PLATE 77 "Then you take beeswax and you rub that up and down your thread. That makes the two strands stick together and makes it sound louder."

PLATE 78 The finished songbow. During the interview Babe used Doug's knife: "He handed it to me open and I'm giving it back the same way, because it's bad luck if you close it yourself and hand it back to him. You're supposed to give it back to him the same way he gave it to you."

PLATE 79 Before Babe played the songbow she licked the string, saying it would make it sound louder. Here Babe shows the correct way to hold a songbow in your mouth.

It appears that the musical bow may have come to America by way of both Africa and Asia. Sybil Marcuse says that musical bows found on the East Coast of Central and South America may have African derivation, yet she points out that musical bows of northwestern American Indians bear a relationship to those of Asia and the Pacific (*A Survey of Musical Instruments*, pp. 179–80. As far as we know, there is no tradition of musical bows in Europe or the British Isles, so such an influence can be sufficiently ruled out here.

According to David Evans, the mouthbow is one of a variety of African derived one-stringed instruments in this country. He has recently recorded a black musician in the Deep South who plays such an instrument (Eli Owens, *South Mississippi Blues*, [Rounder 2005]). The bow is single-stringed, has a tin-can resonator at one end, and is pressed against the mouth when plucked. (For a photograph of Owens, see John Vlach, *The Afro-American Tradition in Decorative Arts* [Cleveland: The Cleveland Museum of Art, 1978], p. 23.) Of the handful of traditional mouthbow players who have been commercially recorded, Charles Everidge, a white musician from Mountain View, Arkansas, seems to have been the earliest to be recorded and the best known throughout the country (see *Ballads and Breakdowns from the Southern Mountains* [Prestige International 25003], recorded by Alan Lomax in 1959, one of several LPs featuring Everidge). In Evans's estimation, Everidge's mouthbow music "almost certainly derives ultimately from Negro tradition" ("Afro-American One-stringed Instruments," p. 239).

Because of the commercial recordings of Charles Everidge, James Morris, Jimmy Driftwood, and others, the most widely recognized use of the mouthbow among white cultures has been in the Ozarks. However, the mouthbow is also distributed throughout the southern Appalachians, where there is a widespread belief that the mouthbow came into the white culture by way of the Cherokee Indians. Though the mouthbow has never been officially documented among the Cherokees, a legend persists among mountaineers, which must be taken into account. For example, one of our old friends, Alex Stewart, a mouthbow player from Norris, Tennessee, has been quoted as saying, "The Indians used to live around on Newman's Ridge in my Grandpa's time and they'd set around their campfires of a night and they'd play their hunting bows and the White's sort of took it up from them" (John Irwin, *Instruments of the Southern Appalachian Mountains*, p. 59).

Appalachian musical bows we've discovered so far are basically the same—a bent stick two to five feet in length to which a string is attached on either end, forming a bow. The player uses the mouth as a resonating chamber. In Macon County, North Carolina, Babe Henson makes a "songbow" out of a sapling and cotton string. In Madison County, North Carolina, they make a "tune bow" out of split hemlock tobacco-curing sticks and wire string (one appears in the Smithsonian collection). In the area surrounding Hancock County, Tennessee, they make instruments out of red cedar or hickory and wire and refer to them as "music bows," "mouth bows," or "tuning bows." We are told that musical bows exist elsewhere in the Appalachians as well. The Library of Congress recorded a mouthbow player in Marrow Bone, Kentucky, and Roscoe Holcomb of Daisy, Kentucky, is also reported to have played one (see the notes accompanying *Roscoe Holcomb and Wade Ward* [Folkways FA2363]). Instruments known as "sambows" are also reported to have been played by blacks in the Blue Ridge Mountains of South-central Virginia. The only published source to date about the Appalachian musical bow is a catalog of musical instruments found in the extraordinary collection of John Rice Irwin in the Museum of Appalachia in Norris, Tennessee. Irwin states, ". . . use of the mouth bow in Appalachia, like the dulcimer, was known throughout the region. But like the dulcimer, it was known by relatively few in any given area." There may be exceptions to this, but for the most part this rings true. The mouthbow is said to be used sometimes in the absence of more sophisticated instruments. At other times it functions as a novelty or as a children's instrument. In order for anything so ancient to survive through the generations it must have a function. In this case the function is obvious. As Babe said, when she played her first tune on the "songbow" for her mother, ". . . you know, that made me feel awful good."

GEORGE REYNOLDS WITH BOYD QUEEN

WOODEN LOCKS

The idea for this chapter came from one of our magazine subscribers, Mrs. Hazel DeMent, who now lives in Pontiac, Michigan. She remembered as a child seeing wooden, hand-carved locks with wooden tumblers and whittled wooden keys on various buildings around her grandfather's farm in eastern North Carolina. Her letter read, in part, "My grandfather, who was born in eastern North Carolina in 1842, used to make them, and I'd be so glad to know if they were his invention or if he learned to make them from some older person. We had those locks, measuring 6 1/2" by 9", on the great house, kitchen, and corn crib. All these locks got lost, strayed, or stolen except one, which my father took off one of the doors for safekeeping. That one also disappeared. So none of us knew whether Grandpa made them (invented them) or not because when he was living, and when my father who could probably have told us was living, we were not interested in such things."

We had never seen such locks, but we began looking. Two years later, we still had not found anything resembling what she had described on any farms in our area, when another letter arrived from her. It included a copy of a newspaper article that appeared in the September 28, 1976, edition of the Rocky Mount, North Carolina, *Telegram.* The article told of an exhibition of locks on view in that town sponsored by the Schlage Lock Company, and it pictured a wooden pin-tumbler lock in use before the birth of Christ. The caption below the picture read, "The first mechanical locks—made of wood—were probably created by a number of civilizations at the same time. This wooden lock was found in the Tenimber Isles (Dutch East Indies). The key is the smaller stick."

With renewed interest, we went to see John Rice Irwin, who owns the Museum of Appalachia in Norris, Tennessee. True to form, John Rice, who always seems to have the answers to any questions we can throw his way, walked out with us to one of his buildings and showed us two wooden locks in a display case. The locks were

PLATE 80 Inside view of
one of the wooden locks at
John Rice Irwin's museum
with the tumblers, key, and
bolt in place.

PLATE 81 The same lock with the tumblers, key, and bolt removed.

PLATE 82   The same lock as it would look mounted on a door. When the key is inserted (at arrow) and pushed upward, its teeth lift the tumblers up out of the notches in the bolt, allowing the bolt to be slid back out of the doorjamb, and the door to open.

nearly identical to the one pictured in the *Telegram*, and they had been used on farms in the mountains near John Rice's museum. He told us that such locks were fairly common in the Appalachians and were usually found on the smokehouses—the only buildings that people felt really needed to be locked. We photographed the museum's locks and returned home.

Several months later, while interviewing Hershel House in Morgantown, Kentucky, about making flintlock rifles [*Foxfire 5*, pp. 296–343], we mentioned the lock search, and he laughed and took us to a nearby farm, where a wooden lock was still in place on a barn door. We photographed that one also.

A continued search for such locks in our own county remained fruitless, however, for another year until Mrs. Isaac Lovell, not even knowing we were searching for such an item, called us completely independently to tell us that her husband had just made something that we might like to see. Benson Justus, Tim Henderson, and Pat Marcellino went to the Lovell home in Tiger, and Isaac pulled out a wooden lock. It was nearly identical to those we had already docu-

PLATE 83 A lock in place on a barn door near Morgantown, Kentucky. An unusually long bolt (arrow) passes through a second block of wood adjacent to and to the right of the lock.

PLATE 84 The top of the lock (arrow) is visible in this view of the upper section of the barn doors.

PLATE 85 The doors, pegged together by wooden pegs, open and close on wooden hinges (see Plate 86).

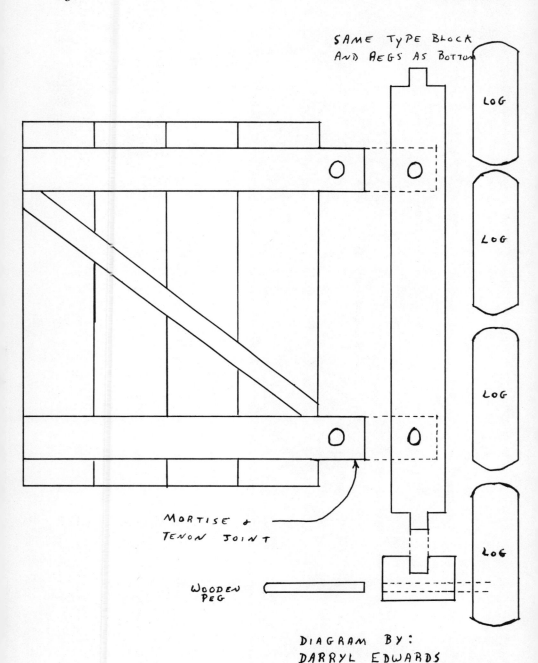

SAME TYPE BLOCK
AND PEGS AS BOTTOM

LOG

LOG

LOG

LOG

MORTISE +
TENON JOINT

WOODEN
PEG

DIAGRAM BY:
DARRYL EDWARDS

PLATE 86

PLATE 87   The Isaac Lovell lock from the inside.

mented. As Benson took photographs, Pat took notes and wrote the following: As far as Isaac knows, his great-grandfather was the first in his family to move to Rabun County. Isaac himself was born in 1915 on Timpson Creek in the Lake Burton area. When the Lake Burton dam was built in 1918, the family was forced to move. They settled in Clarkesville, Georgia, and Isaac in later years moved back to the Bridge Creek section of Tiger, where he and his wife live today.

Isaac's father, Carlton Lovell, was a farmer and used a wooden lock on his smokehouse door. Isaac got interested in the lock when he was a boy, and so his father showed him how to make one, and he made one by himself. During the same period, he noticed them on many outbuilding doors in our area.

PLATE 88   The same lock with the bolt removed to show the slot and pin (arrow), which prevent the bolt from being completely removed from the lock. The block on the left represents the doorjamb.

PLATE 89   The same lock from the outside.

Not long ago, he asked his wife if she had ever seen one. When she said no, he said he would make one to show her how they worked. When it was finished, she was sure we would be interested and so she called us.

There was one significant difference between the other locks we had seen and Isaac's: The addition of a pin on the bolt and a corresponding slot in the floor of the lock to prevent the bolt from being completely removed (see Plate 92).

Isaac was also able to tell us how the locks he saw as a child were attached. Four holes were drilled in the lock—one at each corner—and through the door. Two long pieces of wrought iron were then bent into a "U" shape so that the two prongs of each would fit through two of the holes in the lock (one through the top two holes and one through the bottom two), and through the door with plenty to spare on the inside of one door. Then the two pieces of iron were heated, set in place to pin the lock to the door, and their ends, while hot, were bent over inside the door. Water dashed on the metal caused it to shrink and bind the lock tightly into place, making it almost impossible to get off. The key, which was hung by the kitchen door, was essential to get the door open.

PLATE 90   Isaac Lovell.

THE ISAAC LOVELL LOCK

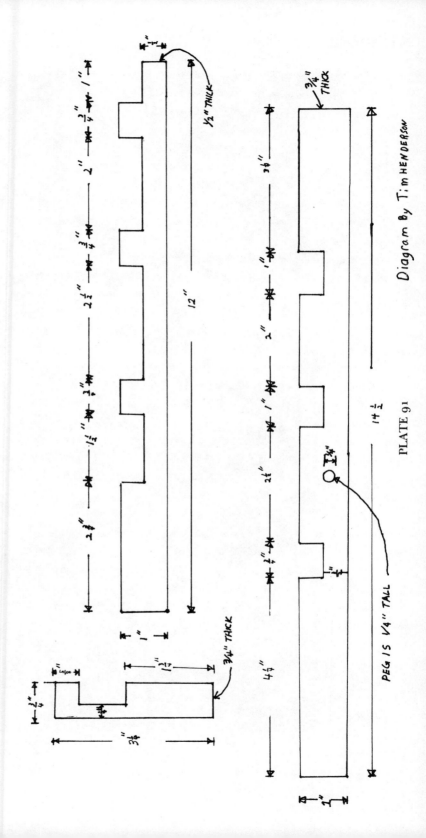

Diagram By Tim HENDERSON

PLATE 91

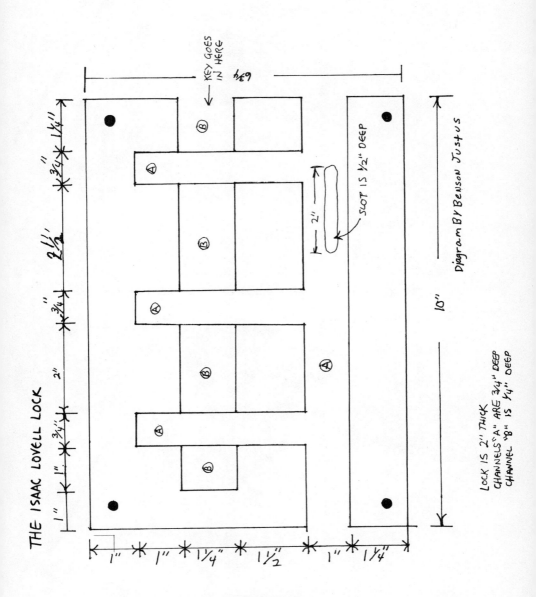

THE ISAAC LOVELL LOCK

KEY GOES IN HERE

SLOT IS ½" DEEP

2"

6¾"

10"

Diagram By Benson Justus

LOCK IS 2" THICK
CHANNELS "A" ARE ¾" DEEP
CHANNEL "B" IS ¼" DEEP

1" ¾" 1¼" 2½" ¾" 2" ¾" 1"

1" 1" 1¼" 1½" 1" 1¼"

PLATE 92

PLATE 93   The lock Shayne and Marty made with the key removed.

PLATE 94   A tumbler being removed from Shayne and Marty's lock (see Plates 95–97).

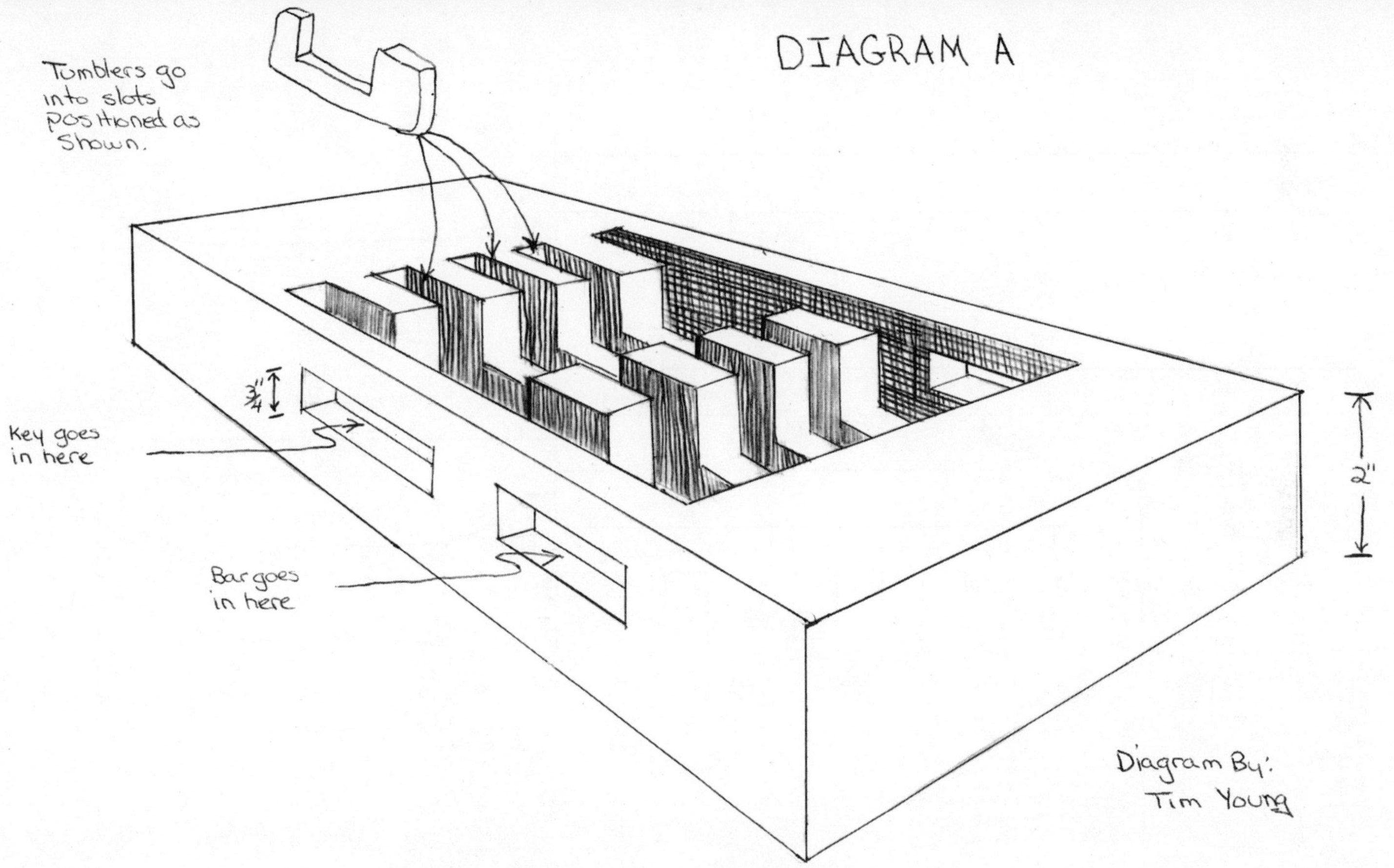

DIAGRAM A

2"

Tumblers go
into slots
Positioned as
Shown.

Key goes
in here

3/4"

Bar goes
in here

Diagram By:
Tim Young

PLATE 95

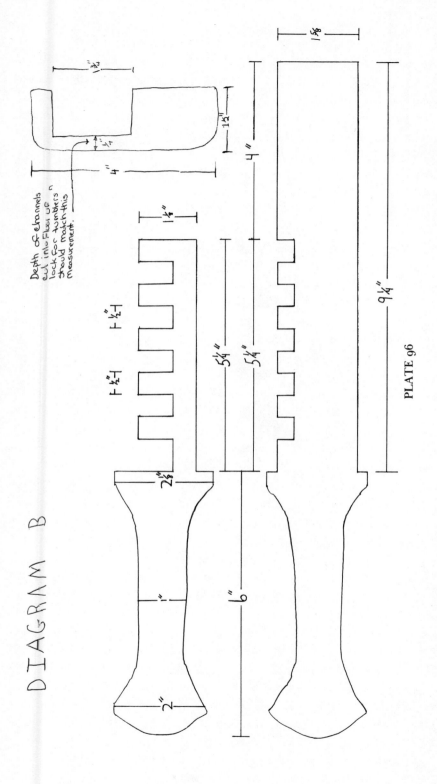

DIAGRAM B

Depth of channels cut into flue up lock for tumblers should match this measurement.

PLATE 96

DIAGRAM C

DIAGRAM BY:
Jim Young

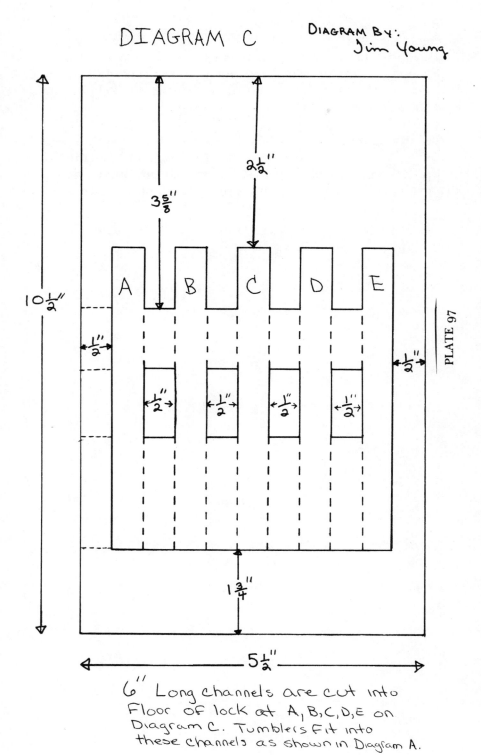

PLATE 97

6" Long channels are cut into Floor of lock at A, B, C, D, E on Diagram C. Tumblers Fit into these channels as shown in Diagram A.

Isaac told us that the function of the locks was not so much to keep out robbers, but to keep out the children who might leave the door open allowing dogs to get into the smokehouse and eat the meat inside.

Using a pattern from one of John Rice's locks, two of our students, Shayne Beck and Marty Henderson, made a lock in the school's shop. Photographs of that lock, along with the other photographs we made, and several diagrams, are included here for your interest.

Article by Bensen Justus, Tim Henderson, Pat Marcellino, Shayne Beck, Marty Henderson, and Ronnie Welch.

SHOEMAKING

ERNEST RIDDLE

When Harvey J. Miller [see pages 453–87] heard that we were looking for someone who could talk to us about how shoes used to be made completely by hand, he thumbed through his notes and came up with the name of Ernest Riddle near Spruce Pine, North Carolina. Harvey came along with us, and we found Ernest at work in his cement-block shoe shop—a shop that he now keeps open only several days a week by choice, even though he has enough requests for repair work to keep him busy full time. While we were there, a constant stream of customers came through the door interrupting our interview, but giving us a firsthand look at the reasons his reputation has spread throughout his part of the state: If a shoe can be repaired at all, he can do it, and he'll do it more inexpensively and more carefully than anyone else around. It seemed to us that many of the shoes he was working on were getting much better treatment than they deserved.

Ernest learned the craft from his father. He can remember many times when his father would eat supper after working all day in his shop, and then, in the three or four hours left before bedtime, sit down with the tools and the leather he had in the house and make one more pair of shoes by hand for another customer. Ernest still has his father's tools, and he allowed us to photograph them for this article.

Ernest lives just up the gravel road from his shop with his wife, Ena Foglesong Riddle. They live in a beautiful stone house with an immaculate front yard surrounded by a privet hedge that screens out the outside world. Flower beds are everywhere. Though three of their children—Helen, Kenneth, and John—have moved away; one daughter, Ernestine, lives next door to provide welcome family company.

PLATE 98　Ernest Riddle holding a pair of shoes he made for himself.

Though Ernest does not make shoes for customers anymore, he still makes a pair for himself occasionally, saying, "I'd rather have the homemade shoes because they're more comfortable (the lasts are made to fit the shape of your foot exactly, and then the shoes are shaped around those lasts) and they last longer. I usually get anywhere from three to five years out of a pair I make myself."

He worked with us for most of the morning showing us, with paper patterns, how the various pieces of the kind of shoe his father made fitted together, despite the fact that he was skeptical as to

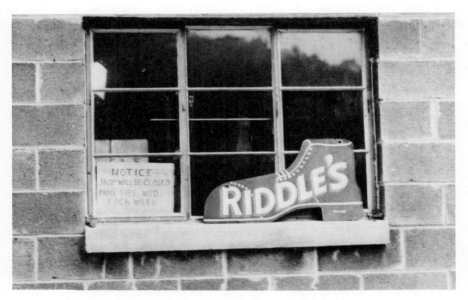

PLATE 99   A sign in the window of Ernest's shop.

whether we could ever explain the process clearly enough so that someone might be able to make a pair of his own. "I don't care how many books you read," he said, "it takes actual experience to really know how to make a pair."

True. But thanks to Ernest, we know a lot more about the process now than we did when we began the search for an old-time shoemaker.

Article and photographs by Tina Smith, Karen Jones, and John Bowen

My grandfather was a farmer. He and my grandmother were of Scots-Irish descent, but they were born and raised in the mountains here—North Carolina natives. My grandfather was not a shoemaker, but my father was. He was twelve years old at the close of the Civil War, and when he was fourteen, he agreed to work a three-year apprenticeship for a tanner that was on Bear Creek between Spruce Pine and Bakersville. He got eight and one-third cents a day for the first year, sixteen and two-thirds cents a day for the second year, and a quarter a day for the third year. During the second year, he got married and saved enough out of his wages to buy a cow so he and his wife would have milk and butter.

When he finished the third year of his apprenticeship, he went down to Marion and took charge of a tannery for a dollar a day. He said he thought that he was making the best money of anybody in the country. At that time, there was very few people who got over twenty-five cents a day, and he was making a dollar a day to manage this tannery, which was a good-sized tannery at that time. But he quit tanning altogether in 1911.

I was born in Bakersville, where my father had a tannery. Then, when I was one year old, we went to Erwin, Tennessee, where he had another tannery for several years. Then we came to Burnsville, where he was a shoemaker. I was raised up in his shoemaking shop. In the evening after school I could either go home and work or go to the shop and work. I'd rather go to the shop than go home to chop wood or work in the garden. I didn't like that.

To make a pair of shoes, the first step, of course, is to get the leather. Neighbors would slaughter a beef and bring the raw hides in to my father and he would tan them on the shares—tan the hide and take one half as his fee and give them the other half. That was a common setup back when I was a child. Then he'd sell his half of the hide, or work it into shoes or harness or whatever he wanted to use it for to get his money out of his labor. And there was more to tanning a hide than you might think. My father always figured that it took about a year from beginning to end because there was a lot of lost time in there. He'd never promise a finished hide in less than a year.

I remember the process they used. They'd take the raw hides when they first came off the animal and put them in a strong solution of lime water. That was made with unslaked lime shoveled into water in a big vat dug out in the ground. The vat measured about eight feet wide by ten feet long—big enough so the hides would go in flat—and it was lined with heavy oak or locust boards. Every tannery would have five or six of those vats.

They'd usually process more than one hide at a time, and those hides would be pegged together by their ends with wooden pegs. They'd be set in the vat accordion-fashion, and there was a windlass over the vats. Every day they'd wind the hides out—since they were pegged together, they'd follow each other out in a long string—and then stir up the solution with a long pole with a paddle on the end of it. Get it stirred up good and then wind the hides back in again.

The hides would stay in that lime water about three to five days—whatever it took for the hair to come loose. Then they'd put the hide over a special bench. Usually it was made out of a log. They'd go to the woods and find a big log—hollow if possible, as this would cut down the weight a lot—and peel the bark off of it and have it smooth. Then they'd cut about a six-foot section out and put two legs into one end. The legs would be long enough so that that end would be about waist high. The other end would be cut at an angle so that it would fit flush against the floor. They'd drape the hide over that and, leaning against the end of the log, they'd push the hair off with a special knife that had a blade about two feet long. The knife had a dull blade, and the log was oval and smooth, so the hide wouldn't be cut in any way.

When the hair was off, they'd turn the hide over and push the flesh off the same way. Then they'd put those hides into a clear, strong saltwater solution in another vat for three or four days. They'd still be wet, and they'd be pinned together like before. That step was called pickling.

Then they'd take them out of there and put them in another vat that was set up so that fresh water ran through it constantly. Sometimes they'd run a creek through it. That would wash the hides and get all the salt and lime out of the pores of the hide.

Then they'd grind up tan bark, which was either chestnut oak or hemlock bark that was gathered in the spring of the year when the sap first came out. People would peel that bark off and haul it into the tanneries, and the tanneries would buy enough of that in the spring to run them for the complete year. And the bark mill that they ground the bark up with was pulled by a mule hooked to a long sweep, and the mule would walk in a circle around and around that mill [just like making syrup] and the man would drop bark down in the hopper of the mill and it would come out down at the bottom ground up real fine.

I guess they used those particular trees because the tannic acid in them was stronger in their bark than it was in any other trees in the area. They'd cut those trees and get the bark off of them and then let the logs lay there and rot—or they'd burn them. Just the bark was what they were after. Then a *few* of them would drag the logs out to sawmills, but not many. That was a real waste.

Then they'd take that ground bark and put it in another vat in a layer, and then put in a hide, and then more bark and then another hide and keep building that up with hides and bark until it was full. The hides would still be pinned together like before. Then they'd run water in over that and keep those hides in there for about ninety days. Every few days they'd wind the hides out and add a little more bark and water and stir it up and put the hides back in. The ooze out of that bark made a liquid that penetrated the pores of the skins and that's what tanned them.

Then they'd take the hides out and hang them up to dry just like clothes on a clothesline, and then put them on a big table and work grease into them to soften them and make them pliable. That grease was mostly a mixture of fish oil and tallow rendered out of any animal like a beef. The hides had to be dry, though, before they'd take that oil. Then if they were going to make black leather, they'd use lampblack, also, and later they'd work that into the grain side—or the side the hair had come off of. They'd work that in by hand on a big table where they could spread the whole hide out.

Then they'd split that hide right down the back following [where the backbone] had been. They'd make two pieces out of it, and each one was called a side.

Now to make a good pair of shoes, the leather has to be carefully selected. Where the best steaks come out of the animal is where the best quality of leather is. For instance, on the hips, that makes better sole leather. Down in the belly and flanks (the cull leather)—that went into harness, bridles, blinders, and stuff like that. It wasn't too good quality, but it worked. But the leather off the hips was better quality and would wear longer and had more form and didn't have near the stretch in it that the thinner leather had. It would hold its shape better.

The thread used was made from flax. I still use flax thread here. It's made in Louisiana or Mississippi, I believe. Cotton thread will work, but it doesn't have nearly the durability as flax has. And the old shoemakers, they'd twist that thread together to make heavier strands, and then they'd run that over a chunk of wax to make the strands hold together so they could sew with it.

PLATE 100 From left to right: lasting nippers, a pegging awl, and a peg rasp.

PLATE 101 A peg rasp with a long handle and a head that swivels to fit the inside of a boot. Peg rasps are used to rasp off the points of wooden pegs that come through the insole into the inside of the shoe or boot.

For shoelaces, they'd cut a narrow strip of leather out of the soft part of the hide. It would be a square strip—not round, of course. And then some people used ground-hog hide for laces. They tanned it the same way, and it was supposed to be the toughest and the stoutest of any hide.

In making shoes, Dad used mostly hand tools such as hammers and knives, nippers, pegging awls, etc. Nippers are used to pull the upper of the shoe over the last to shape it before attaching the sole. Pegging awls are used to make the holes to drive the wooden pegs in. The hammers or mallets are used to drive the awls with.

PLATE 102 Heel shaver for shaving off the outside edges of soles and heels, especially on women's shoes, where the heels are higher and more curved.

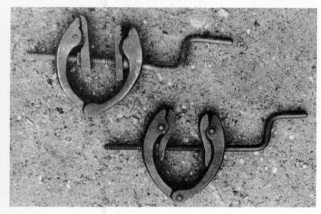

PLATE 103 Shank lasters for drawing the uppers over the last and getting out all the wrinkles in the leather.

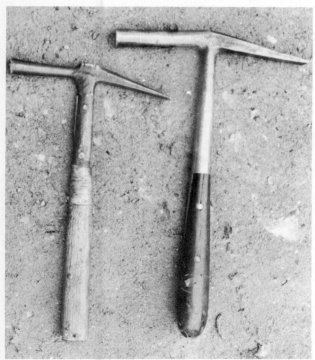

PLATE 104 Saddle hammers for tacking wooden pegs into leather, especially on saddles where the long heads of the hammers help the shoemaker get into difficult, hard-to-reach places.

PLATE 105 A round knife for cutting leather. The tool, used mostly in harness work, is pushed through the leather.

PLATE 106 A gauge knife for cutting leather into strips of a certain width. The blade is set to the desired width using the metal rule, and then the leather is pulled through between the blade and the handle.

PLATE 107 The gauge knife in action.

PLATE 108 A rounding tool. Square strips of leather are pulled through one of the holes, thus rounding them off to the desired diameter.

PLATE 109 The bristle is twirled between two fingers to wrap its end tightly with thread. Then the bristle is twirled backward a half turn to open a loop of thread at the end. The point of the bristle is fed through this loop to make a knot, and then the thread is waxed over to hold it tightly in place.

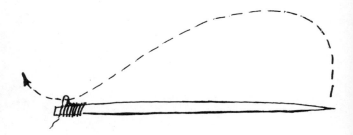

It's all hand work. There weren't any mechanized tools at all at that time. You did the sewing by hand with two needles that were steel needles or bristles. Bristles out of a hog's back. Wax that on the end and it will follow the hole you made with the awl—even if it was a curved hole. That was the object in using a bristle. It was flexible and would follow that curved hole. I hunted for some here yesterday. I've got a pack somewhere that I've had for years, but I never did find them. I wouldn't know of anybody anymore now that'd know how to put a wax thread on a bristle and make it stay so they could sew with it.

Now many people had their own lasts—that's the wooden form in the shape of a foot that the shoe is shaped around. They'd find a shoe that fit them and they'd tear that shoe apart when it was worn out and make a wooden last to fit that foot. Then they'd save that and bring their lasts when they brought their hide in to have it tanned to have their shoes made.

PLATE 110 The wooden lasts Ernest uses to make shoes for himself. Metal lasts are used only for repair work—not for making shoes.

PLATE 111 To remove the last from the shoe after the shoe is made, a metal rod is inserted into the hole, and, with a sharp pull, the two halves of the hinged last snap together, allowing the last to be slipped out heel first.

PLATE 112 A paper pattern Ernest cut out to show us the shape of the vamp . . .

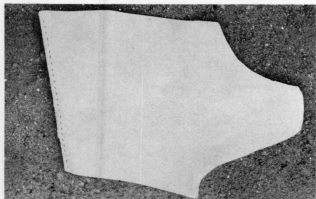

PLATE 113 . . . the quarter . . .

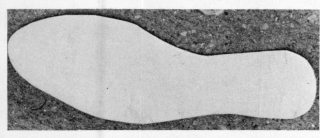

PLATE 114 . . . and the insole.

PLATE 115 First the two quarters are sewed together at the back. The two narrow flaps up the back stay to the outside of the shoe and are covered later by another strip of leather.

If they didn't have lasts, the shoemaker would measure their feet and try to find a pattern that fit. They'd use the lasts they had. My father had patterns. Back when he made shoes he had to have patterns for different sizes and so on. I can remember patterns hanging in the shop against the wall for different size shoes, different styles, whatever he had orders for. And I remember when he had tables full of lasts—I guess all you could haul in a pickup truck—all different sizes. But there weren't many styles. Mostly they were all just plain lace-up shoes. A lot of women's shoes had buttons on them. And then there were rough, heavy work shoes called brogans. In the morning sometimes it would be so cold you couldn't put them on stiff. On those, the leather for the uppers would be turned inside out with the flesh side or the fuzzy side to the outside, and the smooth side next to the foot. They'd turn water better if the leather was turned inside out. I don't know why, but it would turn water better. And it makes the shoes smoother inside, too, to turn the outside in.

A shoe usually had four main pieces of leather not counting the sole, the insole, or the heel. That's the vamp (or the toe and tongue part), the two quarters, and the leather cap that covered the toe. For the vamp, he'd select the best part of the leather. That's where almost all of the wear comes because that's where the shoe bends and wrinkles. An inferior piece of leather would give way.

Here's how you put a shoe together: You stitch the vamp and the quarters together first. Then the quarters are sewed together in the back of the shoe with the edges out (or the flaps out), and then a small strip would be added up the back of the shoe to cover that seam where the two pieces are joined.

Then the insole is cut out to fit the last. Actually, you can cut the insole out first, fit it to the last, then sew the two quarters together with your flax thread and then add the vamp. If you use a cap on the toe it goes across next. Then you start shaping the upper over the last. Wet it and stretch it to conform to the shape of the last and the size of the shoe you want. When you get that stretched and shaped over the last, you should have about a half-inch to three-quarters-inch lap on the underside of the last to attach the sole through. On the bottom of the last, the insole piece comes first and is tacked down in place with a couple of tacks (one in the toe and one in the heel). Then the upper is lapped around, and as it is stretched into place, it is tacked down through the insole into the last. The sole goes onto the top of that; and if you want a heel, you add that onto the top of the sole.

PLATE 116   Next the vamp is added.

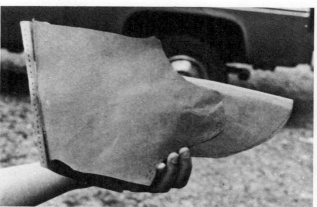

PLATE 117

PLATE 118 With the insole already tacked in place on the last, the upper is pulled down over the insole with the lasting nippers and pegged. The hammer built into the nippers is used to drive the pegs.

PLATE 119 Another type of last (the top section is pulled out of the finished shoe freeing the bottom section). Ernest used two pieces of scrap leather to show us how the lap of the upper is pegged through the insole into the last.

PLATE 120   A stitching horse was usually used to free both hands for stitching and pegging.

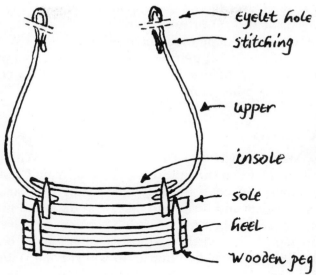

eyelet hole

stitching

upper

insole

sole

heel

wooden peg

PLATE 121 A cross section of a shoe from the back showing how the top of the shoe is looped and sewed for the eyelet holes.

Before the sole is put on, you remove the tacks that are in the insole, as you wouldn't be able to get at them to take them out after the sole is in place. As you draw the upper over the last, you can begin putting on the sole, pegging it down right through the lap of the upper and the insole as you go through holes punched with the pegging awl. Or you can fasten the upper's lap with wooden pegs as you shape it, and then as you add the sole, remove the wooden pegs and replace them with new ones that go through the sole and the upper. That way you only have one row of wooden pegs all the way around the shoe, and not double and triple rows. As tacks are removed and replaced with pegs, the tacks are kept for the next job. The heel is made of layers of leather pegged to the sole with longer pegs.

For stitching the uppers, holes for the thread are punched through the leather with the sewing awl. They didn't do any more of that than they had to. When you're doing it by hand, you don't want an excessive amount of stitching—decorative stitching would be left off completely. Nor would there be any stitching around the top of the uppers—that would be left plain.

Where the eyelets went, they'd double the leather over and stitch the back part inside the shoe. Holes would be punched through for the laces. If the leather was real heavy, that section wouldn't have to be doubled at all. To soften the leather on the shoes, Neat's-foot oil was often used, or fish oil or mutton tallow.

How long the shoes lasted depended on how much you wore them, but most people figured on getting a year out of a pair of shoes. If you wore them out before the year was out, you went barefooted until you got another pair.

WILLIE UNDERWOOD

My grandparents, Willie and Bessie Underwood—"Papa Willie" and "Mama Bessie" to all us grandchildren—live just a half mile off a well-traveled highway. It seems much longer, though, because their graveled driveway twists and turns and takes you up and down bumpy little hills till you reach their house sitting alone in a cleared area on a mountainside. They live in a house built of hard oak boards. It was originally an "L"-shaped house, to which Papa Willie has added two more rooms. At least six generations of Mama Bessie's family have lived in this house.

It is a warm, comfortable, homey place. Walking in the front door, the first thing you see are deer horns on the opposite wall. Behind the door is a gun cabinet with three or four guns standing up inside. There are also turkey claws and a turkey's beard in there. Fishing poles stand in the corner between the wall and the gun cabinet. In the big old kitchen, there are old-timey dish cabinets, an antique pie safe, an old treadle sewing machine, and lots of other interesting utensils and furniture.

Before getting to the house, there is a rock storage cellar on the right and dog houses along both sides of the driveway with a coon or deer dog chained to each one—seven in all. Papa Willie's favorites are Queenie, a coon dog, and Beagle, a deer dog. He's had both of them for as long as I can remember. His hobbies are fishing, hunting, and gardening. He hunts mostly in Rabun County. My brother, Bobby, and I often go fishing with him down on Tugalo Lake, camping out overnight. We usually catch catfish, and sometimes a bream or two.

When Papa Willie was a boy, he usually worked in the garden. He has told me that when he was very small, his mother made him a little hoe using a cornstalk as a hoe handle. For as long as I can remember, he has always had a garden with plenty of corn and tomatoes.

As an adult he has worked in many places doing a variety of jobs. While he served in the Army in World War II, he made special

PLATE 122   Willie Underwood with Queenie.

shoes for crippled soldiers. After getting out of service, he worked for Bob Vickers and Bud Scroggs in Clayton, Georgia, repairing shoes. He took agricultural training under the G. I. Bill. Besides farming, he has worked as an auto mechanic in Clayton and Toccoa, Georgia. Although officially "retired" now, he is back working as a mechanic for Rabun County. He's seventy years old but still looks and acts a lot younger than that to me.

The idea for this piece started when I got to asking some questions about the origins of my baby chair. From there we talked about the clocks, other chairs, and some antique tools of Papa Willie's. For me, it was really unusual to see how people used to make shoes.

KIM HAMILTON

Article and photographs by Craig Carlton, Nina Folsom, Kim Hamilton, Dana Holcombe, and Jeff Giles

PAPA WILLIE: "The first shoes I remember around here were rough. I've seen them where what stitching there was was done with whang leather, which is squirrel skin. They'd take the hair off with ashes and water, and then wash it and work it and cut it into strips. Same thing for the laces—ground-hog hide, squirrel skin, cat hide, anything almost. It was rough. Those people were up in the *woods*.

"And at the time I'm talking about, there wasn't much right and left to a shoe. The lasts were straight and you could wear your shoe one day on one foot and one day on the other. I mean it was *that* straight, now. That's true. Now that is true.

"I was ten years old and you could still buy straight last shoes. 'Course now they cut your feet up. You couldn't hardly tell one foot from the other until you finally broke them. You'd have to get them wet before they'd shape to your feet where you could wear 'em.

"There were four or five people around that made shoes. Usually they swapped them for work. Money didn't amount to too much then."

The early shoes were made using almost no tools. A pocket knife, a punching tool of some sort, and a last are about all that were required.

Leather for the shoes was tanned by soaking the cow hides for months in an ooze made from chestnut oak bark and water. This was usually done in a tanning trough made by hollowing out a log in much the same way a dugout canoe might be made.

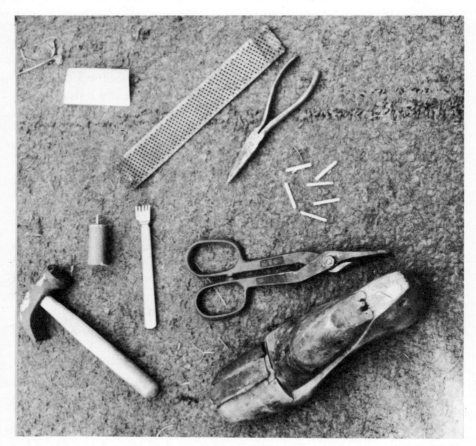

PLATE 123   The tools Willie used to make a shoe for us. The last has a removable midsection so that it can be slipped out of the finished shoe. The strips of leather tacked to its front outer edge were probably added by the owner to increase the size of the last so that the next shoes made on it would better fit his foot.

The other tools, clockwise, are a shoe hammer, pegging awl (made out of a nail set in a block of wood), a punch (which Willie made out of an old Army knife), a package of sewing needles, a forming tool (similar to a rasp), needle-nosed pliers for pulling needles through the leather, wooden pegs, and leather snips.

PLATE 124   A lacing tool Willie made from a dinner knife. The tool punches holes in the leather for stitching.

According to Willie, the best leather for shoes comes from a section about sixteen inches wide by twenty-four inches long on either side of the backbone right over the kidneys. The leather that comes from the neck is thick and can be used for heels, but it is fibrous and not of the prime quality that was preferred. The thinner sections, called flanky leather, could be used if the other was not available.

Early shoes made in this area were extremely simple. Rather than having two quarters, which would have to be sewn together up the back, the quarters were cut out of one piece of leather. The vamp and tongue were also one piece of leather. This meant that the only stitching that had to be done was along the two short "I seams," where the vamp and the quarter were joined. This stitching was usually done with whang leather. The shoes were not reinforced at the eyelets, nor did they have caps. Leather caps were added across the toes when the toes wore through. The toe would be taken loose from the sole, the cap set in and pegged to the sole and toe, and then it was "whanged" (sewed with whang leather) across the top.

A heel spur, or counter, was sometimes used, as this was another area of the shoe that wore quickly, but it was not found on all the shoes.

Leather for the shoes was cut out according to a pattern made to fit the person's foot. Then the pieces were soaked, usually for twenty-four hours, to make them pliable and easy to work. This process was called "casing." Other advantages of working the leather damp were that it was easier to punch the holes; the flax thread (if it was available) or whang leather being used for stitching would pull into the damp leather, making a smoother job; and the leather, as it dried, would dry around the wooden pegs and bind them tightly into place. The pegs would wear down at the same rate as the leather.

The first step was generally to sew the vamp and the quarter together at the two I seams. The hair side of the leather was kept to the inside. Willie explained that this helped the shoes last longer, and also helped them seal up better so they wouldn't leak as badly. Then the insole was tacked to the last in two places (at the heel and toe), and the upper drawn down over the insole and pulled tightly into place with flax thread or whang leather. Sometimes a piece of carved hickory wood was slipped into place at this point to make a crude arch. At the points where the uppers wrinkled or doubled up, swallowforks, or V-shaped notches, were cut to allow the overlap of the upper to lie flat against the insole all the way around.

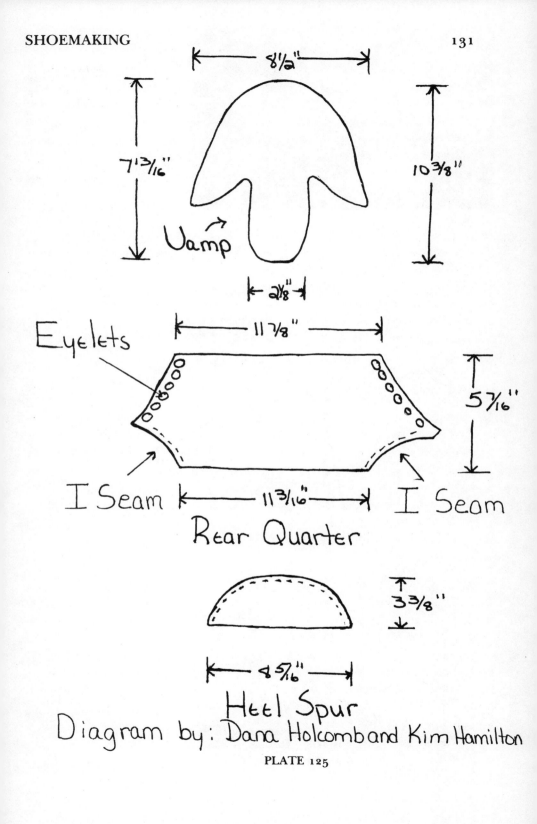

8½"

7¹³/₁₆"

10⅜"

Vamp

2⅛"

Eyelets

11⅞"

5⅞/₁₆"

I Seam

11³/₁₆"

I Seam

Rear Quarter

3⅜"

4⅝/₁₆"

Heel Spur

Diagram by: Dana Holcomb and Kim Hamilton

PLATE 125

PLATE 126 On some old shoes, stitching was done with homegrown flax and hog-bristle needles. Here, with cotton, Willie shows us how to join homemade, hand-twisted thread to the needle in a process called "making a wax end."

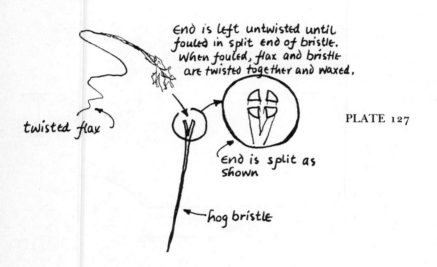

End is left untwisted until fouled in split end of bristle. When fouled, flax and bristle are twisted together and waxed.

twisted flax

PLATE 127

End is split as shown

hog bristle

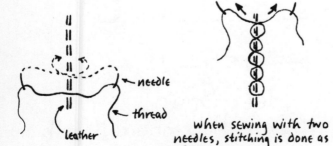

needle

thread

leather

when sewing with two needles, stitching is done as shown.

PLATE 128 Actual stitching with thread was done using two needles or bristles. No knots are tied in the thread, which is crisscrossed through the holes and pulled tight.

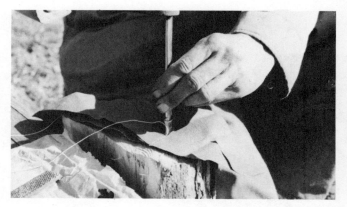

PLATE 129 Punching holes with the lacing tool for the stitching.

PLATE 130 The upper portion of the shoe Willie made for us, as it looked sewn together. This shoe, unlike many older ones, has a heel spur.

PLATE 131 Underneath, thread has been used to hold the leather around the last and over the insole prior to pegging on the sole. A piece of carved hickory is in place to make an arch.

PLATE 132   Now Willie sets the leather for the sole on the shoe and . . .

PLATE 133 . . . pegs it temporarily with one peg at the toe and two in the middle of the sole.

PLATE 134   To make the maple pegs he will need, Willie cuts off small slabs with the grain . . .

PLATE 135 . . . shaves off the edges on one end of each slab so the pegs will have points . . .

PLATE 136 . . . and splits off the pegs about the width of matchsticks and ½" long for the sole and ¾" for the heel.

PLATE 137 Willie makes a mark in the damp sole leather with his fingernail as a guide for pegging. A round block of wood with a nail in the end makes the holes for the pegs

PLATE 138 The pegs are driven in far enough away from the sole's edge that they will go through both the outer sole, the edges of the uppers, and the insole.

PLATE 139 Excess sole is now trimmed off with a pocket knife. Some shoemakers used a lip knife, which had a guard at the tip so the upper would not be cut accidentally.

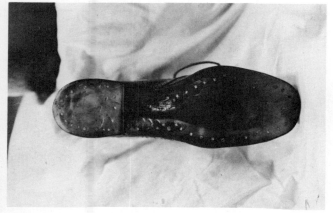

PLATE 140 Then the sole is attached with fifteen to twenty-five long pegs . . .

PLATE 141 . . . and a second row of pegs is driven in at the shank.

PLATE 142 The finished shoe.

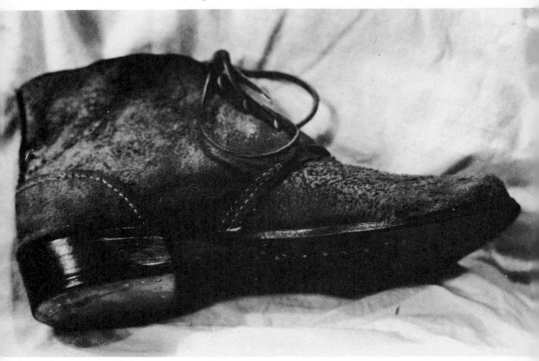

PLATE 143   An old pair of shoes made by Garnett Lovell's·father for his grand-daughter. (Garnett was featured in *Foxfire 4*, pp. 341–46.)

The sole was put into place and pegged with maple pegs, a double row being added at the shank, the narrow portion of the sole and the area of greatest strain when the shoe is being worn. The heel, made of layers of leather and built up to the desired height, was pegged into place with longer pegs.

A tool called a "float" was used to trim off the points of the pegs on the inside of the shoe (or "float the ends of your pegs off"), and a thin leather pad was sometimes added to the inside to make the shoes more comfortable.

To finish the shoes, beeswax and beef tallow or coon oil would be melted together and smeared all over them while still warm. This would help seal them and make them more waterproof, and would help preserve the leather. The older shoes leaked a good bit anyway, but this process helped.

The laces were then cut out. Some people used a gauge knife like the type demonstrated by Ernest Riddle in the previous section, but shoemakers like Willie would just gauge the width with their fingers and cut the laces with a pocket knife. As he said, "I nerve-cut most of mine."

TOYS AND GAMES

Play is in the nature of all children. In some cases, they play with toys and games manufactured and marketed nationally. In some cases they play with toys and games made for them by parents out of love, or lack of money, or both. In the vacuum created by the absence of entertainment provided by others, children create their own.

We began researching the following two chapters years ago with the notion that in our mountains, long before there were stores, the earliest settlers must have developed games and toys for their children that were "typically Appalachian." We soon found, however, that the origins of those we found were hopelessly scrambled. Immigrants had come into the area bringing with them memories of games and toys from numerous other countries and traditions and cultures, had made copies for their children, and had sometimes altered them to fit a new environment and sometimes not. And those children, in turn, had made copies for their children, and had sometimes altered them yet again and sometimes not. People from different backgrounds bumped up against each other in these mountains and traded and combined ideas and produced new off-shoots, the origins of which simply disappeared into the mist. Stanley Hicks, a favorite contact interviewed first for *Foxfire 3* (pp. 139–57), was able to tell us, "Dad would make us little old toy horses, toy steers, toy wagons, wheelbarrows, dancers—all made out of wood. I mean it was all made by hand." But he couldn't tell us where the idea for a toy like a dancer (or top) had come from within his own family. Certainly it would not be considered traditionally Appalachian, since tops have been around nearly forever, but was the specific pattern Stanley's father used handed down within the family or conceived on the spot out of necessity? You see part of the problem we faced.

Also blurring the origins was the crafts revival that hit the mountains before the turn of the century, partly as a means of preserving some of the handicrafts in the face of increasing mechanization, and partly as a well-intentioned effort to give mountain people additional sources of income by building on skills they already possessed. The movement, well documented by Allen Eaton in *Handicrafts of the Southern Highlands* (The Russell Sage Foundation, 1937; New York: Dover Publications, Inc., 1973), was fostered by crafts centers like the Penland Weavers and Potters in Penland, North Carolina, and Berea College's Fireside and Student Industries in Berea, Kentucky. It was given impetus by the formation of the Southern Highlands Handicraft Guild in 1929, originally intended as a means by which such centers could co-operate in working out common problems such as marketing strategies. And then it was given further strength in the 1930s by government agencies such as the Extension Division of the Department of Agriculture (which sponsored 4-H Clubs, for example), the TVA, and the Vocational Division of the Office of Education. Crafts, including the toys that were originally made by children for themselves or by parents for their children, were altered to make them more marketable to the outside world and easier to produce, and new ideas for toys were brought in from the outside and added to older forms, further muddling the origins. As Eaton wrote on page 191 of the original study published in 1937 by the Russell Sage Foundation, ". . . the trend of toy making has been toward more conventional types, often original in design but in treatment resembling those found in city markets. There are, of course, a few examples of toys bearing individuality in both design and execution, but most of those intended for sale outside the mountains are planned and finished to meet market requirements."

What we know for fact, however, is that when our contacts were young, the toys and games they used were homemade and not store-bought. As Buck Carver said, "Nearly anything we had in those days was homemade. To tell you the truth, there was very few toys on the market, and what few there were, we couldn't afford. We just didn't have the money."

And so our research centered on homemade entertainment itself, leaving aside, at least for the moment, the origins of the individual items. All of the contacts we interviewed live within a fifteen-mile radius of us except for Ben Bar (Clarkesville, Georgia), Arthur Davis (Toccoa, Georgia), Margaret Owens (Cleveland, Georgia), Dave Pickett (Winston-Salem, North Carolina), Willard Watson (Deep Gap, North Carolina), Ernest Franklin (Spruce Pine, North Carolina), and Stanley Hicks and Fred Potter (both of Sugar Grove, North Carolina). This is important to note, as it accounts for some regional differences: The fact that Stanley Hicks' jack up a bush and Helen

Justice's hull gull are essentially the same game, for example. Where variations occur, we have included them.

The informants represent all sides of the overall story of toys and games in the mountains. Most of the informants are like Edd Hodgins, whose roots go back for generations in Macon County, North Carolina, who spent most of his life as a logger, and who now, on occasion, makes toys like the whistles he used to make as a child either to please his grandchildren or to satisfy the curiosity of folks like us. It is safe to say that what he makes or demonstrates is unaffected by the crafts revival, and into this same category fall informants like Florence and Lawton Brooks, Buck Carver, and Clyde Runion.

A second category includes contacts like Willard Watson, Kenny Runion, Arthur Davis, and Ben Bar, who now make toys on a small scale, one at a time, for sale as a means of bringing in some extra money, but who have only begun to do it since retirement from another career. Arthur Davis, for example, was born and raised in Toccoa and worked for the Georgia Power Company for thirty-three years as a machinist. In some cases, the toys they make are identical to those they made in the mountains as boys, but more frequently the designs and types are influenced by what craft outlets will stock.

Into a third category would fall Margaret Owens, who makes her apple-head dolls for sale as a hobby when she is not teaching school as a paraprofessional.

Another category would include a Dave Pickett, whom we first interviewed for *Foxfire 3* (pp. 160–67). A young man, he makes his entire living manufacturing toys and crafts in his shop. The toys are handmade, but they are produced in bulk—sawed out in multiple numbers simultaneously—and so their design is naturally influenced by the efficiency and speed with which they can be made, still retaining the quality necessary for them to be marketable.

A final category includes a Fred Potter, whose family moved into Watauga County, North Carolina, from Harlan County, Kentucky, when he was one year old. Hospitalized for twenty-two years with a leg problem that left him disabled, Fred makes his living marketing the toys that numerous mountain craftsmen produce for him at home according to standardized patterns.

The latter two groups, of course, represent the original aims of the crafts revival applied in their most successful forms. The crafts survive, although altered somewhat, and create income. They also are attracting increasing public attention; see, for example, Dick Schnacke's book, *American Folk Toys—How To Make Them* (New York: Penguin Books, Inc., 1973).

The underlying theme that runs through both the sections is that a child could (and still can?) be endlessly entertained by alternatives to the squawking, squeaking, flashing plastic options that confront us from every toy counter in the country. This was brought home to us vividly when Edd Hodgins took us and his grandchildren into the woods behind his house and made them each a simple whistle to their amazement and delight. There was something immensely compelling about both that act and the reactions of the children, something summed up by Kaye Carver (Buck's daughter), who, as a high-school student, wrote in her Introduction to our magazine's first article on toys in 1974: "Thinking back, I know my childhood would have been better for me if I had had a few more responsibilities around the house, had used my imagination a little more, and had used my talking-eating-sleeping-crying-walking doll less."

The information in this chapter was collected by John Bowen, Mark Burdette, Brenda Carpenter, Maybelle Carpenter, Kaye Carver, Kenny Crumley, David Flanagan, Roger Fountain, Anita Hamilton, John Helms, Richard Henslee, Karen Jones, Richard Jones, Julia Justice, Linda Ledford, Tinker McCoy, Dan Melton, Tommy Owens, David Lee Payne, Annette Reems, Robert Repps, Vaughn Rogers, Tina Smith, Scott Stewart, Bill Taylor, Mary Thomas, Ronnie Welch, and Mitch Whitmire.

WILLARD WATSON

Willard Watson has become one of the best-known toy makers in the Appalachians. His photograph appears frequently in newspapers and magazines, and he laughs about how rich he'd be if he had a nickel for every time someone had pointed a camera at him. It's no wonder. The combination of his face and the toys he shapes make him hard to resist.

Willard was born on June 1, 1905, within a mile of where he now lives in the mountains of North Carolina with his wife, who is a fine quiltmaker. He began making toys about fifteen years ago, when he became unable to do the strenuous physical labor he had done all his life. His new work provides him with a steady income and sometimes a tremendous headache, for he is visited constantly by tourists and guided tours and groups of students on field trips.

Willard, like most other men in the mountains, saw his share of hard times while he was growing up. He and his wife got the money they needed for the first four sheets they ever owned when she picked up chestnuts and sold them for two and three cents a pound.

But despite the fact that they are better off now and in much greater contact with the outside world, they still cook on a wood stove and maintain many older mountain beliefs and customs—planting by the signs, for example, and stringing leather britches beans. And Willard still contends that his thumbnail is split like a cow's hoof because his mother was kicked by a cow when she was pregnant with him: "Before I ever come into this world. I told 'em I didn't mark that. The Creator marked that."

The wood Willard uses varies depending on the job and the wood's availability. He favors lind and buckeye for carving, and also likes white pine if it has been air dried, not kiln dried—a process that makes it too brittle. Wild cherry is his favorite for use in a turning lathe, and he sometimes uses black walnut also, but it "fuzzes up," whereas cherry won't.

He claims that the designs he uses for many of his toys come not from patterns as much as from things he imagines. "If you get anything in your head or mind that you want to do," he says, "you'll do it. I see things in my head before I do them. I seen them wagon wheels before I turned 'em out."

He apparently derives as much satisfaction from his work as do the customers who appear at his door. The thing that gives him the most satisfaction, it seems, is the fact that long after he is gone, the toys he made will remain behind, carrying his name. "Things that I'm doing now," he says, "are gonna linger on."

We can't speak for all the things he's made, but we know that's true of the Willard Watson wagon we have just added to our museum. It's one of the finest, and most exclaimed-over, things we own.

Article and photographs by Richard Jones, Ronnie Welch, Dan Melton, and Mitch Whitmire

Right over there, son, I can show you, is the first pieces I ever made. That's them little yokes. That's what got me started making, and I wound up right where I'm at. I've got an ashtray in the house that was about the first thing I ever carved out with a knife. It's a naked woman standing in an ashtray. She's got a red pair of panties on and got her horns covered up with a red brassiere, and that's where I started. And it's *just* what you young folks wants to do. I wish I had somebody that would take this on after I take the final sleep.

PLATE 144 "This mule I'm carving starts with a 12"-square block of dry lind."

I work along when I want to, and when I get tired down here, I'll take something and sit down in the house and work on it there. I've been doing this better than fifteen years, I guess. These dancing dolls were around when I was a little kid, but most of the other things I make weren't around then. We'd make pop guns out of elders, and slingshots. Lord have mercy, I've caused more little boys to get their tails whipped than any other man I know. Make 'em a slingshot and get 'em in trouble. I've got to make some more. When the sap gets a little lower I'm gonna go back to the mountains and hunt me a bunch of forks. I ain't as big as I used to be about plundering around over the woods, but they's a place back down below here and I'll take my little ax and chop me out a sackful of those forks. I keep one here all the time, and my neighbor's dog don't bother me. . . .

Well, go back when I was about six or seven years old. The beginning of this here that you're all gonna tape is every word true just like it happened when I was a little boy.

There used to be an old gentleman over here by the name of Harris Miller, and he went all through the country and to all the neighbors' homes and he made up molasses. He had a little black yoke of cattle, and the cattles' names was Bob and Tom. Well, it was cold of a morning, and I didn't have no shoes. Now this is true. I didn't have no shoes and my granddaddy would get me out of there to drive them little cattle and the frost on the ground. My feet would get cold and I'd run to the house and warm them and then come back and go at it again.

Well, we made up the molasses, and the windup come and everybody'd gather in and have a good time. Lots of times we'd have some old-time string-band music and they'd have one of them old-time square dances—they called them shindigs in them days. They'd move the things out of the house and here they'd go. And they'd play maybe three or four hours. Have a good time. Then we'd do the same thing after we topped the corn and pulled the fodder to feed the cattle in the wintertime. We'd get the corn all done up and have a corn shucking and the neighbors would all gather in and have one of the finest times you ever seen.

Good neighbors is hard to find now. My neighbors is just as good to me as they can be, but some of them ain't actually up in the house there but maybe two or three times a year unless they want something. There's one come here some time ago for a little accommodation and he hadn't been in the house a half a dozen times, but he got his accommodation and went on about his business. I've tried to be good neighbors to everybody, and I guess me and the old lady, if it was tested out throughout the state of North Carolina, has got as many friends as 'ary one or two people they is in this country anywhere. We've had folks here from all over the world. We had some folks here the other day right square out of France. But the furtherest away we've ever had anybody was from Australia. And a man and his wife come in here and bought some little something 'r 'nother and they took it back with them. They was twelve thousand miles from home. Now that was a long way from his bed!

The next thing coming up in the fall was to get the winter's wood. Now I was a young'un, but I knowed all about it and I kept it up and I watched what was going on. [My family] always kept three or four cows and two or three hogs, and they always kept some sheep. Now this happened. I can see this, young folks, just as good

PLATE 145 "One of these days I'm gonna wake up with a dark brown taste in my mouth and—look out! I'll finish that stagecoach."

as if that was yesterday. They had a big pile of wood hauled and put in the yard, and they was a big forked apple tree, and they packed the big wood on the bottom [against the trunk of the tree] and the little wood on top till they got to the fork of that big apple tree. Then, of the days when it weren't bad, why we'd saw and chop up the wood, and my grandma, she'd pick up the chips and put them in boxes on the porch to have when it got snowy and bad. Well, we was there once, and my grandmother and granddaddy went up in a field—it's still there. They call it the old house field now. And my uncle lived there in a little log cabin. Well, they went up there to spend the night with him. My mother was always just as full of fun as anybody you ever seed, and Aunt Isabel—she was the oldest child of the gang—was there, and my mother said, "Isabel," said, "let's put a sack over that sheep's head and see how funny it would be." Well, they went ahead. Caught one and slipped a burlap sack down over its head and you talk about laughing, now, and seeing it go. It would go every which way, and it went to that woodpile and started climbing right up it. I can see that yet today, young folks, and that's been many moons ago. And that sheep went right through the fork of that apple tree and fell off and broke its neck. Aunt Isabel went and got her up a butcher knife and cut its throat and got up an old lantern and went up in the old house field after my grandpa and uncle and told them that a sheep had gone in the woodpile. He had seen a sheep on the woodpile before that [and so he knew it was possible]. And my mother come and humped down to me and said, "Don't you tell Grandpa that that sheep had a sack over its head!" Said, "If you do, he'll kill us all!"

So they come on down and got them a lantern and hung up that mutton, and my grandpa said, "Here," said, "we'll have some mutton." They skinned that sheep out and fixed it up just as nice as you ever seed, and you know I never told that till my granddad was planted!

Well, we'll go from that, then. My grandma, when they'd kill a mutton, they'd tack the hide up on the outside of a building with the flesh side out. Well, the sun would dry that and whenever it got dry on up in the winter, she'd start spinning it—carding and spinning my granddad's socks and mine [out of that wool]. She'd knit 'em. And she'd go get some walnut root bark and beat it up and put it in a pot and she'd throw a handful of salt or two in that walnut ooze and she'd put that yarn in there and dye it and that there salt made that dye stick, and it would be the prettiest brown you ever saw. Then she'd start knitting. She always made me pick the wool out for her to card and spin, and I'd get sleepy and she'd peck me in the head with them cards and say, "Wake up, here, son," she'd always say. And out of that, she'd knit us four pairs of yarn socks. Hand knit, and they'd stay, too, let me tell you. They wouldn't give way like they do now—just blow a hole through 'em.

Well, after that was over with, they'd dry some old leather britches beans and they'd dry pumpkins. Peel that and cut it in rims and hang them on little sticks by the fire. And they'd always dry some fruit. Now dried apple pie is the only pie I've ever eat. We dry some here every year. And sweet potatoes, she'd dry them. Didn't have no other way of keeping them then.

Then along about February and March, they'd start getting ready for the next crop—the next season. If they had a streak of fence they wanted to build, they'd split the stakes on the old of the moon in January and sharpen them with an ax, and when you drove one of them in the ground, it stayed!

Things have really changed. Now I can remember all out through here when they weren't a house nowhere. They was a old store where we'd get kerosene oil. A gallon of kerosene oil would last six months or more. Buy a box of matches once in a while. My father always kept him a little box right by the fireplace. And we'd go to the mountains and get rich pine and split it up, and he always kept him a box full of that—called it hand pine. He'd start the fires with it. In the wintertime, the fire never went out in the fireplace. He never let her go out. Chewed homemade tobacco all the time. So strong you could spit in a cat's eyes and put its eyes out. He wouldn't have nothing but the old-time bull face. They had some back in them days they called the bull face. Strong, oh man. Used to be a little old lady down under the mountain that growed it. When I got big enough, I had to go after his 'baccer, and he'd make me go down to her place. Five cents a twist. Strong, oh man, it was strong.

I can remember, boys, the first pair of shoes I ever put on, where they come from, and what they was. They had a little shoe then they called the copper toe. Around the toe of them it was copper. You didn't get but one pair a year, and they come from an old store back over here they called the Hennecks' old stand. And my granddad went and got them, and oh I was prouder of them, young'uns, than you would be with anything. And I took care of them, too. But children today don't realize and know now what it was. I've hoed corn, boys, right in the field for ten cents a day. Picked beans for my mother and carried them out on my back.

Me and the old lady, the first field of corn me and her ever tended we planted corn and cornfield beans and she dried some leather britches. That's funny to me now, but if you break them beans up, they ain't got near as good a taste as they have if you string 'em up whole. I don't understand that myself. But her daddy told her that, and he just lacked sixteen days of being ninety-six years old when he left here. And she follows the old-time style. She won't leave it, and I ain't gonna leave it neither. I'm gonna walk to the old mark right on out, and I ain't got as far to go as I have went, 'cause I'm not pulling seventy-four years *more*.

Now I was fourteen years old when I left home and went to a logging job. I thought I was a man. I was just a little slim fellow, and I went with my cousin. I had some shoes and my cousin didn't have no shoes. Now this is true—every word of it. And I slipped and got a pair of my uncle's old shoes. And my cousin's foot was so big we had to cut the toes out so he could wear them. Well, we walked from here to Boone, and they run a little old train from Boone to Shull's Mills. That was where the big band mill was at. And we just got up on that thing and set down. We didn't know nobody. After we got up in the mountains where the camp was, the next morning I went out and asked the tram-road foreman for a job. He looked at me and said, "You're a little light and slim." Said, "What can you do?"

I said, "I'll try anything you've got."

He said, "Come on, I've got the very job for you." Well, I went on with him and started out right there. My job was to keep the angle irons and the railroad spikes along where the men could get them. I done it. Kept my job going and kept up with him.

They had a camp there that the men all stayed in and I never will forget that. Had 140 men in the camp and they done all the logging with horses. We was little, young, green—just green. We didn't know nothing. And that first night they was an old fellow— a peg-legged man—there and he worked in the woods, and he could get through the woods just as good as I could or better. And when it come to beddin' that night, he said, "Watson," he said, "you can bed with me," he said. "And they won't nothing bother you neither." He said, "I keep my snake gun with me all the time." He slept with that gun.

One day while that foreman was gone off somewhere, I picked up a spike-driving hammer and was driving spikes and he come back and caught me driving spikes, but *my* job was done and it was done right. He said, "Watson," he said, "if you ain't careful that spike-driving hammer will stick to your fingers." Well, I just laid it down and went on, but every time I'd catch him gone I would pick up that hammer and drive spikes. He said that would stick to my fingers, and he was right. I wound up driving just right along with the rest of the fellers.

Later they changed me off of that and put me to cutting logs for a big steam skidder, and let me tell you one thing. That there steam skidder would bring 'em out of the brush now! And we sawed and split wood for that there steam skidder after they took me off of the steel crew. Had a good job out of that. There's a few of those men living yet, but most of them's about gone now. A fellow passed here this morning that was in the camp when I was and he's eighty-four years old now.

On Saturdays we'd come down to the commissary that was down at the band mill. See, we was way back in the woods at that camp. And we'd come down and hang around there. Ride that little dinky around—it was a cog engine in place of a rod—and it'd go just about anywhere you wanted to go with it. Ride it, and maybe go

PLATE 146 "I got so mad at a man once I'd a'hit him if he'd been a half brother to Jesus Christ."

to a moving-picture show. Didn't have no talking pictures yet. No sound to it at all. That was it. But we'd sit down and watch it.

Well, we stayed there about ninety days before our folks ever knowed anything about where we was at. They thought we was just completely gone. So we decided that we'd come in, and we walked from there home to see them, and after that we'd come home on weekends and then walk back to the camp on Sunday nights.

After that, I went just about everywhere. I still stayed in the woods. I've helped cut timber all over this country—Virginia, Kentucky.

I've worked at rock crushers, I've felled timber—I stayed in the woods for about twenty years—I've worked in coal mines. I've been under the ground three and one-half miles from daylight. I've

PLATE 147 "A man came back at me one time, though, that was more than I could handle. That learnt me to keep my mouth in my pocket."

ditched, done everything, and I wasn't getting no three and one-half and four dollars an hour, no sir. And didn't have no front-end loaders neither. Just had muscles and blood. On that logging job, I remember well the first payroll I drawed just as good as if it had been yesterday. We didn't get in in time to get the full payroll, but I drawed $10.52 and I thought, oh I done knowed it then! Two dollars a day and board. I've walked from right here, son, to the New River Bridge up yonder this side of Boone and went down in the water there when frost was on the boards on the outside and water around my neck. We was putting in coffer dams to widen that bridge, and it didn't hurt us too bad as long as our body was under the water, but boy, when we come out of there! Now how many fellas would do that now?

And I helped cut a boundary of timber on Elk Creek. Run a side edger. We cut eighteen hundred thousand feet. Had a big old steam boiler, and it would drill 'em on down the road, boys! Pulled a crosscut saw in on what they called Buddy Branch when it was so hot you could almost spit fire! Two dollars a day and board. There

PLATE 148 "I told 'em when a place got meaner than I was, I wouldn't fool with it no longer."

was a little bitty fellow a little taller than I was, and his back was as crooked as a frog's back, but, boy, he was a tough one. Me and him was crosscut sawing, and we could shore do it. We cut twelve thousand feet a day with a crosscut saw. The knot clipper in front of us was a'catching trouble! It was good old days. Plenty to eat. Now that there crosscut saw would make you eat things that you didn't like! It would make you love it! That thing would make you eat pinto beans like nobody's business!

And I worked with Charlie Ross Hartley some [see *Foxfire 4*, p. 15]. I'd shore love to see him. I worked many and many a day with Charlie Hartley. But now let me tell you about Charlie Hartley. When he got vexed up, he'd say what he thought and it didn't make no difference. We was working then under WPA, and they transferred me to that courthouse at Boone—building it out of stone—and some of them said, "Willard, you're into it now. Nobody can get along with Charlie Hartley." Said, "He's as mean to work for as he can be."

Well, I went on up, and I was in the mason gang, and I helped build that building, and then helped build that high-school building at Cove Creek, and I never worked for a man that treated me no nicer than the old man Charlie Hartley.

I remember he got sort of bad about some of his carpenters—they hadn't suited him just exactly. I never will forget this while I live. When he wanted to be sassy, son, he could. And he weren't afraid, neither. They weren't a drop of 'fraid blood in Charlie Hartley's body, no, sir. But he got mad at his carpenters over something or 'nother. Walked up the gangway, got about halfway up, and wheeled around just as quick and jobbed that peg leg down and said, "If any of you damn carpenters don't want to work for me," he said, "get your tools and go home!" That's what he said. Jobbed that peg leg down and went on about his business. And they never none of them left him. They stayed with him. But I couldn't ask for no better man. I stayed right on with him till we built that Cove Creek building. That thing has a stack on it from the furnace that we built that is sixty-eight feet, four and one-half inches tall, all out of stone, and we had varied one quarter of an inch from the time we left the foundation to where we went out the top. Me and a man named Ben Brewer put cornerstones in that took two and three of us to pick them up, but we went right on out. We handled 'em right! And when we got done on the outside, we went right on to the inside. We was flooring out of No. 1 oak floor. Charlie went and got us some good Bluegrass hammers. Brought 'em in there and throwed 'em down and said just as solid, "Now I don't want no hammer tracks on this!" That meant put her down right! We put that whole flooring down out of clear oak. Boy, it was pretty. The oak flooring that's in that building over there would cost you fifteen hundred dollars a thousand [board feet] now or more.

We had one old fellow there that drunk liquor. Lord have mercy, how that man did love liquor. He was our waiter—he brought stuff to us to work with, you know. And you know, back in '60 when it come that awful terrible bad spell when they took a lot of stuff to people in helicopters? When people wanted something, they took ashes and made a black spot on the snow and the helicopter would land? Well, he got out of liquor. He went and took and throwed him out some ashes and the helicopter come down. Said, "Well, I'm all right for something to eat, but," said, "I just run out of liquor!" He was awful to drink.

I've made liquor. I've made some that would do to drink. I wouldn't make nothing but good stuff. I've got the prettiest little outfit right now that you ever looked at. Never been a drop run off it. If I was gonna do that, I'd do it just like they done it in the olden days. When I come out of there, I'd know I'd been there! I wouldn't fool with an outfit that held less than seventy-five gallons. Now, the government men would *know* that one, but they wouldn't know where the *other* one was at! That's what they done back in the olden days. They sold this bonded liquor. Had it in kegs—called it kegged. The government man would come around about every week and test that barrel and he knowed how much had been sold out of it [so he could tax the maker]. So I'd have one for the government and one for me and the public. Say, "Come get her, boys. I'm ready for you!" But I'd run good stuff. I wouldn't run a thing but good liquor.

That's the way they done it back then. They couldn't make it at the government still and make a good living out of it, but now when they set that big'un up back in the woods . . . If they'd let me alone six months I'd run a million dollars' worth and I wouldn't never need no more money. I would love to make one more run. Take ten bushel of good white corn and a bushelful of good heavy malt—sprout it myself—and a bushelful of good dry rye, and make some old-time double-still corn liquor [see *The Foxfire Book*, p. 301]. Like they did back in the olden days. They singled it out and then doubled it back and, boy, when she come the next time, it was pure stuff. It weren't none of your guessed-at stuff. I could run ten bushel of white corn and never put a drop of it in my mouth. I'd run it just to run it. Now you could get about twelve gallons out of ten bushels, and lucky to do that of pure corn liquor. It takes more to make that than you think it does. I've heard some of them say that they can make it for fifty cents a gallon to run in automobiles, but I don't believe it. It costs more to operate the outfit than that.

I've done just about everything, I guess. Been lots of places. Had lots of good times. But I think our good times are about over for a while. When I reached and got this thing of mine up here and took her by the hand, I meant it, and she did too. She's played her part. But now young folks don't know anything about . . . But they's a'coming something that they're *gonna* know something about, and they'll never forget it neither. There's coming a bad slowdown. I told 'em that they might as well begin to build some new jails— big jails—because this new generation's gonna start stealing. I'm a'thinking they're gonna get hungry. And it's right now a'walking in the door. I don't know. We'll make it somehow. But young folks

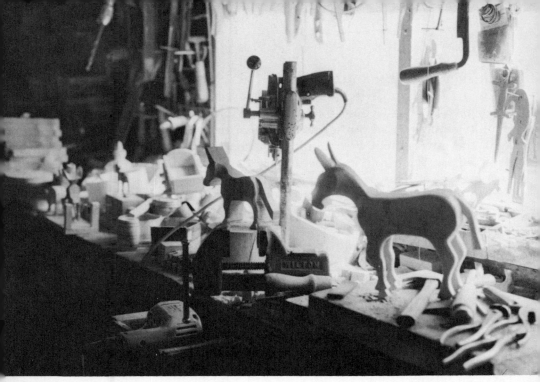

PLATE 149   "I've got enough wood to do me now if I don't live too miserable long."

can learn something from this. It's a'coming. Everything's slowing down now. Slowing down now, and it's gonna gradually get worse and worse till maybe go to bed tonight and trouble in the door in the morning. That's what's gonna happen now, children. I hate it. But they's never been nothing yet went so high but when she come back, she hit hard.

I've been all over this country. And the worst water I've ever drunk yet, folks, and I've drunk her from Norfolk, Virginia, to Arcata, California—and that's just as far as you can get without getting your feet in the water and it too deep to wade—was in West Virginia. West Virginia holds the worst water I ever put my lips in, and Florida is just about as bad. Montana water was good back in the hills there, but I like the Blue Ridge water. If I was back young where I could take it, I'd go to Oregon to live. It's the beautifulest state I ever seed, and if I was back young, I'd go there in one of them logging camps and *be* there. My two choice states is Oregon and Montana. I'd love to live in Montana, but I'm too old now. I'm too old to go back and try it. I can't make it. I ain't gonna leave home no

PLATE 150 "My number's on a big wheel, and when it comes around to it, that's it. You're just a fizzle sprout now, but you'll learn that one of the great satisfactions comes from knowing that the things we're doing now is gonna linger on."

more. In fact, I ain't gonna do nothing only just what I want to. Whenever I want to do something out here, I'm gonna do it, and when I don't want to do it, I ain't gonna do it. If I owed something [it would be different], but I don't owe nobody a dime. If I did, I'd hunt 'em and pay 'em.

I ain't gonna leave home no more. I told the undertakers up here some few days ago, I said, "Boys, when you come down to get this old carcass, don't put no necktie on my neck. I don't want it. I want my shirttail to be unbuttoned just like I've always wore it." When it gets cold enough to make me button my shirt up and cover my ears, it's time to go to the house! I was hatched out about a mile from here on the mountain on June 1, 1905, and I've been back here thirty years and I'm gonna wind it up here. I'm gonna take my final sleep—my last night—up at the house. The old lady, she differs with me a little. She don't want them to bring her home from the funeral home. But I do. I want to spend my last night right here with my children at home. So that's it.

PLATE 151   Mr. Davis glues the cup to the stick.

TOYS

Ball and Cup

ARTHUR DAVIS: I haven't been making these all my life and I don't know anything about their history. It's a good game, though. If you practice a while, you can get pretty good at it.

The pieces are whittled out of mountain laurel or rhododendron, but you could use other kinds. The handles and the cups are glued together, and I make the balls out of pine wood. But you can use whatever you have. The main idea is to swing the stick with one hand so the ball drops into the cup without touching it with the other hand.

PLATE 152 The finished
toy.

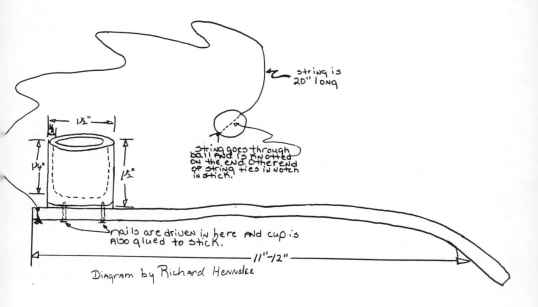

string is
20" long

String goes through
ball and is knotted
on the end. Other end
of string ties in Notch
in stick.

1½"

1¼"

1½"

nails are driven in here and cup is
Also glued to stick.

11"-12"

Diagram by Richard Hennslee

PLATE 153

Blowgun

ERNEST FRANKLIN: Take a hollow weed, or something that doesn't have any sections in it like bamboo, and cut a piece of it anywhere from four to six feet long. That makes your gun.

For the darts, we'd take a round piece of hickory about 3/16 inch in diameter and sharpen one end and put it in the fire and temper it a little bit. Then we'd take a squirrel's tail and cut about a third of it off and fasten that on the other end of your hickory dart. Then you stick that dart in the hollow weed and blow up a storm!

Bouncing Pig

One of the toys Willard Watson (see pages 143–57) makes is called a bouncing pig. A rod runs through the front feet of the pig so that its hindquarters are free to rise up and down. As the crank at the back end of the toy is turned, the man's right arm moves up and down to whip the pig, and each time the pig is whipped, its hindquarters rise off the platform (the man's left leg moves forward, and a rod connected to his left foot and left hand causes his left hand to rise; a rod connecting his left hand and the pig's hindquarters pulls the hindquarters into the air).

Bow and Arrow

LAWTON BROOKS: We made bows and arrows out of hickory wood. We'd take a springy sapling or branch for a bow, shape it right with a knife and put little notches in the ends, and string it with a string. We'd make arrows out of shorter pieces—straight as we could get them. We took umbrella staves one time and made spikes [for the arrows] out of them. We'd tore up somebody's umbrella, got the spikes out of it, and put them in the arrows to kill rabbits, birds, things like that.

LELIA GIBSON: My brother would get a piece of wood, a green sapling—it had to be green so it would bend. He'd cut it to the right length, and string a cord on that. Then he'd get a straight stick [for the arrow] and he'd go to the fields and find stones—old arrowheads the Indians had made—and tie that on the end of the arrow. If they couldn't find arrowheads, they'd use a big twenty-penny nail,

PLATES 154-155   Willard Watson's bouncing pig.

but I don't recall now how they fixed that nail on the end of the arrow. They could make the arrows stick into trees.

HATTIE KENNY: Arrows were made out of sourwood that grows up in the spring. Let 'em stand over the winter and cut 'em to make your arrows.

BUCK CARVER: For the bows we'd use hickory or white-oak saplings. Instead of string we'd use what they called whang leather, which was strips of ground-hog hide. Then we'd wire or tie a nail up in a straight stick for an arrow.

EDD HODGINS: We used string out of cottonseed meal sacks for the string. That's about all the string we ever got when I was little.

Bubble Blower

LELIA GIBSON: We used to get an old sewing-thread spool, take some soap, and make a lather in water. We'd [dip one end of the spool in the lather] and blow through the other end and make bubbles. They'd be different colors. They'd be red, pink, blue—all colors.

Bull Grinder

DAVE PICKETT: The Ozark bull grinder was something people say started in the Ozarks. Of course, bull grinders ain't the only name it had. I've heard them called do nothings and smoke grinders. I call them bull grinders because the guy I got the pattern from, that's what he called it. I asked for his permission to use the label off the back of his and I just changed it a little bit. It's a little toy that's good for absolutely nothing except for passifying oneself with something to do other than twiddling his thumbs. I put a label on the back to tell people just what it is: It's for people going either direction, cutting red tape, breaking conversation ice, relieving nervous tension, advanced stages of thumb twiddling, sharpening dull conversations, a reducing gear for big wheels. The world's most useless necessity is made of selected pieces of well-seasoned outhouse wood by retired moonshiners.

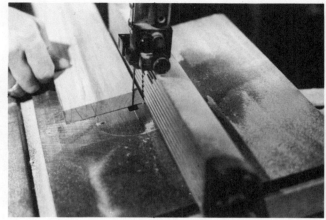

PLATE 156 First Dave cuts strips off a poplar board at a 15° angle for the pistons.

PLATE 157 He then cuts the pistons into 1 ¼" lengths.

PLATE 158 The handles are made of poplar cut ⅜" square and 4 ¼" long.

PLATE 159 Holes are drilled through the center of each piston . . .

PLATE 160 . . . and two holes are drilled 1 ¼" apart through the handles to attach the pistons to.

PLATE 161 A ⅜" dovetail router is used to cut two channels into each 3" square block.

PLATE 162 The toy ready for assembly.

PLATE 163 Dave puts wax on the pistons to reduce friction and keep them from binding, then he screws a bead into the handle for ease in turning. Last, he sets the two pistons into the channels cut in the block and attaches the handle. The screws are left loose so the pistons and arm turn freely.

PLATE 164 As the handle is turned, the pistons slide back and forth in their respective channels.

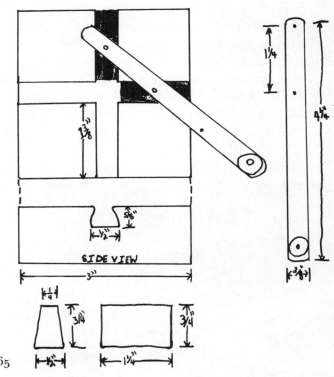

SIDE VIEW

PLATE 165

PLATE 166 Florence threads a piece of thread 36" long through two holes of a button and ties the ends together to form a loop.

Button on a String

FLORENCE BROOKS: We used to make these when we were little girls. We'd play spin the button. You move your thumbs in and out to make it whiz. We used to get them tangled in each other's hair and have fights doing that. We did it just to be mean. We played with them until we wore out the string, then we'd go make us another one or tie the one we had back together. The first person I ever saw make one was my mother.

HATTIE KENNY: You broke you a string as long as you wanted it and you put it in the eyes [of the button] crossways and then you tied the ends together to make the string form a loop with the button in the center. Then you put your thumbs in there and start turning it round and round and round till it was wound up. Then start and it would just "zip" until it broke the string in two. Makes the funniest noise!

PLATE 167 As she increases and then releases the tension in the string, the button spins, making a whistling noise.

Churning Woman

On a recent visit to the Bakersville, North Carolina, area, Harvey Miller (see pages 451–85) showed us a sixty-year-old handmade toy he owns. As a wooden crank on the side of the box is turned, the woman's right arm moves up and down, as does the churn dasher attached to the woman's hand.

PLATE 168   The woman is mounted on a chestnut box. Her body is carved out of wood. The end of the crank that operates the toy is visible (arrow).

PLATE 169 The wooden crank, carved with a pocket knife.

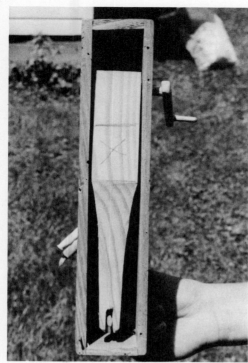

PLATE 170 We removed the bottom panel in order to see how the toy operated.

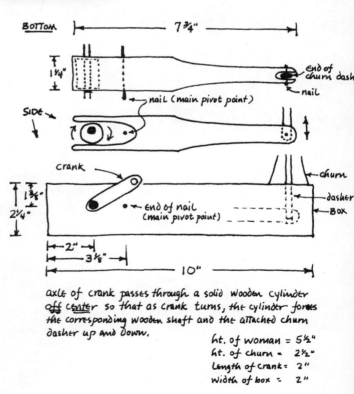

BOTTOM |←——— 7¾" ———→|

↕ 1¼"

nail (main pivot point)

End of churn dasher

nail

SIDE →

crank

↕ 1⅜"

2¼"

End of nail (main pivot point)

churn

dasher

BOX

|←2"→|

|←— 3⅛" —→|

|←——— 10" ———→|

axle of crank passes through a solid wooden cylinder off center so that as crank turns, the cylinder forces the corresponding wooden shaft and the attached churn dasher up and down.

ht. of woman = 5½"
ht. of churn = 2½"
Length of crank = 2"
Width of box = 2"

PLATE 171

Climbing Bear

DAVE PICKETT: The climbing bear is a derivative of a Swiss toy. Sometime in the early eighteenth century, a Swiss toy maker made a little man, and it climbed up a string and worked on the same principle. And he was called a climbing Swiss. And when the Swiss people immigrated to this country, there were no similar mountains in this country to climb. So they made what *did* climb. They made a bear. Some of the Swiss have immigrated to some of the islands, and I've seen monkeys made the same way, squirrels—just about anything that climbed you could adapt to this principle.

The way it works is one side holds while the other side catches the higher hold. It climbs one side while the other side alternately holds.

I usually make them this size. The thing about a bear any bigger than the one I make is that you take a kid two or three years old, and he's standing under it, and he makes that bear climb and he turns it loose, and it's heavy enough that if it fell and hit him in the head, it would hurt him. And that's the reason I keep the bear small. If it did fall, it wouldn't hurt him.

There was a guy came here a couple years ago. One of the representatives of the Stanley Tool Company. He wanted to know if he couldn't have a pattern of this climbing bear to make some. So I said, "Fine." I gave him the pattern, and I saw him three weeks later.

He said, "You know, I made about fifty of those bears and not a one would climb."

And I said, "What did you do? Drill the holes straight through?" And he said, "Yeah."

I said, "No wonder it wouldn't climb." Then I explained how the holes in the arms have to be drilled [see Plate 173].

PLATE 172   Dave makes the bear climb by alternately pulling on one, then the other string.

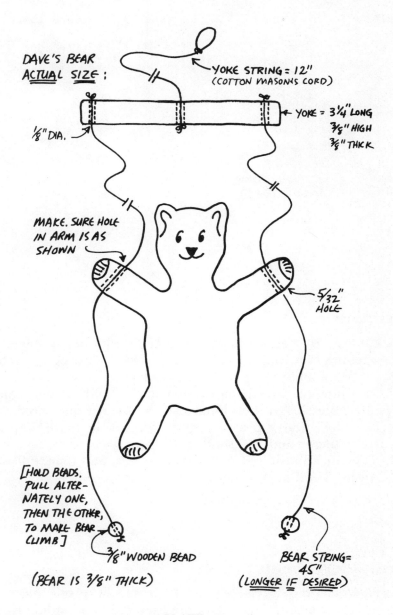

DAVE'S BEAR
ACTUAL SIZE :

YOKE STRING = 12"
(COTTON MASON'S CORD)

1/8" DIA.

YOKE = 3 1/4" LONG
3/8" HIGH
3/8" THICK

MAKE SURE HOLE
IN ARM IS AS
SHOWN

5/32"
HOLE

[HOLD BEADS.
PULL ALTER-
NATELY ONE,
THEN THE OTHER,
TO MAKE BEAR
CLIMB]

3/8" WOODEN BEAD

(BEAR IS 3/8" THICK)

BEAR STRING=
45"
(LONGER IF DESIRED)

PLATE 173

PLATE 174 Buck Carver's
corn gun.

Corn Guns

BUCK CARVER: We had another toy we made with big spools. It had
a big opening that would hold a grain of corn or a pea or a bean.
Well, we'd take a little carpet tack and tack this rubber band around.
We had a plunger in back and this rubber band came around it.
We had a little slot in the plunger so the band would hold in the
slot. Then we'd put a pea or a grain of corn in there and flip it
with that plunger and it'd send it a pretty good ways. We had a
kind of corn with little old slick, hard kernels, and that stuff would
whack pretty good in those little old corn guns.

Cornstalk Animals

ERNEST FRANKLIN: There's nothing to them. Take one piece of a
cornstalk for the body, then take another stalk and split strips off
the outside for the legs and the neck. Then make the head and
tail from other pieces. Kids would play with those lots.

MRS. RAE SHOOK: We used to make horses and sheep out of cornstalks. They'd have long legs and necks. The head would be made from the hard outside of the cornstalk. The body, ears, and face would be made out of the stalk, too. Everything was made from the stalk.

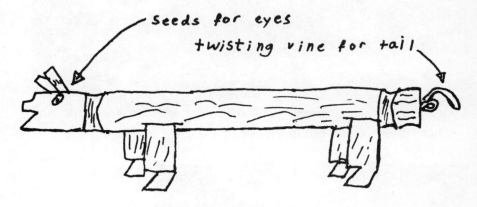

DIAGRAM BY CHRIS JARRARD

PLATE 175

Cornstalk Fiddle

MRS. TOM MACDOWELL: We'd take a cornstalk outside and strip and split it and then fix the bow and we'd just squeak and play.

EDD HODGINS: Yeah, I've made a thousand of 'em. Just cut off two joints out of a cornstalk and use one for the bow and one for the fiddle. Sometimes when they go to gettin' dry, you can spit on them and make 'em squeal real big.

HARLEY THOMAS: There's nothing to it. You just make your little strings and make your little bridge and there's your fiddle. We used a resined stick for our fiddle bows, but you can use a real fiddle bow or a cornstalk one, too. My mother used to make two cornstalk fiddles and use one for the fiddle and one for the bow.

PLATE 176   Harley first decides which part of the stalk he will use.

PLATE 177 He selects a two-joint section of the stalk . . .

PLATE 178 . . . and trims off any ends of leaves, or pieces of foreign matter.

PLATE 179 Next he decides which section to use for the "stringed" portion, and, with a pencil, outlines the areas to be cut away.

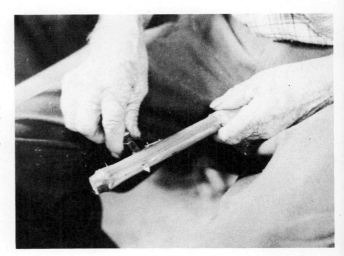

PLATE 180 Then he begins to cut, first slicing away the excess stalk that lies underneath what will become the "strings."

PLATE 181 After cutting out the excess stalk between the "strings," he fashions a tiny bridge out of scrap wood.

PLATE 182 The finished fiddle.

PLATE 183 Richard Hens-lee tries playing the fiddle us-ing one of Harley's fiddle bows . . .

PLATE 184 . . . and so does Harley.

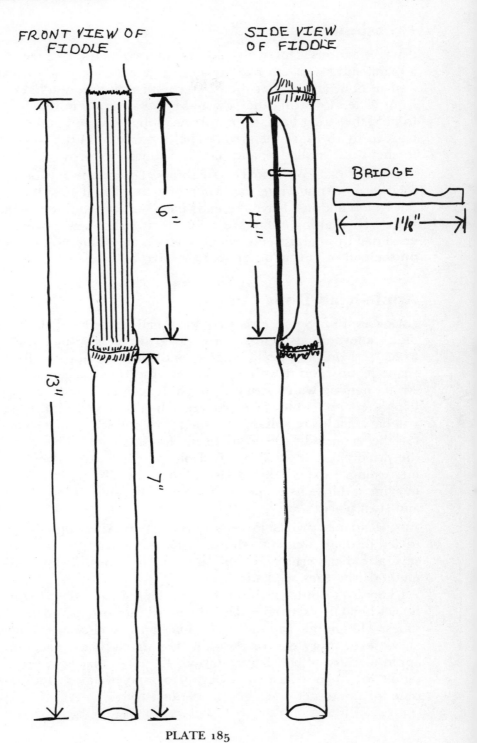

FRONT VIEW OF FIDDLE

SIDE VIEW OF FIDDLE

BRIDGE

PLATE 185

Cross bow

LAWTON BROOKS: I used to make an old wooden crossbow. I'd get a plank and saw it out like the stock of a gun, make a bow like for a plain bow, and mount the bow crosswise to the gun stock at the front. Then I'd string the bow and make a trigger in the gun stock to hold the string back, set my arrow in the bow, and pull the string back ready to shoot the arrow. The trigger'd hold the string ready to shoot till I pulled it, and then it'd shoot the arrow.

STANLEY HICKS: We'd make crossbows. Hickory is the best wood for the bow, but white oak will work, too. We'd hew the arrows out round and just leave the ends flat if we were going to practice. If we were hunting, we'd take a .22-cartridge hull and drive a sharpened nail through its end from the inside and then mount that hull on the end of our arrow. That made a good one.

Apple-head Dolls

LOLA CANNON: [Some girls may have had apple-head dolls] but I didn't know about them when I was growing up. But I know how to make them. You peel an apple, and while the apple is fresh you shape features on it with a teaspoon. And then the best part is to string them up with a string through the center. In a dry, airy place hang them up and let them shrivel. When they shrivel, the features you have made are still there. You put in tiny sequins or something for the eyes and little pearl beads for the teeth. The texture of the dried apple looks like a real old person's skin. They're really interesting. I expect they'd last a long time. If you got one wet, I imagine it'd lose its shape. You see a lot of them in the craft shops and such places.

MRS. MARGARET OWENS: [Mrs. Owens began making apple-head dolls to sell through area craft shops nearly ten years ago. She modified several old patterns and came up with her own designs, but the methods she uses are typical.]

I know very little of the history of apple-head dolls. I read in a book when I first started making them that they originated in colonial times. The mothers would peel apples and pinch a nose and poke at the eyes every day or so until they finally had a face and the apple was dry. When I first started, I tried it that way, but it just didn't look like a face, so I began to carve them. It took a long time for me to get one right on the first try.

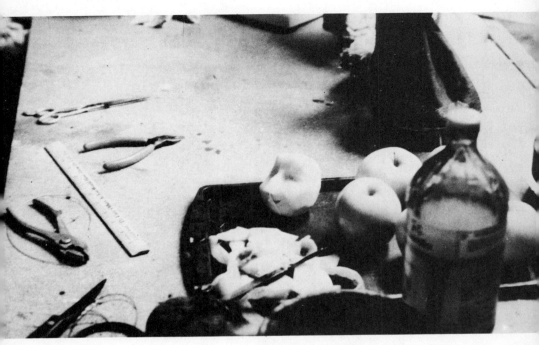

PLATE 186 Margaret first peels the apple with a thin, sharp knife, leaving only
the skin around the stem. She shapes the face with the knife by cutting indentations
for eyes and cutting into cheeks, thus forming the nose. She uses Golden Delicious
apples, and she dips the whole apple in lemon juice to keep it from turning brown.
As the apple dries, it shrinks and takes on an aged appearance and individuality.
After the apple is completely dry she decides whether it will be a man or a woman.
Then she shapes the face by pinching and poking and perhaps snipping off the
nose a little.

It takes about four hours to make a whole doll. The men don't
take as long to make as the women because the women have on
pantaloons, bonnets, and aprons. The hair is fake fur that I buy at
a fabric shop. Some people have used cotton but it doesn't look
quite as real. The face will stay that way for at least four years.
Until the apple dries, I never know whether it is going to be a
man or a woman. I've had to throw away lots of heads. They look
perfect when I carve them, but they dry crooked. You can't make
young people out of the apples because their faces wrinkle as they
dry.

PLATE 187   Margaret strings several apples on a thick thread with a carpet needle, separating them by twisting a small stick under each one. During extremely damp weather, she may first dry them in her gas oven for about twenty-four hours. She turns the heat on a low setting for about ten minutes, then turns it off, the only heat being from the oven's pilot light. She sometimes turns the oven on low again for about ten minutes about twelve hours later, but during this time, the door is not opened. Even though the apples may be dried in the oven first, they are still hung up until Margaret is ready to use them.

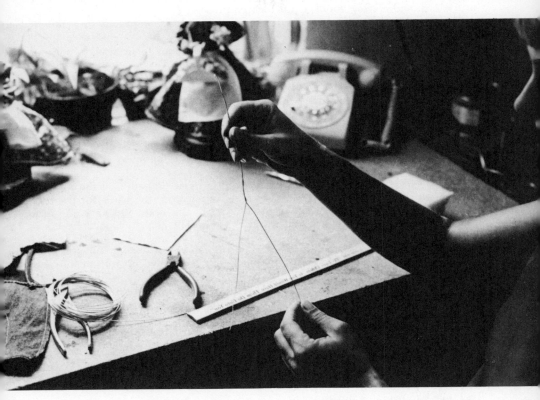

PLATE 188   To make the body, Margaret uses 20-gauge wire. She cuts the wire
24″ long, then doubles it. The wire is twisted together from the top for 6″. To
make the arms, a 10″ length of wire is inserted where Margaret's right thumb is
(about 3″ from the top) and is twisted around the body wire several times to
hold it securely.

PLATES 189–90   *Apron:* Gather waist along dotted lines to about 3 ½". Turn under a ½" hem on both sides and at the bottom.

Make a sash for the apron by cutting a strip of material 1 ½" wide and 17" long. Fold in half lengthwise and turn the ends and edges under with ¼" seams. Sew the sash to the apron, matching the center of the gathered apron to the center of the sash and leaving about 7" on each end to be tied.

The apron will be tied around the waist of the dress, indicated by a dotted line on pattern piece J.

Bonnet Crown: Gather ½" from edge along dotted lines to fit straight edge of bonnet brim. Sew to bonnet brim at ½" seam. Make a tie for the bonnet by cutting a strip 1" wide by 17" long. Fold together lengthwise and turn under edges. Make a casing for the tie to go through by turning under the straight edge of the bonnet crown about ¾" from the edge.

Bonnet Brim: Cut two. Sew right sides together along curved edges and turn. Sew to bonnet crown along gathered edge.

Lady's Bloomers: The pattern allows for ¼" seams to sew the pieces together and for a ½" hem at bottom of legs and at waist. The bloomers are stitched to the stuffed "body" at the waist.

Body: Use one piece of material folded over and sewn together at the top and bottom with ¼" seams. The 4 ½" side is left open until the wires for the legs are inserted through notches cut at the bottom of the body and neck and arm wires are pushed through the notches at the top. The big dots on the pattern indicate places to cut the notches.

After wires are all inserted, a wad of foam rubber, cotton, or any other type of stuffing is pushed into the case and the open side is stitched up with needle and thread.

Men's Overalls: Cut two. For the back of the overalls, cut the material on the dotted line and put in a ½" hem there. The pattern allows for ¼" seams and ½" hems on the pants legs.

Men's Shirt: The pattern allows for ¼" seams and ½" hems for the sleeves. Only the tiny notch is needed for the neck opening. The pattern is cut on the fold of the material, so there is no seam across the shoulders.

Straps for Pants: Cut two. Fold each one in half lengthwise and turn under the edges and hem. Then tack the straps on with needle and thread in front and back just like overall galluses.

Lady's Dress: The pattern allows for ¼" seams down the sides and ½" hems at sleeves and lower skirt. The dotted line indicates waist, and an apron or belt is placed here and gathers adjusted. No other gathering is necessary. The pattern is cut on the fold of the material, so there is no seam across the shoulders.

For the wire forming the body:

1. A 24" length of wire is doubled and twisted for about 6", then spread to make the two legs.

2. A 10" length of wire is inserted about 3" from the top for the arms.

3. The 3" loop of wire above the arms is cut so that it can be separated into a 2" and a 4" length to attach the head.

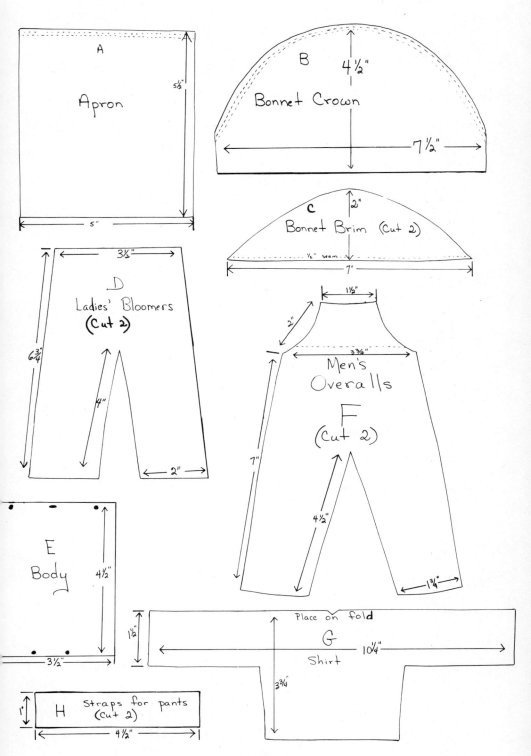

A
Apron
5½"
5"

B
Bonnet Crown
4½"
7½"

C
Bonnet Brim (Cut 2)
2"
½" seam
7"

D
Ladies' Bloomers
(Cut 2)
3½"
6¾"
4"
2"

Men's
Overalls
F
(Cut 2)
1½"
2"
3¾"
7"
4½"
1¾"

E
Body
4½"
3½"

G
Shirt
Place on fold
10¼"
1½"
3¾"

H Straps for pants
(Cut 2)
1"
4½"

PLATE 189

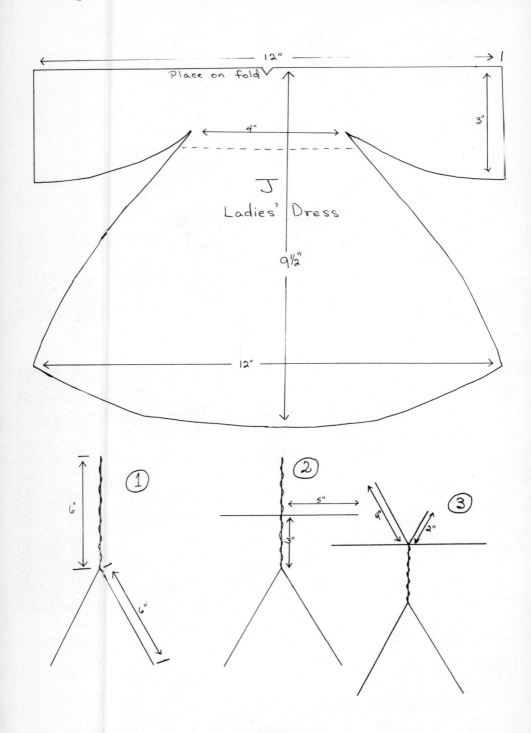

PLATE 190

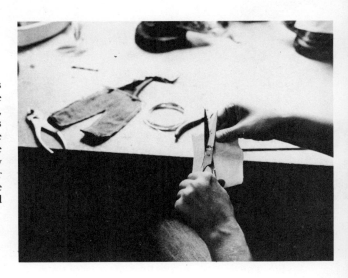

PLATE 191 Margaret cuts five tiny slits in a pillowcase "sort of thing" for the legs, arms, and neck. It measures 4 ½" by ½" doubled. She slips the wire through the holes, then stuffs the body with foam rubber or other material. She sews up the open side with a needle and thread.

PLATE 192 Mrs. Owens makes the dolls' clothes on a sewing machine. She turns the clothes right side out just before dressing the doll, and at that time cuts out a tiny notch for the neck wire to slide through (see pattern pieces).

PLATE 193 — She then pulls the shirt down over the top part of the body and runs the arm wires out through the sleeves. Then she pulls the overalls up over the body and sews the galluses (or straps) into place. The papier-mâché hands and feet are then pushed onto the arm and leg wires and glued on with Elmer's glue. The doll is left to sit for five to ten minutes so that the glue will dry completely.

To make papier-mâché hands and feet, use one-half cup of water to one table-spoon of flour. Use about four sections of toilet paper for the hands and five for the feet. Before wetting the paper in the flour mixture, fold and refold until the shape of a hand (or foot) is made. Cut and shape the hand or foot and then wet thoroughly. Keep shaping while in the flour mixture and then squeeze the water out. Lay on cookie sheet and dry overnight in an oven heated by the pilot light or out in the open for about two days.

PLATE 194 The loop of wire that will hold the head is then cut so that one end is 4″ long and the other end 2″ long. The 4″ piece is run up through the core of the applehead and folded down the back of the head. The 2″ piece is brought up behind the head and twisted with the longer piece to hold the head securely in place. This method also allows for the head to be replaced if it is damaged by insects or rodents. To prevent insects from getting into the applehead, Margaret inserts an insect repellent into the core. She does not know of anything that will prevent rodents from eating the dried apples.

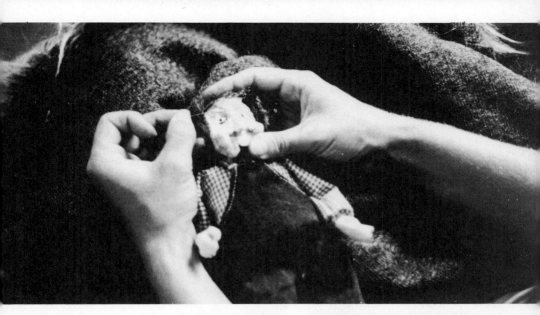

PLATE 195 Matching cucumber seeds are glued in for eyes and black dots painted on the seeds with poster paint. Eyebrows are made by gluing small pieces of fake fur over the eyes, and a small piece of fake fur is cut out and glued on for hair.

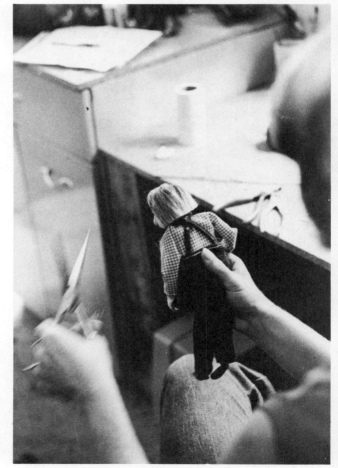

PLATE 196 The hair is brushed and cut to the right length. To hold the hair in place, Mrs. Owens uses spray starch or hair spray. She cuts out a small neckerchief and ties it around the man's neck as a finishing touch. Here is a rear view of the doll when the haircut is finished.

PLATE 197   After the doll is completed, Mrs. Owens decides on an arrangement
and wires the doll to a log or stool or something else on the stand that will hold
it securely in whatever position it looks natural. Mr. Owens made the fiddle; the
spinning wheel was purchased from a shop; the dough bowl is half a walnut shell;
and the biscuit dough is real dough sprayed with insect repellent.

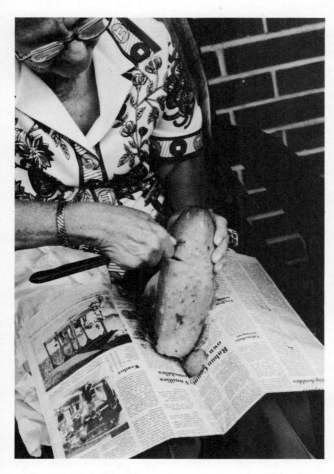

PLATE 198 Any cucumber will do, but Florence prefers to use a long one, 10″ or more. The greener it is, the better. Cut about 1″ off the bottom end of the cucumber, and, using a knife, scrape out the seeds and pulp to the point where you plan to cut the mouth. Then cut a notch where you want the mouth, making sure you cut through to where it is hollowed out. Using the point of the knife, cut out the eyes and nose, and stick small pebbles in the eyeholes to make them stand out more.

Cucumber Dolls

FLORENCE BROOKS: I'll make you a cucumber doll like me an' my sister, Beulah, used t' play with. You need a knife, a cucumber, scissors, some cloth, a needle, and a safety pin. We'd pin a diaper on them, and make a "dress" out of a square of cloth, fold a hem, gather it [with a needle and thread], and tie it around its neck. We used t' have a lotta fun playing with those things. We used t' make 'em t' feed 'em. [The doll is hollowed out, so the "food" goes right through.] We made clay mud with water, poured it in 'em, and then the diaper was in a mess. We'd take it off and change it. We never fed it anything else. Milk would have gone down it, but we was in the Depression and we didn't have enough of that. We'd get mountain moss off a log, make 'em a bed, put 'em in

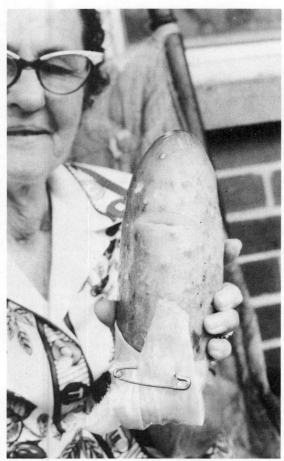

PLATE 199 To make the diaper, take a piece of cloth about 6″ square and fold in half diagonally and pin it on as you would any diaper.

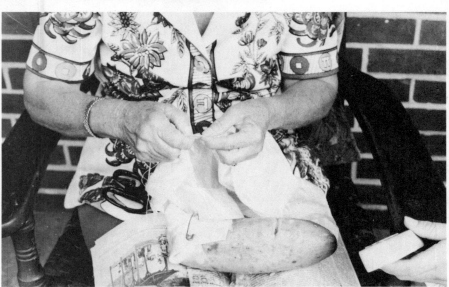

PLATE 200 To fashion the dress (really a skirt), use a piece of material about 10″ square. Fold down the waistband, and gather it with a needle and thread.

PLATE 201 Tie the dress around the "neck" of the doll using the ends of the thread you gathered the waistband with. The doll is now finished.

the bed. We didn't put hair on it, but you know if we'd thought of it, we could a'got corn silks and made 'em some hair. The doll wouldn't last more than a day or two, because drunkards [fruit flies] would get after it.

I don't know of anybody ever doing that but me and my sister, Beulah. She was four years older than me but she had to play with me or else.

Other Dolls

HARRIET ECHOLS: We had Raggedy Ann dolls, and my older sister made dolls; my father wouldn't buy dolls. Back then people had to work for a living and Dad didn't believe in foolishness, and so we didn't have any toys. My older sister made my first doll and I guess I was eight or ten years old. We made rag dolls and cornshuck dolls, and then we learned to do potato heads. You take potatoes and make a doll. You got one big potato and get sticks and make its legs. Then you get a smaller potato and make its head, and find sticks for his arms. A potato will last a long time.

ETHEL CORN: Mama used to make dolls and then you could also get rag dolls in the stores. Then they went to making dolls with just their heads filled, and then sleepy dolls. I was a pretty good-sized young'un before I ever saw any sleepy dolls. There weren't many toys back when I was growing up.

I can remember my first doll. They had just come out with what they called the "Dutch Doll." The body would be stuffed with straw, but the arms and legs and faces would be delft. My sister and I had sleepy dolls, and mine wouldn't go to sleep. Mel [my brother] was always doing something, and he told me to take my doll and hit it over the plow handle and it would go to sleep. I did, and it broke that doll's head all to pieces. It was made out of the same thing that cups and saucers were made of.

We'd cut [doll clothes] like we'd cut dresses for a baby, and after I got older, that was the way I learned to cut and sew.

BERTHA DOCKINS: At Christmas usually Mother would make rag dolls for us. We used to have these old black stockings and made rag dolls from them. We'd take a needle and some white thread, and make their eyes and nose and mouth. We stuffed them with bran or something like that.

MRS. E. H. BROWN: The only toy I ever owned in my life was an old doll. I played with that thing, y'know, and I'd worn out several dresses, and it had to have more dresses made. You had to make [the body], and fit it to that little head. That's all there was. Now that was Pard—that was her name. That was my partner, y'know, and I called her Pard.

LOLA CANNON: Most times [when we made rag dolls] we took a little knob of cotton and packed it tightly in a cloth, and wound it around for its neck. Then we rolled another roll and fastened it to that for arms. Sometimes we made legs the same way. But most times we just made heads and arms and let them have a long dress.

I had one doll that was big enough to wear my baby clothes. It was too big for me really, but they wanted me to have it. I didn't have china dolls. Some of the neighbors' children did. They were more expensive. Later on I had bought dolls—with papier-mâché heads and legs and everything—but there weren't the commercial toys available in those days that there are today.

NANNIE ANN SANDERS: We had cornshuck dolls [see *Foxfire 3*, p. 453], apple-head dolls, and just regular old rag dolis. The heads for the apple-head dolls were made from apples that we would shrink and make them look like an old person. Our rag dolls were made out of regular cloth and stuffed with bran left over from where you sifted corn meal. For the face we would just mark 'em with a pencil.

MRS. RAE SHOOK: I guess rag dolls were about the first toys. They were made out of wool and old stockings. Their faces were made from buttons and black markings. We'd make the clothes for them.

BLANCHE HARKINS: We made our rag dolls out of white flour sacks stuffed with rags. Arms and legs were made out of rags and were straight. Then we would take fire coals and make the eyes, eyebrows, mouth, ears, and hair.

VELER MARCUS: All I had to play with was rag dolls that Mama made for us. Way back then we enjoyed that. We hung onto that one doll because Mama just made us one a year. The best I can remember, Mama would cut the cloth out and stuff the arms and legs with old cloth rags, then sew it. I can't remember exactly how she fixed it to get the leg shaped up. She embroidered the eyebrows a little—the best she could. The eyes, nose, mouth were made of thread. I don't believe it had any ears.

HATTIE KENNY: I was fifteen years old before I ever had a doll bought out of a store. We made our dolls out of wool cloth, unless we spun some cotton cloth and made them. We made the faces from wool thread—eyes, nose, hair, mouth. And we made dresses for them.

HELEN JUSTICE: We would use just white material to make our dolls with. We would take a pencil to draw the face. Sometimes we would even make a cap for them.

MRS. TOM MACDOWELL: Our dolls were just big, long rocks. We'd get a long rock and we'd say, "Oh I'm just so tired of carrying my baby," just like we'd heard women say.

PLATE 202   Stanley demonstrating how a dumb bell would be used if the hide and string were in place.

Dumb Bell

STANLEY HICKS: Take a section of a hollow log and tack a piece of hide over one end. Then punch a small hole in the center of the hide. Then take a long string and tie a knot in one end and feed the string through the hole in the hide so that the knot catches against the outside of the hole and the string comes through the log and out the other end. Then wax the end of the string with beeswax. When you pull against the waxed part of the string it makes a sound just like a bull a'bellering. There ain't as many haint stories in the mountains as there used to be. That's because there ain't as many dumb bells being made!

Dumb Bull or Bull Roarer
or Buzzer

ETHEL CORN: Bill Lamb, my uncle, was bad to make things. He'd make what they called the "dumb bull." It was made in a way that when you whizzed it around, it would make an awful racket. He'd take a plank and whittle it down thin [about ten inches long by three inches wide] and sharpen the edges in some way, and bore a hole in one end. You'd attach a string to it [about five feet long], and whirl it around, and it'd make the awfulest racket you ever heard.

EDD HODGINS: We just called it a buzzer. I've made a lot of them. Take a flat piece of this wood and tie a string to it and tie that to a stick and [swing it around and] it'll buzz. I reckon that string a'twistin'll make it roar. It don't take but three minutes to make one. I've made them and about scared the dogs to death!

BUCK CARVER: John Dillard taught me how to make a dumb bull. Back in those days when I was a boy nearly anybody could make them, because we learned lots more from each other then than they do this day and time. If one person learned something, he was always tickled and glad to show it to somebody else.

Bill Lamb was a man I scared to death with a dumb bull. I lived right across the river from him in the old Bill Lamb House. I got to slinging that thing around and it was howling and making noise. Bill was going to a Woodmen of the World meeting. He had gotten up the river a ways and ran back to the house. There was an old rail fence coming down the ridge there. He sat down on that fence for a while. Then he got some rocks and ran up to the house and [his wife] opened the door for him, and after he got safe in the house, he threw his rocks back out in the yard!

The next time he heard the noise he and his wife and children were in the field plowing and weeding corn. Bill sent them to the house and came back out with his shotgun. His wife got to looking off the back porch and saw me and John Dillard down there and told Bill that every time she heard the noise John or my arm was swinging around. So he walked around back behind us and saw that it was a dumb bull. He had never heard one before.

The last one I made was in 1929 to scare someone with, but I slung it a few times and it burst. They burst real easy if you hit them on the ground or against a tree limb.

The way you swing the dumb bull is how to make it work. I find the easiest way to do it is make an X motion with your arm.

PLATE 203 Buck with the finished propeller he whittled for the dumb bull.

PLATE 204   Linda Ledford trying out the finished toy.

Fluttermill

One of Lawton Brooks' favorite childhood toys was the fluttermill. Tinker McCoy, Linda Ledford, and Richard Henslee spent a rainy day with him making one, and, because of the rain, they didn't get to set it up in the creek as they had hoped they would be able to do. Lawton was able to show them how it worked with the use of an outside faucet, though, and he described the things he and his friends used to do with them.

LAWTON BROOKS: You get forked sticks and drive them in the ground. Then set your mill down to where the creek will pull it. Drive it down far enough so that the water is hitting the paddles. It will go just as fast as the water goes. If the creek's running it will just keep on going from now on.

Sometimes we'd make them and put them in the creek and we'd get great, great old big wide planks for paddles, and we'd get a sluice of water about as big as your arm and we'd put a pipe in the branch out here so it would hit the end of a paddle. Then

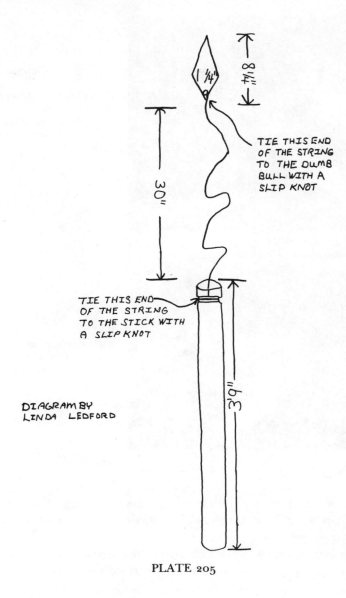

1 ¼"

8 ¼"

30"

TIE THIS END
OF THE STRING
TO THE DUMB
BULL WITH A
SLIP KNOT

TIE THIS END
OF THE STRING
TO THE STICK WITH
A SLIP KNOT

3'9"

DIAGRAM BY
LINDA LEDFORD

PLATE 205

we'd whittle us out some little round pulleys and cut a groove in
them all the way around for the string to go in and put them on
the side of the fluttermill. Then we'd put a string across the pulleys.
Then we'd put up three or four fluttermills on down through there
and have this first one up here pulling the others on down there
where there wasn't any water. We'd make it look like a sawmill

PLATE 206 Lawton finds the centers of two 12" boards and then cuts a notch into each board and fits them together.

PLATE 207 Then he puts a nail in either side to act as an axle, and, holding it under a stream of water, shows how it spins.

working. Sometimes we'd make it pull something else way down yonder. It worked like a belt. It wouldn't take but one pulley each to pull them.

We'd leave these in the creek and when it came a hard rain they would wash away, but we would make us some more.

EDD HODGINS: Get you two boards and mortise them together sort of like a grist mill, and have nails for axles and set that in two forked sticks. Then let water pour on them blades and it'll turn. I made the Florida folks one over here and it was still turnin' when they came back the next year. Then what you want to do if you want to make a little racket is put you little pieces of tin on those blades and that water will make a racket on that tin when it hits it.

PLATE 208

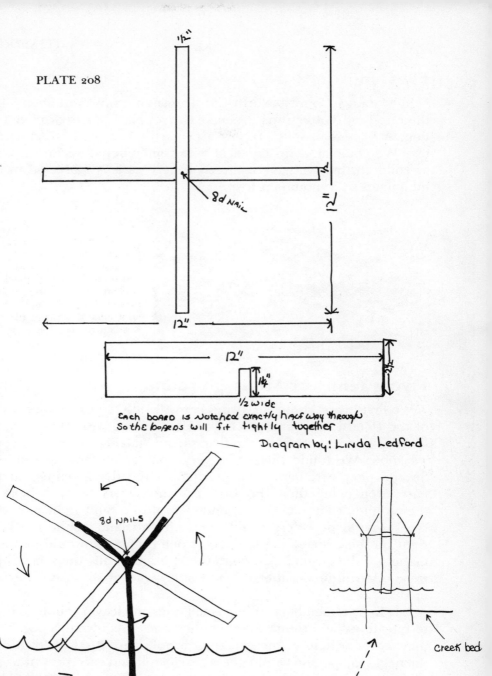

12"

12"

8d NAIL

12"

12"

1¼"

½ wide

Each board is notched exactly half way through
So the boards will fit tightly together

Diagram by: Linda Ledford

8d NAILS

water flow

prongs anchored
in creek bed

creek bed

Two forked prongs hold the flutter mill up in the water.
The mill is held upon the prongs by 2 nails which extend
2" from each side. As water flows, it hits the paddles
and makes it turn.

Diagram by: Tinker McCoy

PLATE 209

Fly Gun

In Watauga County, North Carolina, numerous craft shops, like the one Fred Potter runs in Sugar Grove, market a toy called a fly gun. A white-oak split propels a projectile out of the end of the toy. We could find no contacts who remembered seeing this toy as children, but we have included it here as it is marketed in the mountains as a mountain toy.

PLATE 210 A wooden pin pushed through from the underside (arrow) holds the white oak split ·bent back, or cocked. When the pin is pulled down, the end of the split hits the projectile and sends it flying.

Flying Jenny or Merry-go-round

We first heard about the flying jenny from Oscar Cook, principal of the Dillard Elementary School. After talking with Mr. Cook, we decided to do a survey on the flying jenny, talking to several people we know. We found this was a very popular toy among children. Several people remembered playing on the flying jennies in the past, even tieing their tiny brothers and sisters on with belts so they wouldn't fall off. Flying jennies could be built right next to a creek where the riders could jump off and land in the creek, or right on the edge of the bluff so at one point one would be much higher off the ground. Although they were basically the same, there were often little variations. These are some of the ways they are made:

Ada Kelly remembers cutting small trees and leaving about a three-to-four-foot-high stump. They whittled one end down to a peg. They then bored a hole in the center of a pole and fitted it down over the peg. One person would get on each end, and each person would push with his foot. She doesn't remember anyone getting hurt or a flying jenny ever breaking.

Richard Norton called it a "merry-go-round." They cut a tree leaving a four-foot-high stump, and used a board about ten to twelve inches across and eight to ten feet long. They drilled a hole in both the board's center and the stump and screwed a nut and bolt

PLATE 211   Fred Potter outside his shop with a limberjack.

down in the board and the tree trunk. One person would get on each side close to the tree trunk. Then one would get on each side close to the end and all would push until they had it going real fast.

Oscar Martin remembers the log was shorter on one end than it was on the other. A person would be astride the long end and someone would push on the shorter end to make it go.

Mimi Dickerson remembers one person riding on each end and two people near the center pushing it. It was constructed the same way as the one Ada describes.

Mack Dickerson remembers a small oak stump about four feet high. They used a plank with a hole drilled in the center. The flying jenny would last longer when they used axle grease. He also said they were located all over the settlement, not just around creeks or gullies.

The hole drilled in the horizontal piece may be either in its center or drilled off center so that one end extends out further than the other.

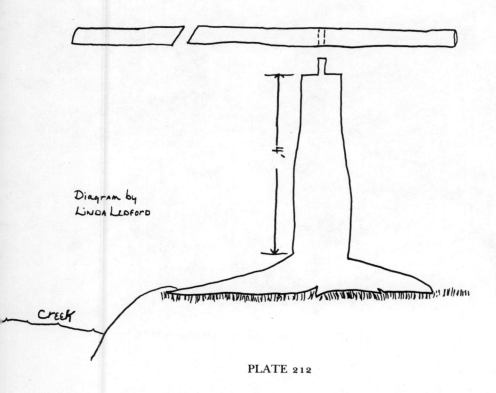

Diagram by
Linda Ledford

Creek

PLATE 212

EDD HODGINS: You made it in the woods. Cut you off a white oak. They make the best ones. Cut you a mortise in a pole and set it [on a dowel] on top of that stump, and have your stump up as high as you want. Set the pole down right in the middle. I've rode 'em many a Sunday with four or five kids on each end. Somebody has to push, but he better keep his head down when he gets it started! That pole is just like a merry-go-round. That's pretty much fun. I like it because you can ride awhile, pull awhile, or you can sit off and watch another bunch. All kids liked that. Grown men made good pushers for little fellows. They were stout and they could make that thing run!

A new one might be a little hard to push, but when that gets wore slick, and maybe you put a little grease around it, you can just take your foot and kick it and it'll go four or five rounds by itself.

VELER MARCUS: We would spend the weekend with our neighbors and play. Their daddy always kept them up a flying jenny and it would be out [in the woods]. We always hoped it would be a pretty, moonlit night, 'cause we could see how to get out there good. They would fix up a post about three feet high and then get this great long pole and bore a hole in it and notch it out to fit down over this post.

They would stand here next to the post and make it go around. You can imagine how it come around. It wouldn't be a little bitty short pole, either. It would be a great long one. There would be two that would have to get in next to this post and push. There would be one person that got on the far end of the pole and one over here on the back end. After the pole got worn and got slick, it would move fast. Those in the middle would be running and it would make those ends go around real fast. Law, it would make your head swim!

Up at this place where we were playing one night, it was my time and they started before I got my balance good, and it went 'round and 'round. Some of 'em would sit up on it, but I would always lie down on it. Law! They got that thing just a'flying! I kept telling them, "Stop! Stop! Stop!" I was getting ready to turn loose and boy! They slung me off that log out to an apple tree that was there. I looked like a lizard lying out there. You can imagine! I've always been long and slender and they just slung me up in that apple tree. They had to work with me awhile. They didn't dare let [their parents] know I got hurt, or their daddy would of taken it down so we couldn't play on it no more. I said if I lived through this I would be the most worked-over young girl there ever was in this world!

PLATE 213   A walnut doll's bed made by Willard Watson.

PLATE   214   This child's rocking chair has a corn-shuck bottom put in by Harry Brown, Sr. [*Foxfire 4,* pp. 461–65].

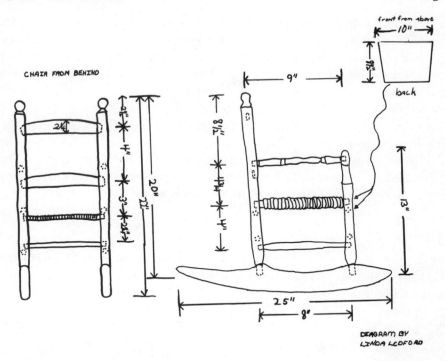

PLATE 215

Furniture

In many houses, miniature pieces of furniture gave away the presence of a girl whose doll had a bed of its own, or a child who had his own rocking chair to pull close to the fire. Stanley Hicks told us that he had often made crude beds for his sister's dolls, and Willard Watson still makes beautifully carved ones today. The photographs in this section illustrate several such pieces.

Hoops

CLYDE RUNION: We rolled rims, you know. I don't know if anybody knows how to roll rims now or not. Old Model T's had spoked wheels, you know, and that rim came off it. You'd get a little old piece of wood and get it under that rim and just see how fast you could run with that thing. It's a lot of fun. I'd sometimes leave over here rolling that rim and I'd roll that thing all the way to school and never let up on it till I got to the schoolhouse.

LAWTON BROOKS: We'd get small steel bands like those that go around a wheel, and we'd get two sticks and put them together in the shape of a *T*. You go along and guide the band. We got a lot of kick out of running them things. Just had old dirt roads to run them in. There weren't any cars to run you out of the road, so then you had the whole road.

LELIA GIBSON: We'd get a hoop off a wooden barrel; a wooden hoop. Then we'd get a stick with a bend in it. We'd start off and roll the hoop with the bent stick. Just run and roll till we gave out. The stick had to have a little bend in it; you couldn't stabilize the hoop just standing still. The crook in the stick would stabilize it.

Jumping Jack

FRED POTTER: We used to have these when I was a child in Harlan County, Kentucky. The ones I saw when I was little were homemade out of cardboard.

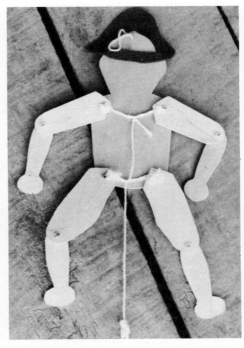

PLATE 216   The toy is hung by a string loop through the top of its head.

PLATE 217   Seen from behind: When the hanging string is pulled, the arms and legs flex and jerk upward.

Kicking Mule

PLATE 218   Willard Watson with his kicking mule.

Another toy Willard Watson makes using an old pattern he has in his shop is similar to his bouncing pig but is called a kicking mule. As the crank is turned, the man's legs "walk." As each leg approaches the mule, a rod connecting the man's foot and the corresponding mule's rear hoof makes it "kick."

PLATE 219 Dancing dolls can be as fancy or as simple as the maker wants. This carved, hand-painted doll, complete with bow tie, was made by one of Dave's friends.

Limberjack or Dancing Doll

DAVE PICKETT: One story behind the dancing doll goes that sometime in the seventeenth century, a Bohemian puppeteer broke the string to one of his puppets and he didn't have a replacement string for it. So in order for him to perform, he put a stick in the puppet's back and found a limber board for him to dance on. And it was so funny and hilarious that he decided to incorporate this into his act. What makes it so funny is that there really is no control on the motions that the doll goes through.

So it evolved from a stringed puppet. Actually the dancing doll, which is a jointed toy, has been around for about five thousand years. Jointed dolls as such have been found in tombs in Egypt.

It probably got into the mountains like the majority of the toys. People immigrated to this country and they brought it with them. I'd say ninety-nine per cent of the folk toys we have in this country originated in Europe. The people just brought their ideas with them. The various sizes of dolls were up to the individual. Just whatever size he happened to cut out that day with his knife was what he made. It was something that was relatively easy to make. It could be made completely by hand. People didn't have the places to go and buy toys for their children, so what they did was make their own toys.

When I first started making dancing dolls, I made them out of pine, or anything I could find—pine crating material, for example. But then I started making them out of poplar. It's a little harder wood, and the wearing ability of it is better. I make these dolls to dance, and poplar is much easier to work with because it is a little harder than pine and doesn't splinter as badly. The body, the legs, and the thigh pieces are primarily poplar, and the arms I normally make from scraps left over from the rockers off my rocking horses, which are made of beech or maple or any kind of close-grained hardwood.

For the paddle, I've gone to using Luan plywood. The reason for that is that I found this makes as good a paddle as you can use. I've made them out of solid poplar, and that makes a good paddle, but I found you get more spring out of a Luan than you do a solid paddle. Luan is a type of soft mahogany. Taiwan's a big producer. I don't like the imported woods, but sometimes we have to resort to them.

The kind of wood you use doesn't make as much difference in the action as it does the sound of it. With poplar, you get a real good sound. Pine is soft and you don't get the real good crisp sound when the doll is dancing on the paddle that you do with poplar legs.

All you need to work it is a little practice.

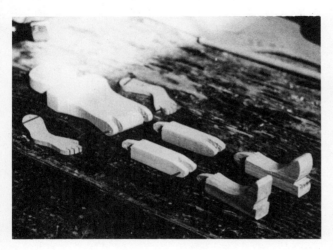

PLATE 220 The disassembled doll.

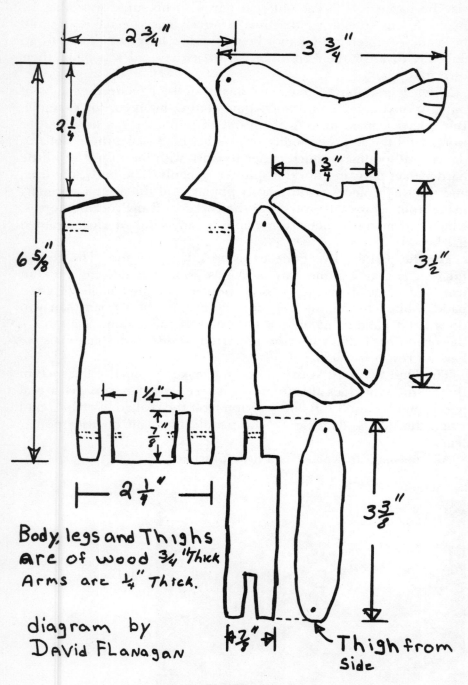

2 ¾"

3 ¾"

2 ¼"

6 ⅝"

1 ¾"

3 ½"

1 ¼"

⅞"

2 ¼"

3 ⅜"

Body, legs and Thighs
are of wood ¾" thick
Arms are ¼" Thick.

diagram by
David Flanagan

¾"

Thigh from
side

PLATE 221

PLATE 222 After cutting out the body, Dave nails the arms on but leaves the nails protruding about $\frac{1}{32}''$ instead of driving them in tight so that the arms will swing free. The small heads on the nails keep the arms from swinging off.

PLATE 223 Dave continues assembly by attaching the legs to the thighs. Before driving any nails, he drills tiny guide holes to keep the wood from splitting. Then, using serrated nails (he found that after a while the slick wire brads he used work loose and work out), he joins the pieces.

PLATE 224 He clips off the points of the nails that go through (arrow) and sands the area down to remove any rough edges. "I've seen people use wire nails and just drive the nail through and bend it over, and I don't like this at all. I don't like anything projecting like that."

PLATE 225 Dave checks to make sure the thigh fits and will swing freely.

PLATE 226 After drilling guide holes, he nails on the legs, being careful not to get a leg on backward.

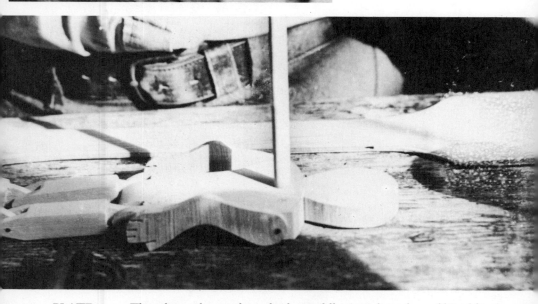

PLATE 227 Then he makes and sands the paddle (29″ long by 4 ¾″ wide at the ends), and inserts the dowel in the doll's back. He does not glue the dowel in so that it can be easily removed.

PLATE 228   David Flanagan using the doll. As the end of the paddle
bounces beneath the doll's feet, the legs dance and the arms swing.

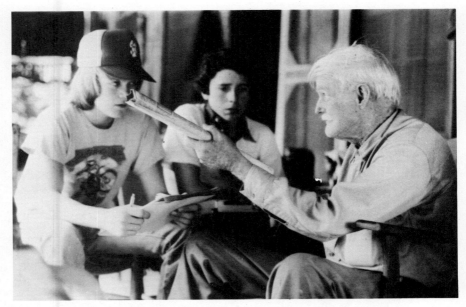

PLATE 229   Mitch Whitmire and John Bowen watch as Edd Hodgins demonstrates one use of a pop gun with a rolled-up newspaper.

Pop Guns

BUCK CARVER: We had our pop guns; we'd get an elder—that's pithy. First thing, it had to be good and straight. We'd hew us out a stick to punch that pith out with. Sometimes that pith would pack up in that and maybe jump out three, four feet when it did pop out. You get all that pith out, and then you loaded them with spitballs. They'd make a pretty, cracking racket. We always had one load in front; then pack another one in the other side with a ramrod. 'Course that's compressed air in there. Lots of time we'd blow in the barrel, but that didn't help any, I don't think. When you pushed the back spitball up [with the ramrod], it threw the front ball out. Some of them shoot pretty doggone hard—I've nearly had blisters on me from those things.

HATTIE KENNY: You went out and cut your elder and between the joint they's about a foot. You couldn't have a joint too thick 'cause the paper wads wouldn't go through. You cut it behind the joints and then you got you some wood and made you a ramrod. Then you got some paper and went to chunking it in. You had to have two balls. One stayed in and the other went out. One stayed at

PLATE 230 Mr. Davis with the barrel in his left hand and the plunger in his right.

POP GUN

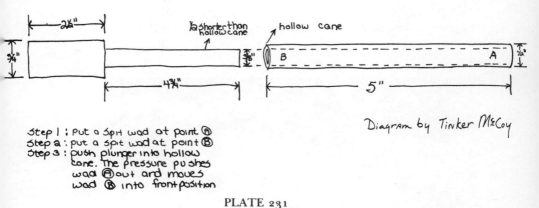

Step 1 : Put a spit wad at point Ⓐ
Step 2 : put a spit wad at point Ⓑ
Step 3 : push plunger into hollow
cane. The pressure pushes
wad Ⓐ out and moves
wad Ⓑ into front position

Diagram by Tinker McCoy

PLATE 231

the end at all times. It would burn you like fire if it hit you, too.

EDD HODGINS: You load them like loading a muzzle-loading gun. You put your first load in there and push it to the end. Ramrod it to the end. Blow a little air in there [from the back end] and chew up another wad of paper and stick it in the back end. [Then push that back wad with your ramrod] and it'll pop like a .22 rifle!

ARTHUR DAVIS: The first one I ever made was sixty-five years ago. I took them to school many times and got into trouble with them. We'd use a wad of newspaper and put it in there and make it shoot.

I'd have to sit on a slat with my back to the crowd because I shot somebody with one. Our teacher would take every one away from us that she saw. We never got them back neither. We'd go home, make some more, take them back the next day.

The plunger is made out of pine. The other part is made out of cane. I get my wood from the woods.

You chew a little wad of paper, put it in one end of the cane. Then chew another, put it in the other end. You shove the plunger in the cane, and the air between them pushes one of them out and leaves the other one for the next time. It will pop you so hard that it will blister you.

Puzzles

Some of the most vivid memories Foxfire students have are of the times Kenny Runion visits our classes with a suitcase full of puzzles he has made—puzzles that keep us occupied and frustrated sometimes for hours. Kenny claims that homemade puzzles like the ones he makes have been around in the mountains to fascinate children on rainy days for as long as he can remember.

PLATE 232   The six curved cuts made in this block of wood cause it to come apart into sixteen pieces (four rows of four pieces each). The object is to put the scrambled pieces back together.

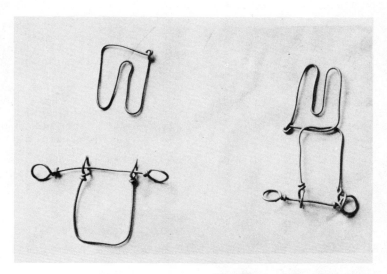

PLATE 233   The object here is to remove the heart-shaped piece from the rest of the puzzle without bending or untwisting any of the wire.

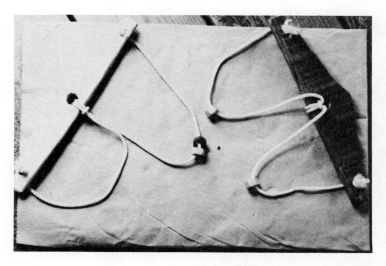

PLATE 234   This ox-yoke puzzle has two loops of cord with one nut or washer on each loop. The object is to get both nuts onto one loop without untying the cord.

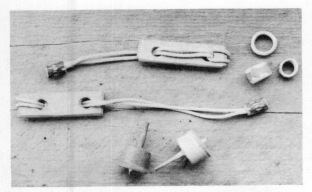

PLATE 235 This puzzle consists of a block of wood into which two holes have been drilled, and a length of cord, the ends of which are glued into a section of mountain laurel that is big enough so that it will not pass through the holes in the block. The object is to remove the cord from the block of wood. Also shown are two of Kenny's tops and three mountain-laurel rings.

PLATE 236 Kenny with one of his newest creations: a redheaded woodpecker door knocker. Pull the cord and the bird pecks.

PLATE 237 Dave Pickett makes his furniture puzzle by first cutting around three sides of the original block to make the large table.

PLATE 238 The sixth cut yields a small table from between the legs of one of the large chairs.

PLATE 239   In less than a minute, all the necessary cuts are made.
Here, John Helms looks at the disassembled puzzle, all pieces of which
came from one block of wood.

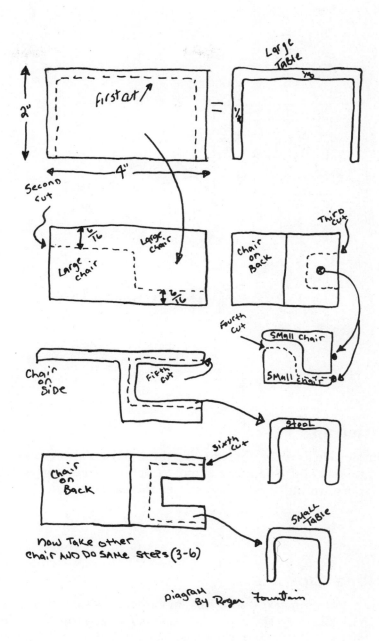

first at 1"

2"

4"

= Large Table

½ ¼

Second cut

Large chair

6/16

Large chair

Large chair

6/16

chair on Back

Third cut

Fourth cut

Small chair

Small chair

Chair on Side

Fifth cut

Stool

Sixth cut

Chair on Back

Small Table

now Take other chair AND DO SAME steps (3-6)

Diagram By Roger Fountain

PLATE 240

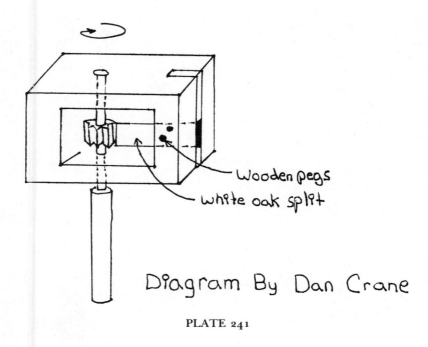

Wooden pegs
white oak split

Diagram By Dan Crane

PLATE 241

Rattletrap

Stanley Hicks remembers having these noisemakers as a youngster. A white-oak split snapping against a handcarved cog wheel as the box spins around the handle causes the racket.

Rolling Clown

Fred Potter markets this toy in his craft shop in Sugar Grove, North Carolina. As the two handles are squeezed together, the thread loop that passes through the clown's hands twists and untwists, causing the clown to flip over.

PLATE 242 The rolling clown. One end of the horizontal peg fits loosely into a hole in one of the arms (arrow).

PLATE 243 When the ends of the two arms are squeezed together, the loop of thread through the clown's hands forces it to spin.

PLATE 244 A child's sled in John Rice Irwin's Museum of Appalachia in Norris, Tennessee. It is identical in construction to the large farm sleds [*Foxfire 4*, pp. 134–49].

Sleds

BERTHA DOCKINS: The children had sleds, but these were made just about like the big ones [which were used for hauling loads]. Whenever it'd snow, they'd get out their sleds and they did have a time with them. Why, even my children did that! They'd go up on a mountain and turn those sleds loose—two or three of them would get on—and come down the mountain.

LAWTON BROOKS: We made sleds to ride when the snow was on the ground. We made the runners out of sourwood. [They often grow with the proper "crook" in them for runners.] One time we didn't have a sled and there come a big old snow and we had a big ladder. We drug it up the hill to make us some tracks. Me and my brother got on it and started back down the hill, and the thing left the road and run aground a stump and it swapped ends—like to have killed both of us! [It was] my daddy's ladder. It tore the ladder up and tore us up, too. My brother—he was hurt pretty bad for quite a while.

HATTIE KENNY: We had little sleds to ride in the snow. My father made them. They were like farm sleds only you had a bigger crosspiece to sit on so you didn't fall off.

VELER MARCUS: We'd get a wide board and nail a piece across here to put your toes against. Get up on the hillside up here and come down the steep hill to the bottom on that board. Whenever you slid down those hills long enough to get the bottom of the board slick, you'd have a time sticking on that board. I've rode down many of a time. My uncle always used to keep us one made.

STANLEY HICKS: We used to hollow out a piece of a log and then ride it down the mountain on the snow. That was our snow sleds.

PLATE 245   The bed lifts off just like its full-sized counterpart . . .

PLATE 246 . . . and the standards lift out.

PLATE 247 Willard Watson makes an even smaller version of a farm sled, complete with mule and farmer, for a child's toy.

PLATE 248 Willard's sled includes farm tools such as a single-foot plow and a hoe with a tiny metal blade.

PLATE 249 Lawton Brooks with his slingshot.

Slingshots

ARTHUR DAVIS: Mountain kids have played with slingshots for years. I used to kill birds with them, and I knocked the windows out of a schoolhouse one time, but not on purpose. I used shoe tongues to make the slings because they wouldn't break easily. I use leather now; it's the best. Canvas or tough cloth will make a pretty good one, too. You can throw a rock three times better with a slingshot than you can with your hand. You can also put a piece of lead in the slingshot and you can kill a bird with it. If you have a good round rock, it will go as straight as a bullet. I use old bicycle inner tubes now for the rubber strips.

LAWTON BROOKS: I've killed many rabbits with a slingshot. Marbles are the best things to kill them with. A rock won't go as straight. If I get close up to what I'm aiming at, I can hit it; but when it's a ways off, it goes to wobbling. Lead bullets is the best thing of all. I've shot the eyes out of a rabbit before.

I don't like bought rubber on my slingshots. I like raw rubber. I like raw rubber because it's got more power to it. It's got a kick

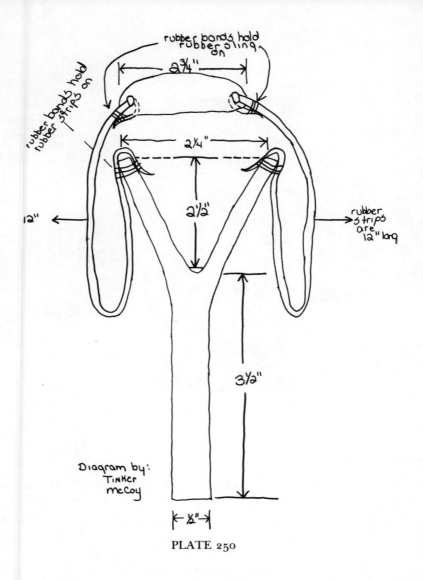

rubber bands hold
rubber sling on

2¾"

rubber bands hold
rubber strips on

2¼"

12"

2½"

rubber
strips
are
12" long

3½"

Diagram by:
Tinker
McCoy

½"

PLATE 250

to it. We used to use inner tubes. I got some of that raw rubber out of some old T Models. Some of that would be red.

And then we'd carry these things with us to school. We'd get about to the school and they'd make us hide them. After school, we'd pick up little round rocks just laying in the road. Once we had a whole pile of rocks and we was standing there in front of the store just flipping them. And Edith said, "Lawton, let me shoot, let me shoot."

I said, "Here it is. Now don't flip yourself."

She said, "I ain't." She drawed back and it knocked her right between the eyes and, boy, did I laugh!

PLATE 251 A smoke grinder. Pump up and down on the horizontal bar with two fingers, and the disc and shaft spin back and forth inside the bar.

Smoke Grinders

Another locally made toy Fred Potter stocks in his shop is this smoke grinder. The point of the toy is set in a slight depression, and as the horizontal bar is pumped with two fingers, the influence of the string twisting around the shaft and the weight of the wooden disk make the toy spin back and forth in the depression.

Squirt Guns

STANLEY HICKS: We made them like those pop guns—a hollow piece and a plunger. Pull the plunger back and suck water up in there and then push the plunger to squirt it out. Sometimes kids would fill their squirt guns with hog mud and manure and squirt that mess all over us!

Stick Horses

LELIA GIBSON: In playing, we'd have stick horses—get a stick or a broomstick, tie a string on it [for a bridle], and straddle it, and lope! Now, that's the kind of playing we had.

PLATE 252 To make a pair of stilts, Clyde Runion first cuts two rhododendron trunks, leaving forks as shown.

Stilts (Tom Walkers or J-walkers or Walking Crutches)

EDD HODGINS: We just called 'em walkin' crutches—that's all we called them. Get you some forked sticks over there in the woods and cut 'em off. Keep your feet in those forks and walk in them. I got to where I could get a way up there. When you're not up too high, it won't bother you much, but you get up pretty high and you better know what you're doing pretty good. [If you don't] it'll pitch you plumb across that pickup.

STANLEY HICKS: We'd wade the river on those. Then we'd see who could walk the furtherest without falling. We had a prize we'd give the one that walked the furtherest with 'em. It wasn't much—a toy or something we made. We'd make little old horses and little old dogs for prizes.

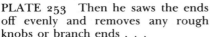

PLATE 253   Then he saws the ends off evenly and removes any rough knobs or branch ends . . .

PLATE 254   . . . and tries them out.

MRS. TOM MACDOWELL: We'd cut sticks with forks in them, and we'd get old socks and wrap them around right there to keep them from hurting our feet, and we'd walk with those stilts. We'd wade the creek with them—go right on down the banks of the creek and then get out on a big flat rock.

VELER MARCUS: My brother and me would walk in those things and just ruin the sides of our shoes. We started off about a foot high, then go on up. We would get over here by Fred Lovell's right along the creek. They was an old road there. That creek was about up to your knees, and we would carry them Tom Walkers down there—our high ones—and, boy, we had to get steady or we would fall. Once we got balanced we could go right on.

So we would get down there and if we heard a wagon coming round the bend, boy, we would get out of that water and get back

PLATE 255   Benson Justus caught on quickly.

up [on the bank] and hide so they wouldn't see us down there playing in the creek. We didn't want to be down there walking 'cause we might scare whatever they were driving [horses or oxen]. They would think, "Oh no, that's those rude young'uns down there." Of course, they were everybody's rude young'uns that got out and waded the branch and all that!

Grape-vine Swings

NANNIE ANN SANDERS: Go to the woods and find a wild grape vine growing up into a tree. Cut it in two at the bottom and then hold onto that free end and swing. I liked to have broke my neck on a grape-vine swing once. I fell into a creek—the best place you ever fell. It didn't break my neck but it sure shook me up!

HATTIE KENNY: Oh yeah, swing up in there and back. I remember one Sunday there was two men that fell off and broke their legs. They tried to swing at the same time and it pulled out with them. Both men broke their leg in the same place. One·of 'em died with cancer and the other one got well and went right on.

Rope Swings

VELER MARCUS: Daddy would make us rope swings. Tie a rope in a loop on a limb in the yard where our shade trees were. Then he'd fix us a board for a seat. Notch the board so it wouldn't turn us out. You had to be careful or it would turn you out and you would get hurt.

MRS. RAE SHOOK: We used to make swings. Somebody would climb way up on a tree and tie the ropes, and you'd get in it down here and somebody would swing you way out over yonder. You'd go a long ways. We'd have a piece of hickory bark across it for a seat.

Tops or Dancers

BUCK CARVER: [We had] homemade tops. They usually consisted of a spinner. You take a spool and whittle it to a sharp point. Then take out a round peg and plug it in the hole [of the spool] and slope it to a sharp point. Take that in your fingers and spin it on the floor.

PLATE 256 Kenny Runion had a top similar to the one Buck describes.

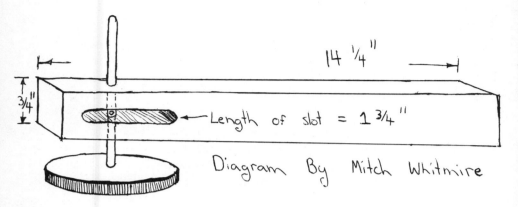

14 ¼"

¾"

Length of slot = 1 ¾"

Diagram By Mitch Whitmire

PLATE 257 The launcher Stanley uses.

PLATE 258 With the dancer set in its launcher as shown in the diagram, Ronnie Welch threads a string through the hole in the dancer's shaft . . .

PLATE 259 . . . and then twists the dancer inside the launcher to wind the string around its shaft.

STANLEY HICKS: We made dancers out of round wooden discs [4″–6″ in diameter and 1/4″–1/2″ thick]. We'd drill a hole in the middle and drive a sharpened stick through there, and they'd spin on the point of that stick. We would get three or four spinning at the same time and see which one would spin the longest. I've made some that would dance over five minutes, but if you've got one that dances that long, you've got a pretty good one. Then we'd play a game where we'd get them spinning together in a marked-off area, and the one that kicked the other ones out of there was the winner.

PLATE 260 With a sharp pull of the string, Stanley launches the dancer, letting it drop out of the launcher and spin freely.

PLATE 261 Dan Melton, Ronnie Welch, Stanley, and Richard Jones watch as it spins.

PLATE 262 Roger Fountain and Bill Taylor saw off a 2'-long piece of locust while Clyde holds the log. This piece will form the two wagon axles.

Wagons

LAWTON BROOKS: We used to make wagons. [We'd] saw the wheels out of old black-gum trees—saw them about three inches thick. I had a big old auger to bore a hole through the wheels, and we'd take soap and grease them things with old homemade soap. We'd get the axles slick, and they'd stay slick.

We'd tie a rope to the front axle, and have our seat over the back wheels, and we'd guide it with the ropes. You get started down the mountain, and you could just fly!

BUCK CARVER: We made wagons. We made the wheels out of old black gum. Made many of them—used to haul wood on them. We'd make the darn things and get up on a mountain—you steered 'em with your feet. And to pull them, you tied a rope on each end of the front axle. We kept those wheels greased with axle grease till they rolled pretty easy. We'd get on that mountain and sometime the thing would get going so fast where we'd see we couldn't make the curve, and we'd bail off and leave the thing and let her go. I guess we got up to twenty miles an hour, maybe more.

EDD HODGINS: My granddaddy and my daddy was wagon and buggy makers. Had a pretty good shop. So when my boy wanted one, I knowed how to do it. I made that oldest boy one and, boy, was it a dandy. He was just about six or seven years old and he'd ride it around here and pull it. Sometimes there'd be two or three out there playing with it.

But it was a nice wagon. I made every piece about it from sawed-off blocks. It was about eight inches high, and it had the bolsters, the hounds, the rocking bolsters, and everything just like a regular wagon out of a factory. Every bit of it was made from wood—wheels and all. I used to do all such stuff as that every chance I got.

Then I made my grandchildren a little bitty covered wagon and a yoke of steers to pull it. They took it to school. You couldn't get it from 'em for nothing. I mean they wouldn't take anything for it.

CLYDE RUNION: My father was a blacksmith. When they were building the Black Rock Road up here in 1903, he was the blacksmith on that road. He sharpened all the tools, shod all the mules. Then

PLATE 263 Clyde halves the piece of locust, and shapes each half into a rough axle using his ax.

PLATE 264 Final shaping of the axles is done with a draw knife. The top surface of each must be flat to hold the bed of the wagon.

PLATE 265 Clyde uses a wood rasp to round the ends of the axles to fit the wheels.

PLATE 266 Using a homemade gauge, he checks the diameter of the axle ends to make sure the wheels will fit on without binding, and will roll smoothly. He then drills a hole in the end of each axle for the wooden pegs that will hold the wheels on.

PLATE 267 Using first a saw and then a hammer and a chisel, Clyde notches the top of the rear axle for the support beams (see Plate 284).

PLATE 268   While Clyde worked on the axles, John Helms and Roger Fountain sawed four 2″-thick wheels. Ideally, the wheels would be made of black gum, but since none was available at the time, Clyde decided to use poplar he had handy just for purposes of demonstration. Poplar should be avoided if at all possible, however, as it splits easily.

PLATE 269   With a crude compass, Clyde marks a perfect circle of identical diameter on each wheel. The wheels should be *at least* 12″ in diameter.

PLATE 270 With a hammer, chisel, and a draw knife, he removes the wood that lies outside the circles he has scribed on the wheels. After rounding the wheels and drilling a hole in the center of each, he puts them on the axles, adding the wooden pegs to hold them.

PLATE 271 At one end of the center-support beam, Clyde chisels out a small notch on both sides so that the beam will fit exactly into the center notch cut previously in the top of the rear axle.

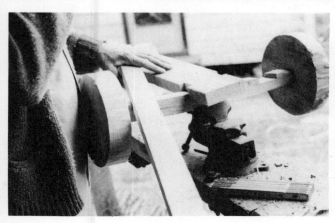

PLATE 272 He next marks the angle he will have to cut in the end of each side brace (the end that will have to be angled for the left brace is under his hand in this photograph) and the length to which each side brace will have to be cut.

PLATE 273 Using one of the side braces as a guide, he marks the top half of the rear axle (the rocking bolster) for the notches that will fit down over the side braces (see Plate 284).

PLATE 274 The rear axle assembly, including the rocking bolster, minus the two side braces.

PLATE 275 Next Clyde drills a hole through the center of the rear axle assembly and drives a wooden peg into the hole to hold it all together. The peg should go all the way through, and any excess should be cut off where it comes through the bottom of the axle.

PLATE 276 He then puts the side braces in place and drills and pegs them also.

PLATE 277 To complete the rear axle assembly, he drills and pegs the side braces into place through their angled ends.

PLATE 278 The next step is to turn the wagon over, and shave off the sharp edges of the underside of the main support beam at the point where it will rest in the top of the front axle. This will allow it to turn on the front axle without binding.

PLATE 280 To complete the front axle assembly, Clyde drills a hole through it for a metal bolt that will hold it together loosely enough so that the front axle will turn with ease.

PLATE 279 The wagon is turned back over and the main support beam is set into place in the sloped notch that has been cut in the top of the front axle. Note that a support brace for the wagonbed has been added to the main support beam.

PLATE 281 Clyde nails the bed of the wagon to the top of the rocking bolster and the top of the support brace, and then shapes the two sides for the wagon and nails them firmly to the side of the wagonbed.

PLATE 282 To complete the bed, Clyde cuts out a back rest and nails it into place at a slight slant behind that portion of the bed that serves as a seat.

PLATE 283 To finish the wagon, he nails a foot rest onto the main support beam, and attaches a steering rope to the front axle. Axle grease can be used to make the wheels turn freely, and a coat of paint can be added if desired.

when he first come to Mountain City, he built a blacksmith shop in 1925 and ran it to 1950. Back in them days, blacksmithing was a good business.

I used to watch him make horse wagons, and from that I got the pattern to make my wagons to play with when I was a boy. When I took to schooling, seemed like everyone tried to style his own wagon, and the one I'm going to make for you all today is styled the way I made mine, except the one I hauled wood on was different from that. It was built stronger with brakes and all, and the bed would come out to the front wheels. It was bigger, and me and my brother would pull it. We'd haul wood out of the mountain all the time.

For these wagons we rode on, we'd have trails, and miles to ride on Sunday. That was all there was to do. Bunch of us get together and race off the mountain. They'd style them every which way, you

REAR AXLE FROM TOP AND SIDE

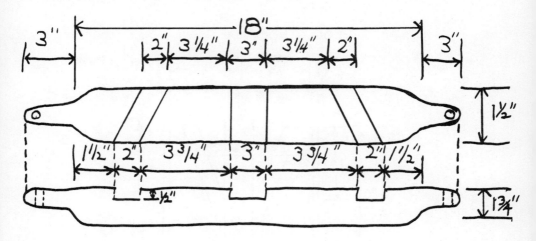

FRONT AXLE FROM SIDE

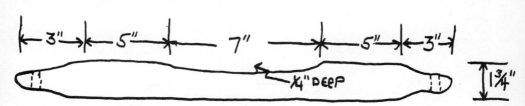

DIAGRAM BY ROGER FOUNTAIN

PLATE 284

know. Some made them one way and another made another way. There's a lot of ways to fix them. Put steering wheels on them, or put another seat behind, or change the bed. About anything you want to. Now, I used to make a goat wagon with bigger wheels and shafts like a regular horse wagon except a goat would pull it, and that's lots of fun to pull people in. We'd always make the wheels out of black gum, and use locust for the axles on account of it wouldn't wear. The wheels would wear some, but all you have to do is saw you another set of wheels and put them right back on when the wheels wear out. Instead of using an auger, we'd heat up a pipe in the fire and burn our holes in the center of the wheels for the axles. Sometimes we'd put old black axle grease on the axles, but not too much or it will swell the wheels up and make them tight. You'd want just enough to make them slide good. But that makes a pretty rig. Never painted them. Just left them natural.

FROM UNDERSIDE:

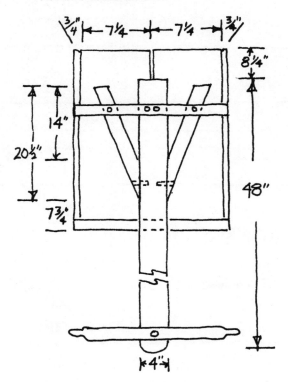

PLATE 285

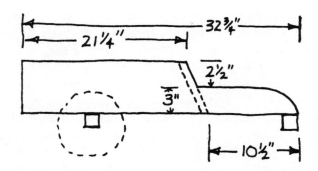

PLATE 286

PLATE 287 Clyde on the finished wagon.

I quit school in 1946, and when I quit school, I quit my wagon business. I hadn't never thought of another wagon until I saw you all the other day. But we really used to have a time on them. I had several hurts on one of them things. Get a big bunch on it and get on the mountain and hang around a curve and right down off the side and run into a tree and throw us off. Best one I ever had, I had made one out of wheelbarrow wheels, and got a way back up on the mountain about a mile or so, and there was a big old sawbriar patch out yonder; and just before we got to it, I jumped off and let the wagon go on through the sawbriar patch. There was two people on it. But we got a lot of kicks out of something like that. We'd get together and get our wagons and ride all day long on Sunday—play in the woods. Now you almost don't want that. It'd be dangerous to get on the road nowadays, too. Every morning I used to pull my old wagon all the way through here all the way to the old schoolhouse up yonder. I'd take my wagon with me every morning, and at recess we would race and have a big time.

PLATE 288   Happy Dowdle with a wagon he had as a child.

PLATE 289   Close-up of Happy's wagon.

PLATE 290   Benson Justus with a wagon in John Rice Irwin's Museum of Appalachia in Norris, Tennessee. The wagon was made for John Rice by his father.

PLATE 291 The same wagon with the bed lifted off.

PLATE 292   A covered wagon Willard Watson made.

PLATE 293   Dan Melton, Willard, and Ronnie Welch looking at the harness that hooks the mules to the wagon.

PLATE 294 The front axle assembly.

PLATE 295 The rear axle assembly.

PLATE 296 A one-horse cart Willard made.

Whimmy Diddles or Jeep Sticks

ARTHUR DAVIS: First one I ever saw was about twenty-five years ago. My friend found one up in Mountain City. Then he finally gave it to me. First one I ever saw made, I made it myself.

When I first started making jeep sticks I told everybody I could tell their fortunes with them. The idea is to put your thumbnail right up against the stick and it will go one way. If you want it to go the other way, put your thumbnail under the stick. You can make one of these in thirty minutes, or forty at least.

The ridges are what makes it turn. You could take a pencil and do the same thing. They can be any length; they're usually about five inches long. Inside is just a piece of hard wood. You get the propeller as loose as you can get it. You can use any kind of wood. I usually use ivy because it usually has a crook in it. The crook makes it easier to hold.

PLATE 298

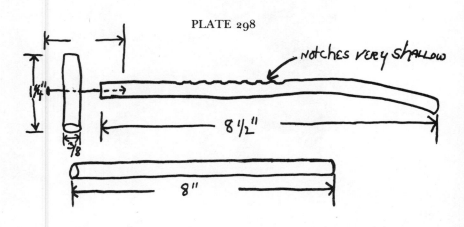

notches very shallow

1¾"

⅜

8½"

8"

I've always called them "jeep sticks," that's all I ever call them. Some people call them "gee-haw whimmy diddles." [The "gee haw" part of the name that many people use comes from the fact that you can make the propeller go in either direction, just as the same commands make a mule or a steer turn to the right or the left.]

Hollow Whistles

HATTIE KENNY: We made hundreds of whistles out of willow along the creekbanks. We would get a slick, pretty one and cut it off as long as we wanted it. Then we would make a notch to blow through and put a piece of wood back in the end of it to plug the end. You had a whistle you could hear a mile. You can even learn to make little songs on 'em.

PLATE 299 The piece of wood that goes in the end of the whistle is in Mr. Davis's right hand.

PLATE 300 Trying the whistle out.

MRS. RAE. SHOOK: Used to, in the spring, we'd go up and get some small pieces of young sourwood. Cut a sprout and rub the bark of it loose with another sprout and pull that bark off. Cut a mouthpiece where you blow into it. Then fix you a piece to go back down in the end to plug it up.

ARTHUR DAVIS: I've made them ever since I was a kid. The whistle is the easiest toy I've ever made because it only takes fifteen minutes to make. I used to make whistles with little holes on top of them, but I haven't made one of them in a long time. Those make a different tune than the ones I make now.

I get my river cane out on Broad River. It's smaller than bamboo. It's better to cut them when they're green because they're easier to work with, but you can work them when they're dry.

You stop one end up with a piece of wood to keep the air from coming out. You can use any kind of wood for the plug. The plugs will get tighter as they dry out. Sometimes they dry out so good that you can't get them out again. But this doesn't change the tune of it.

You want them dried out when you blow them. The length makes the difference in the tune, but you can have them long or short. Cut a little air hole in one end to blow through so it will whistle.

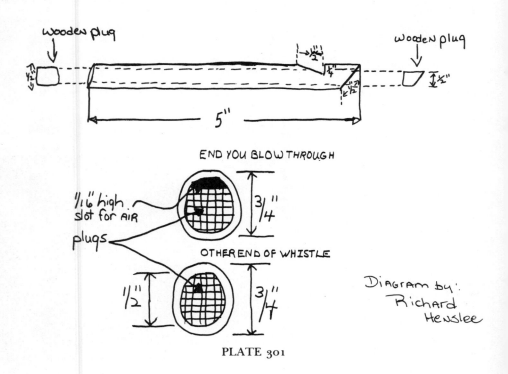

PLATE 301

PLATE 302   Edd Hodgins took us to the woods behind his house to show us how to make a whistle.

PLATE 303   First he cuts a laurel branch and . . .

Split Whistles

ERNEST FRANKLIN: We made our whistles out of goose quills. You split the feather and blow against it.

EDD HODGINS: I could make you one in a few minutes if you want to see one. You just split an ivy stick and put you a leaf down in there and trim it off and then blow on that.

PLATE 304   . . . shaves off two sides and splits it about halfway down the middle.

PLATE 305   Then he inserts a laurel leaf into the split, trims off the excess with his knife, and . . .

PLATE 306 . . . blows against one side to make the noise.

Whittled Animals

One tradition firmly associated with the Appalachians is that of whittling birds and animals, often for children to play with; more often, now, for sale to tourists and collectors through area crafts shops. One area whittler, Ben Bar, who lives in Clarkesville, Georgia, was selected for this chapter because of the appropriateness of many of his works for children's play.

BEN BAR: I've been carving about thirty or thirty-five years. I did a little when I was sixteen or seventeen years old. I like to whittle. When I started off, using a big knife, I'd shave off sticks letting the shavings fall down. But then an old man told me one time, says, "You've got a nice stick there, but you whittle it all away and

PLATE 307   Ben Bar with one of his creations.

it's gone. Make something out of that stick you can save instead of whittling it all away."

I drive a lumber truck for a local sawmill for a living, and I can get lots of my wood—slabs, knots, and such that they can't sell— from the mill. I also collect laurel wood to use in lots of my toys. I collect that in the woods during the winter when the sap is down so the bark won't peel off later and ruin the toy.

PLATE 308   Ronnie Welch with two of Ben's carvings—a bird, and a dog with a treed raccoon.

PLATE 309   Ben's versions
of a rooster . . .

PLATE 310   . . . a steer . . .

PLATE 311   . . . a horse
and wagon . . .

PLATE 312   . . . and a dog with three treed possums.

Kids can play with all my toys. They like them because they're sturdy and there's nothing about one to hurt them in any way.

I've never been trained to do my carving. I just do a little more and a little more getting ideas here and there. And I buy Barlow knives by the box, taping the handles so they won't hurt my hand. I wear those knives out fast. This one here is about two and a half months old and it's about wore out already!

Windmills

Though not technically a toy, these creations powered by wind
are among the most lighthearted, entertaining, and fascinating creations in the mountains. Mounted on stakes in a front yard or on
a roof, and constantly pointed into the wind thanks to a ball bearing
and a tail rudder, the motion and light clatter of these works can
be satisfying in a unique way. Some families are so drawn to them
that their yards will be literally filled with windmills all representing
different activities: churning, boxing, sawing, splitting wood, milking—a list limited only by the maker's imagination.

The principle is simple. Heavy-gauge wire runs from the propeller
along the base. At various intervals, crooks are bent into the wire.
The moving portions of carved animals or people are hooked to
these crooks by other pieces of wire. As the propeller turns, the
base wire with its crooks also turns, forcing the moving portions
of the figures back and forth or up and down in a constantly repeating
motion, the speed of which varies, of course, according to wind
velocity.

KENNY RUNION: I put up a windmill here—one with a big wheel.
There was seven things on there a'workin'. The first was two fellows
on a seesaw. One would go down and the other would come up
just thataway, you know. And the next thing was a man churning,
and the next thing was a man milking. Then there was some other
things on there. When that thing turned, it was something to see!

CLYDE RUNION: These windmills have been around for a long time
in the mountains. I just build them for a hobby thing, myself. I
just like to see them run, you know.

I made the pattern for this one [see Plates 313–24] myself. Another
way I made one once was with a man riding a horse. Every time it
would turn, the horse would go. I just had one on it. It didn't work
too good, though. You had to have it all hooked up together to
where as the horse went one way, the man went backwards. You
had to bend one crank down and the other up 'cause one pulled
the horse down and at the same time, the other one pushed the
man backwards. It's real complicated to make one of them. And
when it got wet, it wouldn't work.

I used to make them with lights on them with a generator. When
the wind blows, it would light up, you know. The generator would
put out, and the lights would come on. It's right pretty to have
different kinds of bulbs in there. And when the wind would blow,

PLATE 313 Clyde's windmill has one man who bends at the waist and appears to split a log with a wedge . . .

it would light up. You have to have about a six-foot propeller to do that with, and a car generator. You can run you a wire all around the propeller, and make your bulbs around in it like Christmas lights. Then when it's turning, you don't see the propeller at night. You just see the lights turning. People wonder what that is. The faster it turns, the more light it lights up. It's real pretty. I like to do something like that. I've always had windmills.

You can have them milking a cow or fighting or about anything you want to put down there. One's just about as easy as the other [to make]. But the cow milking is hard to make because you've got to have the cow moving and the man [moving, too]. Then you can have a woman churning. That's no trouble to make.

PLATE 314 . . . and two men who move back and forth sawing a log with a crosscut saw.

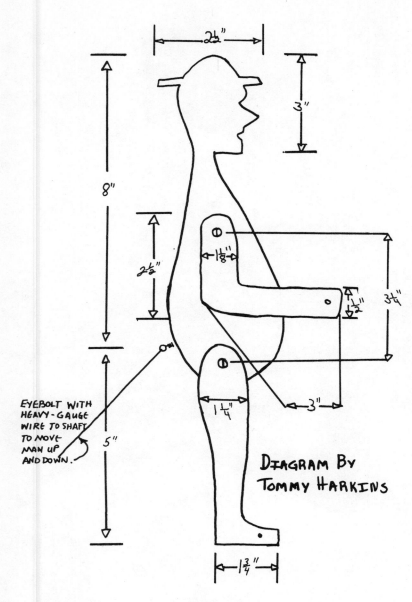

2½"

3"

8"

2½"

1⅛"

3¼"

1½"

EYEBOLT WITH
HEAVY-GAUGE
WIRE TO SHAFT
TO MOVE
MAN UP
AND DOWN.

5"

3"

1¼"

DIAGRAM BY
TOMMY HARKINS

1¾"

PLATE 315

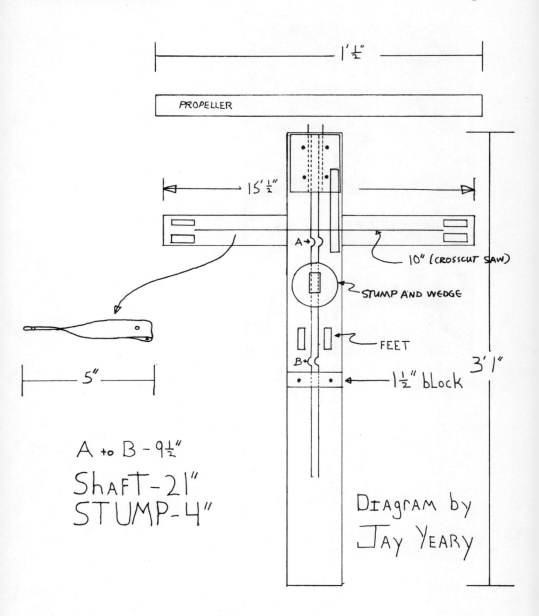

1' ½"

PROPELLER

15' ½"

A→

10" (CROSSCUT SAW)

STUMP AND WEDGE

FEET

B→

1½" bLock

3' 1"

5"

A to B - 9½"
ShaFT - 21"
STUMP - 4"

DIAgRAM by
JAY YEARY

PLATE 316

PLATE 317   Clyde saws the blades for
the propeller out of 1″ x 2″ white pine.

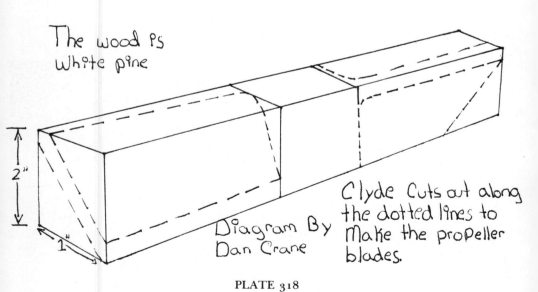

The wood is white pine

2″

1″

Diagram By
Dan Crane

Clyde Cuts out along
the dotted lines to
make the propeller
blades.

PLATE 318

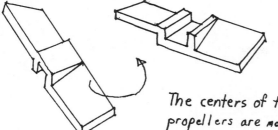

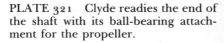

PLATE 319

The centers of the propellers are mortised out so that they will fit together flush.

DIAGRAM BY CHRIS JARRARD

PLATE 320 The finished propeller.

PLATE 321 Clyde readies the end of the shaft with its ball-bearing attachment for the propeller.

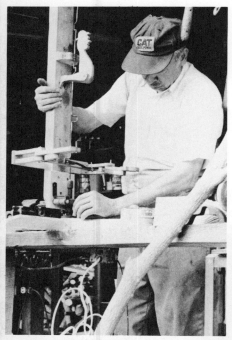

PLATE 322   Holding the front end of the windmill against the propeller, he attaches it with four screws.

PLATE 323   Then he reattaches the men to the shaft.

PLATE 324   After testing the propeller to make sure all three men are moving, Clyde attaches a plywood wind rudder to the far end of the shaft to keep the propeller turned into the wind.

PLATE 325 Another type of windmill. The rabbit used to have wings so that when the wind blew, it would spin.

You've got to use a hard wood on account of it busting. Something like maple or oak. Pine won't hardly work on it. And you've got to be pretty particular about making that shaft there [with the cranks]. You got to figure out not to make them the same way, you know. If you do, they will all work together. You've got to have them offset so one will work different from the other. I use copper wire for that shaft. I take a pair of pliers and a vise and bend it the way I want to. And you've got to leave the arms loose enough to work. If you tighten them up too much, they won't work.

On the propeller, you cut one slope one way and the other the other way, and when the wind blows in here, why, it turns it. I like to make the propellers out of poplar because it's the lightest wood and it doesn't soak water in as bad as pine. It sheds the water off and doesn't get heavy. On a double propeller, if you ain't careful, you'll get one cut wrong and it will fight itself and won't turn at all. You've got to get them all cut the same, and you've got to

PLATE 326 This windmill, made by Preacher Charlie Woody of Spruce Pine, North Carolina, is a churning woman.

PLATE 327 A windmill with a six-bladed propeller. Like the others, it is mounted on a locust post and turns on a ball-bearing system.

PLATE 328 Close-up of the propeller from the front . . .

PLATE 329 . . . the back . . .

PLATE 330 . . . and the side.

balance them. If you get one side longer than the other, the wind won't blow it good. Two propellers are stronger than one. But something else. If you get too big of a propeller, it turns too fast and then it'll fly apart. I had one on top of the house once, and I had it with two men fighting on it. In come a big windstorm one night, and it got to turning too fast and they all flew off of it. The faster the wind would blow, the faster they would fight.

I've tried to paint them but I can't paint them just right so I leave them natural. Anybody that was a good hand to paint could paint them good. Sometimes I take my knife and round off the bodies real good. But that one there I just sawed it out and never did round it off. You can use a three-quarter-inch board and can whittle out the man to look pretty much like a man, you know. That's just a half-inch board there. It takes a long time, though, to round one off.

GAMES

Anty-over (or Anthony Over or Ant'ni Over)

ESCO PITTS: Half would be on one side of a house and half on the other. One side would have the ball. The side that didn't have the ball would say, "Anty," and the one that had it would yell, "Over." Then he would throw the ball and if anybody on the other side caught it he would run around the house and throw it and try to get somebody out. They would go till everybody was out, then change sides.

VELER MARCUS: We would get us a ball and we'd go down to the schoolhouse. There would be eight or ten on this side, then eight or ten on that side. The school building was pretty high but we managed to throw the ball over. We'd holler, "Anty-over." We'd have two people down at the end so we could tell pretty well who caught the ball. [Our team] would divide and half of us would run on each side of the building toward the other side of the schoolhouse. The person who had caught the ball would throw it in the crowd, and whoever the ball hit had to go over on the other side and then we'd start all over again.

HATTIE KENNY: You would throw the ball over, and if one caught it and ran around and hit you with it, you had to go to that side and let him stay over here. They would be a whole team of people. Sometimes there would just be two and sometimes there would be ten or twelve. We played this a many of times.

PLATE 331   Veler Marcus.

LAWTON BROOKS: You see, if you threw the ball over the roof—one team on one side and one on the other—whoever caught it would run around the other side of the house and hit a person with it. That person was out, if you could slip around and hit him with it before he could get out of sight of you. We always had to play with old yarn balls. They wouldn't hurt you—if you got hit on the head with one, it wouldn't hurt, just bounce off.

MARINDA BROWN: When I was in school, along when I was about sixteen, our main game was anty-over. We'd throw the ball across the schoolhouse. We'd divide up the crowd—part would be on one side and part on the other. We'd throw the ball back and forth, and if anyone on one side caught the ball, they'd all run around and try to tag the ones coming from the other side. Everyone they tagged had to join that side. Sometimes they'd play till maybe just one was left, and sometimes not any left on that side. They just kept working like that way; that was a lot of fun. We spent all of our time as far back as I can remember doing that.

I got my nose hurt one time. We had a new boy come to school— his first day. It was kind of a cold, bad day and we were playing anty-over. We ran into each other, and oh! It just smashed my mouth and nose. I was sick for about a week.

KENNY RUNION: I like to got killed playing it one time. I threw the ball over and a girl hollered. She ought not to have done that. I started around the corner of the schoolhouse and we met. I'm telling you the truth—I bet I went ten feet out through those rocks. Like to killed her too. We just run face to face. Teacher didn't whip us, though. We said it was just an accident. I never played no more ball.

Base

ERNEST FRANKLIN: I've known a game of base to last two or three hours because some of the runners were so good. The game was usually played at school and took the place of our baseball today. Most one-room schools could about make a good team if they used all the kids they had. You have to have an umpire because the game gets pretty confusing.

Any number of people can play. They are divided into two equal teams and each team is assigned to a base. The two bases face each other twenty to thirty feet apart or more depending on the running ability of the players, the terrain, etc. The bases are long enough so that each player can touch the base simultaneously [see Plates 333–36].

The object of the game is to circle the opponent's base and return "home" without being caught and tagged out by one of the opponents. There is usually no restriction on how far a player runs. [Ernest remembers one time that a player circled so far through

PLATE 332   Ernest Franklin uses pebbles to show Tina Smith, John Bowen, Wig, and Harvey Miller the layout for base.

the woods around an opponent's base that he didn't get back until after school was finished for the day.] Play continues until all the players on one side are out—or until the referee stops the game.

The rule to remember is that if a player has touched his base since you left yours, he can tag you out unless you beat him back to your home base or he is intercepted and chased away or tagged out by one of your teammates.

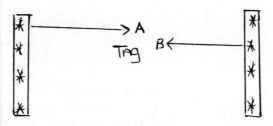

PLATE 333 A approaches the opposite team and tries to entice B into chasing him.

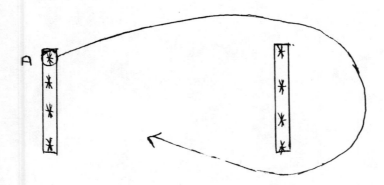

PLATE 334 A then tries to circle the enemy base and get "home" without being tagged.

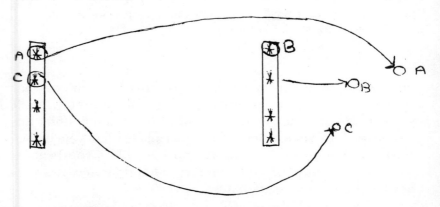

PLATE 335 While A is circling the base, B can move in pursuit to tag A out. C can come to the aid of A and tag B out as long as C leaves his base *after* B.

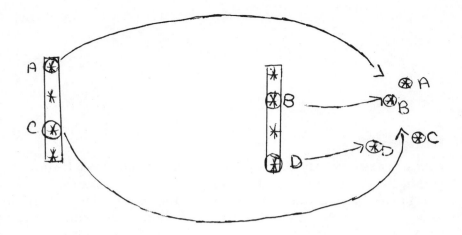

PLATE 336 While C is helping A, D may chase C and tag him out as long as he leaves his base after C. Two or three men may be chasing A, but C can tag only one of them out [and only one that left his base before he did]. Then he has to get back to his own home base to be safe.

When C gets into enemy territory, B can leave pursuit of A, tag his own base, and then chase C if he wants.

A player tagged when off his base is out of the game. The side that loses all its players first loses the game.

Play usually begins with a player from one side approaching the enemy base and getting as close as he can to it without being tagged out. When a member of the opposite team is taunted into chasing him, he gets back to his home base as quickly as he can. If he is tagged before he gets home, he drops out. Meanwhile, another player from the same base may be trying to circle the opposite team's base. If this player makes it back home safely, the opposite team has to eliminate one of their men. They usually pick one of their slower men and make him drop out and save their strongest runners for as long as they can.

At least one player stays on a base at all times to protect it.

Blindfold

MRS. RAE SHOOK: One person has his eyes blindfolded. All the other players stay just out of his reach as he wanders around trying to touch one of them. The players call out to him and may run past and touch him and tease him, but they try to dodge fast enough so they won't be tagged. The first person touched or tagged by the blindfolded one is then "it," and his eyes are blindfolded and the game begins again.

Bullpen

ERNEST FRANKLIN: My dad would play this game, and I guess my grandpa did too. It's been handed down for generations. The last year I played was in 1929, which was also the last year I went barefoot to school. I was a sophomore in high school then. You'd have at least eight players: four on a side. The game was played with a ball made of yarn, and we always got our mother to sew around it to keep it from unraveling. If the ball was too light, sometimes we'd wrap the yarn around a core like a piece of wood to give it extra weight.

[The object of the game is to get all the men out on one team by hitting each one of them with the ball. One team of four players mans the bases, and the other players get in the center or in the bullpen. One man on base throws the ball diagonally across the field to another base to get the ball into play. Then it is thrown around the bases. At any point, a man on base can catch the ball and try to hit a man in the center with it. The man in the center tries to dodge it. If the man who throws it misses, he is out of the game. If he hits the man he was throwing at, that man picks up the ball as quickly as possible and tries to hit one of the basemen. who by this time have scattered and are running in all directions. Though the basemen are allowed to run away, a man in the center cannot leave the bullpen unless the ball bounces or rolls out. Then he can leave the bullpen to retrieve the ball, but he has to throw it at one of the fleeing basemen from that point. He can't run with the ball. If the man in the center misses the baseman he is throwing at, he is out. If he hits the baseman, that man is out, and the thrower can stay in the bullpen for the next round.

When a baseman is out leaving three men on base, those men can move from base to base at will. When there are two men left on base, those two, at the beginning of each round, meet together out to one side, and one conceals the ball so that the players in the center don't know which baseman has it. They return to their bases, each one acting like he has the ball, and each moving from base to base to keep the players in the center confused until the ball is actually thrown at a man in the center beginning the round.

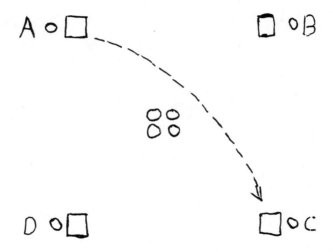

PLATE 337 The ball must pass diagonally over the players in the bullpen, from one base player to another to begin the game.

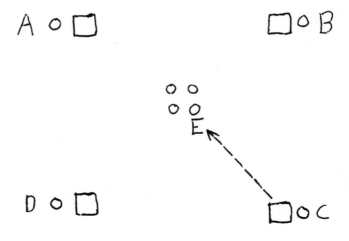

PLATE 338 If C throws and hits E, E can throw at any of the players on the bases (who are running by this time), and if he hits one, that base player is out. If E misses, he's out.

When there is only one man left on base, he can move along the baselines at will and throw at any time at a man in the center. The game ends when all the players on one team are out. Then those who were in the bullpen take the bases, those who were on the bases move to the bullpen, and a new game begins.]

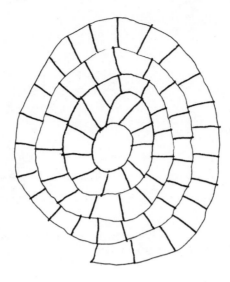

PLATE 339

Chase the Rock

JEAN RAMEY: The object of the game is to hop all the way around the circle on one foot without stopping or changing feet. Throw a disk into one of the squares. Hop on one foot around to it and jump over the square it is in and onto the circle. When you get to the circle you may change feet and hop back to the square that has your disk in it. Stop, pick it up, and then hop back to the starting line.

There are two ways of playing this game. You can play with a disk, or without. The way you play it without a disk is you hop around it without stopping or changing feet. Whoever goes all the way around it without stopping is the winner.

Checkers

ERNEST FRANKLIN: Checkers has been around as far back as I can remember, which was about sixty years ago. We would usually use Coca-Cola tops after they came out. Turn the caps one way and the other person would turn them the opposite way. For the board we would use cardboard and draw out the squares on it. The game was played then the same way it is now as far as the rules go.

Club Fist

MRS. IVY MCCALL, DAISY JUSTICE, AND MRS. GERALDINE OWENS: The players stack their fists, with their thumbs up, each player grasping the thumb of the fist below. The leader, whose hands remain free, starts with the top fist in the stack and asks its owner, "You want to take it off, knock it off, or let the crows pick it off?" If the owner doesn't take it off the stack himself, he tells the leader to either knock it off, or let the crows pick it off, whereupon the leader either knocks it loose or pulls it off, following the command. This continues until only one fist remains. At this point the leader and the owner of the last fist say the following dialogue:

Q.:   Where's the water?
A.:   The ox drunk it.
Q.:   Where's the ox?
A.:   The butcher killed it.
Q.:   Where's the butcher?
A.:   The rope hung him.
Q.:   Where's the rope?
A.:   The rats gnawed it.
Q.:   Where's the rats?
A.:   The cat caught them.
Q.:   Where's the cat?
A.:   The gun shot it.
Q.:   Where's the gun?
A.:   The hammer broke it.
Q.:   Where's the hammer?
A.:   Behind the door cracking hickory nuts!

The first one that shows his teeth (grins) while this is going on gets so many hairs pulled out of his head or so many pinches or hits. We always said ten boxes and a pinch.

Corncob Jail

WAYNE WALL: We used to play this game in the barn, and my father says he played it as a child in Rabun County, also.

One player is chosen as the sheriff, and an area four or five feet square is marked off as his jail. The other players are fugitives. The sheriff throws corncobs at the fugitives, and each one he strikes has to come to jail. While the sheriff is busy trying to "capture" the other players, they try not only to dodge, but also to set the prisoners free. A fugitive can set a prisoner free by slipping past the sheriff and handing the prisoner a corncob, which becomes his ticket to freedom, releasing him to become a fugitive again.

The game ends when the sheriff has all the fugitives captured and in jail.

Cracking the Whip

ERNEST FRANKLIN: Everyone would join hands and form a long line with the biggest man in front as the anchorman, and the smallest man on the end. Then we'd run together in a curved line and at some point the anchorman would stop and the rest of the line would keep going around in a curve just like cracking a whip. If you went fast enough, that little one on the end would almost be airborne when he came around. They finally stopped us from playing that at school. Too many kids got their shoulders dislocated and their arms broken. That one on the end really fared rough!

Devil in the Promised Land

LAWTON BROOKS: We played a game called "The Devil in the Promised Land." A big branch went down through our pasture. Some places it was wide and some places were narrow enough to jump across pretty good. There'd be about eight or ten of us on one side. We'd put one on the other side and he was the devil. Now we had to cross the branch and go around him and jump the branch back. Now if he caught us before we made the run around him, we had to go on to the devil's side.

Dodgeball

MRS. BUCK CARVER: Get some people and bunch them up in a circle. One person would get on each side of the circle and roll a regular rubber ball through the center of the circle and try to hit the people in the circle. The people in the circle tried to dodge the ball, but when a person was hit, he had to go out and sit down. The game was over when everyone was out. When the game was over, the people that were playing picked two more throwers. Then they started again.

Dropping the Handkerchief

VELER MARCUS: We would have a big ring with everyone facing into the middle, and one would be out of the ring. The one out would go around and drop the handkerchief behind someone. They could watch our side and we could watch theirs. If they dropped the handkerchief over there, then our side couldn't help but to start grinning, same with their side. Then one would look down and see if it was behind him. If it was, he would jump and grab the handkerchief and run and try to catch this one going around the ring to get back where this one left from and take his place. If he caught the one that had dropped the handkerchief, that one had to go to the middle. If he didn't catch the one that had dropped the handkerchief before that one got to his place in the circle, then that man had to keep the handkerchief and start a new game.

Fieldball

ETHEL CORN: Everyone played ball together. We raveled up socks and made our own balls. We'd take a rag and ball it up in the center (some people used rocks for the center) and sometimes we'd make them out of pure yarn, then sew them good after we got them wound up. It was balled up just like you would ball up yarn to knit.

[For the bat] you'd get a common-sized little hickory and trim it down, but generally we'd get a plank about five inches, gauge it down to make a handle for it.

VELER MARCUS: Two teams are chosen—evenly divided. Number of players is not important. Each team has a catcher, a pitcher, and the rest stay in the outfield to catch the ball after the batter hits it. All people on a team get a turn at bat before the sides change.

One team goes up to bat. Every person on that team has a turn at bat and *then* the other team comes to bat. Every time the pitcher throws the ball, the batter strikes at it. None is considered a "ball." If the batter misses the ball, he is out and the next player comes up to bat. If he hits the ball, he starts running toward first base. If someone in the field catches the ball before it hits the ground, or after only one bounce, the batter is out. If he hits the ball far enough, he may make a home run, running around all the bases and back to home plate.

When the ball is caught by a person in the field, he either tries to tag the runner or throw the ball to someone closer to the runner who can tag him. The runner is out when tagged, unless he is touching a base. He can run on to the next base or home when the next batter hits a ball. If the remainder of the players on his team strike out before he can run into home, he is considered out and doesn't get a point.

The game can end at any time the players agree on, so long as both sides have an equal number of times at bat. A point is made each time a runner successfully bats a ball and runs around all the bases and returns to home plate without being tagged.

Fireball

EDD HODGINS: You tie a bunch of old toe sacks up good. Soak one in kerosene oil and set it on fire. Then you can whack it or throw it. Boy, it's dangerous. It'd take it half the night to burn out, and it could set something afire, but it used to be nothing never got fire much. We'd get a bunch out in a field Christmas or something afire balling. Throw 'em just as far as you can throw 'em. Couldn't burn your hand because you'd grab 'em quick and throw 'em quick. Never get burnt. Play with 'em all night. That ball of fire goin' through the air bigger than anything was something. And that was the sport—to see who could throw it the fartherest. That was the fireball—soaked in kerosene oil.

Fox and Dogs

BUCK CARVER: This was a rough game usually played just by big boys, and often at school. One was the fox, another carried an ax, and the rest of the players were the dogs.

The fox would start running and try to find a small tree about six to twelve inches in diameter and climb it. The dogs would be chasing him. When they caught up with him and treed him, the person with the ax would come along and chop down the tree. If the fox could get away without getting caught, he'd start running again and climb another tree. The game continued until he was caught. Then a new game could start with another person as the fox.

There was usually a lot of noise with the dogs barking at the fox and yelling as they chased him.

Fox and Geese

KENNY RUNION: This was one of the first games I learned to play. [It] was usually played at the mill while people were waiting to have their corn ground. I guess this is one reason they used corn instead of something else for playing the game.

The miller was usually the fox and he was usually the winner because he got so much practice at it. It was always exciting to see if anyone could beat the miller at playing the game.

[Twenty-two pieces of white corn represent the geese. Two pieces of red corn represent the foxes. Foxes may catch the geese, but

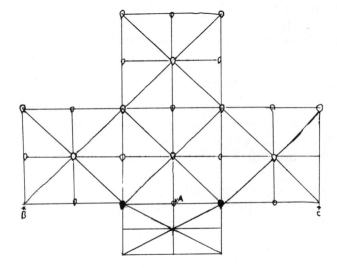

PLATE 340   Geese are set on each corner and intersection as shown. The two dark grains are the foxes.

The two lower corners on the right and left sides of the foxes (points B, C) are left open. The first move is always made by one fox. He has two choices: (1) capture one of the geese by jumping one into an empty space, or (2) move to the center line (at point A).

The fox may, at any time, move into an adjacent empty space, or jump over one goose (in any direction) into an empty space beyond, thus capturing that goose. A fox may also move or jump into a space occupied by the other fox.

Geese may move in any direction into an adjacent empty space, but cannot jump other geese or foxes.

The small end of the board belongs to the foxes and they cannot move back down into it; nor can the geese move down there. The line separating the foxes' end of the board from the main playing surface is called the "fence."

Again, the object of the game is to stop the foxes so that they cannot make another move. It is very difficult to corner the foxes after ten to twelve geese have been captured, so the geese must act quickly to block the foxes.

the geese may not at any time capture the foxes—only use their greater numbers to corner them. The object of the game is to be able to stop the foxes so that they have no other place to move.]

STANLEY HICKS: We played that game a lot. You had to hem those foxes up to beat them. And the way we played was every time a fox jumped a goose, he'd go, "Qua-a-ack!" real loud. Our dad would do that—"Qua-a-ack!"—and he made us so cussed mad!

Frog Trouncing

M. S. YORK: Place a flat board on a block or stump or something of that nature (in a seesaw position). Put a frog on one end of the board, the end that is touching the ground. Take a mallet or sledge-hammer and hit the end opposite that that the frog is on. The object of the game is to see who can get the frog the highest.

Fruit-basket Turnover

HELEN JUSTICE: Everyone sits on chairs in a circle. Someone gives each person the name of a fruit—two or three people should have the same [one]. One person is standing in the middle without a chair. He calls out one or two fruits at a time. When they call out your fruit you try to change places without the one in the middle getting a seat. The one left standing calls out names next. If "fruit basket turnover" is called, everybody has to change places.

Green Grass

JULIA SMITH: Miss Jinks, our first woman teacher, taught us this one. She had us sitting around on seats in one corner at the wall. She sat back on one of the desks, and told us how to play green grass. You start off with "Here's a crooked crab tree." And the one that had it said to him had to say it to the next one. And that one would have to turn around quickly and say it to the next one. Each person added something on—like "the crooked grass that grows under the crooked crab tree," and we had to say it every bit every time. One would say it to the next one and he'd say, "Is it the crooked crab tree?" And he had to say, "Yes, it's the crooked crab tree."

Here's how I think it went:

Person No. 1:   Here's the crooked crab tree.

Person No. 2:   Is it the crooked crab tree?

Person No. 1:   Yes [etc.].

Person No. 2:   Here's the crooked grass that grows under the crooked crab tree.

Person No. 3:   Is it the crooked grass that grows under the crooked crab tree?

Person No. 2:   Yes [etc.].

Person No. 3:   Here's the crooked [something] on the crooked grass that grows under the crooked crab tree.

Person No. 4:   Is it the [etc.]?

And they'd make it up as they went along.

Green Man's Garden

JULIA SMITH: We'd play two sides and have one crowd over here and one over there. They said some little something like, "Where are you?" and the other group would say, "In the green man's garden." The first would say, "What are you doing in the green man's garden?"

"Eating the green man's grapes." Then the reply came back something like, "The green man will get you."

The ones over here would run over to the other side, and the ones over there try to catch the ones that have been in the green man's garden. And as many of them as they could catch, they'd put in the soup pot.

Ghost

HELEN JUSTICE: Most everybody would be in one room, then maybe three or four in another. We would hang a sheet over the door and have all the lights out. Set a lantern in front of the sheet and somebody would step between the lantern and the sheet and move around, and the rest of us would be on the other side of the sheet and we couldn't see who it was. We would all have to guess who it was from watching the shadow.

Hiding a Needle in a Haystack

STANLEY HICKS: Some of us would hide stuff and then the rest would go hunt it. If they found it they got to go hide it, and if they didn't find it, they didn't get to hide it.

Hide-and-Seek or Hoopy Hide

BERTHA DOCKINS: We used to play hide-and-seek a lot. It's been a long time since I thought of that. We'd all hide and [the person who was "it"] would holler. He used to yell, "Bushel of wheat, bushel of rye, those ain't hid, holler 'I'!" [Then any person who wasn't hidden yet would holler "I" and the person who was "it" would wait a little longer before beginning to hunt for the others. Other than the rhyme, it was played the same way then as it is now.]

STANLEY HICKS: We would hide and then holler, "Hoopy hide!" and somebody would have to come hunt us. If they caught you before you got back to your home base, they got to hide in the next game. If they didn't catch you, you got to hide again.

Hide the Thimble

FLORENCE BROOKS: We played hide the thimble. One person gives out the thimble—pretends to give it to everyone, but only one person gets it. Just drops it in her hand with everybody sitting there. Everybody closes their hands and makes like they have it. The person who gives out the thimble asks everyone who has the thimble. If no one guesses who got it, then the person who gave it out that first time has to give it out again. But if they guess who got it, the one who did get it gets to give it out. If nobody can guess it, the person who gave it out says, "Rise up, thimble," and the one that has it rises up. Then they have to give it out.

PEARL BATES: As many as wants to can be in the game. Everybody playing sets down but one, [and] the one that didn't set down has the thimble. The others hold out their hands as if someone was going to give [them] something. The one with the thimble holds the thimble in his hands. He goes to each person sitting down and acts like he's going to put it in everyone's hands, and he *will* drop it in someone's hands. Then when the thimble boy drops the thimble in someone's hands, each one will go down the row guessing who has the thimble and even the one who has the thimble guesses and acts dumb. The one who guesses who has the thimble [becomes the next] thimble boy. And you play till you get tired of it.

Hopscotch

This game is played outdoors on a court or grid of sequentially numbered squares drawn with a stick in dirt or with chalk on a sidewalk. Simply defined, hopscotch is a progressive game in which the first player tosses a marker (a small rock, a glass shard, or a stick, for example) into the first square, then hops on one foot over that square into No. 2 and on through all the squares, using both feet in side-by-side squares, to the end of the grid. Some grids provide a "rest" square at the end in which the player may put down both feet, others simply require turning around on the "hop" foot before starting back. When the player reaches the No. 2 square on returning, she picks up the marker and hops over No. 1 to the outside. The player must not skip any square other than the one containing the marker, step on any of the lines, put down both feet in a hop square, or, if she stumbles, touch the ground with the hands. If the process is successful, then that player may have another turn and begins by tossing the marker into the No. 2 square, and so forth. When the player steps on a line or commits any error, then her turn is over and she will begin in that same square at her next turn. The player's marker is left in that square. The first player to complete tossing into and hopping through all the squares is the winner. The game may be extended by coming from the last square back down to No. 1.

There are many variations on the theme of hopscotch. While the rules of errors and "out" are always the same, the rules of hopping over designated squares are very flexible. In one basic version of the game *all* squares containing markers must be hopped over by all the players, but when there are so many players participating that it is physically impossible to do this, then each player may skip only the square containing her marker. When player size is a factor, the rule for skipping several squares at once may be suspended for little players and at the same time upheld for the larger ones.

MRS. ERNEST FRANKLIN: The girls used to play that. You layed it off—took a stick, and layed it off and made squares. Then you took a piece of glass or a rock. And you throwed it and if it landed in

the block you had to jump out to it and pick it up and turn around and come back to the start. The thing you threw had to land in a square or you were out. If you hopped and landed on the line, you're out. The squares would be from two feet to thirty inches square.

CAROL BATES: Our hopscotch courts could have either two or three squares at the beginning and they usually had a rest circle at the end. The first player threw a pebble into the first square, hopped over that square, and hopped through all the squares. You jumped on both feet into the side-by-side squares and you could put both feet down in the rest circle. Then you hopped back to the second square and picked your pebble up out of No. 1. You could put

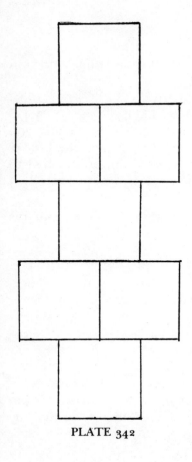

PLATE 342

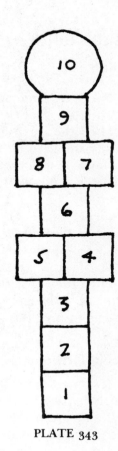

PLATE 343

one hand down flat on the ground and brace yourself as you reached into the square to get your pebble. But if you accidentally put both hands down you were out for that turn. If you picked up your pebble and hopped out right, then you would have another turn and you'd throw your pebble into No. 2.

You would be out if you stepped on a line, or if you skipped any empty squares. You'd also be out if you stepped in a square with a pebble in it. You would be out if your pebble missed the square or rolled out of the square. Then you would pick your pebble up and put it into the square you missed to mark where you'd start the next time. All the players had to hop over all the squares with pebbles in them. If they couldn't do it then they just had to wait until someone else moved their pebble. The first one to go through all the squares was the winner.

Hull Gull or Jack up a Bush

HELEN JUSTICE: We would have some chestnuts in our hand and the first person would say, "Hull gull."

The second person would ask, "How many?"

Then the first person would say, "A handful."

Then the second person was supposed to guess how many you had. For each one they missed the guesser had to give the holder however many it was. If they guessed it exactly, the holder had to give them all to the guesser. The object was to try to get all of the hulls.

STANLEY HICKS: One person puts some marbles (or none) in his hand and says, "Jack up a bush."

A second person says, "Cut it down."

The first person says, "How many licks?"

Then the second person guesses how many marbles the first person has. If he gets it right, he gets all of them, and if he doesn't, he has to give the first person the difference.

Jack Rocks

ERNEST FRANKLIN: You have five round rocks 'cause flat ones were much harder to pick up, and one rubber ball. You throw up the ball and reach down and get one rock while the ball is in the air, then catch the ball before it hits. Then you put the first rock back and throw up the ball again and this time pick up two rocks and catch it before it hits. Then you put them back and try to get three rocks, and so on until you get all five. If you miss, you start over or the next player tries. The one who can get the most rocks wins if you're playing with more than one person.

Jack Straws

LOLA CANNON: This was one of the first games I learned. I learned to play it with Daddy before I even went to school. That was our amusement on rainy days or Sunday.

[We had little straws that] were probably six inches long. They were all colors. We also had two little wire hooks. We would shuffle the straws out in a big heap on the table. Then each player, with his hook, would try to pull out as many straws as he could without disturbing all the others; he [couldn't let any of them] shake or fall or his turn was up. The person with the most straws won.

Jumping Jack

STANLEY HICKS: We'd draw a line on the ground and then just see who could jump the furtherest. Whoever did, won. It was a simple game, but we'd play it.

Jump Rope

VELER MARCUS: We would get a vine that was limber and about as long as this room and play jump rope. This is happening in school. That was one of our main games in school. We would have one on each end of the vine, swinging it. The rest would line up and run through or jump as many times as they could without missing. I stood and jumped sixty-four times and then one of my school friends jumped in and jumped sixty-five times.

JUDY PAYNE: There's one called going through school, and in this type of jumping rope you have two people to twirl the rope and then a person will jump in and count to eleven [as] he or she jumps. If that person hits the rope and stops at number nine, then that person is supposed to quit school in the ninth grade. That counts for any grade or count, not just nine. The reason I said to just count to eleven is because [back then] they only went to the eleventh grade. If this person goes all the way through eleven, then he or she will jump out and another person will jump in.

Kitty Walks a Corner

MARINDA BROWN: That's a game we used to play a lot. One person is "Kitty" and he goes around to everybody in a circle. He meows and pats you and tries to get you to laugh. If someone can't control their emotions and smiles or laughs, he has to become "Kitty."

Kitty Wants the Corner

MRS. RAE SHOOK: We'd all get around somewhere and someone would say, "Kitty wants the corner, click, click, click. Kitty wants the corner, click, click, click."

And then dodge. They'd try to steal places because they'd be going from one place to another—dodging from one to another. You'd try to get in their home and if you beat them and got in there, then you beat them and that'd put them out. Every kid but

PLATE 344   Mrs. Rae Shook with John Bowen and Mitch Whitmire.

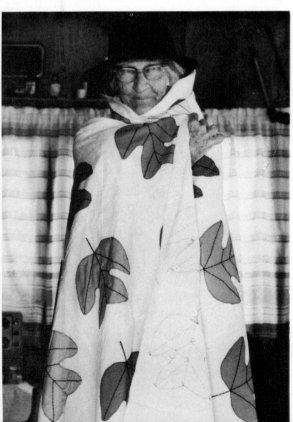

PLATE 345   Nannie Ann Sanders.

one had a spot in the house, and he had to go around till he got a place. He'd get in when they changed over. He had to beat them back to their place.

NANNIE ANN SANDERS: Each person would have a corner except one. That one would walk around and say, "Kitty wants a corner," and they would run to change corners. While they were changing, the one in the middle would try to get a corner. If he didn't, he had to stay in the middle; but if he did, that one whose corner he got had to go to the middle.

Leadbelly

M. S. YORK: Place a flat board on a block or stump in a seesawlike fashion. Place a frog on the end of the board that is touching the ground. From the opposite end roll buckshot or BB's down the board. The frog should eat the buckshot. After the frog is full you try to see how far it can hop. After playing with the frog, take it by its back legs, hold it upside down, and the shot will fall out.

Lost My Handkerchief

LELIA GIBSON:

> I lost my handkerchief yesterday
> I found it today
> All full of mud
> And I threw it away.

[Someone would hide the handkerchief] and they'd all hunt for it, and the one that got it would hide it and call out the rhyme and it'd start over.

Marbles

VAUGHN ROGERS, SR.: Draw a line in dirt, then get about twelve feet from the line. Each man pitches one of his marbles, and the closest to the line goes [gets to play] first, second closest goes second, etc. Draw a circle in the dirt. Each man puts x amount of marbles in the center of the circle. The first man shoots his marble (shooter). If he knocks a marble out without the shooter going out too, he keeps going (called a stick). But if he doesn't knock a marble out or he knocks a marble out and his shooter both, he passes his turn to the next person. Keep this up till all the marbles are knocked out of the circle. The one with the most marbles at the end of the game wins.

There are two ways of playing this. You either play for keeps, which is almost like gambling, the ones you knock out you keep; or then a game for fun, in which you give the marbles back to the owner after the game.

CARRIE CUMMINGS: Draw a circle and have an equal amount of marbles for two people [along a line] in the circle. Each shooter tries to knock them out of the circle. Whoever gets the most marbles is the winner.

JOHN AND BURMA PATTERSON: First of all, you get a large marble and put it in a ring about a foot or two in diameter; around the ring you will have put about ten marbles and then get about five feet back and try to knock the large marble out of the ring. If you do, you automatically win. Every other marble you knock out of the ring, you get to keep. But if you knock the large marble out first, all the marbles are yours.

BILL PHILLIPS: [Dig a fist-sized hole in the dirt.] Use twelve marbles [placing only one at a time] in front of the hole. Each player gets one shot. When a player shoots the large marble in the hole he gets another shot. Whichever player shoots the most marbles into the hole is the winner.

LELIA GIBSON: I've played marbles, but they were bought marbles. We'd make a square in the dirt, and put a marble in each corner, and one in the center. You first tried to shoot one corner marble to the center marble. Then you tried the next corner, and so on, till you got all of them together. That was pretty hard to do. Maybe we'd play with three, four, or five other children. One person got to continue shooting as long as he got the marbles to the center. And then the next person got to go. Whoever had the most of his own in the center won the game, and won the marbles that were in the center.

BUCK CARVER: Now a lot of times we made our own marbles with packed clay. You see, the only heat we had was fireplaces. And if you lived next to a patch of white pipe clay, you got a bunch of that and made it up in a stiff wad. You worked out your marbles— rolled them in your hands till you got them perfectly round—and you got some hot ashes on a shovel and buried a row of marbles and then covered them with more hot ashes. Let them bake till they were good and hard; it didn't take too awful long. Change

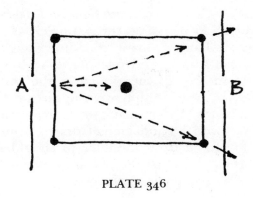

PLATE 346

the top ashes two, three times. It'd take an hour maybe. We'd always make one bigger than the others—we used that for the middle man.

To play the game, player A, using a shooter marble, aims at the marbles on B's side. He tries to knock the corner marbles over B's line. He gets one point for each of them, and he gets two points if he can also hit the middle man across B's line [see Plate 346].

B then has a turn and tries to knock A's corner men and the middle man across A's line.

Marching Around the Level

LELIA GIBSON: We had a game we played called marching around the level. We'd all catch hands and we'd sing:

> "We're marching around the level,
> We're marching around the level,
> For we have gained today.
>
> Good-bye, I hate to leave you,
> Good-bye, I hate to leave you,
> For we have gained today.
>
> One kiss and I will leave you,
> One kiss and I will leave you,
> For we have gained the way."

While we sang that, we'd march. We'd catch hands and go in pairs and march like soldiers. We'd always get on level ground to do it because that went with the song. We'd march in the level.

[*The Frank C. Brown Collection of North Carolina Folklore,* Vol. 1, (Durham: Duke University Press, 1952–1964), pp. 119–22, gives several different versions of what is probably the same game. Players would join hands and form a ring, and one player in the center of the ring would do all the things mentioned in the song. To "go in and out the window" meant simply weaving in and out of the ring under the clasped hands. To "measure my love to show you" meant to measure a lover with a handkerchief drawn from the shoulder to the waistline and then from shoulder to shoulder. The one in the ring chosen as the lover by the one in the center would stand in the center for the next game. The verse:

> We're marching around the levee (or love ring),
> We're marching around the levee
> We're marching around the levee
> For you have gained the day.
>
> Go forth and face your lover, (etc.)
> Go in and out the window, (etc.)
> I measure my love to show you, (etc.)
> I kneel because I love you, (etc.)
> It breaks my heart to leave you, (etc.)]

Mumble Peg

CARRIE CUMMINGS: [Draw a circle in the dirt.] You take a knife, flip it off your arm, and try to make it stick in the ground. You have three turns and the one who makes it stick inside the circle the most wins.

DELMO PATTERSON: You start by balling up your fist and placing the knife on the flat surface of your fingers. You start with your right fist and try to stick the knife in the ground and then you switch to your left and repeat. After using your fists, you go to your fingertips, going from right to left, trying to stick the knife in the ground. After the fingertips, you then go to your elbows and your shoulders, repeating the same procedure from right to left. After completing the elbows and shoulders, you place the knife on your nose and [then place it] just above your forehead and once again try to stick the knife in the ground. When the knife fails to stick in the ground, you then give your competitor (or competitors) their turn. When the time comes for your turn again you begin at the place where you left off. The first person to stick the knife in the ground from his head is the winner.

5 POINTS

GROUND → DIAGRAM BY DAVID LEE PAYNE

PLATE 347

5 POINTS

PLATE 348

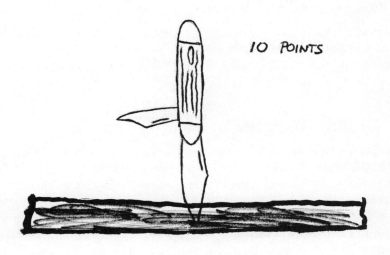

10 POINTS

PLATE 349

PLATE 350

You need a double-bladed knife [with blades that open as shown in Plates 347–350]. Now, if your knife lands upright with the big blade sticking up in the ground, that's ten points. If the small blade ends up in the ground and neither the big blade nor the other side of the knife is touching the ground, that's twenty points. But if either side touches the ground, it's only five points.

Old Granny Hum Bum

VELER MARCUS: There would be a bunch of us children get out and get to playing and one of them would act like Old Granny Hum Bum. She would be all humped over and have a stick. She would come along, and we would say:

"Old Granny Hum Bum,
Where did you come from?"
"Pretty girl's station" [Granny Hum Bum would answer].
"What's your occupation . . . ?
Well get to work a'doing it!"

Then she had to do [pantomime] something like sew, chop wood, etc. . . . Then the rest of us had to guess what she was doing. She couldn't talk. Little old games like that are fun. We had lots of fun.

Old Granny Wiggins Is Dead

PEARL BATES: You get as many players as you want sitting or standing in a circle. We usually sat outside in the grass.

Then the lead person says, "Old Granny Wiggins is dead."

And the next person says, "How'd she die?"

And I say, "She died this way," and I do something like wave my left hand up and down, and keep on waving it, and that next person has to start waving his or her hand the same way.

I repeat the same sequence with every person in the circle until they are all waving the same hand. When we've come all the way around the circle and they're all waving, I start a new round and add some motion this time like waving the *other* hand the same way. We go all the way around the circle until everyone is waving both hands, now. Then we used to add patting one foot and go all the way around, and then add patting the *other* foot, and then bobbing our heads. When everyone in the circle then is waving both hands and patting both feet and bobbing their heads, I give a signal and we all fall over dead on top of each other. We'd get a big laugh out of how we'd fall.

We always did pretty much the same sequence with the hands and feet and head, but I guess you could add other signals like wagging a shoulder or something if you wanted to.

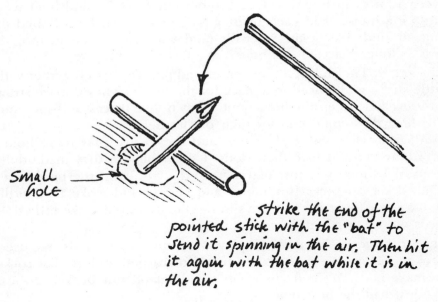

small hole

strike the end of the pointed stick with the "bat" to send it spinning in the air. Then hit it again with the bat while it is in the air.

PLATE 351

Peg

LLOYD CRUMLEY: You find a stick about one inch through, any length. Set this stick on the ground and on the backside of the stick dig a small hole. Take a stick about eight inches long and on one end put a point and on the other make it square. Then you take the eight-inch stick and lay it across the stick laying on the ground [with the square end in the hole]. Find a three-to-four-foot-long paddle stick. You take the three-to-four-foot stick and hit the eight-inch stick on the end that is not touching the ground. When you do this it will make the eight-inch stick spin in the air. While the eight-inch stick is spinning in the air, you take the three-to-four-foot stick and hit it again and when it lands you take running jumps, and how many jumps it takes to get to the peg (the eight-inch stick) is how many points you get; and if the eight-inch stick sticks up in the ground, you automatically win. You usually play to a score of about five hundred. The sticks should be made out of oak.

Playhouses or Playing House

HARRIET ECHOLS: When we moved to Georgia, my father bought land with lots of pine trees on it, and he was clearing it. He left a piece just behind the barn so the cows would have shade and there were a lot of little poles. Our brother cut us poles and built us a little log house, and each of us girls had a room. He whittled us out all kinds of cooking utensils (and I learned to do it, too). It was as long as across this house. We just played house.

ADA KELLY: The children took leaves and pinned them together with little sticks, and fenced in a place for the house. They'd make straw brooms and sweep the house out. They'd take pieces of dishes and anything they could find for their playhouses.

All little girls had a playhouse and they'd just play there hours at a time. They'd take their dolls. I don't believe they made doll-houses; I think they just played with their dolls in the playhouse. They'd set up rocks [for tables and chairs] and make their little doll a chair to sit in. The boys in the family would make little doll beds out of corn stalks.

LELIA GIBSON: We'd make our playhouse out in the woods. We used broken dishes. We'd get green moss for carpet, and get flat rocks to make beds. We'd fix us a table and eat off our broken dishes. We just had the best time.

HATTIE KENNY: We had playhouses. Get moss and make beds for the dolls. Great big beds! For our dishes, we used broke pieces of dishes that we found through yards and about.

HELEN JUSTICE: Oh yeah, we had playhouses. We would sweep it out and put moss down for the beds. Have an organ made out of moss and put chalk on it for keys. For the pans, we would use lids and then we had weeds that we would play like they were green beans and other food.

NANNIE ANN SANDERS: We played in playhouses a lot. We had little tables with moss scattered all over 'em. We used moss for our beds, and for dishes we used acorn cups.

LOLA CANNON: We went all over the mountains to get pretty rocks and bits of moss to decorate the playhouses. We had whole families and then somebody kept a boardinghouse and took in boarders. I remember those days real well. And we liked to play dolls then in a game that we girls played. When we were right small, we made a whole congregation of little rag dolls. Then we went somewhere by the branch or somewhere and made a pond and we baptized them all. We had them sitting up on the side. Somebody in the crowd was the preacher, and we sang, and then they'd baptize all these dolls.

We had a graveyard where we'd bury the dolls. Maybe when we were together one time we'd bury some. And the next time we'd go dig them up to see how they were. I guess [we were checking] to see if they were still dead.

Please and Displease

LAWTON BROOKS: We used to play please and displease. Get a whole bunch of us sitting around like us here. I'd say, "Are you pleased or displeased?" If you didn't have nothing on your mind for someone to do, you'd say, "I'm pleased."

Then I'd ask the next person, and she might say, "I'm displeased." Well, I'd ask what it takes to please her. "Well," she could say, "for Florence to get up and walk around the house barefoot," or something, and you'd have to follow whatever they put on you. It went around the circle—one person asked a question for his turn. Then it went on around the circle. Sometimes if there were boys and girls, they'd say for this boy to go over and sit by that girl, and that girl to go sit by another boy. Change things around. It was a nice little old game. I always enjoyed playing it.

Poor Old Tom

PEARL BATES: As many can play as wants, [but there must be] three or more. Everybody sits except the one that's going to be the cat. The one that's going to be the cat gets down on his knees and crawls to one of the people sitting down and meows three times and tries to make them smile. Every time the cat meows, the person sitting down pats him on the head and says, "Poor old tom." Then the cat goes to the next person and all the rest of the people and does the same. If one of them smiles he has to trade places with the cat and on and on. You can play as long as you want to.

Ring Around the Mulberry Bush

ETTA HARTLEY: You'd make a big ring with one person on the outside and everyone in the ring facing in. That person on the outside would make three rounds around the ring and then tap someone and those two would race around the ring to see who could get back to that empty place first. The one who lost had to be the one on the outside of the ring for the next round.

Rooster Fighting

STANLEY HICKS: What we would do, a whole bunch of us would get out there and choose up sides and see which side could outwhip the other one. We'd all just come together in the middle and poke each other with our elbows and shoulders and punch at each other that way [without using hands] and try to drive the other side off or make them give up.

Shakespears

DR. REXEL BROWN: All of my relatives are from Butler County, Kentucky, which is in the mountains of western Kentucky. They played a game called shakespears, which is much like our modern game of pick up sticks, except that the point value was determined by the shape of the sticks rather than by color, as in the modern version.

My father made a set out of cedar according to instructions from his father. The first person to get five hundred points won the game. I have checked with both my brother and sister, and we think the point system we have outlined here is accurate [see Plate 352].

Skin the Cat

STANLEY HICKS: You'd go to a limb that was a little over your head and grab ahold with both hands, and then hang on and swing your legs up through [the space between your arms] and come on over your head and see if you could touch the ground behind you and then get back through the way you were without turning loose of the limb. It's pretty hard.

Snake in the Grass

STANLEY HICKS: We would make snakes out of sticks or anything that looked like snakes. One bunch would hide with those snakes in the tall grass, and the other bunch would go look for them. We would hide with those sharpened sticks. We wouldn't hurt nobody bad, but when they got close, we would stab 'em and holler, "Snake in the grass!" and boy, you talk about gettin' gone! They'd get scared and run and fall down and laugh. We'd try to surprise them like that, and then after a while they got to hide and we'd hunt.

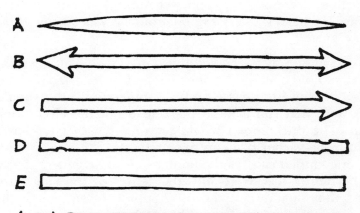

A = 1 ROUND, TAPERED STICK WORTH 100 POINTS.
B = 2 ARROWS WORTH 50 POINTS EACH.
C = 4 1-POINTED ARROWS WORTH 25 POINTS EACH.
D = 5 ROUND, NOTCHED STICKS WORTH 20 EACH.
E = 10 FLAT STICKS WORTH 10 POINTS EACH.

PLATE 352

Tap Hand

MRS. BUCK CARVER: We formed a ring. One stayed on the outside and went around and chose a person to tap and that person tried to catch the tapper. If he didn't catch the tapper by the time he came back to his place in the circle, he got back in the circle. If he did catch the tapper, then the tapper went around and tapped somebody else.

JULIA SMITH: Occasionally we'd have a Saturday night to play. We'd get out and hold hands and make a big ring and play what we called tap hand. One would stay out of the ring and walk around and tap someone, and that one was supposed to run and try to catch the one that tapped him.

One time they had a [water] tap out in the yard and one of the boys had a birthday. Some of the older girls found it out and one of them was going to tap him, and instead of just running right on around the ring, she was going to the water tap. One of the other girls was supposed to help her, and they were going to get him, put him under the tap, and wet him good. It turned out the other way. He wasn't a very big boy, but he was strong enough to outdo the girls.

PEARL BATES: The way we played this game is we'd all get in a circle facing in and hold hands. The one on the outside called the "tapper" would walk around the circle and tap someone on the shoulder or the back and then run around the outside of the circle as fast as he could. The one tapped would try to catch that tapper before he got into the vacant place in the circle.

If the one tapped catches the tapper before he gets to that vacant space, the tapper has to go into the center of the ring into what we called the soup pot. If the one tapped doesn't catch the one who tapped him, the one tapped has to become the tapper.

You might have several people in the soup pot. The only way they can get freed and get back in the game is by holding their hands out through the circle, and if the tapper chooses, he can "tap out" one of those people by hitting his hand as he goes around the outside of the circle. Then that one in the soup pot whose hand got tapped can come back into the circle and into the game. Or the tapper could "tap out" two or three people if he wanted to. That would make the game last a long time. If you wanted it to be shorter, you just wouldn't tap anybody out of the soup pot. They'd just be out.

Teacher

CAROL BATES: This is a guessing game usually played outdoors on a bank, porch steps, or schoolhouse steps. One person is elected teacher and the other players sit side by side along the lowest step, which is first grade. The teacher stands in front of each student, in turn, puts her hands behind her back, and conceals a small pebble in one fist. She then presents both fists to the student, who tries to guess where the pebble is and indicates her choice by pointing to or touching that fist. If the guess is correct, that student moves up to second grade; if not, she remains at the same level until her next turn. Players advance through the grades only by guessing correctly, and the first player to "graduate" becomes the next teacher.

Totin' over the Mark

KENNY RUNION: The oldest game I know of is totin' over the mark. Two boys face each other over a line, and they grab ahold of each other and one tries to pull the other over the line.

Now that's the hardest work you've ever done in your life! Those two'll run together just like cars a'couplin'. It was a good game if you didn't mind putting out all the strength you had. You'd have to do everything in the world to keep from being toted. It was fun!

Townball or Catball

BUCK CARVER: Townball was our biggest sport. We played it with a bat. Take the bat—somebody on the opponent's side pitched the bat and you caught it. Then you stacked hands—whoever came out on top (you had to leave about one half to one inch) had to be able to throw that bat so far before it was called a legal hold. Then they'd choose their players for each side (the one that had the top hold chose first). Each side could have few as three or as many as three or four dozen if they had that many. And, of course, you have your three bases, a pitcher, sometimes a catcher if there's enough.

If you caught a ball on the bounce or if [the catcher or fielder] caught it on a fly, [the batter] was out. Usually in running the bases, there was nobody holding base, and they just threw the ball at you—it was usually a homemade ball made out of twine—when you were between bases, and if you were hit, you were out. I've been burnt with them things pretty bad. The ball's center was made from an inner tube when you could get the darn stuff, and the rubber gave it life. Or you could take strips of inner tube and wrap them around a hard core like a marble and then wrap cotton thread around that and sew it all over the outside to hold that thread in place.

That game was the main thing at school for us boys.

VELER MARCUS: We would choose two sides, and then they would hold up the bat and the captains would put one hand on top of another and the one whose hand was on top got to bat first, and the other team would take the field. Each one on a side would bat till he got caught out. When the side was all caught out, the other side would come and bat. When one side would beat the other, we would just jump up, holler, and scream.

EDD HODGINS: We called it catball. You get you a wad of paper and wad it up just as tight as you can about one third the size of the ball. Then you wrap it with yarn just as tight as you can. It made a good ball. I believe you could knock it better than the baseballs they play with now.

Trip to Alaska

PEARL BATES: Any number of players can play. You all stand in a circle and the first player says, "I'm gonna take a trip to Alaska, and I'm gonna take some _____." In the blank you put a word that, say, starts with the first letter of your last name. Like I might say, "baloney."

Then the next person says, "Well, I'm gonna go, too, and I'm gonna take some _____." But if the word that person uses doesn't start with the first letter of his or her last name, I say, "No, you can't go," and that person has to keep standing there in the circle [and guess again when his turn comes around). If the word chosen *does* start with that person's last name, that person gets to sit down and wait for the next game to start.

Then the next person goes, and so on around the circle until everyone has caught onto the trick and has sat down. You keep going until everyone is out.

Then with the next game, the lead person chooses another trick that the rest have to figure out. Like I might decide to use the first letter of my first name this time, and say, "I'm gonna take a trip to Alaska, and I'm gonna take some peas." And the next person tries to figure out what trick I'm using and choose a right word.

Tug of War

STANLEY HICKS: First we would get a rope and I would put five boys behind me on one end and put six on the other end. Then we would see who could outpull.

Sometimes we'd play tug of war across a creek. Get boys on both sides of the creek holding to a rope and one bunch would see who could pull the other bunch into the water. And sometimes we would get the girls to come with us in their long dresses. We'd drag them through the creek with us and get mud in their nose holes and sand down their dresses!

William Trembletoe

MRS. RAE SHOOK: Any number can play. You sit in a circle, and all but one player puts one finger from each hand out on a table or flat surface. The person who is "it" goes around the table tapping each finger as he says a verse [see below]. The person whose finger he taps as he says "out" is put on a pack saddle formed by the arms of two of the bigger players. He is taken toward the door and is asked, "Where'd you like to live? Thorn bed or feather bed?"

If the one who is being carried answers, "Thorn bed," he is let down easily. If he says, "Feather bed," they bounce him three times and set him down. The game could get rougher depending on who was playing.

Then we'd say this rhyme:

> William, William, trimber, trucker
> He's a good fisher
> Catches him hens
> Puts them in pens
> Some lays eggs
> Some none
> Wire, briar, limber lock
> Three geese in a flock
> One flew east
> One flew west
> One flew over the cuckoo's nest
> Y - O - U - T
> You're out

HATTIE KENNY: Here's the rhyme we used:

William Trembletoe
He's a good fisherman
He catches hens
Puts them in a pen
Some lays eggs
Some none
Wire, briar, limber lock
Three geese in a flock
One flew East
One flew West
One flew over the cuckoo's nest
There I met my father
He had rings
Many pretty things
Be gone, you dirty dish dog
O - U - T, out!
[See also *Foxfire 5*, p. 69.]

[*The Frank C. Brown Collection of North Carolina Folklore*, Vol. 1, pp. 134–37, gives more complete directions for playing the game, as collected in western North Carolina between 1915 and 1928: The player on whom the word "out" falls, leaves the group. The remaining players each choose some type of animal or bird to become, such as a camel, bear, horse, etc., and also assign one of these terms to the "out" player. The "out" player is then asked, "What would you rather come home on?" All the choices are named, including the one assigned to him. If "out" chooses what the group has assigned him, he is told to "hop home." Otherwise he is carried home (back to the group) by the player whose bird or animal he has named.

Next the leader asks the bearer, "What've you got there?"

The bearer answers, "A bag of nits."

And the leader says, "Shake it till it spits."

Finally the "out" player is asked, "Which would you rather lie on, a feather bed or thorn?" If he chooses a feather bed, he is thrown down hard; if he chooses a thorn bed, he is laid down gently.]

"UNCLE JOHN WAS IN THE CRIB
STEALING CORN"

One day my mother, Rex Duvall, and Wig were talking about what was going to be in the next issue of *Foxfire*, and Rex asked us to interview a ninety-three-year-old woman named Ethel Meadows, who is his great-aunt. Before we went to her house, he told us a little about her: "Her daddy was my Grandpa Morgan. He fought in the Civil War. And her mother, when she was nursing [her], was killed accidentally by her brother with a hog rifle. And so they raised her, and she never knew her mother. And then she raised her own family in this old house they live in now. I think they say it's 125 years old. And she's never had modern plumbing and she uses an old cookstove—she's never had modern conveniences.

"At one time, she raised turkeys and paid their taxes and bought everything, and she could tell you more if you'd just listen to her talk. When the flu epidemic hit in 1918, she lost a son. She almost died herself. She can tell you about really *living*. She gets up every morning and eats a good breakfast. I've been there, and she cooks her some eggs and she sits down and eats her a good breakfast.

"And she's got Deweze in her. Deweze is long-lifed people. And she's got Morgan in her, which my grandmother had in her. In other words, my grandmother was a full sister to her. She only lived to be eighty-seven, but she had a brother die up in the state of Washington not very long ago that was in the Gold Rush in Alaska and was ninety-six or ninety-seven years old. Those people just kept *a'living*.

"So it's remarkable just to be around her. And she takes these rags and she tears 'em all up in strips and rolls them in a ball and then she'll make a little throw rug or something just out of old rags that most people take to the dump. Not that she *has* to do that, but she amuses herself that way.

"She'll amaze you. I love her, and she can really tell you some history."

We got in the car and drove to her house. It had snowed and it was cold, so she and her son, Billy, were in the one downstairs room that is heated by the wood stove. There were four wooden chairs in the room, two beds with homemade quilts on them, a light bulb hanging from the ceiling, several shotguns propped up in the corner, a kerosene lantern on the fireboard, and several spools of thread on the windowsill. Aunt Ethel was wearing a dress and an apron and a pair of red tennis shoes. She couldn't hear us, and so we'd write out questions one by one and she'd read them and answer them. She seemed glad to have us there, and she said that it would be nice to have an article about her so she'd have something to pass on to her children. I hope she'll be proud of this article.

RONNIE WELCH

We knew that several of her relatives had been in the Civil War, and so we began the interview by asking her to tell us what she could remember of the stories she had heard them tell. Here is how she began:

They never did get my Uncle Riley's body back [from the Civil War]. My grandmother never did give up [admit] that Riley was dead. She cried so when he started. She was an awful fool about a horse, and he told her that when he come back, he'd bring her a big black horse. She died and never did admit that he was dead.

At that time, they wove their cloth and made their underwear. She made hers with great big sleeves. And when she'd hear somebody a comin' a'ridin', if it was night or day, she'd run out to see if it was Riley a'comin' with her black horse. [One time] she run out and there was a man a'passin'. He was on a black horse and she throwed up her arms. Old John Byrd was our closest neighbor then. This man went over there and told 'em he wanted to stay all night with them. They asked him what was the matter. He said he seen an angel. And what he seen was when she raised her arms and them big white sleeves fell down and he thought they was wings. His horse had got loose and run on in home, and his folks got up and set up all night. Next day he come walking in and told them about the angel.

Everybody around there knew that Grandma Morgan was still a'watching for Riley, and did as long as she lived and could get to the road. When she seen somebody a'comin a'ridin', she'd be out on the road.

[Uncle John Deweze and my father were in a Civil War battle near Gettysburg.] Our soldiers was camped on one side of a moun-

PLATE 353 Aunt Ethel at work with her strips of rags.

tain and the Yankees on the other, and they come across the mountain. Ours was out of anything to eat at all, and they had took possession of an old mill and were taking off all the meal they had, and Uncle John, he was in the crib stealing corn for the horses and some of the Yanks come up to the door and Uncle John hollered, "Surround 'em, boys! Here they are!" And the Yanks run—thought

our boys were really a'surroundin' 'em. And Uncle John, they got
their meal and corn and got away. It was close to Gettysburg. Dad
was in that battle.

[He didn't talk about it much, but I guess they had a hard time.]
Billy, my son, once at the table we had got some old tough beef
and we was talking about it, and my sister said she thought it was
mule meat and asked Daddy if he'd ever eat any mules, and he
got up and left the table and never answered it. So he really had
eat mule's meat.

He'd talk about the Civil War once in a while with old Aunt Mat.
She was an old-maid sister of his. She lived with us. She'd tell us
the stories. One time the Yankees came in on her and Grandma,
and they went in and took a whole lot of their cloth and all, and
my mother was living with 'em, and she was afraid of 'em. But I
reckon from what they said, my grandmother wasn't afraid of anything, and my mother started to run and grandmother, she got the
iron poking stick and says, "Stay here! You'll be safer in here with
me than anywhere's else." She was gonna kill 'em all with her poking
stick. And they just took what they wanted and took what money
they had—ten dollars in money. I think they had sold a cow or
horse or something for ten dollars to get money.

They used to have a Confederate reunion up here at the campground where they used to hold their revival meetings up in the
woods. I was at some of the revivals, and one of Daddy's old soldier
friends would come home with him. [They had a game they'd play
where they'd sail their hats out onto the ground, and then ride
past as fast as they could on their horses and bend down and try
to grab their hats up off the ground as they rode by.] Grandpa
Meadows was the only one in the bunch who could grab his hat.
The others was all out of practice. I heard my daddy say that one
time they all sailed [their hats] down into a wheat field, and they
was gonna ride down in there and get 'em. You know what an army'd
do to a wheat field? And that man that owned the field was standing
there with a gun, and he said he'd let one man go down there on
foot and gather up all them hats, but they wasn't riding into his
field. So that stopped that.

My father was a one-eyed man. He was a'shootin' at a hawk on
Sunday and a cap busted and put out one of his eyes. He was a
schoolteacher, and he was unusual-looking, but he was just a good-
looking old man. He had red whiskers on his head and the blackest
hair you ever seen—had two colors of hair on the same head! And
he taught school here and there, and then he ordered books and

peddled 'em. He sold Bibles and Testaments and histories and so on. [My brother killed my mother by accident, and so my father married again. We didn't like our stepmother.] I've seen the rivers rose over twice in my lifetime. My stepmother and Daddy was over in Briertown visiting her people, and my sister, Betty, and her husband come in and stayed with us, and we had the best time. Lord, we'd a'been so glad if our stepmother hadn't a'never got back.

When she had finished talking about her parents, we asked her to tell us about how she and her brothers and sisters were raised.

When we got up in the morning, we milked the cows, and then as soon as we'd had breakfast, we went to the field to hoe corn. And sometimes we was a long ways from home and had to climb a mountain to get to the field. And water was scarce on that Breedlove's Mountain. When we'd go in home for our dinner and get back after climbing that mountain, we were just exhausted, my sister and me. And we'd come in home and milk the cows that night and wash our feet and go to bed and we'd just fall into sleep exhausted.

We just had a three months' school, and all the communities around us had five months', and so after our school was out, I'd go to Oak Grove or Sulfur Springs another two months. I'm supposed to be the best speller they is in Macon County.

Now we used to play ball and tap at school. You form a great big ring at school holding hands, and one stays outside and he taps you and breaks and runs, and if you catch him, you can kiss him! We always let the boys outrun us.

[After I got married, I raised my family in this old house.] My brother-in-law, a couple of years ago, said the house was 104 years old. And Margaret Ann, his sister, was born here and she was 89 years old when she died. It's mortised and pinned together with locust pins. It wasn't sealed overhead out on the porch, and we never would seal it on account of showing people how it was put together with locust pins. Bore a hole and put one of them in. Oh, they wasn't big around as my arm there hardly. This house has four fireplaces. One upstairs in this room and one upstairs in that room, and two fireplaces down here.

We had this place rented when [the family that owned it] moved to Iotla community, and I was putting out potato plants down in the little bottom next to the river, and Rebecca'd seen me grease the baby's feet with Vaseline. So her Hoke was a baby then, and her and Rex got Hoke down and greased his feet. Then they greased

PLATE 354   Aunt Ethel's house.

theirs. And I had a clean white bedspread on the bed, and they
got in on that bed with them greasy feet and kicked the wall and
left tracks of all three of them on the wall. And Seth [who owned
the house] and them, they was awful particular. That was their living
room, but I had two beds in there. And he found them greasy tracks
on the wall and he just rared and he said I'd just messed up the
house till they wouldn't be able to live in it after I'd had it. And I
told him how I'd take a rag and wash them off, but I never did. I
made a marker round 'em and kept 'em, and they stayed there till
after they was grown and the ones who owned the house was painting
the room. And I think Becky was teaching school then—she was
about twenty years old. And they painted over them tracks. And I
tried to get her to paint around 'em and she wouldn't do it. Said
nobody wanted to see 'em but me.

[I lost one of my sons in the flu epidemic of 1918.] Deneezer
McCoy, Verlin's wife, died one day, and Donald, he heard the death
bells and he says, "I'm not dead yet." And he never died till the
next morning. They was in the kitchen a'gettin' breakfast, and I
was in there with Donald. I seen he was a'dyin', and I run in and
told 'em, and they got Amos up and he went to Neal Bryson's after
Ben Matlock, and Neal Bryson come and was here when he died.
Them death bells were to notify the people. They had to dig their
own graves then. They didn't have no insurance or anything, and
the members of the church would dig the graves. And that was to

call 'em together to see who was dead and where to dig. There.
was no cure for the flu—not at that time, they wasn't. And then
Donald had had a fall. He was thrown off a wagon against a tree a
few days before he had it, and one of his lungs was busted. He
coughed up a piece of one of them. That was the first time that
flu had ever been through here, and Deneezer and Donald was the
first deaths in the county.

I had nine children. And I had three full brothers and six sisters,
and I was the seventh, and so I was supposed to be able to take
off moles and warts and all such as that—and cure the thrash—
and I didn't know it till I was too old and people had learned better!

[The way I found out I could do it] was Edna Parrish over here
had six sisters, and she was the youngest and seventh. She said
that whenever her mother saw anybody coming with a baby, she
was supposed to blow in its mouth and that'd cure the thrash when
all it really needed was a dose of oil, you know, to clear up its
throat [laughing]. But I did make catnip tea and ground ivy tea
for the babies when they was little.

I never did cure no bleeding. Gray fell off where they was building
a bridge down in Swain County somewheres and broke his nose,
and it'uz a'bleedin' him to death. So we sent for Joe Martin across
the river over here [who could cure bleeding] and thought he had
to come. Joe went and told him that Gray's nose was a'bleedin'
him to death and the doctors couldn't stop it. And Joe was a'waitin'
on him [to come with him] and he told Joe, said, "You can go
on." Says, "It's stopped now." And we looked at the time of day,
and it worked. But we'd heard that it would before ever we sent.

We asked her how she raised the money that she needed for her family.

One year I raised $119 worth of turkeys, and the other years I
didn't raise so many. I generally just about raised what I hatched
off. They'd come up and I fed 'em twice a day, and I kept their
water. Had to water 'em. I kept water pans out up above the house,
and kept their pans just as *clean*. And I took 'em sand. I don't know
whether they used it or not. And I didn't feed 'em any wet feed. I
fed 'em dry. Baked bread for 'em. Or else bought a little chicken
feed for 'em. And me and one of the young'uns'd haul 'em to market
at selling time.

I don't think we ever got as much as three dollars out of one. I
know I've got over two dollars and some. I generally didn't have
no late'uns and little'uns. It was where an old turkey had raised a

gang and we maybe stole her nest out and come off with five or six or seven. And we built houses, and, Lord, their nests was hard to find. You've never seen nothing any harder than finding a turkey's nest!

At this point, she seemed to be getting tired, and so we asked her if she wanted us to leave for now and come back some other time.

No. I'm so glad to have your company. I stay by myself so much sometimes and I get so lonesome I feel like climbing the wall.

I belong to the Snow Hill Church, and their singers come one time to sing for me, and me deaf and couldn't hear? I tried *awful* hard to hear 'em. I couldn't, but they made a picture that I never did forget, and I just kept 'em as long as I could. But it was one of my bad days, and I just had to get to bed.

[I fill up the time the best way I can.] I piece quilts and crochet. Did you see that spread out there? They give me their old rags and I cut them up. Takes longer to cut the stuff than it does to crochet it. And them old knots is a bothersome thing! My grandmother's sister crocheted, and I watched her and made me a needle out of some wood and started. I piece quilts and do some of the awfulest sewing now that you've ever seen, but it holds together. I've got good strong thread.

And I get breakfast and dinner, and Billy, he cooks when I can't. And we've got canned stuff. All you have to do is just open it and heat it. We had chicken noodles for dinner today, and stew beef.

My daughter-in-laws, they keep me busy all the time a'making something. They keep me supplied with stuff to work with. I was raised on a farm and taught to get up at daylight, and if I don't have something to do, I don't like it. It's worse now. The other day I just answered somebody. I was imagining that I had company and I was a'answerin', and I was working on an old pan that the taters was cooked in and stuck to, and I couldn't hardly get 'em loose. And I thought she said, "That's enough. You've got it." And I turned around to speak to her to tell her that I could still feel stuff sticking to the pan. That was the second time that I had imaginary company and I thought they said something to me and I turned around. But I never did see nobody nor imagine who it was. But I've had company twice when I was all alone! I was so confident [that there was somebody here the last time that] I told her that I just about had it off.

We asked her about advice she might have for young people.

I don't want none of 'em to live together anymore without being married. It leaves a woman in such a helpless condition. I know a man who took up with this other woman, and they was just a'livin' together and not married, and his first woman [who he was not married to either] is down sick now and she's back home with her parents. They ain't no protection for a woman to live with a man without being married to him.

And I don't want the boys to be covered with hair! I like to see their faces. I hate to see a hippie so bad. My granddaughter come to see me, and she had a husband and I couldn't see him. His beard was way down here on his belly, and I don't know. It just about pukes me to see them hippies living the way they do.

We also asked her about her feelings on religion and death.

I guess that'd be hard to explain, although I still hold onto my childhood faith in religion. And as for dying, it'd be almost a relief. But I'm like old Miss Cody. I dread it! One Sunday evening I found out there was a crowd up there [for a worship service], and I hurried over—never washed the dishes—run over there. And she said how she had prayed for me and my boys all through the war and they all got back home, and she wanted everybody to pray for her to die quick and easy. She didn't want it to hurt too bad while she was at it. And we all put up our hands that we'd pray for her.

And her daughter-in-law was living with her taking care of her, and she had a child in school and a baby. Miss Cody, she got up and got her a piece of cornbread one morning and went and fed her little chickens. And she had a row of gladiolas along the garden fence, and she looked at her gladiolas. She'd reach out and put her hand in under 'em and pull 'em towards her. Then she come in and set down by the couch and played with the baby some. And she had a heart condition. She hollered, "Rosy, get my pill!" And Rosy said she got it, and said when she got there, she was just a'drawin' her last breath. She was dead. So I have faith in prayer. And I'm like Miss Cody. I want to die easy, too!

But I've outlived my usefulness. The young'uns could divide up here and do what they wanted to do and I'd be out of the way, at rest. One day I was studyin' about Carrie Cody. And it was a bad time, and my feet was cold, and I was just a'havin' a hard time,

PLATE 355 Aunt Ethel feeding her chickens.

PLATE 356 Kenneth Law and Ronnie Welch say goodbye.

and Billy was out. I was just a'sayin' to myself, "Now, Carrie's a'layin' down there at peace and rest, and here I am just still a'strugglin' around when I could be at peace, too, if I was out of it."

There's been a time or two, though, when I thought I was gonna die and I didn't want Billy to leave me at all. I didn't want to be left by myself. He couldn't have kept me here or nothing, but anyhow, I *wanted* him.

"I DID THE BEST I COULD
WITH THE BRAIN NATURE GAVE ME"

This is a very small biography of a very big person. His name was Ben Ward, and he lived in the mountains of North Carolina about as far away from the culture of the city as is possible in the eastern United States.

He was an inventor whose inventions are still in use in some modern sawmills. He was a political observer whose ideas were not contained by the shallow, street-corner gossip of some. He was a reader who, despite only a ninth-grade education, read Voltaire, Shakespeare, and Thomas Wolfe. Because living out in the mountains made it hard for him to get many works of literature and philosophy, he built a two-thousand-volume library of his own from which he read, and made notations in every book. He was a philosopher, but he never retreated from the world to pursue his ideas in seclusion. He was also an inventor and political observer in his spare time. Most of the time he ran a sawmill and generated electricity for himself, his neighbors, and the community church.

You might imagine that building and running a sawmill might not be that time-consuming, but consider some of the things you'd have to do starting from scratch as Ben did: You'd have to be enough of an engineer to dam a river, designing it yourself and mixing the cement and pouring it by hand; then you'd have to rig and hook two turbine wheels—one to generate electricity and the other to power your saw, carriage, log turner, edger saws, conveyor belts, and sawdust chains; then you'd have to figure out a system for transferring all the scrap wood to a large bin so it wouldn't pile up and get in the way; and then, because you were building from scrap, you'd have to invent ways to transfer the power from your turbine wheel to the machinery through a system of truck rear ends and transmissions and other junked automotive parts to save money; and then you'd have to figure out how to buy your timber and market your lumber, all the while keeping all the machinery repaired and in good working order, and all the while adding new inventions to the mill to make it work more efficiently. All this Ben did.

But even all this wasn't enough to occupy Ben's mind entirely. He also spent a large amount of time tinkering with perpetual-motion machines, even with the knowledge that many great minds before him had tried until frustration got the best of them.

And on top of all that, he took up a hobby that became almost an obsession: baseball. He wasn't the best player on the team he played for, and when members of that team blamed him for some of their defeats, he took his bulldozer to a nearby mountaintop and built his own baseball field, recruited his own team, and outfitted it completely.

This put a lot of stress on Ben, and it didn't help when the doctors said he was abnormally tense, or when people in the community regarded him as odd and somewhat crazy. Who could be considered normal and do all the things Ben did, including raising a son?

Ben will serve as an inspiration to me and countless others in the Appalachian region, for he disproved every stereotype of the southern Appalachian mountaineer as being an ignorant, shiftless hick. To my mind, he was a genius.

JOHN SINGLETON

This article was researched and written by John Singleton, Darryl Edwards, and Tim Young, with initial interviews conducted by Stanley Masters and John Garrard. Our special thanks to Ray Ward and his family for giving of their time and effort to make this article full and accurate, and to Roy and Milton Hodges for introducing us to the Wards.

Ben Ward was born on January 28, 1896, in a house roughly 150 feet from the spot where he eventually settled permanently. He was the fourth of thirteen children, eleven of whom lived to adulthood. His father was the community blacksmith, miller, and sawyer, and he had built a dam out of hemlock logs across the Watauga River in about 1905 to provide water power for his mills. The dam was so well built that it was the only one on the Watauga River to survive the huge flood of 1940, and it is still standing today.

Ben always attributed his inventiveness to his father. As Ray, his only child, said, "Many of the Wards were inventive people. My grandfather Ward, who was a blacksmith, invented a stirrup. He was in the process of patenting it with the idea of selling it to the cavalry, but then they did away with the cavalry and I don't think

PLATE 357 The original hemlock log dam built about 1905 across the Watauga River by Ben Ward's father.

he ever got the patent. The way it worked, when the rider would fall off his horse, the stirrup had a little spring on it that would release and let the rider's foot go. Ben always said he got his inventiveness from the Wards and his grit and tenacity from the Harmons [his mother's side of the family]. When he got an idea in his head, he wouldn't give up on it until he had it figured out.

"I understand my grandfather had a little water wheel out in the branch that powered a washing machine he had built. They said it would wash pretty good. I've heard Dad say when he and some of the other boys were around and Grandpa Ward would try to get them to work, he'd get aggravated at them and say, 'You lazy little devils. Get away! I'd rather do it myself than be bothered with you!'"

Ben went to grammar school at the one-room Johnson School near his home. "I believe he said he went to school for five years and couldn't learn anything. He said he'd just sit there and look at a book and it didn't mean anything to him. He'd sit and chew the corners off his books. But then everything just unfolded for him and he moved ahead of many of the kids.

"In many ways, he was an average kid, but he dared to be tested, I guess you could say. If he believed something, he had to have his way and he wouldn't follow friends. In other words, he was his own person. He would question. He didn't believe things just because other people said they were so."

As a teen-ager, he only rarely ventured out of the area, and so his knowledge of the outside world was limited, a condition typical of many young mountain people at that time. "On his first trip out of this county, he went to Johnson City, Tennessee, and stayed in a little hotel that was more or less a house of prostitution. Of course, he was so green he wasn't aware of it. He was just a pure old mountain boy. He wasn't aware of anything like that being in the world.

"Later he was in the Navy and he spent the night with a friend, and he started to tell this boy's folks about spending the night in such-and-such a hotel in Johnson City, and the boy said, 'Sh-h-h!' Later he got Dad out and told him where he had stayed, and until then he hadn't been aware that he had been in a house of prostitution and the only reason he was telling the story at all was that he was so proud of having stayed in a hotel in a strange town by himself.

"Of course, I guess if you didn't go in there with that intention, you could probably get a room. He said, 'I thought the girls were stuck on me.' That was their job, you know—to be nice to the boys. He didn't know. He was just that ignorant of the situation. I think Thomas Wolfe writes somewhere about having a similar experience. That's just how green some of the mountain boys were."

Despite his rather limited contact with the outside world, his absolutely remarkable inventiveness surfaced early. "His first real project was in about 1914. He made a small steam engine that worked just like the big ones, and it had a little circle sawmill that would saw little pieces of soft, rotten wood. They had it in a museum over at Appalachian State University. It was in the old music building that burned down in the early forties. I never did see it, but I have heard many people talk about it. They said it would pop off just like a big steam engine. He built it from scraps in his father's blacksmith shop.

"Sometimes he would take interest in some gadget and work all

day on it, but most of the time he'd just tinker with things in his spare time. Just play. Change this and change that. When he died, he was tinkering with a perpetual-motion machine. Grandfather Ward had started playing with one. He never figured it out, but he believed that if he could ever find a perfectly round wheel, he could solve it. Ben took up where he left off. He would set one up and then tear it down and set it up a different way. He had magnets on one mounted somehow on an old phonograph along with pieces of lead to break the magnetic field. Somebody is liable to stumble on the solution one of these days. He just played with ideas like that.

"And sometimes he'd lose patience. I remember once he was working on an old motor block. He welded and welded on it, and every time he put water on it, it would leak. He got mad at the thing and he said, 'Well, I'll fix the G—— d——— thing.' And he took a sledgehammer and just beat the whole side of the engine in. He would get mad at something and beat the dickens out of it. Sometimes he would get mad at it and throw it. His patience would wear thin after he would work with something a while and it wouldn't work. He'd just throw it, and then he would go pick it up and calmly start working again.

"I cleaned this machine shop up a lot after he died. When he worked, he seldom cleaned up anything. He picked up just enough so that he could get to something the next time he wanted to work on it. He could send me after something and tell me where it was, and I wouldn't be able to find it. But he could walk right in and pick it up without even looking twice. It was like he had an index in his head of where everything was, even with everything scattered around. He would lay something down, and if somebody didn't bother it, he was like a bee that could go right back to the hive. It was just like an instinct of some kind.

"And about everything he saw, he could see something useful in it. Every usable piece of junk he could find, he would pick it up and bring it in here. He loved to go to junk piles and hunt for useful things.

"He was an artist, and like a great artist, he used machinery to express himself." This was a trait that he carried all his life.

Another trait that surfaced early was a hatred of hypocrisy. He recognized the human tendency to be hypocritical in himself while he was in grammar school. At the old Johnson School, his family was rather poor and they could only afford to pack him a lunch of milk and cornbread and butter and molasses. It embarrassed him so much that he would slip off and hide to eat. Later, when he was boarding with a family and attending another grammar school, he was fed very well and would sit up on a rock and eat so that everyone could see him. He told Ray often how much he. hated the fact that when he was poor, others were cruel to him and teased him, and when he had been well off, he had done exactly the same thing to others.

After finishing grammar school, Ben went on to the Appalachian Training School, which later became Appalachian State University. His education was cut short, however, after a total of nine years (not much by today's standards, but enough to qualify him to teach in a one-room country school). "All the schooling he had was just nine years. Most of it was just self-education. When World War I broke out, he was at the Appalachian Training School working toward some kind of program that General Electric had for boys who were talented in electronics and science. At that time, patriotism,

PLATE 359 A portrait taken of Ben while he was in the Navy.

I guess, was high, and so he talked to Professor Dauphin Dougherty, one of his teachers and one of the founders of Appalachian State, about joining the Navy. Professor Dougherty said, 'You can learn more there than you can in our school. They will teach you more that you can use when you get out in the world. I would advise you to go on.'

"So he did. He first went to Newport, Rhode Island, for his boot training. Then he was aboard a troop ship, the U.S.S. *Powhatan*. He served first in the boiler room passing coal. That was where they haul coal from storage to the boiler room and put it into the boilers. He did that for two or three weeks and got sick. It was caused by running from the hot boiler room to the cold weather outside. He practically took pneumonia. I remember him saying that there was a boy who worked with him that took pneumonia and died. After Dad got sick, they moved him to an electrical gang, where he served the rest of the war.

"On his first trip across the ocean, they got into a big storm. They were out in the mid-Atlantic somewhere, and he said the old ship would just roll and creak. Some of them were getting seasick, and this old sailor got mad and said, 'I wish old bald-headed Jesus Christ would sink the G—— d—— ship to the bottom of hell and do it right now.'

"It scared my father to death. He said he had never heard anyone talk about the higher power like that and he was sure he was a goner. He said he thought his hair stood straight up. But it wasn't long until he had the same feeling as the sailor. From that time on [his feelings toward Christianity and all-powerful God were demystified, and he never regarded religion with the kind of awe he had once reserved for it].

"About two years ago, there was sort of a coincidence. An old gentleman came from Charlotte to see the mill. I asked him if he was a veteran, and he said, 'Yes.' And he got to talking about going over to France. I questioned him a little, and he said he was on the *Powhatan.* And he got to telling me about the ship and the storm, and he described it just as my father had. He knew all about the ship and even had a picture of it."

After the war was over, Ben returned home. "I have been told many times that when he came back from the service, he was very popular and looked up to because he had a big Harley Davidson motorcycle and a car before those things were common, and he'd drink some just to be one of the boys. He said, 'A poor man ought to get drunk at least once a year just to know how a rich man feels all year.' He was kind of a daredevil on his motorcycle. He took one fellow for a ride on it and went across a footlog, and the fellow got so scared he swallowed his tobacco. He had the byword 'Wonetime,' that he prefaced everything he said with, and he jumped off the motorcycle and shouted, 'Wonetime Ben Ward is crazy and doesn't value his life!'

"He didn't like to fight, but he wouldn't back down either. Once in the Smoky Mountains he got into an argument and both went to get their guns. But halfway back, he thought about what he was doing and said to himself, 'I don't want to kill anyone. If someone's got to be killed today, I'd rather be killed myself than kill him.' The other man came back with his gun and sauntered around Ben and poked at him and taunted him, but Ben just stood his ground and took it. He said that later the man became one of his best work hands and a good friend.

"Another time he got into one after the war and almost killed a man. The way he told it, it happened in front of the old Pastime Theater in Boone, North Carolina. There was this big fellow who was kind of the bully around Boone—an all-conference football player and Golden Gloves boxer. Dad had been in the T&L Tavern right beside the theater and had had a couple of beers. Then he went in to see the movie and sat down by a young lady, and this fellow came over by them and said something to my father about him sitting next to this lady, and Dad asked him what business it was of his—or something like that. So he invited my father out on the street.

"Dad said as soon as he walked out to the street, this fellow hit him and knocked him about ten feet, but he never did go down. One thought that struck him said for him to run, and the other said to stay with him or die. Dad was only 5-8 and 150 pounds, but he went back, ducked his head down, got hold of the man's throat, and held on just like a little dog hanging onto a big one. The fellow grabbed him, beat him with his fists, broke his nose, knocked his teeth loose, and blacked both of his eyes. He just about beat my father to death, but Dad said, 'For some reason, I just couldn't feel any pain,' and he didn't let go.

"Finally the fellow went down from lack of breath. There were a couple of friends with Dad, and when they finally pulled him off, he had his finger around this man's eyeball trying to pull it out. Then the law came and they ran into the alley.

"Later on, somebody asked this fellow why he didn't hit him or something. He said, 'I *did* hit him. I don't know what kind of a man he was. I hit him with everything I had and I still couldn't put him down.'

"My father said he came home the next morning, and his niece, Kate, was staying with him, and when he came into the room where she was, she just ran backwards and screamed, 'Uncle Ben, what has happened to you?'

"And he said, 'I don't know. Why?'

"She told him to go look in the mirror, and he said his face was nearly beat off. He said it was just scary. The doctors say that a person with his mental diagnosis produces up to three times the normal amount of adrenalin, and I guess that's what happened.

"That man must have really gotten desperate, though. Dad said that the next morning the bottoms of his feet were sore where the man had bounced him up and down against the sidewalk trying to shake him loose."

Shortly after Ben returned from the war, he sawmilled in Silverstone and other communities around Watauga County, and then in 1925 moved to the Cable Cove section of Graham County, North Carolina, where he sawed timber for a large lumber company that operated a circle mill in the area. In the late twenties his inventiveness surfaced again, and he built his own band mill out of parts of two or three old ones that were out of commission. A saw filer told him he could never do it himself, which made him even more determined. Mr. Johnson, a saw filer for the Bemis Lumber Company in Robbinsville, North Carolina, helped him a great deal, and Ben never forgot him.

Ben had several extraordinary experiences in the Smokies. "He was driving along Lake Cheoah below Fontana Lake one day, and he was on this mountain road that goes around the lake, and there was a rocky bluff up above the road. He said the vision of a house appeared before him, and later on [in 1938–39] he built it just the way he had seen it then. That's this house that we live in now. Four of the millstones that are around the house came from Grandpa Ward's old mill, and two are Grandfather Harmon's. The rest he just picked up in other places. But he said he saw the outside rock parts of the house in this vision and planned the inside later. A cousin of his named Junior Simpson was talented in radio, and he helped Dad set up a system of speakers all through the house. When you stood between two rooms, it was just like stereo sound, which hadn't even been invented yet. And Dad had mercury switches in the house. They were real quiet, and people couldn't understand why they didn't click."

When the Depression hit, Ben found himself in debt over a thousand dollars, with no way to get the money. To make matters more difficult, his young wife was pregnant with Ray, their first child. "My father was going on a Fourth of July fishing trip when I was born on July 1, 1930. He was with Jack Morphew, a prominent Robbinsville, North Carolina, attorney and one of his best friends. He decided he'd better see how she was doing before he went, and so he called the hospital and asked how she was getting along. They said, 'Hold on a minute. Your wife wants to talk to you.'

"He said something to her about fishing, and she said, 'Get on over here. You've already caught a big fish. Bring me some clothes.'

"I had just been born, so he told Jack, 'I guess my fishing trip is over. I've already landed a big one.'

"I can remember his paranoid streak. He said he had lost all interest in women at one time, but my mother appealed to him and changed all that, and Jack advised Dad to marry her. He said there wasn't a finer family of people in these mountains. I can remember his saying that when he was with my mother, all his jealousness and suspicions completely left him, but as soon as he was out of

PLATE 360   The stone house Ben built. Between the millstones are granite plaques into which are carved his favorite quotations.

her presence, they'd return and haunt him. And when she was pregnant with me, they weren't married. I can remember that he doubted for a while that I was his child, but I used to have a little mole on my ear, and he had one in the same place and my mother pointed to it and said, 'Look here, Ben, you can't deny this!' and that finally convinced him.

"My mother had had rheumatic fever when she was a child, and it damaged her heart. Two months after I was born, it reoccurred and killed her just before her twentieth birthday."

On his wife's headstone, Ben carved a quotation from *The Rubaiyat of Omar Khayyam:*

> Yet Ah, that Spring should vanish with the Rose!
> That Youth's sweet-scented manuscript should close!

The death of his wife triggered a nervous breakdown, and for a period of several years, Ben was in and out of VA hospitals, once being locked up in a ward for the criminally insane after attacking a doctor who called him antisocial, a term they apparently used to mean that he was lazy and wouldn't work. He underwent some fifty shock treatments in those VA hospitals, and he wrote of that experience, "Death can't be any different. It's just like turning out a light. The light just slowly dies away. There is no memory. They would take me before breakfast in the morning, and I'd come back to reality and think it was still early morning but it would be suppertime. I've been dead fifty times."

At a VA hospital in Perry Point, Maryland, he was declared incompetent and given a service-related full-disability pension and sent home.

Soon after leaving Perry Point, he became a strong advocate of Bernard Macfadden and his physical-culture magazine. Macfadden advocated eating natural foods and fasting for health, and so from the early thirties to about 1960, Ben's daily diet consisted only of four or five whole-wheat muffins crumbled into a bowl of whole unpasteurized milk at every meal. Whenever he felt his system to be out of sorts, he would go on a five-to-seven-day fast, living on water and fruit juices. He felt this cleansed his system and gave Nature a chance to correct the problem. In the late 1950s, his stomach began to give him problems and so he gave up the diet. But in 1960, he came upon a book called *The Art of Living Long* by Louis Cornaro, a celebrated Venetian centenarian who lived from 1464 to 1566. Cornaro advocated the use of wine as a main source of food for people with stomach and digestive problems, and so Ben began using Chianti and bread along with a few cashew nuts as his main food source. The wine seemed to solve his stomach problems, and strong men working along with him could never understand how he could do as much or more work as they did on such a small amount of food.

After his release from Perry Point in the early thirties, Ben went to the Smokies, retrieved his band mill, hauled it home, and set it up on the spot where his father had had the little circle mill that had been the first mill in that community. He set it up not so much to make money as to play with and keep himself occupied. When money began to circulate again after the Depression, and things picked up, he went into sawmilling and eventually earned enough money to buy the old homeplace for himself and his son. "The first load of lumber he hauled after moving from Graham County to here he got $11 for. He said he looked at his check and said to himself, 'I made $111,' and he thought he had really done well. But when he got back to his truck, he looked at the check again and saw that it said $11, and he had $30 or $40 invested in the load.

"When he got home, he said, 'Well, I can't operate like that.' So the next week, he started with a good worker and got out some more logs and cut them, and that load of lumber brought about

PLATE 361 Ben's original sawmill, which was completely washed away in the flood of 1940.

$40 and he made a little profit. So he started from there. Back then, people were willing to work hard. He said that even during the Depression, people would work hard, but before he died he said, 'Nowadays people won't work. I just don't know what to think.'

"He always had a few average workers, but they were good men. He would pay the man that did good work good pay. The ones that did not do much did not get as much pay. Sometimes two men would work and do the work of one good man, and he would pay them accordingly and they were happy. But he had to quit doing that when the wage and hour laws came in because he couldn't afford it. I know one or two men kept on working, and he paid them accordingly by the hours they worked.

"He bought timber from people. People would sell him the timber from their land and he would cut it. The way he got most of his land was that he would just buy the land and then cut the timber off it, and then he would harvest the timber and maybe pay for a lot of the land from the profits.

"And he always said he replanted as many trees as he cut. He replanted about a hundred thousand trees, and he cut about twenty-five million feet of timber during his life, so that should replace what he cut. I more or less got him interested in that. We had pastureland in these old fields, and they were steep, so we set out about a hundred thousand poplars and pines. Some of the pines are big enough now to where you could make small logs out of them. It was about '56 when we started setting. At that time, most people that had land in here just cut the timber off and let it reforest itself. Then the Forest Service started giving out seedlings. When we got started replanting, it really interested him.

"He used to have a gristmill here also, and a hammer mill for cow feed. He ran it on Saturdays when he wasn't sawing. Back in the late thirties, his brother ran it most of the time and he did right well with it then because corn was something like a dollar or a dollar and a half a bushel, and a man would work all day then for a dollar. The miller would get an eighth of the corn ground as his payment, so it paid then. But later it got so it didn't pay well at all—not enough to hire a man to do it—and so he ran it for a while as a community service and then discontinued it altogether in the late forties.

"I remember Ben was talking once to an old gentleman who was a real fine old man that used to run a gristmill. And Dad said to him, 'Did you ever dip up a dish of the toll out of the hopper where a grain of corn would just balance on the side of the dish about to fall back into the hopper and be ground for the other man, and it would just be hanging there, and you would ease it back just as easy and into your pile to save that kernel of corn?'

"And the man said, 'God, yes, I have many a time!' You know, it's just human nature, that selfishness or whatever. He would hold the dish so that one grain of corn wouldn't slide off back into the hopper. You wanted to be honest, but yet you wanted that grain of corn also for yourself. That seems funny to us now, but I guess it was common then."

In addition to the sawmill and gristmill—all water-powered thanks to his father's dam, which was still intact—he added a generator and began to produce electricity for the community. "He had a franchise to sell electricity in a five-mile radius because back then there were no major producers around here. He wrote to the utilities board and they granted him a five-mile radius. He produced electricity for fifteen houses, charging them one dollar a month, and he gave power to the church for free. He had a set of governors made out of the governors off an old steam boiler. I don't know exactly how it worked, but he had it fixed somehow so that when the people began to kick their power on, those governors would turn a little more water in to the turbine wheel automatically and provide more power to the generator. But the power company came through here and took over all these little franchises, and they said then that he could only generate power to within a two-hundred-foot radius of the mill, and so he generated just for himself after that."

On August 13, 1940, a disastrous flood washed the mills away, along with a hundred thousand feet of lumber, but it left the old dam standing. "Right after the mill washed away in the 1940 flood, his Uncle Oscar was telling him how it was an act of Providence. Dad said, 'Aw, it has nothing to do with that. I just had my mill too damn close to the river. I didn't like the way it was built anyway, and besides it left me a good, clean place to start over.'

"The first person he saw after the flood was a neighbor named Wilborn, and his first words to him were, 'Wib, damned if it didn't wash our ball equipment away.' [His interest in baseball is explained later in this chapter.]

"After the flood had washed everything away, he looked around and got up some lumber to take to town to buy a little stove, since we had cooked with electricity and didn't have any power. It was getting dark, and he didn't have any lights on his truck. When he got to Cove Creek, the patrolman stopped him and told him it wasn't safe for him to drive without lights. Dad told him his misfortunes and how he couldn't do any better, and the patrolman wouldn't listen to him. Finally he got mad and said, 'If nothing else will do you, just take me to the damn jail and lock me up.' The patrolman got tickled and got one of the men up there to bring him home."

Since the dam was left standing, he rebuilt the mill in 1941. He was constantly looking for ways to improve it, though, and in 1947, while attending a World Series game in New York, he bought the machine-shop equipment with which he began to add the improvements that are on the mill now.

In 1953, for example, he replaced the four-foot bandmill with the present saw, which is a six-foot bandmill (a thirty-six-foot-long blade set around two six-foot-in-diameter wheels or narrow, hollow drums). The Bristol Steel Company cut the steel for the wheels, and Ben hired a skilled welder to weld the pieces together. Then he trued the drums/wheels himself (since no local machinists knew how to help him) by building a frame next to the machine-shop

PLATE 362 Ray holding the punch Ben invented. It fits on a hydraulic press and is used for punching out saw teeth.

lathe, mounting a bandmill drum on the frame, and letting it turn against the lathe bit. "He balanced them himself, and they are just about perfect."

He also improved a log-turning device he had patented earlier, designed and built a saw filer, and made a hydraulic punch so that he could make his own saw blades out of Swedish saw steel.

The next major improvement to the mill came in 1963. "Grandpa Ward had always talked about someday building a concrete dam to replace the log one. That project became my father's last big ambition in life. One day I was sawing, and he was out in the yard sunning. Suddenly he came over to where I was and sat down on the steps to the filing room and looked out over the river. The water was kind of low and the dam wasn't running over because we were running all the water through the water wheels. Then he walked down and shut the mill off.

"I asked him why, and he said he was going to build that dam. This was in the last part of August 1963. About Labor Day, we

PLATE 363 Ben on the day water first came over the top of the new cement dam. He is holding his grandson.

PLATE 364 At the far end of the dam, Ben had a cement fish ladder built in for trout and bass to climb. The writing in the wall of the ladder says, "June 1964," the date the dam was completed.

started the main project. We first built our coffer dams and everything to cut the water out. Roy Hodges worked in water up to his
chin for two days, driving and nailing the piling boards to four
poplar logs to make the main coffer dam. Without him, we might
not have made it. We used the old dam for the upper coffer. When
the coffer dams were finished, we had the job licked. Then we built
the dam. He said later, 'Something just told me that if I was ever
going to build that dam, this was the time.' Fortunately, we just
had one little freshet and it didn't bother us hardly at all. The only
thing that happened was that Henry Hicks, who was running the
concrete mixer, got hit in the eye with a rock when we were busting
rock. He was out all that fall, and that slowed us up a lot. We worked
on Thanksgiving Day, and that was the last day. We must have
poured over five thousand bags of concrete. There was one boy,
Paul Rominger, who was real strong and hauled just about all the
sand for it himself in a wheelbarrow. He got it out of the sand
that had piled up behind the old dam. His younger brother, Larry,
hauled the bagged cement in another wheelbarrow. We'd pour about
seventy-five to eighty bags a day, mixing it all in a one-bag mixer."

With the dam completed, Ben continued the sawmill business
and continued generating power for himself. His inventive streak
turned to the problem of how to mount a four-foot bandmill on
the back of a truck to make it portable so that it could be carried
to small boundaries of timber, thus saving the expense of hauling
the logs to the mill.

And he also continued a lifelong passion for baseball. "He always
liked to play ball when they played in school. They called it town
ball. You had two bases and you throw the ball between the runner
and the base. They had a community team before he went into
the service, and when he came back from the service, I don't think
he played much. Once, in a VA hospital, he had given up and death
was all that was on his mind. They had him out one day with a
group playing volleyball. There was an old fellow standing there
that was sort of like him, and someone hit the ball and it hit him
on the head and he didn't flinch or anything. My father said, 'If I
look like that fellow, I ought to be dead.' So then he got into the
game and started playing. He became interested and they had a
pretty good team. He was first substitute on the hospital team, which
beat the best team in Baltimore. He also was proud of the fact
that when the world-champion volleyball team came by to entertain

PLATE 365   The Watauga River team of 1912, the first team Ben ever played on. Ben is fourth from the left on the front row.

the patients at Perry Point, he was on the hospital team that got to play them.

"Up in the filing room [in the mill building] is the old box he hauled his baseball equipment in. During the Second World War, you had to deliver wood or lumber if you went from one place to another. That was to conserve gas. So on weekends he would put that box on top of a load of stove wood and go to little communities around here and play baseball. He kept the gloves and bats in the box—outfitted the team.

"He wasn't a good player. When some of the better players objected to him playing, saying he was making them lose, he packed up the equipment and left, saying, 'The next field I play on, no one can kick me off of'; and then he built his own ball field, making it exactly the same size as the ball field in Cleveland Stadium—a favorite of his. He built the field between 1947 and 1950 with the help of Dexter Rominger, who operated the dozer, and put over ten thousand dollars of labor and materials into it.

"When local team players would brag about how many games they had won, he would laugh and say, 'I can brag that I've been beaten more times than anyone who ever played in Watauga County.' He was probably right. In the early thirties, for example, he played on a community team called the 'Old Stag Team' in which all the

PLATE 366 Ben's ball field.

PLATE 367 The backstop and dugouts.

players were from thirty to fifty years old, and they didn't win a single game all year and often got 'greased' [shut out]. All the other teams in the area wanted to play them because they were such good sports and so easy to beat. 'It was the most fun I ever had,' Dad said. One of his biggest thrills was hitting a home run one day, thus saving the team from being shut out, and his fellow players carried him on their shoulders. He said, 'I felt bigger than the President.' His one goal for the team was that it get at least one run, after which he would exclaim, 'God, they can't grease us now!'

PLATE 368 The view from Ben's ball field.

PLATE 369 At age fifty-seven, Ben releasing his favorite pitch, a slow, round-house curve. (Photo by Palmer Blair, Palmer's Photo Shop, Boone, N.C.)

"He loved to pitch. He could do rather well at times. He never would strike many people out, but he would throw an old slow junky ball and you couldn't hit it very hard. It was slow, and you'd hit it into the ground or pop it up. He would pitch five innings most of the time if he could get by that long, and then he would quit. Sometimes he would pitch longer. Nineteen fifty-six was the best year he had, when he won thirteen games and lost none, and his team was Watauga-Avery County league champions. After he won the thirteenth, he wouldn't pitch anymore because thirteen was his number.

"He considered man walking on the moon the highlight of man's achievement during his lifetime. On the same day of that feat, he pitched a seven-inning baseball game and won, 5–4. He was seventy-three years old, and he considered this game his most memorable baseball feat. But it was during this period that his physical and mental health began to deteriorate, and after trying to make a comeback by playing baseball one Saturday evening, he told my wife while they were leaving the ballfield, 'It looks like I'm going to have to hang up my spikes.'

"The game remained one of his favorite things in his later life. And fishing for native speckled trout ran a close second to baseball. But he sometimes said, 'When I go to the Pearly Gates, if I find they don't have a ball team, I'll put in for a transfer.' "

When Ben died on June 15, 1970, he was cremated, as he had requested, wanting "every atom in his body released to get back into Nature's workshop." The memorial service was free of religious ceremony and prayer, as he had wished.

His ashes were scattered over his ball field.

Ray, in an attempt to help us collect additional stories about his father, invited Clay Ward and Henry Hicks over to his house to talk with us. Both used to work for Ben, Clay for eight years and Henry for fifteen, and both played on his ball team. The following is part of the conversation we had:

CLAY: I'll tell you what a sharp thinker the man was. Them fellows were out here dozing one time, and Henry there crawled under the dozer and it sunk down and caught him across the chest. And Mr. Ward didn't know which way to pull the lever to raise or lower the blade. He stood there a minute and thought which way it should work and then he lowered the blade against the ground and lifted the dozer up in the air off Henry. He said he thought, "I've got to be right this one time." He was that kind of man. He'd stop and think before he did anything. He could figure things out in just a minute, whereas you and me wouldn't.

HENRY: One wrong move and I would have been dead. If he had moved that blade up one little bit, I'd have been dead. He'd never been on a bulldozer before, but he said he knew he had to make the right move.

RAY: There was so much pressure on you it busted blood vessels in your eyes. The doctors said that if they'd busted around your heart, it would have killed you. When Ben got in a close circumstance like that, he was just as calm as a human can be. But get him in normal places and he couldn't even talk he got so nervous.

HENRY: He was really smart. He could memorize anything. And he could figure out things that I just couldn't understand. He'd tell me what the moon weighed while we were working. He had it figured up in his mind. And what the earth and all that weighed. He had it figured right, too. And I'd try to understand it and he'd try to explain it all to me. He'd say, "Do you see into it now?"

And I'd say, "No." He'd tell me three or four times and I'd say, "I just can't focus into it."

RAY: He'd just commit it to his mind and it'd be there. I remember one time he was just about to renew his driver's license. Living by himself, he really needed one. This new boy was doing the examination. The other [officer] and Ben were good friends, and he'd just make him drive a couple of miles and that would be the test. But this new boy asked him all these tricky questions like how many car lengths and that sort of thing—how far a car would bounce if it fell off a building and all that.

Well, he just threw the paper down and the boy said something smart to him, and he said, "Son, I can figure out things in my head that you can't even figure out on paper." Then he said, "I can't pass this damn thing. You just take it and throw it away."

And then the regular [officer] came back and talked to him and just gave him his license and told him not to drive in certain conditions. But that boy was sort of smart and gave him a smart remark.

HENRY: He couldn't stand for that.

RAY: But he was really intelligent in a practical way, too. We'd get down to what looked like solid rock to us when we were building that cement dam, and it would feel like solid rock, and he'd get down there with a crowbar and beat on it and say, "Hell, this ain't solid rock."

HENRY: I tried it many a time and never could do it.

RAY: He'd jump down in there with some dynamite and he'd blast and it would be shell rock. I don't know how he learned it, but he was good with it, wasn't he, Henry?

HENRY: Darn right he was good. He could take a crowbar and move a rock that would take a compressor and drill hours to do. He hardly ever had any drilling done. I've seen people drill for three days on something where he could just take dynamite and a crowbar and do the job and save hundreds of dollars.

RAY: I guess he poured more concrete by hand than anyone in this area.

HENRY: And that mill is something. I don't think anyone but him understood how that mill worked. I didn't know what was going on.

RAY: I don't even think he understood it all the time. Dad said his mind was like a funnel with all the stuff coming in at the big end and it would all get crushed together at the little end and couldn't get out. I've seen him come to the house just sick.

HENRY: He'd work with us, though. There were about eighteen people working on the dam, and all the time I worked with him, he never asked me to do something he wouldn't do himself.

RAY: A man came by one time and asked to see him. The man was all dressed up, and Ben came out from under the mill all covered with grease and stuff and his old hat pulled sideways and his overall leg torn up to about his knee, and that man looked at him for a while in disbelief and said, "Are *you* Mr. Ward?"

And he said, "Yeah, I reckon I am."

HENRY: There was a lot of difference working for a man like that. You feel different working for a man like that. He went to work and you followed him.

RAY: Then when he'd get stuck, he'd give you something else to do and just say, "Go over here and do this while I figure this out."

And then sometimes he was forgetful. Once he left a man holding something heavy and told him that he'd be right back and went off to do something and forgot about that man, and when he came back, the man had fallen over.

But I'll tell you what. He could take three men and do more work and handle a bigger job than an ordinary man could take a dozen men and do. He'd get them all to work together. You get a crowd together and everyone lifts at their own time and nobody gets anywhere. But he'd take three men and all would lift together and there wasn't much they couldn't do if everybody would stay with him and pull their share of the load.

And sometimes he'd get mad. I've seen him yell and cuss himself when something went wrong. But things usually worked out. He was just like a little kid with a Christmas tree full of presents when he filled the dam up and the water came over it just as even. And he did that just with his eye. He sighted across that thing [to make it level on top] and the water came over completely smooth.

HENRY: If you was going to contract [to have a dam like that done today] it would cost a half a million dollars trying to figure out how to do it. That's right, too.

RAY: He would sight with his thumb and it would always be right. Funny thing happened to him when he was building a fence up at the baseball field. He had two stakes set up, lining them up, you know. He said [to the man standing there], "What the hell are you laughing about?"

And the man says, "Well, Ben, any fool knows you can line up two stakes at one time."

And he says, "Damned if you ain't right, ain't you?"

HENRY: Most people didn't have any reason not to like him. Some didn't like him because they were jealous of him, but he carried his own weight pretty well. He'd stand up for what he believed in. It was just that he was so much smarter than other people, and they couldn't understand him. A lot of people were so confused, they didn't know what to think. But if a man got time to study everything, you could see what he was doing. Right off hand, though, it was pretty hard to understand.

Sometimes people felt he would try to cheat them when he'd buy their timber, but as long as I worked for him he never told me to be dishonest. A man would price a boundary of timber for us, and on the way back I'd tell him that the man would take less than that, and he'd say, "No; I ain't gonna do it."

RAY: He'd never dicker. A man would price something and he'd either buy it or leave it.

HENRY: Yep. If he thought it was worth it, he'd take it. Otherwise, he'd just walk off. But he was honest. I remember one night late we were driving—it was late, but he had it in his mind he just had to go look at something—so we started up the mountain and filled up with gas. We went on up the road, and he said, "Did you pay for that gas?"

And I said, "No, I thought you did." We were way on up the

mountain, and I said, "Let's let it go, and sometime when we're back this way we'll pay for it."

He said, "Hell no." He thought I was meaning to never pay for it. He said, "I never have done it and I don't aim to start now." He said, "Find a place to turn and let's go back and pay for it." We found the man there, and he never even knew we hadn't paid for it.

RAY: He was just like Mark Twain in that manner. Said, "You can clear me legally, but you can't clear my conscience."

You were talking about him buying timber—like how fair he'd be with people. [A woman who lived in the community] had the finest boundary of timber in this county. And nobody could go and get a tree from her without her giving it away. She and her brother lived together, and he was retarded in some ways. This fellow that she almost married one time—Dad was a good friend of his—went with Dad to try and buy some timber from her. So they talked a little while and told her that she would be helping out in the war. She told him that she had a certain tract and told him to go look at it. So he went out and looked at it, figured out how much he could pay for it and how much there was. She had other people there that wanted to buy it.

She asked him how much he could give her, and he figured it up. Said he could give twenty-five hundred dollars for it. She agreed that she would sell it to him. So she wrote out a little contract— she was a very intelligent person, and people looked on her as they did him; they thought they were [both] strange.

So as soon as he made the payment for it, she began to laugh, and he asked if he had hurt her feelings or said something funny. She said, "No, no. You know, I'm just thinking that the most anybody has ever offered me for that boundary of timber was a thousand dollars." So that was just how honest he tried to be with people.

HENRY: They would come and ask Ben for a job like, say, they wanted to drive a dump truck. He wouldn't hire them [to do that] because he said they'd have to start at the bottom and work their way to the top just like the other men did. And the bottom was the wood saw, and he wouldn't ask you to do it if he thought you couldn't do it. That was just the kind of man he was.

RAY: Well, he always had his men working for him here, and as long as he had that, that was what he got a lot of enjoyment out of. People working and talking to him and telling jokes, and there was no difference in human beings to him. Everybody was the same. Actually, if somebody tried to frown or make fun of someone, he would stand up for them, saying, "They're playing their part in Nature's plan just the same as you and me."

HENRY: I will tell you the way I see it; most likely he talked to the ones he enjoyed talking with in the evenings when the men got off work, and he enjoyed that, I guess, more than anything in the world, and once he got onto you, you couldn't hardly get away from him, you know, 'cause he was always talking to you, and he made sense when you was talking to him.

He talked about politics, but he didn't take sides. He just told it like it was, and as long as I worked for him he never one time told me how I should vote.

The only problem I ever had working with him was getting away from him. [He liked to talk so much that] he was hard to get rid of!

I'd liked to have seen him be President for just one term. There was no man that could have solved things like he could. Fifteen years ago he talked about the way the government should be run, and every day something comes up that [makes me] remember what he said. Hardly a day passes that I don't think of him [in connection with] something. If it hadn't been for him, many a man in Watauga County would have went hungry.

RAY: He helped a lot of boys like you get you a home.

HENRY: Helped me get everything I've got. If I'd listened to him then, I might be something now. And I still remember the last words he ever spoke to me. He said, "Henry, it's a dog-eat-dog world. Look out for yourself."

CLAY: He helped more people in this community than any man that's ever been in it or ever will be in it. I've heard fellows say that they'd come and tell Ben that they were down and out and didn't have nothing to eat. And he would hire them to work when he didn't need help, just to help them. I don't see why anybody in the county could down him in any way. Well, I know he's been good to me.

One of the more remarkable aspects of Ben's personality is the amount of serious reading he undertook in philosophy and science and literature, and the number of passages he memorized and carried with him like talismen— lanterns to illuminate what for him was often a confusing, but always fascinating, world. Ray talked to us at length about this aspect of his personality, illustrating continuously with points he remembered his father making to him or to others in his presence.

He had a photographic memory. When he read something interesting, it was committed to his mind. Professor B. B. Dougherty
made all the students learn a poem called *Building the Bridge for Him*
by W. A. Dromgoole when they were at Appalachian Training
School, and Dad learned it and could quote it right along.

One day he was getting a water wheel from Professor Dougherty
that the college had replaced with a bigger one. They were riding
along in an old truck and Dad mentioned this poem to Professor
Dougherty and started quoting it to him. He grabbed Dad on the
leg and said, "Hush! Hush!" He said the professor sat a minute,
and then he started quoting the poem to perfection—just right.
My father could quote it, but he said he could not quote it like
Professor Dougherty. The professor said, "You know—it's been
twenty years since I have thought about that poem. I'm glad you
mentioned it."

Dr. Dougherty was compared in *Life* to Horace Mann, the father
of our education. They called him the Horace Mann of the mountains. The training school he and his brother started became Appalachian State University. He taught over there for a long time, but
in his later years he didn't teach because he just ran the school.
I've been told they tried to raise his salary one time when he was
making ten thousand dollars a year. They wanted to give him more
money and he said, "Give it to the school. I don't need it. I've
already got all I need."

Ben's older brother, John, was a teacher and encouraged him
to read books by people like Darwin. He was about six years older
than my father. And Dad also credited Professor B. B. Dougherty
for helping him to be able to read and understand the great authors
and thinkers. Dad found out once that a family member owed Appalachian some tuition money, and when he heard about it, he paid
it off. He said, "Dougherty was too good to our family to be treated
this way."

Ben said the first time he ever saw Voltaire's name in a book, it
glittered like gold. He said it just stood out. He said he didn't know
why because he had never seen or heard it before.

He thought Einstein, Newton, Copernicus, and Darwin were the
four greatest minds that ever lived. Of the philosophers still living
then, he said that after Bertrand Russell, he couldn't think of a
first-rate mind left in the world. Once he said, "Einstein left his
footprint on a little ball of mud." And he thought Madame Curie
was the most wonderful woman who ever lived. Mark Twain was
his favorite author, and he also liked Clarence Darrow and Thomas

Wolfe and Burns and George Bernard Shaw and Jack London.

Altogether, he had somewhere in the neighborhood of two thousand books. He had a lot of what we called little blue books. That's really where he got started in books. They cost a nickel apiece, yet they had all the information of a big book. A young friend of his up here at the Johnson School was a thinker, and he took some of Ben's books about evolution home with him and his father found them and burned them because they were against the Bible. Of course, he thought that burning those books was the right thing to do.

So this boy came back and asked Ben what he was going to do. Dad told him not to worry about it because they had only cost a nickel apiece.

I would say he had about fifteen hundred hardbacks, though.

Dad constantly quoted from books he had read. I remember one thing he used to quote about the mob. It goes, "I have stood upon a precipice and heard them cherish and praise my name. I have gone down into the valley and heard them heap scorn and ridicule upon me." The same people will praise you, and when you get down, they will down you, but you are still the same person. I don't know where that came from, but Dad often quoted it.

My father read the Bible a lot, but he thought that it was just the history of that period and that the smartest men of that era wrote it. Einstein said, "You're at full liberty to call any power you believe in God." Dad believed this.

Once a new preacher came into this community and everybody told him about Dad being close to the Devil. The preacher was a rather broad-minded fellow, and he came up and looked at my father, and looked him over just like I would be looking at a cow or something at the county fair. He looked all around and he said, "I don't see any difference in you and anybody else." He said that everybody had told him what an awful fellow Dad was, but he said, "You look just like anybody else to me." After that, they became good friends, and they would often discuss the Bible and other things. He wouldn't criticize others for what they believed. He'd disagree with them, but he respected their rights to their thoughts. He'd disagree with the ideas—not the person.

I remember another thing Ben used to say: "There are no mysteries, only lack of understanding." He was fascinated by the nucleus of a cell, and he thought that when that was understood, we'd have the mysteries of life solved.

He had a thing with number thirteen because there were thirteen children in his family, and he had made thirteen round trips across the ocean, and his mill washed away on the thirteenth of the month. And so he tried to make a lot of things correspond with that. His baseball uniform was number thirteen; thirteen steps to the house; thirteen rooms in the house; he put thirteen millstones around the house, and he put thirteen rear ends and transmissions in the sawmill, etc.

He was very shy. He often got stage fright. But now you get him out with an individual and he would talk day and night. But to get up in front of a group, I don't guess he could have said anything. And he refused to talk on a telephone.

I wasn't interested enough to listen to him much then, but now I could listen to him for days. It bored me then because when he'd say things like, "There is no such thing as memory, only recognition," I didn't understand him. I could more understand now what he was talking about. But he often would say, "Nobody wants to talk about what I am interested in."

He was very interested in politics. He had a lot of admiration for Herbert Hoover. Thomas Jefferson and Abraham Lincoln were two more he liked. And he thought a lot of Roosevelt, but he didn't think much of Harry Truman. He said he was the biggest rascal we've ever had—another Machiavelli. He didn't like his attitude toward Russia after World War II. He always said that if we had had someone like Roosevelt after World War II that would try to make peace instead of stir up trouble, we could have really had a United Nations. But instead, we split and then divided Berlin. He liked Wendell Willkie's one-world philosophy, and he admired Henry Wallace's socialism and thought Roosevelt's success was in part due to Wallace. My father said Eisenhower always promised to straighten up our situation but never did. He had a lot of respect for Ike at first with the way he handled the McCarthy problem, but he was disappointed in the end, especially by the U-2 incident and our nation's loss of face. He at first was a little leery of Kennedy because he was a Catholic, but later he changed his mind and thought we lost a great man. Under a portrait of John that hung on his bedroom wall, he wrote, "John, by God, I hope your brother Bob wins in November."

He liked a piece Mark Twain wrote about how he once decided to write and use his influence to purify his party and draw all of the corruption out of it and make it a party he could be proud of. He went on to say that after about a year, he gave up, saying the Devil ruled all the world politically and three quarters of it spiritually.

At Appalachian, a teacher was talking about communism, and one of the kids asked the teacher what it was. He explained that it was where everybody worked and everybody shared and everything belonged to the people. My father said that it just seemed to him that that was the ideal thing. He spoke out in class and said, "Wouldn't that be better than the system we have?" And all the kids just laughed him under. In his lifetime, I've heard him remark, "I can still remember that, but now over half the population in the world lives under communism, and after all, aren't the best parts of our government, like our schools and roads, rather communistic?"

Another thing I often heard him say was that if he was setting up an ideal government and he was the ruler, he would feel like he had as just and as fair a country as possible if he could go into even the most humble home and spend a comfortable night and have a good meal. "Then," he would say, "we could boast of being on the threshold of civilization."

That's not to say that he was anti-American. He was for his country all the way, but he wanted it to work for peace and be honorable and trustworthy in its dealings with other nations. Clarence Darrow's writing greatly influenced his political views and ideals, and he quoted from Darrow more than anyone he read other than Mark Twain. In a copy of *Darrow for the Defense,* Ben underlined the quotation, "How to cross nineteenth-century capitalism with twentieth-century socialism so as to retain the best qualities of both, kill off neither parent, and breed a healthy, happy, lusty, economic child?"

He also had an appreciation for opera and classical music. His favorite piece of music was *Il Travatore Al Nostri Monti* as sung by Ernestine Schumann-Heink and Caruso with orchestra, but when working, he usually hummed, "When You and I Were Young, Maggie."

One of the things especially interesting is the intensity with which Ben read. The books he devoured are filled with margin notes that reflect how he reacted to certain passages. The flyleaves are filled with his thoughts. For example, written on the back flyleaf of Thomas Wolfe: A Biography, *by Elizabeth Nowell (Garden City, N.Y.: Doubleday & Company, 1960):*

"It takes a bit of an idiot, a bit of genius to begin some jobs. An idiot to start, a genius to finish it. I built my cement dam in 1963–64. It was almost too much for me. Delerium [sic] set in during the winter but let up in the spring."

B. O. WARD

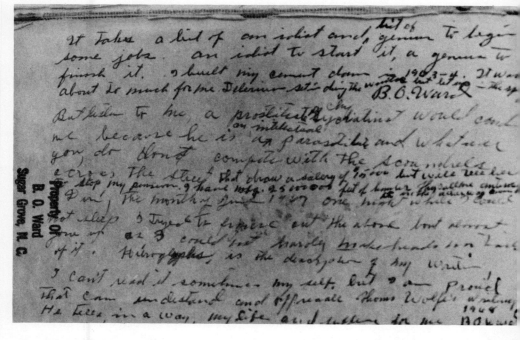

PLATE 370 The back flyleaf of *Thomas Wolfe: A Biography*, filled with Ben's thoughts.

And written underneath it later:

"But listen to me. A prostitute psychiatrist would condemn me because he is an intellectual parasite and whatever you do, don't compete with the scoundrels across the street that draw a salary of $15,000 but will tell lies to stop my pension. I have mfg. [sic] 25,000,000 feet of lumber. They call me antisocial. It is the other way around.

"During the month of June 1967, one night while I could not sleep, I tried to figure out the above but almost gave up as I could hardly make heads or tails of it. Hieroglyphics is the description of my writing. I can't read it sometimes myself. But I am proud that I can understand and appreciate Tom Wolfe's writings. He tells, in a way, my life and suffering for me."

B. O. WARD,
1968

On page 155 of the same book, beside a quotation that reads in part, ". . . the story of the sensitive young man in conflict with his environment, driven out at last, forced to flee and escape from his own town . . . ," Ward wrote: "I have been in conflict with my neighbors about religion and politics as far back as I can remember."

In Clarence Darrow for the Defense, *by Irving Stone (Garden City, N.Y.: Doubleday & Company, 1941), on a flyleaf, Ben Ward wrote, "p. 486 I agree." Page 486 reads, "I have more and more come to the firm conviction that each life is simply a short individual expression and that it soon sinks back into the great reservoir of force, where memory and the individual consciousness are at an end. I am not troubled by hopes and still less by fears."*

In other books other passages appear:

"How can judges and jurors pass sentences on their fellow men when in most cases they have done the same offense that they are passing out punishment? I as a boy stole apples from two neighbors' orchards. Later I bought the orchards and was advised that thieves were carrying off my apples by sack loads. I started on my way to commit harm, but after about ten steps, I recalled my stealing apples from under the same trees. I stopped in my tracks."

B. O. WARD,
1947

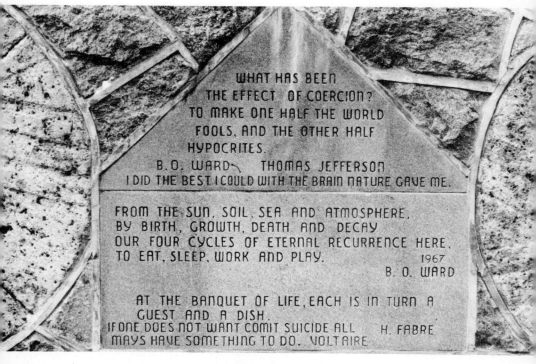

PLATE 371   One of the granite slabs Ben had engraved and set into the stone wall in front of his house.

"We never die—just change from once a guest, then a dish. All the universe is alive, some things are cold, some things are hot, and sometimes between, but always in motion and in many directions at the same time. Time is the only thing that is stationery [sic] and fixed."

"To try and raise the moral and intellectual standards of a neighborhood you live in is a gigantic task that will try your mind."

B. O. WARD,
1969

"We know our lives better than we know others', so we set out to find others that have done worse than we have, and it makes us madder than hell because we can't. Scandal-seeking is our greatest pasttime [sic], so learn to bear with us. For every sweet there is a bitter, so I have been told.

"Life, with its ups and downs, is a most wonderful experience."

B. O. WARD,
1970

Ben was so impressed with some of the literature he read that he had it printed to give to others who were visiting with him. The following pages include some of these selections, the first two pages being a document that Ben called, "My Letter."

My Letter

BY B. O. WARD

Dr. Frued says that Dementia is not a disease that destroys the intellectual capacities but to a massive blocking of the feeling process. Jung on the other hand merely repeated his opinion that the disease was an organic condition of the brain produced by a hypothetical psycho toxin. I claim they are both right. The massive blocking causes the patient great suffering which causes him to have evil thoughts against his enemies. Then psycho toxins flood the blood stream which in turn interferes with the proper actions of the many glands. Then poor digestion results and auto-intoxication followed by delerium.

I once thought of a fool remark I made months earlier and struck my jaw a blow that later abscessed, layed me up in Banner Elk Hospital for three weeks.

Not more than six months ago I was having trouble getting to sleep. In an imaginary fight I let go a haymaker and hit my right leg a fierce blow that caused me much pain. So a dog caught in a steel trap will bite everything in its reach, even its beloved master. A snake with a broken back will fight everything in its reach, even its own body. Schopenhaur says the bull dog ant of Australia, if cut in two, the head will seize the tail and the tail will sling the head, fight until dead or carried into the den by other ants. You can repeat this experiment as many times as you like with the same results every time. They are in great pain and their instinct tells them to fight.

As an automorphism, the judgment of others by analogy from the knowledge of ones self, words realize nothing, vivify nothing to you unless you have suffered in your own person the thing which the words try to describe.—Mark Twain.

Sometimes in my great suffering, my head feels like it is in the universe and my brain is the earth and dark hot vapers are coming up through the pores and whisking over the surface to eternity. These attacks last for hours. Sometimes the surface seems to be an eternal splashing sea. This must be as near Christian hell as one can get in life. No wonder some patients scream to the top of their voices. An old lady in the Smoky Mountains told me that she felt like running up and down the road hollering and screaming to the top of her voice, I told her I felt the same but we have to fight that thing. Soon after that she was confined to an asylum. I was admitted to Perry Point Veterans Hospital in 1930. A doctor told me that if I did not hold my head up and fight I was a goner. I told him I wanted all the help I could get. The morning my wife lay a corpse the rising sun looked like a boiling mass of blood. Nothing could be worse. That was August 26th, 1930.

Bodily suffering, dangers from the outer world and disturbances in our relations with our fellowman perhaps the most painful of them all. "Life can be so delightful." But the moods could change. On the 12 of March 1885 we read "I never felt so fresh in my life," and on the 21, "I can't stand it much longer." I remember thinking he was taking the matter rather personally. Suddenly, to our consternation, he fell on the floor in a dead faint. When he revived his first words were "how sweet it must be to die."—Dr. Freud.

He needed a loved friend and a hated enemy. As an automorphism and his self analysis he knew more about the suffering of mankind than any man that ever lived. He said all neurotics were in a certain sense malingers but only unconsciously so. So is a crying baby and a squealing pig. They want help and attention.

Under compulsion I speak and act
By compunction I am tortured to detraction
Then a compurgator I seek
Wishing to get compurgation
But I only get more fear and self condemnation.

Oscar Levant, being advised by someone that he needed to exercise, said it is hard to exercise without an objective. How true. Your trouble is in your head, Oscar. What a place for it to be!

A neurotic when in a disturbed state will act in a way that offends his companions and makes enemies. Something he can ill afford. If they could only know the awful suffering that he was going through they would be more forgiving. Charles Darwin was a neuroasthemic and was accused of being a shamer. He was one of the four world's greatest men. Copernacus, Newton and Einstein were the other three.

In great pain one will feel mean and act badly and his conscience will condemn him without mercy.

Few love to hear the sin they love to act.

I am afraid to think what I have done. Look on it again, I dare not.—Shakespeare.

You people want to hear me speak. While I am just a human being, tna-being, and beside if you could know some of the things I have done, you would politely leave this room. In a speech at Miami, Fla., 1924 Associated Press.—G. B. Shaw.

Tachylogia produced by scopophopia causes me discomfort and causes me to suffer with depression. Unreality is a very unpleasant feeling when it crowds.—B. O. W.

. . . It don't make no difference whether you do right or wrong, a person's conscience ain't got no sense, and just goes for him anyway. If I had a yaller dog that didn't know more than a person's conscience does I would poison him. It takes up more room than all the rest of a person's insides and yet ain't no good, nohow.—Huckleberry Fin.

I have never murdered anybody, but have read obituaries with pleasure.— Darrow.

God is life.—Leo Tolstoy

At the banquet of life each is in turn a guest and a dish.— Henry Fabre.

Everyone tells me that I look quite blooming and beautiful and most think I am shamming. But you have never been one of those and must be remembered. At this time he was miserably ill, far worse than later years, in a letter to Sir Joseph Hooker, June 13, 1849. He studied earthworms while bedridden.

If one does not want to commit suicide always have something to do.—Voltaire

He must have thought about it often. He wrote more than eighty books. If he could bear his great suffering and do great and useful work why can't I? The most effective remedy against suicide. If he could, so can I until death releases me from my miserable life.—B. O. Ward.

The most humane treatment I ever received was at Perry Point Veterans Hospital at Perry Point, Md. by the famous staff of doctors headed by Dr. Frank Leslie, Dr. Bradford and Dr. Robbins and all the personnel. But I did not get any encouragement at the three other hospitals I was in. They were malingering hounds. Their noses could not smell any other game. I have created two million dollars of wealth, crossed the Atlantic Ocean 26 times on U. S. S. Powhatan with three thousand troops, built three band sawmills, manufactured twenty five million feet of lumber, built up three run down farms, planted 100,000 young trees, built a ball diamond and a cement dam across Watauga River, took 28 insulin shocks and 22 electric shocks, yet my enemies, including doctors, condemn me. But I don't mind. When Charles Darwin had to face these jealous critics, I know what his suffering was like (automorphism) but he is one of the world's four greats. I feel better to know that suffering is a part of the game of life and must fight these things.

PLATE 372

From the sun, soil, sea and atmosphere (Eros)
By birth, growth, death and decay (Thantos)
Our four cycles of eternal recurrence here
To eat, sleep, work and play.

B. O. Ward, 1970

"The proof of how much more the world contains of pain than of pleasure is in the spectacle of two beasts, one of whom is eating the other," someone has said.—Marilyn

Love is perhaps no more than gratitude for pleasure.

I have got world game, a ranch with cattle on it, a wife and kiddies and purple grapes growing over my door, yet I am not happy—Jack London.

In a nervous breakdown one does not come to grip feelings. One just lets go everything.—Virginia Wolfe.

Inasmuch as most good things are produced by labor, it follows that all such things of right belong to those whose labor has produced them. But it has so happened, in all ages of the world, that some have labored, and others have without labor enjoyed a large proportion of the fruits. This is wrong and should not continue. To secure to each laborer the whole product of his labor as nearly as possible, is a worthy subject of any good government.

A. Lincoln

"Now, make believe you are in debt, and eaten up by relentless creditors; you are out of work—which is horse-shoeing, let us say—and can get none; and your wife is sick, your children are crying because they are hungry—"

Words realize nothing, vivify nothing to you, unless you have suffered in your own person the thing which the words try to describe. There are people who talk ever so knowingly and complacently about "the working classes", and satisfy themselves that a day's hard intellectual work is very much harder than a day's hard manual toil, and is righeously entitled to much bigger pay. Why, they really think that, you know, because they know all about the one, but haven't tried the other. But I know all about both; and so far as I am concerned, there isn't enough money in the universe to hire me to swing a pickax thirty days, but I will do the hardest kind of intellectual work for just as near nothing as you can cipher it down—and I will be satisfied, too.

Intellectual "work" is misnamed; it is a pleasure, a dissipation, and is its own highest reward. The poorest paid architect, engineer, general, author, sculptor, painter, lecturer, advocate, legislator, actor, preacher, singer is constructively in heaven when he is at work; and as for the musician with the fiddlebow in his hand who sits in the midst of a great orchestra with the ebbing and flowing tides of divine sound washing over him —why, certainly, he is at work, if you wish to call it that, but lord, it's a sarcasm just the same. The law of work does seem utterly unfair—but there it is, and nothing can change it; the higher the pay in enjoyment the worker gets out of it, the higher shall be his pay in cash, also. And it's also the very law of those transparent swindles, transmissible nobility and kingship.

Mark Twain

"What is it that makes the poor man think it is quite natural that there are fires in my palace while he is dying of cold? That I have 10 coats in my wardrobe while he goes naked? That at each of my meals enough is served to feed his family for a week? It is simply religion, which tells him that in another life I shall be only his equal, and that he has actually more chance of being happy there than I. Yes, we must see to it that the floors of the churches are open to all, and that it does not cost the poor man much to have prayers said on his tomb."

Napoleon Bonaparte

"The present position which we, the educated and well-to-do classes occupy is like that of the Old Man of the Sea, riding on the poor man's back; only, unlike the Old Man of the Sea, we are very sorry for the poor man . . . we will do almost anything for the poor man, anything but get off his neck."

Leo Tolstoy

"The inherent vice of capitalism is the unequal sharing of blessings: The inherent value of socialism is the equal sharing of blessings.

Winston Churchill, 1945
National Observer

"Everyone without any discrimination has the right to equal pay for equal work."

United Nations
Article 23

HOW TO KEEP SICK

I recently read an interesting little pamphlet on how to get sick, how to keep sick and how to make others sick.

This is welcome information and fills a long felt want.

Among the other suggestions, I note that the leading one is "Think Sickness." That is, if you want to have any particular disease, concentrate your mind upon it. There are times when a disease is very handy. When you want to dominate your husband it is often very effective to use the tyranny of tears. If you have worked up a lather of self-pity and want your wife's sympathy, it will be much easier to get it if you can come home, fall limp into a chair and roll your eyes.

Hence, if you wish to have a bad spell, say to yourself, "Day by day in every way I am feeling worse and worse."

Another valuable piece of advice is—Talk sickness.

It is well known that our words affect our opinions by a sort of reaction. Therefore, make it a point to talk about every sort of pain, itch, megrim or gripe that you may have or have had or expect to have.

Talking sickness is easy and pleasant. It gets you sympathy and attention. It is the shortest road to being conspicuous. Other pertinent hints are:

No work of any kind. Work greatly interferes with the progress of disease and sometimes even stops it. People who work right along do not seem to find time to be sick.

Eat as much as possible. Always eat a little more than you want. Particularly eat plenty of pastry. This food produces unhealthy fat and is full of various poisons which will be of great value in promoting your ailments.

Always drink ice water after meals so as to chill your stomach and prevent digestion.

When traveling, drink strange waters freely. This gives you a fine chance to get typhoid.

Don't chew your food. Bolt it. Wash it down with plenty of liquids. This saves time and is a good health preventive.

Don't think about what you eat. Eat what you like. Comfort yourself with the saying that what is one man's food is another man's poison and that nobody knows anything about diet anyway. Scorn all information regarding calories, vitamins and such nonsense.

Eat plenty of candy and drink quantities of soda water and ginger ale and the like. This will help you get rid of your teeth and also assist in securing diabetes.

Never visit a physician when you are well in order to find out how to keep from being sick. Wait till you are very ill and then call him in.

Worry as much as possible, read plenty of gloom literature and don't forget that everybody who is cheerful is a hypocrite.

PLATE 373

How can we have peace in the world when we worship a god like him?

My grandfather was a bastard so my son and four grandchildren are out of luck.

BIBLE

EXODUS 20:13 Thou shalt not kill.

DEUTERONOMY 32:2 A bastard shall not enter into the congregation of the LORD; even to his tenth generation shall he not enter into the congregation of the LORD.

I SAMUEL 15:3 Now go and smite Amalek, and utterly destroy all that they have, and spare them not; but slay both man and woman, infant and suckling, ox and sheep, camel and ass.

EXODUS 2:12 And he looked this way and that way, and when he saw that there was no man, he slew the Egyptian, and hid him in the sand.

EXODUS 4:24 And it came to pass by the way in the inn, that the LORD met him, and sought to kill him.

NUMBERS 31:16-17 Behold, these caused the children of Israel, through the counsel of Balaam, to commit trespass against the LORD in the matter of Peor, and there was a plague among the congregation of the LORD.

Now therefore kill every male among the little ones, and kill every woman that hath known man by lying with him.

MATTHEW 18:21-22 Then came Peter to him, and said, Lord, how oft shall my brother sin against me, and I forgive him? till seven times?

Jesus saith unto him, I say, not unto thee, Until seven times: but, Until seventy times seven.

MATTHEW 10:34-35-36 Think not that I am come to send peace on earth: I came not to send peace, but a sword.

For I am come to set a man at variance against his father, and the daughter against her mother, and the daughter in law against her mother in law.

And a man's foes shall be they of his own household.

MATTHEW 13:42 look it up.

LUKE 19:27 But those mine enemies, which would not that I should reign over them, bring hither, and slay them before me. Satan talking

LUKE 12:5 But I will forewarn you whom ye shall fear: Fear him, which after he hath killed hath power to cast you into hell; yea, I say unto you, Fear him.

REVELATION 2:23 And I will kill her children with death; and all the churches shall know that I am he which searcheth the reins and hearts; and I will give unto every one of you according to your works.

MAN AND HIS GODS

being just to a Christian kindness, Witch

Page 286

The accused was usually first tested in the ordeal by water, which consisted of throwing her into a river or moat; innocence was proved by sinking, guilt by swimming, the principle being that the water refused to receive those who had shaken off the baptismal water through a renunciation of their faith. Even when the ordeal by water immediately revealed that the accused was guilty, it was imperative to obtain a full confession, to which end a variety of very ingenious devices were afterward applied. There were heavy pincers to tear out the fingernails, or to be used red-hot for pinching; there was the rack, a long table on which the accused was tied by her hands and feet, back down, and stretched by rope and windless until the joints were dislocated; to this were added rollers covered with knobs or sharp spikes, which were placed under the hips and shoulders, and over which the victim was rolled back and forth; there were the thumbscrew, and instruments designed for disarticulating the fingers, Spanish boots to crush the legs and feet, metal shirts lined with knives, the Iron Virgin, a hollow instrument the size and figure of a woman, with knives so arranged inside that when the two halves of the figure were closed under pressure the accused would be lacerated in its deadly embrace. This and other devices were inscribed with the motto Soli Deo Gloria, 'Glory be only to God.' In addition there were a variety of branding irons, horsewhips, pins to be thrust beneath the nails, and various devices for suspending the accused in space, head up or head down, with weights attached. These instruments were sprayed with holy water to fortify them against the devil, and to weaken her power of silence the suspected witch was forced to drink an infusion prepared from objects that had been blessed. Official records reveal that suspects were put to eighteen successive tortures in one day, and a witch namd Holf was 'continued' fifty-six times. Then the torturer and his assistant grew tired, the hands and feet of the accused were tied, the hair was cut off and brandy poured over the head and ignited, or sulphur was burned in the arm pits or on the breast. At night the victim was chained closely to the floor or wall where she was a helpless prey to the rats and vermin which populated the bloody torture chambers.

Page 294 Billy Graham's God likes to smell burnt flesh

In 1647 the mania spread to New England and culminated in the Salem witch trials of 1692. Before it had spent itself hundreds of persons had been arrested and nineteen had been hanged, eight in one day. The Salem epidemic is notable chiefly because the shamed reaction that followed it broke the power of Cotton Mather and ended theocracy in the Colonies. During the Salem trials a dog was put to death at Andover for bewitching several people, which balanced accounts between the Eastern and Western Hemispheres; in the year 1474 a diabolical rooster, for the heinous and unnatural crime of laying an egg, had been solemnly tried, condemned and publicly burned at the sake by the church authorities of Basle.

Dr. Albert Einstein approved this book

FUNK AND WAGNALLS NEW STANDARD ENCYCLOPEDIA

Page 114 XXIV

TYNDALE, WILLIAM (1490-1536), English translator of the Bible, born in Gloucestershire. At Cambridge he came under the influence of Erasmus. In 1525 at Cologne, he began the printing of his English version of the New Testament which was completed at Worms. His translation was vigorously combated by ecclesiastical authorities in England.

Tyndale's combined translations were published as Matthew's Bible. He was taken into custody at Antwerp, and, after fifteen months' imprisonment, was tried in 1536, and on October 6 was burned at the stake.

Page 383 XXV

WYCLIF, JOHN (c. 1320-84) The influence of his teachings was widespread, and in England made him the champion of "national rights as against foreign aggression," the bulls issued against him by Pope Gregory XI in 1377 were not enforced. Tho the attitude of the government changed with the shifting of parties consequent upon the death of Edward III and the accession of Richard II, Wyclif continued to enjoy the protection that had carried him so far. Thirty years after Wyclif's death forty-five articles extracted from his writings were condemned as heretical by the Council of Constance, which ordered the bones of the heretic to be dug up and burned, a sentence executed thirteen years later.

IF I WERE GOD By Dr. William J. Robinson

Page 177-78

Jonathan Edwards (1629-1712), a gentle Christian soul, wrote as follows:

"The world will be converted into a great lake or liquid globe of fire, a vast ocean of fire, in which the wicked shall be overwhelmed, which will always be in tempest, in which they shall be tossed to and fro, having no rest day or night, vast waves or billows of fire continually rolling over their heads, of which they shall for ever be full of a quick sense within and without; their heads, their eyes, their tongues, their hands, their feet, their loins, and their vitals shall forever be full of a flowing, melting fire, fierce enough to melt the very rocks and elements; and, also, they shall eternally be full of the most quick and lively sense to feel the torments: not for one minute, nor for a hundred ages, nor for ten thousands of millions of ages, one after another, but for ever, without any end at all, and never, never be delivered."

God holds sinners in his hands over the mouth of hell as so many spiders; and he is dreadfully provoked, and he not only hates them, but holds them in the utmost contempt, and he will trampel them beneath his feet with inexpressible fierceness, he will crush their blood out, and will make it fly so that it will sprinkle his garments and stain all his raiments—Jonathan Edwards (Sinners in the Hands of an Angry God.).

Beautiful, loving sentiments!

Now no one believes in witches. Who is responsible for the torture and death of 11,000,000 that were not witches. There is no such animal. (Mark Twain

Petronius - The Satyricon

we are heading for this a great change comes ever 2000 yrs.

Nor less in Mar's Field Corruption swayed,
Where every vote was prostitute to gain;
The People and the Senate both were sold.
E'en Age itself was deaf to Virtue's voice,
And all its court to sordid interest paid,
Beneath whose feet lay trampled Majesty.
E'en Cato's self was by the crowd exiled. *song*
Whilst he who won suffused with blushes stood,
Ashamed to snatch the power from worthier hands.
Oh! Shame to Rome and to the Roman name!
'Twas not one man alone whom they exiled,
But banished Virtue, Fame and Freedom too.
Thus wretched Rome, her own destruction bought,
Herself the merchant, and herself the ware.
Besides, in debt was the whole Empire bound,
A prey to Usury's insatiate jaws; (1)
Not one could call his house, or self, his own;
But debts on debts like silent fevers wrought,
Till through the members they the vitals seized.
Fierce tumults now they to their succour call,
And War must heal the wounds of Luxury;
For Want may safely dare without a fear.
And sunk in hopeless misery, what could awake
Licentious Rome from her voluptuous trance,
But fire, and swords, and all the din of arms?
Three mighty chiefs kind Fortune had supplied,
Whom cruel Fate in various manners slew.
The Parthian fields were drunk with Crassus gore;
Great Pompey perished on the Libyan main;
And thankless Rome saw greater Julius bleed. *J.F.K .*
Thus as one soil too narrow were to hold

Their rival dust, their ashes shared the World.
But their immortal glory never dies.
'Twixt Naples and Dicharchian fields extends
A horrid Gulf immensely deep and wide,
Through which Cocytus rolls his lazy streams,
And poisons all the air with sulphurous fogs. (2)
No Autumn here e'er clothes himself with green,
Nor joyful Spring the languid herbage cheers;
Nor feathered warblers chant their mirthful strains
In vernal comfort to the rustling boughs;
But Chaos reigns, and ragged rocks abound
With naught but baleful cypress are adorned.
Amidst these horrors Pluto raised his head,
With mingled flames and ashes sprinkled o'er,
Stopped Fortune in her flight, and thus addressed:
Oh! thou whose sceptre Heaven and Earth controls!
Who had'st the power which too securely stands,
And only heap'st thy favours to resume;
Dost thou not sink beneath Rome's ponderous weight,
Unable to sustain her tottering pride?
E'en Rome herself beneath her burdens groans,
And ill sustains Monopoly of Power.
For see elate in Luxury of Spoils,
Her golden domes invade the frighted skies!
Sea's turned to land, and land is turned to sea,
And injured Nature mourns her slighted Laws.
E'en me they threaten, and beseige my Throne;
The Earth is ransacked for her treasured stores,
And in the solid hills such caverns made, (3)
That murmuring ghosts begin to hope for day.

(1) U. S. Debt $2,000,000,000,000.
(2) Fallout.
(3) Fallout Shelters.

We are in debt five(5) times what we are worth. If you own a piece of property worth $1000 then you would have to put up $4000 and you died to square you with the financial world. I hope I am in the land of delirious I am sending these leaflets to Sen. Fullbright. Jan. 22 1967

PLATE 375

On a summer day in 1970, Ray found his father lying across the front seat of his car in the garage of his home. He was dead of carbon-monoxide poisoning. He had connected a hose from his exhaust pipe to the front window of his car. Ray said later he looked like a child who had simply gone to sleep.

Ben left a suicide note in his mailbox for his son that read:

Ray,
Have my body cremated and spread my ashes over the ball field. It is nonsense to suffer this awful pain longer. Take my body from here direct to the crematory.

B. O. WARD

At the bottom of the note, he left Ray a set of directions for the mounting of the granite plaques and millstones in the walls in front of his house. Under the directions, he wrote, "The way the house will look when finished."

On one of our visits, Ray talked openly about his father's action: "He had bad nerves that were probably inherited and then aggravated by his military service. His diagnosis was dementia praecox. A professor at Appalachian State had died the same way a year or so before. Ben was looking at a local paper called the *Democrat,* and he read about it and commented to my wife, 'What an easy way to go.' He was going on seventy-five, and his physical health had given completely away. He had said that after his 1930 breakdown, for a long time there it was a lot harder to keep from committing suicide than it was to do it. And I can remember him looking at my children, his grandchildren, and saying, 'Lilly and I are not dead. See? We're living again.' "

A note Ray found later on a scrap of paper in his father's things read, "After your health breaks down, you look up into the sky and wonder how in the hell you can stand it until you can die."

B. O. WARD,
1970

At the memorial service held at Ben's baseball field, Alfred Adams, a local banker, gave a summary of Ben's accomplishments; Dexter Rominger, the same man who helped build the ball field, scattered Ben's ashes around home plate, and Ben's brother-in-law, Floyd Millsaps, read, "Building the Bridge for Him." In addition, Ben's brother, John, read a passage selected by Ray. The passage was first read by Robert C. Ingersoll at the funeral of his brother, Ebon C. Ingersoll, on May 31, 1879. It reads:

". . . This brave and tender man in every storm of life was oak and rock; but in the sunshine he was vine and flower. He was the friend of all heroic souls. He climbed the heights, and left all superstitions far below, while on his forehead fell the golden dawning of the grander day.

"He loved the beautiful, and was with color, form, and music touched to tears. He sided with the weak, the poor, and wronged, and lovingly gave alms. With loyal heart and with the purest hands, he faithfully discharged all public trusts. . . . He believed that happiness is the only good, reason the only torch, justice the only worship, humanity the only religion, and love the only priest. He added to the sum of human joy; and were everyone to whom he did some loving service to bring a blossom to his grave, he would sleep tonight beneath a wilderness of flowers.

"Life is a narrow vale between the cold and barren peaks of two eternities. We strive in vain to look beyond the heights. We cry aloud; and the only answer is the echo of our wailing cry. From the voiceless lips of the unreplying dead, there come no word; but in the night of death hope sees a star and listening love can hear the rustle of a wing.

"He who sleeps here, when dying, mistaking the approach of death for the return of health, whispered with his latest breath, 'I am better now.' Let us believe, in spite of doubts and dogmas, of fears and tears, that these dear words are true of all the countless dead.

"The record of a generous life runs like a vine around the memory of our dead, and every sweet, unselfish act is now a perfumed flower.

"And now, to you who have been chosen, from among the many men he loved, to do the last sad office for the dead, we give you his sacred dust.

"Speech cannot contain our love. There was, there is, no gentler, stronger, manlier man."

As a memorial to his father, Ray planted thirteen white pines around the periphery of the ball field, planted twenty-six white pines—one for each of Ben's trips across the ocean—along the road leading to the ball field, and he wrote the following to be engraved on a metal plate and set in a stone in center field:

PLATE 376 A stone, once intended to be cut out for a millstone, set up as a memorial to Ben.

THE BEN O. WARD BALL DIAMOND

BUILT: 1947 to 1950 by Ben. "I never claimed to be a good player, but I loved to try." He said, "If they don't play ball in heaven, I'll put in for a transfer."

MOST FUN: 1932 as a regular on the "Old Stag" team. "We never won a single game."

BEST RECORD: 13–0 as the pitcher for his team, the Avery-Watauga League Champs, in 1956.

MOST MEMORABLE GAME: On July 20, 1969 (the same day man first walked on the moon), at age seventy-three, Ben pitched seven full innings for a 5–4 win over Rich Mountain.

A disabled World War I veteran, his life was a living symbol of victory over dementia. He built a cement dam across the Watauga River, designed and built three water-powered bandmills, invented and held patents on machinery still used in the bandmill business, manufactured twenty-five million board feet of lumber, and planted over a hundred thousand trees to replace what he had used.

He studied the Bible in depth, and absorbed the works of many of our greatest thinkers. By the end of his life, he had found his touchstones: Voltaire, Darwin, Ingersoll, Burns, Darrow, Freud, Fabre, Swift, London, Russell, Shaw, Tolstoy, and Thomas Jefferson. Mark Twain was his literary idol, and he met Tom Wolfe.

He said, "I have been in conflict with my neighbors on politics and religion for as far back as I can remember."

Of the following, he was in agreement:

"The inherent vice of capitalism is the unequal sharing of blessings; the inherent value of socialism is the equal sharing of blessings."

WINSTON CHURCHILL

"I cannot conceive of a God who rewards and punishes his creatures, or has a will of the kind we experience in ourselves. The presence of a superior reasoning power which is revealed in the incomprehensible universe forms my idea of God."

ALBERT EINSTEIN

He believed that Nature had never made a mistake, and he often said, "Only change is permanent. The Universe that embraces life and death is the God I adore."

Ben died as he lived—a realist. On June 19, 1970, his ashes were scattered on this, his ball field.

In the following section, we have done our best to unravel the mysteries of Ben's sawmill and, in the process, give you some feeling for his inventiveness. Though it would take a professional engineer to explain exactly what happens in the inner workings of the mill in terms of gear ratios and force developed by the bewildering maze of recycled auto and truck transmissions and rear ends and brake drums, we have, at least, after four visits, been able to pin down the placement of all the parts and—though we still don't know why—what each does.

Not knowing all the whys still frustrates us and increases our determination to keep plugging away until we have the answers, but for the time being, we must be content with letting an air of mystery envelop the mill and increase our amazement at what Ben wrought with his ninth-grade education—a sense of mystery enhanced by the sensation that sweeps over one when Ray turns that truck steering wheel to open the water gates, and a previously silent building comes to life as every machine begins to whir and spin and the lights flicker on and the floor trembles.

The two patents in this article were obtained through the help of Charles McMullen in the U. S. Patent Office. Ray had told us some time ago that Ben had taken out several patents but he had no copies of them that he could put his hands on. On a trip to Washington where Wig had business with the National Endowment for the Humanities, student editors Stanley Masters and Boyd Queen went to the Patent Office in Crystal City, where Mr. McMullen met them and showed them how to locate the information they needed. When Wig was finished with his meeting, he went straight to the airport. At the prearranged time, Stanley and Boyd came running into the airport lobby grinning and waving copies of the patents in the air. We have included them in this section for your interest.

PLATE 377   The barn, still in use today.

Ben's inventiveness apparently found its way into any job he undertook. Bothered by a huge 50-foot-high rock outcropping right in the middle of his finest field, he solved the problem not by removing the outcropping but by building his barn around it. The barn, which is shown in Plate 377, is 140 feet long, 80 feet wide, and 60 feet high. Against the rock outcropping, Ben built two silos of poured concrete 16 feet square and 30 feet high. Plate 377 shows the sliding double doors through which they are loaded: The trucks or wagons back into the top of the barn from the back side and dump their loads directly into the silos, the open tops of which are nearly flush with the upper story's floor.

Putting this section together has been a memorable experience for all of us. We hope we have been able to capture enough of the story so that you will be as amazed as we have been at the accomplishments of a man of whom we stand in awe.

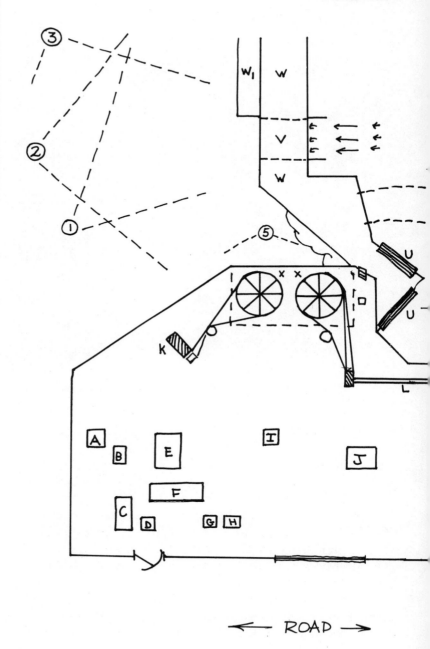

PLATE 378   Floor plan of machine shop and mill complex: (A) Shaper. (B) Key
cutter. (C) Lathe. (D) Drill press. (E) Milling machine. (F) Work bench. (G) Drill
press. (H) Power hacksaw. (I) Welder. (J) Hydraulic press for cutting out saw
teeth. (K) Generator for electricity. (L) Shaft that powers main line drive (M) via
belt (N). (O) Road providing access to log pond (P) into which logs are dumped
and floated down to log buggy (further explained in later diagrams). (Q) Fence

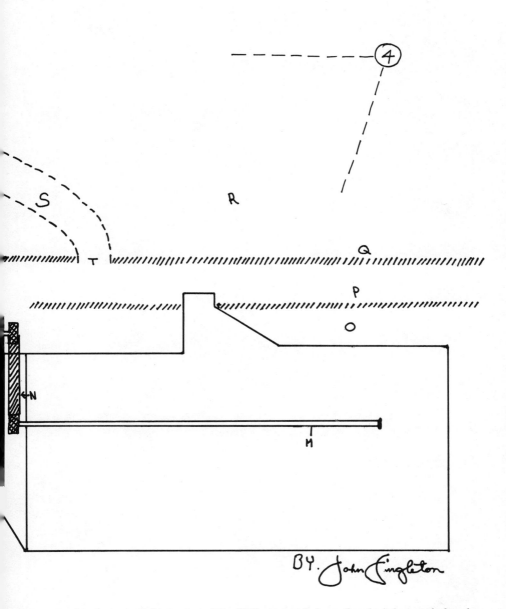

separating log pond from river (R). (S) Log pond chute for draining and cleaning
mud and trash out of log pond. (T) Gate used to open log pond chute. (U) Trash
gates for keeping debris out of waterhouse and turbine wheels. (V) Opening in
dam (W) to let excess water out. (W1) Slanted portion of dam's outside wall. (X)
Wheels connected by shafts to turbine wheels in waterhouse (see photographs
and diagrams on following pages).

PLATE 379   The dam taken from angle 1 in Plate 378.

PLATE 380   From angle 2.

PLATE 381 From angle 3 (note Ben's house visible in background).

PLATE 382 The machine shop and part of the mill taken from above the dam (angle 4 in Plate 378). Note the top of Ben's house in the background. The water is low, as Ray had the dam open when this picture was taken so he could clean out the log pond.

PLATE 383   The sawmill building as seen looking upriver from the lawn of Ben's house.

PLATE 384   The end of the sawmill building as seen from upriver looking down the length of the log pond (P in Plate 378). The square hole in the end of the wooden building is for leading scrap wood from the mill into trucks. People from the community would use it for stove wood.

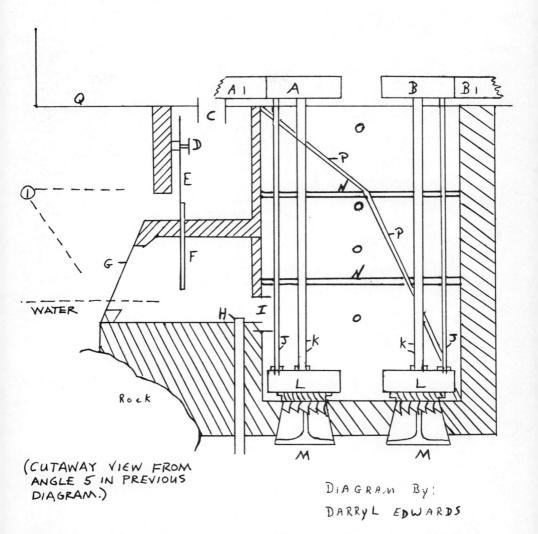

(CUTAWAY VIEW FROM ANGLE 5 IN PREVIOUS DIAGRAM.)

DIAGRAM BY:
DARRYL EDWARDS

PLATE 385   (A) Wheel that powers main line shaft in mill via belt A1. (B) Wheel that powers generator via belt B1. (C) Opening into room where main iron gate is raised and lowered manually by crank (D). (E) Threaded rod welded to top of iron gate. When gate crank is turned, it raises and lowers the gate. (F) Iron gate. When closed, the water cannot get into the waterhouse. (G) Trash gate that keeps sticks and debris out of the waterhouse. (H) Drain that drains out any water that gets past gate F when it is lowered. (I) Opening to let water into waterhouse. (J) Shafts that, when turned, open or close the gates in the turbine wheels. (K) Main shafts turned by turbine wheels. (L) Thirty-inch Sampson turbine wheels. (M) Exits for water. Set at level of water below dam. Water that exits here is called "tailwater." (N) Support beams. (O) Ends of additional support beams. (P) Ladder providing access into water house. (Q) Floor of machine shop. When the gate (F) is opened, water flows into the water house and fills it to a level of fourteen feet. The only exit, then, for the water is through one or both of the turbine wheels. When the gates in the wheels are opened, water exits turning blades, shaft (K), and upper wheels (A and B).

PLATE 386   A discarded Sampson wheel lying outside the machine shop. The top lip of the metal cone is visible on the left. Just to its right can be seen three of the metal turbine blades and the upper part of the wheel (L in plate 385). For use, the lip of the cone is bolted to the lip of the upper part of the wheel (thus concealing the blades inside the cone), and the whole assembly is set into place in the bottom of the water house and hooked up to the machinery above.

PLATE 387   The wooden spindle on which the Sampson wheel turns.

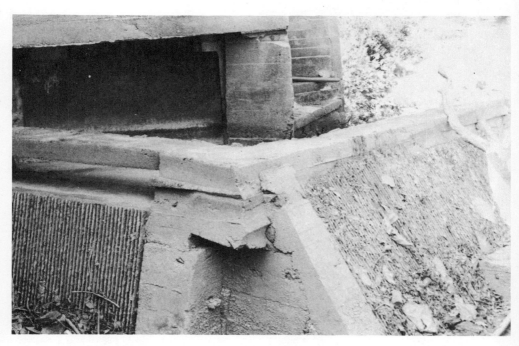

PLATE 388 The trash gates from the outside. The dark rectangular shape at the upper left is the upper third of the metal gate (F in Plate 385). The photo is taken from angle 1 on the same plate.

PLATE 389 Close-up view of a trash gate from inside the water house.

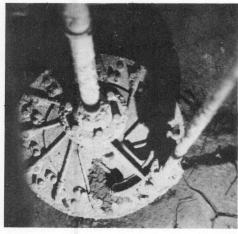

PLATE 390 The top of one of the Sampson wheels as seen looking down into the water house from an opening in the floor of the machine shop.

PLATE 391 Wheel B and belt B1 (see Plate 385) looking toward the generator.

PLATE 392 In the foreground is wheel B, and in the background is wheel A. The view is from the generator.

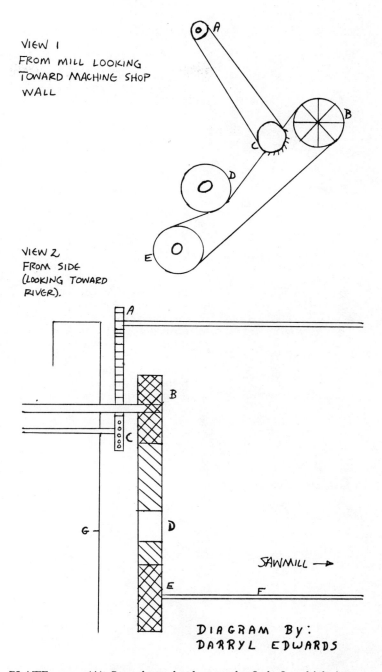

VIEW 1
FROM MILL LOOKING
TOWARD MACHINE SHOP
WALL

VIEW 2
FROM SIDE
(LOOKING TOWARD
RIVER).

SAWMILL →

DIAGRAM BY:
DARRYL EDWARDS

PLATE 393   (A) Sprocket wheel at end of shaft, which is turned by a steering wheel in the mill building. A chain connects it to sprocket wheel (C), which turns the shaft that opens the gates in the turbine wheels. (B) Wheel turned by shaft from turbine wheel. Connected by belt to wheel (E), which turns shaft that is the main line drive for the mill equipment. (D) Pressure wheel. (G) Machine-shop wall.

PLATE 394   Same as view 1 in Plate 393. The wheel that is visible is wheel B in Plate 393.

PLATE 395   In the background is the wheel (A in Plate 385) that turns the main line drive for the sawmill. Its belt turns the wheel in the left foreground, which turns a shaft (visible coming from the center of the wheel). This shaft is the same one that turns wheel B in Plate 385, and thus shaft F, the main line drive itself.

PLATE 396   A side view.

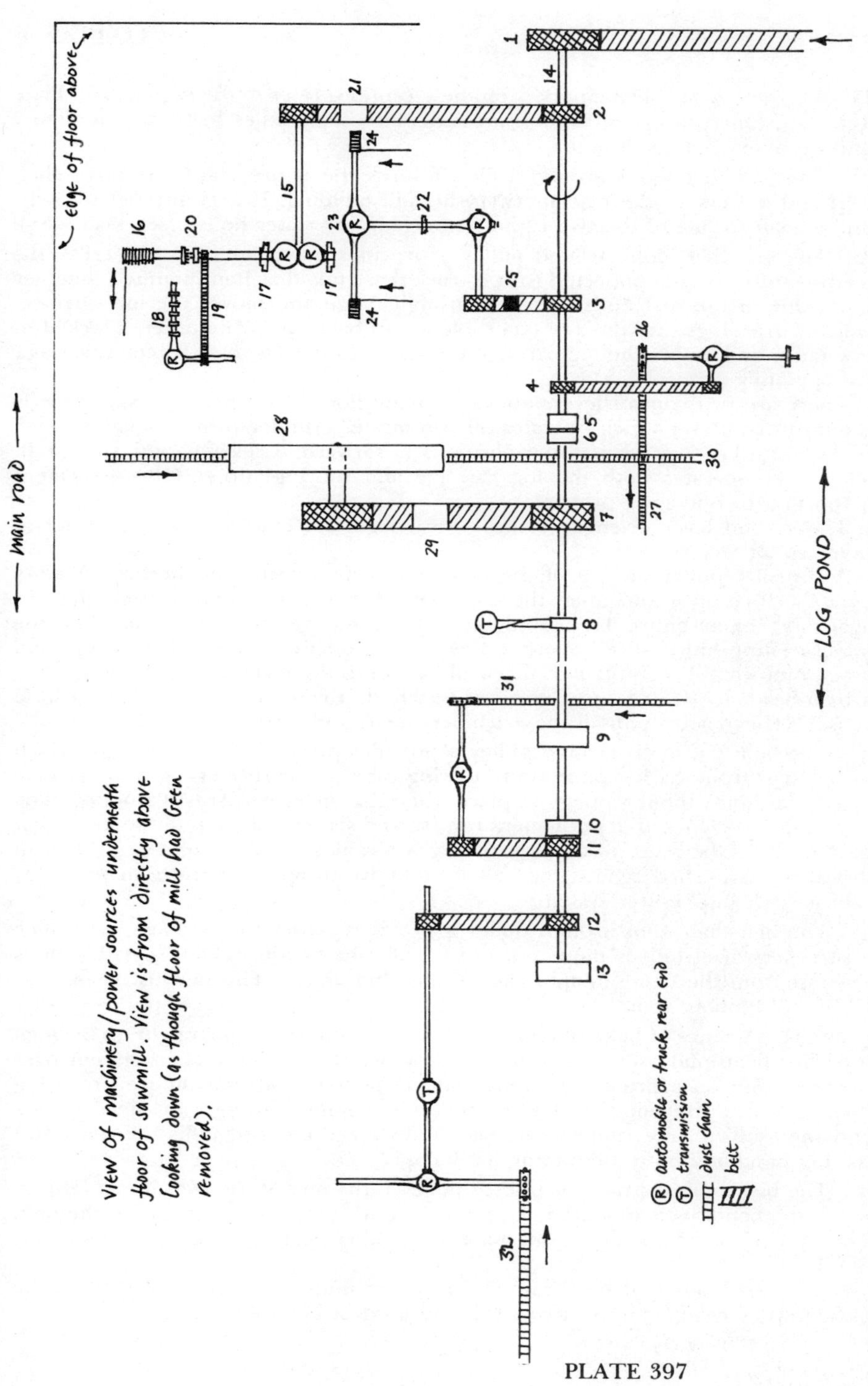

View of machinery/power sources underneath floor of sawmill. View is from directly above looking down (as though floor of mill had been removed).

← main road →

← edge of floor above

← LOG POND →

® automobile or truck rear end transmission
Ⓣ dust chain
▥▥▥ belt

PLATE 397

SEE FOLLOWING PAGES FOR CAPTION.

PLATE 397 *Note:* The numbers on these captions refer to the numbers on Plate 396. Ben called the metal wheels around which the leather belts run "pulleys," and we have used his terminology.

1. The belt that loops around pulley 1 turns the entire main line drive shaft (14) and powers all the machinery in the mill building. It is connected via belts and a shaft to one of the two turbine wheels in the water house (see Plate 385).

2. The belt that loops around pulley 2 provides power to what Ray calls "the feed"—a drive shaft connected to two truck rear ends that Ben mounted together (15). One of the rear ends is locked in high range and moves the log carriage, which carries logs into the saw (via cable at 16) backward. The other is locked in low range and moves the log carriage forward into the saw (see Patent 1,691,834 for operating principle).

There are two control levers above (at main floor level) near the saw. One is the main feed lever which operates off two master cylinders (one hooked to each brake drum [17]) giving it three positions (a forward, a reverse, and a neutral). This lever operates both the log carriage and the log turner (18—see Patent 2,100,115 for operating principle).

The second lever disengages the log carriage and engages the log turner at point 20, or vice versa.

A pressure pulley on top of the belt (21) keeps tension on the belt. A story goes that Ben once took apart the main feed to repair it and put it back together again. It took an entire day. As he finished putting everything back together, the man assisting him noticed a metal sleeve lying on the ground, held it up, and asked him what it was for. Ben threw his hat onto the ground and shouted, "I'm a bald-headed J—— C——! I'm a *registered* fool. *You're* supposed to have a little sense!" They had to pull all the machinery apart and start over again.

3. The belt that loops around pulley 3 provides power to the log buggy, which brings logs from the log pond up to the log carriage via three rails; 22 is a brake drum that holds the log buggy in place when the operator wants it stopped. The rear end (23) is locked in permanent reverse and serves only to pull the log buggy back up from the water to the log carriage via cables on two drums (24). A small drum (25) is pushed against the belt from above to apply pressure in what Ray calls a "jack slip" power system.

4. The belt that loops around pulley 4 provides power to a rear end on which a sprocket wheel (26) is mounted, which pulls the sawdust chain (27) that pulls sawdust from the bandsaw into the sawdust bin above. The sawdust chains are all one continuous loop.

5. and 6. A series of belts (the belt feed off of an old mill) go straight up through the floor from pulleys 5 and 6 to provide power to a cable that hangs out over the log pond on a drum. The cable can be pulled down and hooked to a log floating in the log pond, and when power is applied through another car rear end (not shown), the cable winds back onto the drum and pulls the log down the log pond and onto the waiting log buggy.

7. The belt mounted on this 24-inch pulley turns one of the two drums (28) on which the bandsaw is mounted. A pressure pulley (29) keeps tension on the belt. The drum's shaft turns on an old bulldozer's roller bearings, which are immersed in oil.

A sawdust chain (30) pulls sawdust out from under the saw so that it can be picked up by chain 27 and carried into the sawdust bin above.

8.   A small 2-inch belt hooks to 6-inch pulley 8 and provides power to a four-speed transmission that powers the feed rollers in the edger saw directly above. The transmission has a reverse so that boards can be fed into the edger's saws through the rollers at four different speeds, or, if fouled, can be backed out of the edger.

9.   The belt hooked to 24-inch pulley 9 goes straight up to the edger above and turns the edger saws. A pressure pulley against the belt keeps it taut.

10.   The belt that runs off pulley 10 goes straight overhead and powers the trimmer saw from above. Another belt powers the main sawdust chain (3). Plate 401 explains how this works.

11.   The belt from 12-inch 11 powers the sawdust chain (31) that removes the sawdust from beneath the edger saw blades and carries it into a bin. A sprocket wheel drives the chain, as in 26, for chain 27.

12.   The belt from pulley 12 powers a three-speed A Model transmission linked to an A Model rear end. A sprocket wheel pulls the conveyor chain (32) that carries wood scraps from the wood saw and trimmer saw up a wooden chute into the storage bin at the far end of the building.

13.   The belt from 24-inch wheel 13 goes straight up to and provides power to the wood saw above.

14.   Main line shaft.

15.   The "feed."

16.   Cable that pulls the log carriage backward and forward.

17.   Brake drums.

18.   The log turner (see patent, Plates 406–7).

19.   The chain that is the power source to the log turner.

20.   The spline that engages or disengages the log turner or log carriage.

21.   Pressure pulley.

22.   Brake drum.

23.   Rear end that pulls the log buggy.

24.   Drums with cables hooked to log buggy.

25.   Pressure pulley.

26.   Sprocket wheel that pulls sawdust chain 27.

27.   Sawdust chain.

28.   The lower hollow drum that pulls the bandsaw. The second drum, above, simply turns with the bandsaw and is called the "idler."

29.   Pressure pulley.

30.   Sawdust chain.

31.   Sawdust chain.

32.   Wood scrap conveyor chain.

PLATE 398   A view from underneath the mill's main floor of the cable that pulls the log carriage back and forth (16 in plate 397). One of the wheels of the carriage is visible on the left side just above the horizontal wooden beam that runs across the middle of the photograph.

PLATE 399   A view of the main line shaft and one of the wheels mounted on it.

PLATE 400   The end of the main line shaft. The wheels visible on the shaft are, left to right, Nos. 13, 12, and (on the right side of the small upright wooden support beam), 11/10 and 9 in plate 397.

PLATE 401   This photo is taken from angle 1 of Plate 402. Visible is wheel 10a and its belt, shaft 33 (running from upper center to the upper right corner of the photo), and the horizontal belt that runs off wheel 35.

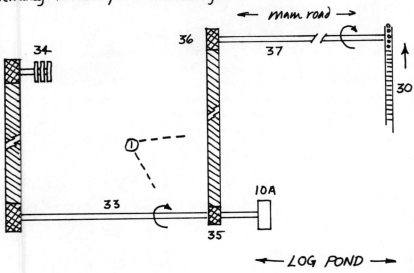

View from ceiling level looking down
at overhead power sources. Keyed
numerically to main power source diagram.

PLATE 402   (Diagram) (10a) Belt from wheel 10 in Plate 397 goes straight up
to ceiling overhead and around wheel 10a. This wheel turns a shaft (33) and, via
a belt and wheels, provides power to the V belts mounted around wheels 34.
The V belts that run on these wheels go straight down to turn the trimmer saw
below. As shaft 33 turns, it also turns wheel 35, which provides power via belt
and wheel 36 to shaft 37, on the end of which is mounted a sprocket wheel, which
pulls the main sawdust chain (30), which pulls the sawdust out from under the
bandsaw. Shaft 37 runs suspended just under the ceiling and nearly against the
posts that support the mill roof.

PLATE 403   The cable and drum arrangement described in captions 5. and 6. of Plate 397.

PLATE 404   Ray Ward, Ben's son, shows John Singleton how to activate the log turner, the patent for which is shown in Plates 406 and 407.

PLATE 405   The log turner elevated and in action.

UNITED STATES PATENT OFFICE

2,100,115

LOG TURNER

Benjamin O. Ward, Valle Crucis, N. C.

Application June 16, 1937, Serial No. 148,557

1 Claim.   (Cl. 143—102)

This invention relates to mechanical means, the general object of the invention being to provide means whereby one driven member may be driven in one direction and another in the oppo-
5 site direction at the same speed, the device being used to turn logs on a saw mill carriage.

This invention also consists in certain other features of construction and in the combination and arrangement of the several parts, to be here-
10 inafter fully described, illustrated in the accompanying drawing and specifically pointed out in the appended claim.

In describing my invention in detail, reference will be had to the accompanying drawing where-
15 in like characters denote like or corresponding parts throughout the several views and in which:—

Figure 1 is an elevation of the invention.

Figure 2 is a section on line 2—2 of Figure 1,.
20 showing how the hooks come in contact with the log.

Figure 3 is a side view of the planetary gearing.

In the drawing the numeral 1 indicates a shaft which has its ends journaled in the beams 10.
25 A pinion 2 is keyed to shaft 1, and the planetary gearing, Fig. 3, is rotatably mounted on shaft 1. Another pinion 3 is also rotatably mounted on shaft 1 and it meshes with planetary gearing 4 which meshes with pinion 2. Pinions 2 and 3 are
30 the same size. Beams (or arms) 5 and 6 are rotatably mounted on shaft 1. Sprocket 7 is rotatably mounted on shaft 1 and is fastened to the back of pinion 3. Another sprocket 8 is mounted as an idler at the top of the beams 5 and 6 in
35 line with sprocket 7. On shaft 1 a thrust collar 13 is fastened against the hub of sprocket 7 to hold the gearing in mesh and the planetary gearing is fastened to shim 19 which is bolted to beams 5 and 6 by bolts 11. Chain 9 runs on
40 sprockets 7 and 8, between which sprockets 7 and 8 on the log side of shim 19 is fastened an iron track which holds chain 9 and hooks 15 firmly against the log; hooks 15 being fastened to attachment links 16 by bolts 17. Sprocket 8 ro-
45 tates on shaft 21, and braking device 20 rests on the hub of sprocket 8 to produce necessary friction to lift beams 5 and 6 from a horizontal position to a vertical position when shaft 1 is turned toward the log; also when the shaft 1 is
50 turned in a reverse direction it is caused to return to a horizontal position so that logs may be rolled over it to the carriage. When shaft 1 ro-

tates toward the log it lifts beams 5 and 6 with the chain 9 and hooks 15 against the log 23; it then stops and as pinion 2 continues to rotate, planetary gears 22 rotate on shaft 4 meshing with pinion 3 which then rotates in a reverse direction 5 carrying with it the chain and hooks. The hooks catch in the log and turn it toward the carriage. Pinions 22 are held in place by nuts 14 on shaft 4. When power is applied (by power transmission means patented by me under Patent #1,691,- 10 834) to gear 12 it makes a very satisfactory combination.

It is to be understood that I may make changes in the construction and in the combination and arrangement of the several parts, provided that 15 such changes fall within the scope of the appended claim.

What I claim is:—

A log turner comprising a shaft, means for rotatably supporting the shaft, a pinion keyed 20 to the shaft, a second pinion, like the first, with a sprocket wheel fastened to it, rotatably mounted on the shaft, planetary gearing rotatably mounted on a cross-shaft and meshing with the two pinions, the planetary gearing being fastened 25 to two beams which are rotatably mounted on the shaft one on one side of the two pinions and the other on the other side, a second sprocket wheel mounted as an idler at the other end of the beams in line with the first sprocket wheel, an 30 endless chain with hooks attached to it running on the two sprocket wheels, a track supported by the two beams between the two sprocket wheels on the front side so as to force the hooks firmly against the log, a brake on the idler sprocket 35 wheel to furnish enough friction to lift the beams when the shaft is turned toward the log, whereby when the chain strikes the log the beams stop and as the shaft turns on, carrying with it the pinion keyed to it and as the planetary gearing 40 that is secured to the beams that support the idler sprocket wheel and chain also stop then the rotatably mounted pinion and sprocket wheel turn in an opposite direction carrying the chain with its hooks up against the log forcing it to 45 turn; power being applied to the shaft by a spur gear and pinion connected to power transmission means; the beams with the idler sprocket wheel returns to a horizontal position when the shaft is turned in a reverse direction so that logs may 50 be rolled over it to the carriage.

B. O. WARD.

PLATE 406

Nov. 23, 1937.

B. O. WARD

LOG TURNER

2,100,115

Filed June 16, 1937

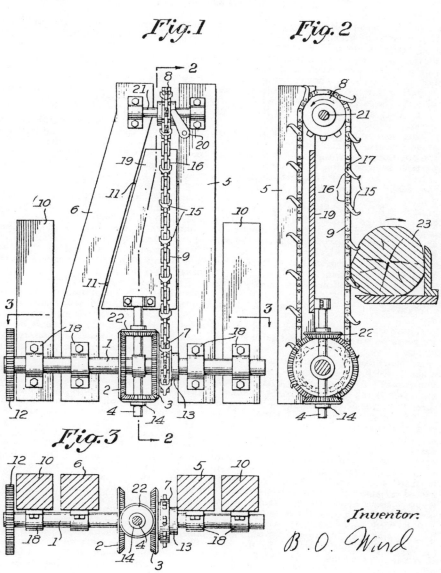

Fig.1

Fig.2

Fig.3

Inventor:

B. O. Ward

PLATE 407

UNITED STATES PATENT OFFICE.

BENJAMIN O. WARD, OF CHEOAH, NORTH CAROLINA.

POWER-TRANSMISSION MEANS.

Application filed May 25, 1928. Serial No. 280,587.

This invention relates to power transmission means, the general object of the invention being to provide means whereby the driven member may be driven in one direction at half speed and in an opposite direction at full speed, the device being useful in operating saw mill carriages and the like whereby the carriage can be moved forwardly at half speed and rearwardly at full speed.

This invention also consists in certain other features of construction and in the combination and arrangement of the several parts, to be hereinafter fully described, illustrated in the accompanying drawings and specifically pointed out in the appended claims.

In describing my invention in detail, reference will be had to the accompanying drawings wherein like characters denote like or corresponding parts throughout the several views, and in which:—

Figure 1 is a longitudinal sectional view through the invention.

Figure 2 is a section on line 2—2 of Figure 1.

Figure 3 is a section on line 3—3 of Figure 1.

Figure 4 is a view of the hollow shaft and its gears to which the central pulley is attached.

In these drawings, the numeral 1 indicates a shaft which has its ends journaled in the uprights 2. A hollow shaft 3 is rotatably mounted on the central part of the shaft 1 through means of the bushings 4 and a pulley 5 is keyed to a central enlargement 3' on said hollow shaft. Beveled pinions 6 and 7 are connected with the ends of the hollow shaft by the teeth 8, the shaft 1 passing through these pinions, as shown in Figure 1. Brake drums 9 and 10 are rotatably mounted on the shaft 1, these drums being placed adjacent the inner sides of the uprights 2 and a housing 11 is attached to the inner face of each drum by bolts or the like.

A beveled pinion 12 is arranged in each housing and one of these pinions is connected with a part of the drum 9 by the teeth 13 which are the same as the teeth 8 and the other pinion is keyed to the shaft 1, as shown at 12'. These pinions 12 are of the same size as the pinions 6 and 7 and are oppositely arranged to said pinions and are spaced therefrom. A casing 14 is placed in the housing of the drum 9 and is rotatably

mounted on the shanks of the pinions 7 and 12 in said housing, this casing enclosing the pinions 7 and 12 and a spider 15 is arranged in the casing 14 and is suitably connected therewith so that it will rotate with the casing. This spider carries a number of beveled pinions 16 which mesh with the pinions 7 and 12 and the spider is keyed to the shaft 1, as shown at 17.

A casing 18 is arranged in the housing 11 of the drum 10 and this casing is connected with the housing and the drum so that it must rotate with these parts. A spider 19 is arranged in the casing 18 and is suitably connected therewith, but this spider is not keyed to the shaft. The spider carries the pinions 20 which mesh with the pinions 6 and 12 in the housing of the drum 10. Suitable packing glands 21 are placed at the points where the shaft 1 and the hollow shaft 3 pass through the housing. A pulley 22 is fastened to one end of the shaft 1. The drums 9 and 10 are provided with the usual brake bands 23.

From the foregoing it will be seen that when the pulley 5 is connected with a suitable source of power and the bands or drum 9 contracted to prevent movement of said drum 9, the pinion 12, which is connected with the drum 9, is held stationary so that the rotary movement of the pulley 5 and the hollow shaft 3 will be communicated through the pinion 7, the pinions 16, the spider 15 to the shaft 1, as the pinions 16 travel around the pinion 12. Of course, the casing 14 will rotate with the spider. Thus the shaft 1 is driven in a forward direction at half the speed of the pulley 5. The drum 10, with its associated parts, rotate as a unit with the shaft 1 as the pinion 12 of this drum 10 is keyed to the shaft, as shown at 12'. By releasing the band of drum 9 and contracting the band on drum 10, the spider 19, associated with the drum 10, is held stationary so that the movement of the hollow shaft and its pinion 6 will cause the pinions 20 to rotate on their axes while their spider remains stationary and thus these pinions 20 will cause the gear or pinion 12 to rotate at the same speed as the gear or pinion 6 and thus the shaft 1 will be driven at the same speed as the pulley 5, though in a reverse direction. Thus it will be seen that I have provided simple means for rotating the shaft 1 at half speed in one direction and at full speed in the opposite direction.

It will, of course, be understood that the

PLATE 408

2   1,691,834

power can be applied to the pulley 22 and the pulley 5 used as the take-off pulley, but the operation will be the same.

The parts are lubricated by placing lubricant in the casings.

By allowing the brake bands to slip on the drums, different speeds can be secured, as will be understood, so that the invention provides a variable clutch and transmission.

It is thought from the foregoing description that the advantages and novel features of my invention will be readily apparent.

It is to be understood that I may make changes in the construction and in the combination and arrangement of the several parts, provided that such changes fall within the scope of the appended claims.

What I claim is:—

1. Transmission means of the class described comprising a shaft, means for rotatably suporting the shaft, a pair of brake drums rotatably mounted on the shaft, a pinion on the shaft connected with one of the drums, a second pinion on the shaft loosely associated with the other drum and fastened to the shaft, a hollow shaft rotatably mounted on the first shaft, a pinion at each end of the hollow shaft, these pinions being of the same size and oppositely arranged to the first mentioned pinions, planetary gearing keyed to the first shaft and meshing with one of the pinions of the hollow shaft and with the pinion which is connected with its drum, planetary gearing meshing with the other pinion of the hollow shaft and with the pinion which is keyed to the first shaft, means for applying power to one shaft and take-off means connected with the other shaft.

2. Transmission means of the class described comprising a shaft, means for rotatably supporting the shaft, a pair of brake drums rotatably mounted on the shaft, a pinion on the shaft connected with one of the drums, a second pinion on the shaft loosely associated with the other drum and fastened to the shaft, a hollow shaft rotatably mounted on the first shaft, a pinion at each end of the hollow shaft, these pinions being of the same size and oppositely arranged to the first mentioned pinions, planetary gearing keyed to the first shaft and meshing with one of the pinions of the hollow shaft and with the pinion which is connected with its drum, planetary gearing meshing with the other pinion of the hollow shaft and with the pinion which is keyed to the first shaft, means for applying power to one shaft, take-off means connected with the other shaft and a housing connected with each drum and enclosing the pinions and planetary gearing associated with said drum.

In testimony whereof I affix my signature.

BENJAMIN O. WARD.

PLATE 409

Nov. 13, 1928.

B. O. WARD

1,691,834

POWER TRANSMISSION MEANS

Filed May 25, 1928

2 Sheets—Sheet 1

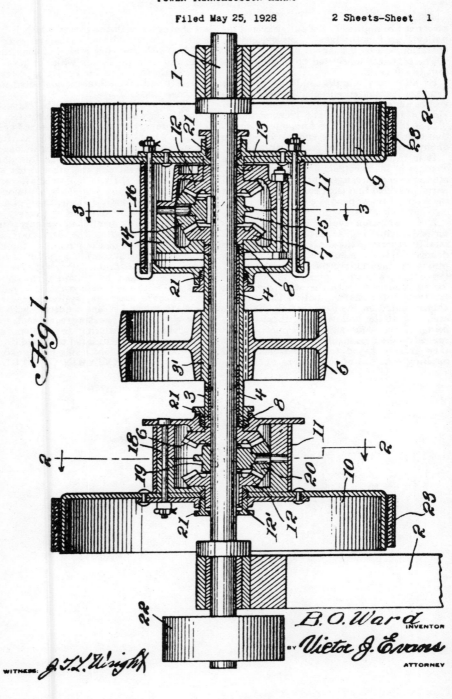

Fig. 1.

B. O. Ward
INVENTOR

BY Victor J. Evans
ATTORNEY

WITNESS: J. T. L. Wright

PLATE 410

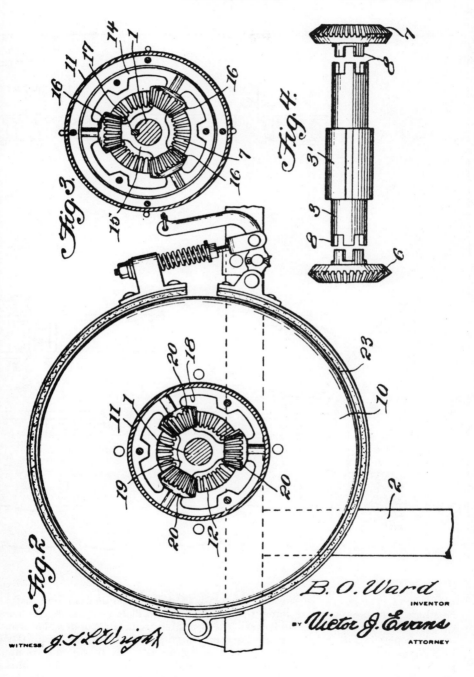

Fig.3

Fig.4.

Fig.2

B. O. Ward
INVENTOR

BY Victor J. Evans
ATTORNEY

WITNESS J. T. L. Wright

PLATE 411

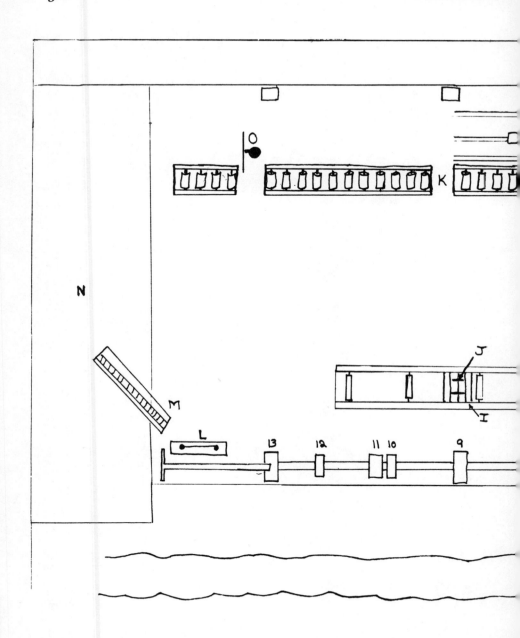

PLATE 412   FLOOR PLAN OF SAWMILL BUILDING: (A) First wheel on main line shaft. Numbers correspond to those along the main line shaft in Plate 397, which detailed the machinery/power sources underneath the floor of the mill. (B) Wooden platform on which person can stand to guide logs into the log buggy. (C) Log pond. (D) Log buggy (see Plates 414–416). (E) Steps going up into saw sharpening room. (F) Sawdust bin—receives sawdust from the bandsaw. Dust can be loaded into trucks from overhead at (G). (H) Shift lever on transmission that controls the

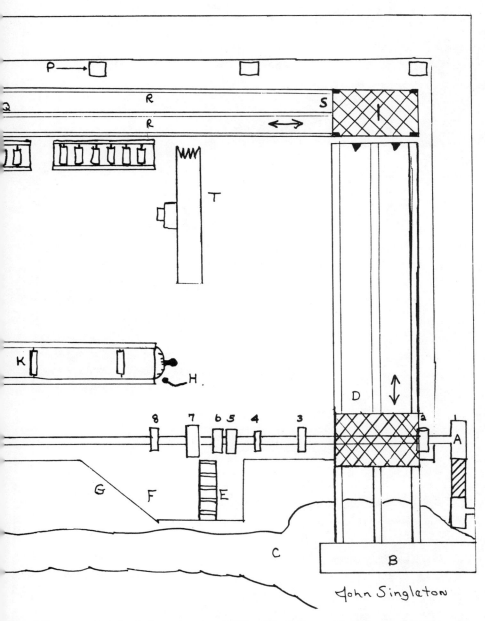

John Singleton

rollers (I) that feed the edger saws (J). (K) Rollers. (L) Wood saw, for cutting the ends off boards. (M) Conveyor belt for pulling scrap ends of lumber up into a storage bin (N) out of the way. (O) Trimmer saw for cutting boards into specific lengths. The rollers are spaced two feet apart to help in measuring. (P) Post holding up roof. (Q) Cable that pulls log carriage back and forth on rails (R). (S) Log carriage. (T) Saw.

PLATE 413   Darryl Edwards standing
on the platform (B in Plate 412) and
pushing logs into the proper position
to be picked up by the log buggy.

PLATE 414   The log buggy being
drawn up out of the log pond with its
load.

PLATE 415   The log buggy at the top
of its incline as seen from Darryl's
viewpoint.

PLATE 416   The log buggy at the end of its run inside the sawmill building. The logs can now be rolled, one at a time, onto the log carriage.

PLATE 417   With Darryl riding the log carriage, John runs a small log through the saw as Ray and his son look on. Note the gears for the log turner in the left foreground of the photo.

PLATE 418 The saw. The huge wooden door that conceals most of the top drum protects the operator in case the saw should jump off the drum. The door can be swung open for easy access to the saw.

PLATE 420 Darryl running a board through the edger saw. The gear shift operates the speed with which the rollers feed boards into the edger saw blades.

PLATE 419   The edger saw.

PLATES 421–22   The trimmer saw (O in Plate 412). The saw swings back and forth as Tim Young demonstrates.

PLATE 423 The chute and its conveyor chain, which carries wood scraps up into the storage bin.

PLATE 424 The wood saw (L in Plate 412). Boards, the ends of which are to be cut off, are laid on the swinging platform that Tim is holding. Then the platform, which is suspended from the ceiling, is swung into the stationary saw.

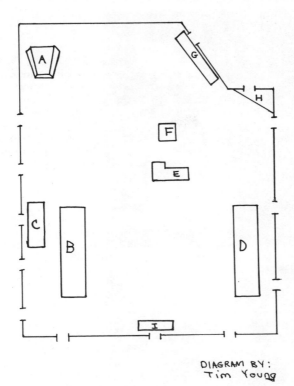

PLATE 425 (A) Stairway to filing room. (B) Saw grinder. The grinder has a carborundum stone, which cuts between the teeth of the bandsaw and lengthens the teeth. (C) Trap door in floor beside saw grinder. Blade can be slipped off saw, raised through trap door, and put onto grinder. (D) Saw workbench, where tension and welding are done to the saw blades. (E) Circle saw gummer, which performs same function as (B). (F) Belt knife, which cuts belts if they are too long or have weak sections that need to be cut out and spliced. (G) Old saw grinder. (H) Workbench. (I) Tool box.

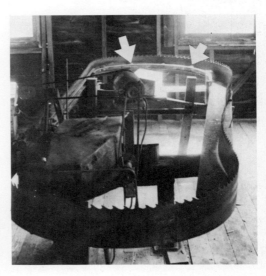

PLATE 426 Saw blade in position to be ground. Note the casters off a discarded bed on which the saw rolls (arrows).

PLATE 427 When the machine is turned on, it automatically advances the saw one tooth at a time. The carborundum wheel automatically drops into place with each advance and grinds the notch between each tooth to a preset depth.

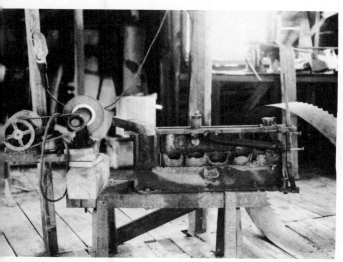

PLATE 428 Circle saw gummer mounted on the engine block Ben once smashed in anger.

PLATE 429 Saw workbench with saw blade in position to be welded.

MEMORIES OF THE AMERICAN CHESTNUT

This article is about the American chestnut tree, which grew predominantly in the eastern part of the United States, and was almost entirely killed by a blight during the first half of this century. It was a very valuable resource, and was used extensively by the people in the areas where it grew.

The article is divided into four parts. The first discusses the characteristics of the tree, and the different ways it was used here in southern Appalachia. The second covers the blight itself, how it killed off the American chestnut, and how the people here felt about it. In the third part people from Rabun County talk about the way they felt after the trees were killed, the changes that were brought about, and the adjustments they had to make. The last part includes information about research being done to develop a blight-resistant tree, and information on how to collect, store, and plant the nuts.

We decided to plant our own small experimental plot of American chestnuts. Bob Bennett, the Foxfire Environmental teacher, and some of his students built a cold frame to plant them in. We planted 25 plain nuts, 75 irradiated nuts, and 100 nuts from trees grown from irradiated nuts, as well as 11 seedlings. Out of the 200 nuts, 139 germinated, and all the seedlings lived. The point of this experimentation is to try to find a tree that is resistant to the blight. On several afternoons after school, Kim Gragg, some of Bob Bennett's students, Suzy Angier (my Foxfire adviser), and I went up to the Foxfire land to plant the chestnuts. We planted the nuts in pots filled with black woods dirt, mulched them with peat moss, and placed them in the cold frame. We plan to distribute the trees next year to people in Rabun County.

VIVIAN SPEED

Article by Georganna Rice, Anita McCoy, Terri Webb, Cam Bond, and Vivian Speed with Kim Gragg and Dovie Green.

PLATE 430 Young American chestnut tree in full bloom. PHOTOGRAPH BY E. O. MELLINGER.

PLATE 431 Foxfire students and staff planting chestnuts in pots and placing them in the cold frame.

Castanea dentata, the American chestnut, was once one of the most valuable trees growing in the United States. Its natural range was from southern Maine, west to Michigan, and south to northern Georgia and Alabama. By the middle of this century, *Endothia parasitica,* a blight that was first noted in 1904, had killed almost every last specimen. The tree grew straight and fast, often reaching heights of over one hundred feet, and diameters of seven feet at breast height. It was heavily relied on for both private and commercial use, as it was a superior source of timber, food, and tannin.

The Japanese chestnut *(Castanea crenata)* and Chinese chestnut *(Castanea mollissima)* are resistant to the blight, but are capable of carrying and spreading it. These two varieties will grow readily in the United States, but they grow much like apple trees, and are not desirable for the production of lumber. They also produce edible nuts, but in the opinion of the people we have spoken to, their nuts are not as tasty and sweet as those of the American chestnut.

The following interviews with people from our area offer some of the various ways people in the southern Appalachians used the American chestnut, and give a clear sense of its importance to the people.

MARIE MELLINGER: The American chestnut, *Castanea dentata,* was a dominant tree over most of the Appalachians. It grew to be huge, [with] a roughly uniform diameter upwards for forty or fifty feet, and that's why it was such a good source of timber. Also, the wood lasted practically forever. In 1859 an American chestnut tree somewhere on the western slope of the Great Smoky Mountains in Tennessee was reported as being thirty-three feet in circumference four

PLATE 433 An old chestnut stump.

PLATE 434 This chestnut log is still solid after being in contact with the soil for years.

feet from the ground. That's about ten or eleven feet in diameter. I was informed that in Greenbriar, North Carolina, in 1934 a large chestnut stump was found that measured thirteen feet the long way across. Wilbur Savage, a forester in the Great Smoky Mountain National Park, reported he measured a fallen, dead chestnut [that was] nine feet, six inches in diameter, and at sixty-five feet from the ground it measured four feet, eight inches [in diameter]. Those were some giant trees. And the nuts were a tremendous source of food for people, [their] animals, and wild animals, such as turkey and deer.

JAKE WALDROOP: I can show you some chestnut stumps now that are six or seven feet through, and they'd grow to be over a hundred feet tall, those chestnut trees would. Grea-a-a-at big, and they'd sprangle out, have a big clustery top to 'em. They most generally grew the straightest timber of any. As the old saying goes, "straight as a gun barrel." They didn't have too many low branches; they'd go way up without branches. On an average you could cut anywhere from three to four sixteen-foot logs out of a chestnut tree before you got into the knots. There was more chestnuts than any other one species of timber. Now you'd find some oaks and poplars once in a while that'd grow bigger than chestnuts, but if you take it on an average, the chestnut grew the biggest of any of 'em. And it grew fast. In fifteen or twenty years you could go to cutting 'em for telephone poles. And them telephone poles'd be anywhere from twenty to sixty feet long. 'Bout as fast a growing timber as there was. I imagine it was as long a lifed tree as any in the forest.

[The wood is] slow to rot. Fact of the business is, if it gets down in there where no air gets to it, I don't know whether it'd ever rot or not. Now it would eventually rot in a ditch where the air could get in there. There's old sogs that you can dig out and they'll be just as sound as can be—logs that have been laying there for hundreds of years. Old sogs. That's an old tree that's fell and gotten buried up in the dirt an' sometimes covered with moss. Now there was timber that was stronger than chestnut, but the one thing about chestnut, it was so much easier worked than the rest of it was. I suppose the chestnut would go in the softwood category.

The nuts grow inside a burr, and it's a big thing, as big as your fist, and 'long about the fall of the year when it starts frosting they'll open. Then the chestnuts fall out, and later the burr itself will drop off. I've seen them a time or two in the fall, it's come a dry spell of weather and the [burrs] would open, but there wouldn't be enough moisture, and [the nut] wouldn't get loose of the burr, and it'd stay in there. I've seen hundreds of bushels hanging up, and you couldn't pick one to eat. Then it'd start to cloud up, rain some, and it was a sight on earth—just in an hour or two the whole earth would be covered with chestnuts. The moisture would hit them, and they'd all drop out. They'd generally start falling along the latter part of September up till the middle of October. October was the main chestnut month.

We'd pick them up in the fall of the year, and whenever they went to falling a wagoner would [come through] and buy 'em and go South with 'em. Down around Toccoa and Lavonia and Athens, all the way to Atlanta, Georgia. Everywhere, selling them chestnuts.

A small little kid could pick up chestnuts. We'd get up before breakfast and go to these trees where a lot of chestnuts had fallen overnight, beat the hogs there, and pick them up. Take them to market, sell them, and get our shoes, clothes, or other things with them. We'd take 'em and boil 'em or roast 'em or just hang them out and let them dry. Now a good way to keep them through the winter—keep you something to eat all winter—was to get a big box and put [in] a layer of chestnuts, then sprinkle some salt on that, another layer of chestnuts, and sprinkle salt, and keep going. If you didn't do something like that the worms would get inside the shell.

I've seen the ground when there were just hundreds and hundreds of bushels of chestnuts on it, just laying on the ground everywhere. They were good for the squirrel, turkey, bear, hogs, and mice. The squirrels and little mice [would] put them up for their winter feed. I've chopped into a mouse den and got a peck to half a bushel. Be a little bit of a hole in the tree where they went down and started to fill it up with chestnuts. They'd put in a layer of chestnuts, a layer of mud, a layer of chestnuts, a layer of mud, and the chestnuts would stay there right like they grew, all winter. Now the chestnut supported everything. There wasn't no kind of game that roamed these mountains that didn't eat the chestnuts. Everything.

[People] used it for acidwood, pulpwood, telephone poles, cross-ties, fence rails, ditch timber, and they made furniture out of it. It made good framing and siding—you could use it about anywhere any other timber could be used. Chestnut timber could take the place of it. Back when there was plenty of it, they would cut it up in ten-foot blocks and make fence rails out of it. Everybody built their own fences with chestnut rails. It was the best splittin' timber there was—wasn't anything equal to chestnut when it came to split-ting. A good workingman, if he understood it all right, [if he] didn't have iron or steel hammers or wedges, would just make a white oak maul, then take dogwood and make a whole lot of wedges. Put them up and let them season. And when he was ready to build a fence, [he'd] take his ax and go out and chop down one of the [chestnut] trees. Then chop his logs off ten feet long and take that [wedge and maul] and split one hundred fence rails a day.

It made good firewood. Now you had to let it season—green chest-nut wouldn't burn at all. It just refused. But when it dried out it was about as good a firewood as there was; you couldn't hardly beat it for nothin'. 'Way back we'd get chestnut for our stovewood. We'd get the dead [logs], bring them in, and bust them up—law, it was the finest wood you ever seen for stovewood.

NOEL MOORE: The chestnut was a tree that before the blight hit it, was just about immune to any kind of disease or trouble of any kind. They grew up to as much as seven or eight feet in diameter, and sometimes it'd be as much as seventy or eighty feet to the first limb; just a straight tree getting up to the light. Most of the trees that were cut for commercial use were three to five feet in diameter at the butt. That makes a lot of lumber. Get five, maybe six logs off one tree. Big logs. Now the trees that grew out in the open, they'd branch out. But the ones that grew in the woods where the timber was thick, grew up very tall because they grew on up to get the light.

In the spring when the chestnuts first came out (they would bloom a little later than any other tree), they had a light, cream-colored blossom, and a big tree that grew up a hundred feet high would have a spread at the top of it a hundred feet wide, maybe. You could see them sticking up out of the woods, and it was just like big, potted flowers standing up all over the mountains. It was really a sight to see. I was just a boy then. They all died by the time I was eighteen years old, and I can remember them just as well now. We'd talk about what a good chestnut crop we were going to have. The blooms were a creamy white, big long fuzzy things, six to eight inches long. There were from one to three nuts in each burr.

The nuts were real sweet, especially if they were roasted or boiled. Didn't taste like a walnut or a pecan; nothin' else tastes like them. And the blossoms gave up one of the best honey crops we ever had. We've never had a honey crop like we did since the chestnuts died, because there's not that much nectar in the wild now. Whenever chestnuts bloomed, in the morning, early, the trees looked like just the whole tops were alive with honeybees working on getting the nectar. They'd really go for it.

We put the nuts out in the sunshine and let 'em dry and that would sweeten 'em. The sunshine would do something to the sugar, sweetened 'em. We'd always gather several bags and put 'em out on a rack and let 'em dry in the sunshine. You'd have to pour boiling water over 'em, though, to kill the eggs that were laid in 'em by some kind of insect. If you didn't, the worms would eat 'em up, and you'd have a sack full of worms. [In cooking, people] used chestnuts principally for making stuffing and they made a bread out of it, too, called nut bread. They'd beat it up [couldn't grind it in the mill because it was too soft and would gum up the mill], beat it up with a wooden mallet and mix it with meal and flour.

There were people who made their living picking up chestnuts and carrying them to the store. I've seen 'em coming out of the mountains [behind] where we lived over where Burton Lake is now. There was a big mountain back of our house with just a tremendous amount of chestnut trees on it. We'd hardly ever see these people at all, except when they came out to go to the store, and in the fall we could see 'em coming, maybe the parents and three or four kids coming down the trail. The old man would have a big coffee sack full of chestnuts on his back, and the little fellers would have smaller sacks, and even the mother would have a small sack of chestnuts caught up on her hip. They'd all trek to the store and they'd swap that for coffee and sugar and flour and things that they had to buy to live on through the winter. That's the way they made their living. You could go in the woods in the fall, and where a log had fallen across the side of the hill, and the chestnuts had rolled down against it, you could reach down and pick 'em up by the double handful.

The hogs and deer and turkeys and squirrels thrived on the nuts. Almost every year was a good year for chestnuts. We had what you call a free range here then and you had to fence your farm and fields to keep out the stock that was turned loose in the mountains. People would let their breeding stock run free in the woods, and the hogs would live on the chestnuts and acorns that they could pick up off the ground. In the fall, after [the hogs] got fat on the mast (they'd get as fat as they could and still walk), the farmers would catch 'em with dogs. That's the way they got their meat. If they wanted to cure the meat and keep it through the winter, they'd put the hogs up and feed 'em on corn for a few weeks, then butcher 'em. But the ones that was killed in the mountains, right off the mast, you had to eat 'em then, [because] you couldn't cure [the meat]. It wouldn't keep—wouldn't take salt and cure like grain-fed meat would. It was better-flavored meat, sweet and tender. You could eat all you wanted and it wouldn't hurt you. Didn't have so much grease, and what it had was mild.

One of the main uses of the chestnut tree when I was a boy was for telephone poles. They call 'em utility poles now, but back then they wasn't nothin' but telephone poles—wasn't any utility lines through this part of the country. They wouldn't use anything but chestnut back then because it would last so much longer than anything else and they could put it in the ground without having to treat it. It was light and easy to handle, and it was all handled by hand, you know. Pine is what they principally use now, but they won't use it unless it's pressure-treated or it won't last any time. But the chestnut would, it would last on and on.

They used it a lot for pulpwood when they first started to make paper—that's about the only thing they made paper out of was chestnut and poplar. They also used it for tannic acid—there's a lot of acid in the wood. Back then they would cut big enormous trees just to get the bark off 'em, and they would leave the rest of the tree just layin' there on the ground to rot. It'd be worth thousands of dollars now if we had wood like that, because it's so much better

PLATE 435 A small chestnut cabinet designed and built by Noel Moore.

wood than anything that grows in the forest now. It made better framing lumber for building houses, [it was good] for siding because it wouldn't warp or split or rot, and it would take a finish good. Then they got to using it for furniture because it takes such a good finish; it polishes good, and the grain shows up good. It's a beautiful wood.

JACK GRIST: Dad had a little grocery store in Dillard which was about fifteen by twenty feet. Most of his stock was kept under the counter because he didn't have room on the shelves to put it. And most of the store work was done by my mother when Dad was in the woods with the men cutting the poles. On his sales, a lot of the time it was a swap. A barter deal. He'd say, "Well, you brought so much chestnut, and it's worth (say) twelve dollars."

The man'd say, "Well, I need a sack of cottonseed meal, I need a dollar's worth of coffee, I need a bag of sugar." It was a swap deal. Lot of times people'd bring wood in, and on top of it they'd have a chicken coop full of hens. "How much you payin' for hens today?" "Well, so much." There was a man came every Thursday, picked those up and carried 'em to Greenville, South Carolina.

In 1924, Dad met a Georgia Power Company engineer, and he needed fifteen hundred poles twenty-five feet in length. He wanted chestnut, and he wanted 'em shipped from Dillard to whereever he wanted 'em. He asked Dad if he could get 'em for him in maybe two months. Dad said, "I'll get 'em before that if the weather's good and I can get things rolling like I want to."

The Georgia Power engineer came back to him (Dad was going along well on his delivery date), and said, "If you can give us the poles in four weeks, we'll give you a dollar for every pole." And they had ordered fifteen hundred, so that was a fifteen-hundred-dollar bonus, and he got 'em. He put everybody he could find with a crosscut saw to work. He lucked out a lot of times like that.

I don't know how many people Dad had working [for him]. I asked Rob (a man who worked with my father), one day, and he said, 'Well, if you take the families, the kids, and the teen-agers, he probably had a hundredsome. A few times I've seen a little boy eight years old, throwing a limb back out of the way, and he was helping.

I'd say that the biggest bulk of Dad's business as far as chestnut went, when it was still green, was for telephone poles, caskets, and acid wood. He was always a timber man from the time he was twenty years old. He was hauling lumber and logs way back that far. This country was literally covered with chestnut. As the saying goes, "You'd cut one down and two'd jump up in front of you." They were no trouble—they would just cut the tree and cut all the small limbs off it and load it on the wagon. In those days they didn't have trucks to haul with, so they had a couple of teams of mules or horses. They'd take the coupling out of the wagon, move it back maybe fifteen feet, and they'd load all the poles they could get on the wagon, then they'd tie a chain around them. That way they could come out the roads and into Dillard and into the pole yard. Then they'd measure twenty-five feet, and take a crosscut saw and cut the ends off. (That's what we used to cook with in the wood stove—it split real easy.)

When they were building the new road through Dillard, Dad became a good friend of the man that was building it. He, in turn, told the city officials [in Commerce, where he lived] when they needed some posts to contact Dad. Well, that spread, so the cities of Commerce, Jefferson, Brazelton, Winder, and some other towns ordered from him, and he shipped poles to each one of those towns, and they replaced the lines they had with new poles. Today you'd call him a broker. Everything he ever did was on a straight contract basis.

My dad always said that he lived out of the store, enough to live on. The money he made he made in the woods. He was just about born in the woods. He's walked just about every foot of all these hills, and he knew where every branch was.

MRS. M. C. SPEED: We used to make medicine out of the leaves, for swelling. Boil the leaves in a pot and get the juice out of them and set [the pot] off the heat and let it cool. Then bathe [the swelled area] with it. People back then had swelled feet and they'd put that on them to get rid of the swelling.

Now my daddy used to—we called it peddling. [He'd] take a mule

and a wagon and go to South Carolina with a load of stuff every week or two. When the chestnuts were in, I'd pick 'em up and get the money for 'em, and I was glad to get to pick 'em up 'cause I'd get the money for 'em. And I was stingy with 'em as I could be, I'll just tell you the truth! When I was little I thought *every* chestnut I picked up had to be sold. I did that starting when I was just a little girl, just big enough to pick 'em up. I'd go in the morning to get the ones that fell overnight. They were [usually] easy to gather, but sometimes you'd stick your finger [on the burr] and it'd hurt. You see, if the nut hadn't fallen out of the burr you could stomp on them, or sometimes you could take your fingers and pick 'em out.

DR. JOHN BROWN: When I was a child, one of my earliest recollections was of going on all-day trips to Scaly Mountain on Sundays to pick up chestnuts and chinquapins. So many of the mountains up there which are bald now at that time had tremendous chestnut trees [growing on them]. I recall one Sunday afternoon we picked up five flour sacks full of chestnuts off the ground within a matter of two hours, then were on our way back down here. We had so many we really didn't know what to do with them. We parched them, we boiled them, we used them in every way possible.

My father had a general merchandise store there at Dillard, and one of the items he carried at all times in a little yard in front of there by the railroad tracks was a little stack of chestnut wood. He got that, I suppose, from some of the sawmills around here, but the only use that I can recall for the American chestnut at that time was to make coffins, or boxes, for people. It's known for its resiliency to water damage and so forth, and the people here capitalized on that. Elb McClure was a carpenter who made most of the coffins, or boxes, around here. I remember his coming and buying enough wood from my father, chestnut wood [for a particular-sized coffin]. He had certain dimensions; he would say that he needed so many feet of chestnut wood because this was for a child, or for an adult, and he had three different-sized boxes that he constructed for burial. My father also carried a certain amount of white satin specifically to line the boxes that Mr. McClure constructed. [Mr. McClure] would take the wood to an old garage out here where there was a shop. He worked during the day and he usually made coffins in the evenings after he got off [work].

That's the only thing that I remember about the use of chestnut at that particular time. It was used to some extent for fenceposts and zigzag fences, but I don't recall any furniture being made out of it, or anyone utilizing it for paneling until it became a fairly rare and endangered wood.

The chestnut blight, *Endothia parasitica*, was first noted in New York in 1904. Some sources say it was specifically introduced via a contaminated Chinese chestnut acquired by the New York Zoological Park in 1904, while other sources say it was introduced into the New England area in the late nineteenth century and not actually discovered until 1904. It spread out from New York at a steady pace, and before the middle of this century had covered the entire natural range of the American chestnut in the eastern half of the United States. There are some isolated survivors which have either lived through the disease, or which for some unexplained reason have never gotten it.

The blight is a fungus whose spores, spread by wind, birds, squirrels, and other animals, enter the inner bark of the tree through openings in the outer bark. It penetrates the sapwood, destroys the tissue, cuts off the flow of sap, and forms cankers in the bark. The cankers may look sunken, or like a rough, corky swelling of the bark, and usually appear on the main trunk or in the crotches of larger limbs. If not arrested, the cankers will eventually girdle the tree, and the portion of the tree above the girdled area will die. The blight does not affect the roots, which may live for years after the top part of the tree dies. Many old chestnut stumps send up vigorous sprouts every year, which usually succumb to the blight after a few years. Some of the sprouts reach bearing size before they die.

Here we present some firsthand accounts from people in Rabun County that illustrate how a population dependent on the American chestnut felt about the demise of the tree.

MARIE MELLINGER: The blight is a parasitic fungus that attacks the American chestnut. In 1904 some Chinese chestnuts [were] brought into New York City and they were the host plants that carried the blight. The [Chinese chestnuts] weren't affected by the blight, but they were the host plants. From New York City, it spread all over the whole country. In 1938, eighty-five per cent of the chestnuts in the Smoky Mountain National Park had been affected or killed by the blight, so you see, it moved westward very quickly. The Latin name for the blight is *Endothia parasitica*. It actually destroys the tissues of the bark and girdles the tree, and cuts off the flow of sap. First the bark is enlarged, forming a cankerous growth, and then [it] sort of breaks open, and yellow, powdery spores come out. Those spores are spread around by the wind and by birds and by animals, and that's why [the blight] continued to spread.

JAKE WALDROOP: The blight hit here around 1938 and on up to '42 or '43. That's when it hit. It came from out of the East and was traveling West. Where we lived up yonder, [there] was bi-i-i-g chestnut country right across from us, we would [watch it], and it went right on and traveled West. You could just almost see [the trees] 'a dying, they died so fast. After that blight hit, the bark went to falling off of 'em. Two or three years after that the trunks began to [weaken] and a windstorm'd come up and it'd be awful to hear them trees 'a fallin' in the chestnut belt.

[The blight would] just hit them trees. A band'd go right around the tree and it'd girdle that tree, just go around it, and the tree would die. When we were clearin' up new ground in these coves, why you could take your ax and go to a chestnut tree and just hack it, didn't have to cut it down, just hack around it, and it would die. Well, that's what that blight did. Just went around that tree and it'd die. It grows on, still tries to grow, and some of the sprouts will get as big as my leg, then that girdle [will] come around it and it'll die. I've known of a few in the last few years that'd get up big enough to bear chestnuts and then they'd die.

People couldn't understand it at first. Finally the Forest Service found out it came from Asia, shipped over in lumber or something, got into the United States, and got started. The worst lick to ever hit the South, and the United States, in the timber line, was when they lost the chestnut timber.

NOEL MOORE: [When the blight hit], you could just see the trees dying. You could see them changing from time to time. One would

PLATE 437   Noel Moore.

die; the leaves would turn brown and fall off in the middle of the summer. Maybe the next would go ahead and finish out the summer. But people couldn't believe it. They thought they'd come back. And it moved from year to year. After people saw what was really happening, it really dawned on them what a tragedy it was. The government did some research on it when it first started getting real bad. But the old-timers in the mountains here blamed it on the worm. You'd go back and cut down a dead chestnut and it would be full of worm holes. And they thought that was what was killing the chestnut. But the worm came after the chestnut died.

The blight is a fungus that gets in the sap, under the bark. It just goes around and cuts [the sap] off, and that kills the tree. The bark is thick and you can take that and peel it off. And there's a layer almost an eighth of an inch thick that's real gummy, [full of] sweet sap. You take a knife and scrape it up and it's real good just to eat—[it has] a sweet, creamy taste. And that's what the fungus strikes. And the fungus can't live underground; that's the reason we still have a few young [sprouts] come up yet. [A sprout will] make a little sapling before the fungus happens to hit it, because the roots underground are still green. And they'll come out and grow. Usually [the trees] died pretty well in clusters. You could see [the blight] moving across the mountains from one side to the other, or from the bottom to the top.

There was a mountain just across the valley from where we were living at that time. It was a ridge like. It wasn't very tall and it was covered up completely with chestnut trees. All of 'em were young trees. They was some of 'em as much as twenty-four inches in diameter. And that's where we'd usually go to get our crop of chestnuts. But they all died in *one* summer. Every one of 'em. They just quit having nuts. There weren't any more. And there [used to be] thousands of bushels of 'em shipped out of these mountains to cities. They was sold in the fruit stands and sidewalk stores in all the big cities because everybody liked them, you know. They were cheap.

That was one of the greatest losses of natural resources that this country has ever suffered. It affected everybody that had anything to do with timber in any way because the best crop of mountain wood was completely destroyed. 'Course, it lasted several years after they all died because people kept going in the woods and getting [dead] timber. But it wasn't like it would have been if they'd kept growing and people could have kept cutting them green. What a money crop that would be on the mountains if the blight hadn't come.

After most of the chestnut in the southern Appalachians died, the gaps it left in terms of the resources it provided had to be filled. The effect on people and domestic and wild animals was great and many adjustments had to be made. In the following edited transcripts, people talk about how the loss of the tree affected them.

MARIE MELLINGER: When you go through the mountains you see what we call sprout forests. The sprouts grow up [from old stumps] and they grow up maybe ten to fifteen feet, and then the blight gets them and they die back again. But there are some big old trees left—there's one on top of Brasstown Bald [in Georgia], and the whole tree is dead except for one branch that sticks out, and that one branch blooms and bears chestnuts. Because of the grain and the silvery color, the [dead] chestnut trees are called ghosts. Wherever the bark was opened up, secondary things would get in— various kinds of fungi, worms, and bark beetles—and all the bark would come off. Chestnut wood lasts longer before it decays than any other wood, and the worm holes that people like so much in chestnut were made after the blight killed the trees.

Several species of oak, and some hickory has come in to take the place the chestnut used to fill. Even though these trees also produce nuts, people say there are fewer squirrels and turkeys than there used to be. But of course, there are a lot of other factors in there, more logging, more developments, more roads, more everything.

DR. JOHN BROWN: In 1937 there were still some chestnuts here, but not too many—not as many as there were back in the latter twenties. Then I went off [to college] and I lost track of [the chestnut] until I decided to build a home in Charleston, South Carolina, when I

PLATE 438   A tenacious old chestnut tree. (Photograph courtesy of Marie Mellinger.)

PLATE 439 Two planed planks of chestnut, light and dark.

was at the Medical University of South Carolina there. This was 1950. At that time I remembered that some of the most beautiful wood that I had ever seen, and some that was not indigenous to the Charleston area, was the American chestnut. So I came up [here] one weekend and tried my best to talk with the sawmill people around and tried to find some chestnut wood to put in the home I was building in Charleston. Lo and behold, I could find none; something had happened to the chestnut during these years of my absence from here. So I went to Scaly Mountain, where I knew that there were the most chestnuts of anywhere in this area that I had seen as a boy. I did find one sawmill man up there who had six thousand board feet of wormy chestnut which he had just stacked over in one corner of his lumberyard; no one wanted it. I mean he couldn't sell it.

So I said, "How much do you want for this?" Snow on the ground (this was wintertime), [and the wood] was covered with snow. We went over and looked at it.

He said, "Gosh, it's been here so long I'd almost give it to you to haul it off, but we do have some labor in this, so why don't you give me four hundred dollars for the whole stack."

Well, this was about four thousand board feet, as it turned out. I rented a tractor-trailer the next weekend. Snow was still on the ground, and we came all the way back up here from Charleston. Left Friday night, loaded up our chestnut, and got stuck in the snow with the tractor-trailer up there. I had to get pulled out, and I *finally* got back to Charleston on Sunday night with this load of chestnut, the most precious wood that I could have found. So we kiln-dried it and processed it. It was enough to do all of the woodwork, including the trimming and including paneling two rooms with wormy chestnut. And it was the only house in the lower part of South Carolina that had wormy chestnut in it. The newspaper, the Charleston *News Courier,* did an article on it and it was publicized quite well. We had a lot of visitors to see our house.

We moved from there in 1958 to Emory University and we had to sell our house. We certainly did hate to lose it. Then [after] I'd been at Emory for eighteen years, I moved back up here, and I do notice a lot of difference in the presence [then], and the absence [now], of the chestnut. First in the game. We used to be able to get turkeys and squirrels everywhere. I'm not certain that we had as many deer then as we do now, as you know deer forage on other things as well. But there were a lot more squirrels, and a lot more of other types of game. Turkeys in particular. I remember getting five turkeys on one hunt. You just don't see that these days. There has been a noticeable decrease in the game.

NOEL MOORE: After [the chestnuts] all died, the principal thing they used [them] for was pulpwood. The ground was coated with dead trees [and there were] dead skeletons stickin' up all over the mountains, big white skeletons. And the timber cutters would cut it in four-foot lengths and split it up and take it to paper mills, where they made it into paper. When it began to get scarce, the demand grew that much more for the worm-eaten chestnut, and all of it that had died was full of worm holes. They got to using that for finish work, for panel work—interior finishing. And the price has skyrocketed. The scarcer it got, the higher it got. You can find just a few places that you can find a tree that is sound enough that it can be sawed into lumber yet. If you can find one, you could sell

it for more than a dollar a foot; that's more than a thousand dollars a thousand board feet.

There's a man in Mountain City who has an orchard of Chinese chestnuts [which are resistant to the blight]. He has a terrible crop of them each summer, more than he can sell. But they're not as good as the wild chestnuts. They don't have a sweet nutty taste. But you can boil those or roast 'em, and that enhances the flavor. But the wild chestnuts you could eat raw, right after they fell, especially when they were green. Before they dried, they were soft and tender and you could chew 'em easy.

JAKE WALDROOP: You just can't imagine how much it changed the looks of the mountains when the chestnut timber all died. When the chestnut was there, why, it was usually a solid growth of it. And when it died, it left great patches that just looked bare. People didn't pay too much attention [when the chestnut first started dying], but later they began to realize what was happening, and they tried to save every piece of it. People go back in these mountains yet and hunt for these old sogs I told you about. Now where that blight hit 'em, first the bark would fall off, and then the wood would go to crackin'. Sun cracks. And them cracks would be about every six inches plumb around that tree, and they'd go plumb to the heart, and all you could do with that then was make pulpwood out of it.

PLATE 441 A grove of Chinese chestnuts.

It wasn't no good for saw logs. Couldn't get enough of it without a crack. But one never did get too dry or too dead but what they could get the acid out of it.

[Instead of chestnut], people'd go ahead and make crossties out of oak. Fact they could use about anything that growed for makin' crossties. But for telephone poles, they wasn't nothin' else here that they could use. Chestnut telephone poles is all they used that grow in this country. They went further down into the swampy country and got cypress. For framing you could take hemlock—it made almost as good a framing as chestnut did. You *could* make framing out of oak or poplar, but chestnut was the best framin' that they was. And people way back yonder, when they built log houses, they was all built out of chestnut. Now they could use poplar after the chestnut died out, but they preferred the chestnut 'cause it was easier worked. Most all the old log houses you see are chestnut. For fencing, now they had to change over to locust, sassafras, and mulberry for posts, but nothin' else took the place of chestnut for rails, because everything else was too hard to split. Them chestnut rails, oh you could make them—I've seen people take their ax and split a great big long log with just an ax.

Seems like the poplar come back more than anything else. Chestnuts and poplar grew more in these bigger dark coves. 'Course the chestnut grew everywhere on the south sides and all, but its main favorite was to get in these dark north coves. That's where the biggest, healthiest chestnut trees were. More moisture anytime than there is on the south side. About the time that the chestnuts disappeared, the oaks grew more, and there were lots of acorns, and the hogs made it good on them, but they usually wouldn't get as fat as they did on chestnuts.

Very seldom do you ever see [a ghost chestnut tree]. They're all down now. You might once in a while find one, but not often. Lots of stumps, and sprouts where young growth tries to come back. Some of 'em will get up maybe eight to ten inches through, then that girdle, that strip come around and it dies. That blight was the awfulest lick that the South ever got. It hurt everybody because so many people could get to work because of the trees. They could get telephone poles, or make crossties, pulpwood for tannic acid or paper. Economically, it was the worst blow this area ever had. It gave all the mountain people employment; they could work at that chestnut. A lot of people log now, but it's nothin' like it was back then when the chestnut was still here.

People have been hunting sound logs awful close, but there are still some. I know of some that are just as sound as they ever were. Cut into 'em and they'd be plumb white inside. You take this downed wormy chestnut (that's what they get out of these old sogs), get that and make paneling out of it, and I guess it's selling the highest now of any lumber on the market.

Ever since the blight affecting the American chestnut was discovered in 1904, many different methods have been employed to control and/or eradicate it, some of them very simple, and some very sophisticated. A few of the approaches have shown promise, but, so far, none of them have met with real success.

The earliest methods were basically mechanical ones, relying on the quarantine concept. The transport of infected trees was curtailed, areas containing newly affected trees were burned, and trees were clearcut in places ahead of the spreading blight. These efforts may have slowed the spread of the fungus in some areas, but were not effective in stopping it.

Much searching has been done to find individual trees that are naturally resistant to the blight, and to use them as breeding stock to replenish the forests. Some completely unaffected trees have been found, but there is a real question as to whether they are truly resistant, or whether they have somehow merely escaped infection. A greater number of trees have been found that have been affected by the blight but that are still alive, demonstrating that they have a certain amount of resistance to it. These trees are usually so isolated that they do not have other chestnut trees close enough to pollinate them, and do not always produce fertile nuts. So far a viable blight-resistant parent tree has not been found, but the search continues.

Experimentation has also been done to clone blight-resistant trees. Twigs from trees demonstrating varying degrees of resistance, but which do not bear fertile nuts, as well as twigs from vigorous sprouts that do not bear nuts, have been grafted onto rootstocks of Chinese chestnuts and chinquapins, a related tree. This method has encountered some problems with the grafts taking, but shows some promise. The point is to raise the grafted trees for seed production, and to see if trees from those seeds demonstrate resistance. Other methods of rooting twigs and sprouts have not been very successful.

Efforts have been made to breed a blight-resistant American-type chestnut artificially by pollinating American chestnuts with pollen from the blight-resistant Japanese and Chinese varieties. The idea is to end up with a hybrid combining the physical characteristics of the American tree with the blight-resistant qualities of the Japanese or Chinese. So far this technique has not resulted in a desirable hybrid that can reliably reproduce itself.

Two methods using biological controls have been experimented with. Each method is seeking to find a fungus that will both counteract the chestnut blight and be able to be implemented on a large scale. In one instance, soil from around the base of diseased trees was compressed onto the cankers, and it was found after two to three months to inhibit the growth of the fungus in each treated canker. This method, as experimented with, is not workable on any large scale. The other method, employing a hypovirulent European strain of the blight to inhibit the virulent American strain, has shown much promise. Cankers inoculated with the hypovirulent strain have either stopped growing, reduced in size, or healed completely in the great majority of test cases. Researchers are trying to determine whether or not the hypovirulent strain will spread by itself, and if not, how to distribute it artificially throughout the range of the American chestnut. Apparently the European chestnut in France and Italy is making somewhat of a natural comeback due to the hypovirulent European strain of the blight combating their virulent strain of it. Exactly what causes the hypovirulent strain to inhibit the growth of the virulent one is not completely understood.

Some researchers have worked to develop a chemical control,

or fungicide. Chemicals have been injected into the ground around the base of diseased trees, and act systemically, due to their absorption by the trees. Chemicals have also been sprayed directly onto the cankers of infected trees. The use of chemical fungicides has met with some success, but neither method would be easy to implement on a large number of trees.

Much experimentation is being done to create artificially a mutant American chestnut with all the desirable physical characteristics and blight resistance. Some work has been done with chemical mutagens, but much more has been done using high-energy radiation, especially gamma rays. The focus of this work is to create a blight-resistant mutant that will pass on its blight resistance genetically to its offspring. The irradiated seeds, called the M_1 generation, are planted and used as experimental parent stock. The trees grown from the seeds of these M_1 trees, called the M_2 generation, are the ones that geneticists are interested in, because it is in the second generation of mutants that particular genetic traits are segregated. Theoretically, it will take only one characteristically desirable M_2 tree, which will pass on these traits to its seedlings [called the M_3 generation], to develop foundation stock to repopulate our forests with blight-resistant American chestnuts. Researchers in this field are optimistic that eventually the sought-after mutant will be produced.

The following information regarding the collection and propagation of the American chestnut is summarized from material written by Dr. Albert Dietz, a research chemist who has worked for over twenty years trying to develop a blight-resistant American chestnut. This summary is geared toward the individual who will collect his or her own chestnuts from the woods and grow them on a small scale.

The best trees to select nuts from are those that have been affected by the blight but that show resistance due to the simple fact that they are still alive and producing nuts. In order to insure proper seed maturity, nuts should be harvested from a tree as soon as a few of the burrs on that tree begin to open. Carefully cut each burr off the limb close to the burr. Place the nuts in a sealed plastic bag in a basement or other cool place. Check them every day or two, extract any nuts from burrs that are opening, and pour out any collected moisture in the bag. Repeat until all nuts are removed from burrs. As the nuts are collected, seal them in a plastic bag and place in the refrigerator—desired temperature is between 0°C and 4°C, or 32°F and 40°F.

Now you may treat the nuts for the presence of the chestnut weevil, which is the larval stage of an insect that lays eggs on the burr or nut and that feeds on the nut meat. Heat a sufficient amount of water to 50°C (122°F), and, stirring gently, add the chestnuts. Maintain this temperature for twenty minutes, stirring continually. Pour off the hot water, add cold water, and allow to stand about twenty minutes, until the nuts cool to room temperature. Pour off water and wipe the nuts dry.

To store the nuts until planting time, mix them with barely moist peat moss (10–15 per cent moisture by weight) in the ratio of four parts nuts to one part peat moss. Seal in a plastic bag and store in the refrigerator at the same temperature mentioned earlier. Check nuts every two weeks for about six weeks, and if the peat moss appears to have absorbed too much moisture from the nuts, replace it with barely moist peat moss. Remove any moldy nuts, wipe them clean, and store separately, but do not dispose of them, as they may still germinate.

Check nuts by the middle of February for germination. Those that have sprouted will have to be planted immediately. Otherwise wait until late March or early April to plant. Chestnuts must be carefully planted in a suitable location. The location should have full sun and well-drained soil at least a foot deep, with a pH below pH 6, preferably pH 4.5. A sandy loam is very desirable. The area should be one in which no human or animal wastes have been allowed to accumulate, due to the possible presence of soil organisms, which can last a hundred years, and which can attack the roots of the seedlings. Work the ground to a depth of eight inches, and remove all clods and stones. Make two-inch-deep furrows six inches apart, and place nuts six inches apart in furrows with the flat side down. Press the nuts firmly into the soil, cover with one inch of loose soil, and press it down so one-half inch of soil covers the nut. Cover the entire seedbed with one or two inches of mulch, preferably peat moss, not leaves or sawdust. The seeds are still edible through August, and may have to be protected from birds and rodents. Sheet metal pounded eight inches into the ground around the bed will keep out mice, and a one-foot-high frame, covered top and sides with one-half inch of hardward cloth, will keep out the birds and squirrels. Do not use *any* fertilizer, either chemical or organic. Keep the bed free of weeds. Give the seedbed two inches of water a week during dry spells. Seeds that have been collected from the woods should sprout in roughly thirty days. Leave seedlings in the seedbed through the end of the second growing season. The next spring, transplant them one foot apart into rows four feet apart.

After two more growing seasons, transplant them to their permanent site, at least ten feet apart in rows at least ten feet apart.

Chestnut seeds may be grown in pots if you wish to give them special care. Use a foam plastic cup six inches deep, large milkshake size; "32 T 32" is stamped on the bottom of the cup, which means it has a capacity of thirty-two ounces. Make three to six one-quarter-inch holes in the side of the cup, one-fourth inch above the bottom for drainage. Place small stones in the cup one-half inch deep and fill the cup to one-half inch of the top with commercial potting soil or a fifty-fifty mixture of a sandy loam soil and peat moss for this purpose. Put one seed in each pot, cover the seed with one-half inch of soil, and water sparingly. Shade the sides of the pot but allow the full sun on the plant.

After the first growing season and in the fall before freezing weather, transplant the seedling (taking care to remove the seedling from the pot without disturbing the roots) to a nursery environment, and mulch with peat moss, wood chips, or bark chips. Do not attempt to hold the seedlings in pots over the winter. The roots will freeze and the seedlings will be lost.

The transplanting site should have the same characteristics as the seedbed. Transplanting should be done while the tree is dormant, between about October 15 and April 1. The weather should ideally be 50°–60°F and cloudy or overcast, but not raining. To protect the trees' roots, avoid days that are windy or below 44°F. Prepare the trees' new site before digging them up. Dig holes nine to twenty-four inches in diameter, depending on the size of the tree. Holes should be at least three inches deeper than the longest root—eighteen inches should be deep enough. The following instructions are for transplanting trees one at a time. Dig up the tree carefully, by first making an incision the full length of the shovel blade all around the tree about ten inches from the trunk. Then reinsert the shovel blade its full length and lift up by pushing down on the shovel handle, being careful to get the blade under the whole root system, so as not to damage the roots. Immediately wrap the root ball in burlap and carefully transfer to the new site. Unwrap the burlap and carefully place the root ball in the new hole in such a way that the tree will be planted at the same depth it was before you dug it up. Fill the hole with dirt, constantly monitoring the depth and making sure the tree is standing straight. Press the dirt down, using your full weight. Thoroughly wet the newly compacted soil with water, cover the wet soil with dry soil, and gently press the dry soil down with your foot. Stake trees that are more than five feet tall so the wind does not bend them so much that the roots are loosened in the soil. Mulch trees with two or three inches of peat moss.

We would like to extend special thanks to Dr. Albert Dietz, a research chemist from Ohio who has done a tremendous amount of research and experimentation on the American chestnut, and Katharine Bryan, the publicity director for Stronghold, Inc., in Maryland, for all the energy, expertise, and support they have given us, both in producing this article and in starting our own small experimental project of growing American chestnuts.

Stronghold, Inc., an organization committed to finding a blight-resistant American chestnut, has a limited number of seeds and seedlings available at a reasonable cost to people seriously interested in joining the effort. Individuals wishing to support Stronghold's activities may take out a membership with the organization. Included in the membership is Stronghold's *Bulletin,* informing members of their activities and the progress made in them. For information on buying seeds and seedlings, membership, and the bulletin, write to: Katharine Bryan, Publicity Director, Stronghold, Inc., 3618 Gleneagles Drive, Silver Springs, Maryland 20906.

THE HOMEPLACE

This three-part section is a result of an almost accidental merging of three separate student activities that were going on simultaneously during our 1978–79 school year.

The first began after the chance discovery of an almost complete, but abandoned, farm on a dirt road miles from any town. The log house and the log outbuildings still stood, but they were nearly hidden by brush and vines, and the sense of loneliness and loss was overwhelming. I told the students in one of my classes about it, and two of them adopted the farm as their project. The story of Hattie and Arthur Dills is the result.

The second came about through a class assignment that I make every year: Find the oldest living accessible member of your family, and with that person's help, draw a complete floor plan of the house in which he or she was raised. Label every piece of furniture, and then take each wall in turn and locate windows, doors, shelves, mirrors, pictures—everything they can remember. John Crane came up with an unexpected bonus when his grandmother, Betty, told him that she thought part of her old log homeplace, now on government land, might still be standing. John and his father spent a weekend hunting, and they found it; and because of that direct connection with a rather surprising, almost impossibly difficult past, I'm convinced John is a somewhat different human being.

The third happened when two of my students were about to interview Harvey J. Miller, an old friend of ours, for the first time, and they didn't know what to ask him. We spent an hour at a motel breakfast that day talking about it, and because Harvey is a journalist and has a keen eye for detail, I encouraged them to get Harvey to help them draw up a floor plan of his childhood home, and a map of the farm on which he was raised, knowing that each time he began to talk about a separate outbuilding, a series of recollections and stories would follow. They used that strategy, and an hour and a half later, all three were still completely engrossed. It was the best interview either of the two has ever done, and the information they collected that day meshed perfectly with what former students had already collected from Harvey.

The three projects were brought together in this section because of a troubling realization: Though for years students have documented isolated artifacts and activities from their culture, they have not yet attempted to bring these artifacts and activities together in their proper context—the total home environment in which they were used or occurred. This section is an attempt to address that need—to create something of a whole out of what, until now, has been a collection of pieces.

BEW

THE ABANDONED HOMESTEAD

At the beginning of the quarter, Wig told us about an abandoned farm nearby that sounded interesting to Shayne and me. Wig said he was riding around one day up near Cartoogachaye, North Carolina, and came to a road he'd never been down before. The dirt road went by an old homestead that consisted of several log buildings—a large main house, barn, cribs, and other outbuildings.

Jake Waldroop, an old friend we consult on many subjects, lives nearby. We went to talk to him about the farm—who owned the place and why they had moved out leaving so many of their things there. He told us that he knew the man who had lived there but that he was in poor health and several years ago had gone to stay with his sister, Hattie. He told us how to get to her house. That's how we met Arthur Dills and his sister, Hattie Dills Kenny. They told us about the farm.

The kitchen was standing when their parents bought the farm, and the main house was added to the kitchen. Hattie said, "I was four years old [when the main house was built], and I'm eighty-seven. So it was built eighty-three years ago by Pa [Vance Dills] and Tom McDaniel and Hyman Carpenter. They cut and hewed the logs and chinked them and daubed them. There was no bedrooms. They was two beds in the kitchen, four in the big house, and that's all we needed. That was a big place in there. [Upstairs in the big house] were old barrels, boxes, and such as that—just junk that they didn't want down for people to see. And Pa had poles hanging up to dry his tobacco on. We cooked on the fireplace in the kitchen. There was an iron piece that went plumb across the chimney, and there was a hook in the middle of it to hold up

PLATE 442 Mr. and Mrs. Vance Dills, parents of Hattie and Arthur.

PLATE 443 Hattie as a young woman . . .

PLATE 444 . . . and her husband.

pots. I was about sixteen years old when we got our first [wood] stove. It was a cast-iron one, four eyes. We had some big round pans that had handles on them. There were four of them."

Neither Arthur nor Hattie had been up to the old homeplace for about five years. When they went back, they found that someone had gone into the house and taken just about everything they had left. Hattie said, "Everything was tore to pieces: They broke in, tore it down, and messed it up, and it was some sight when I last

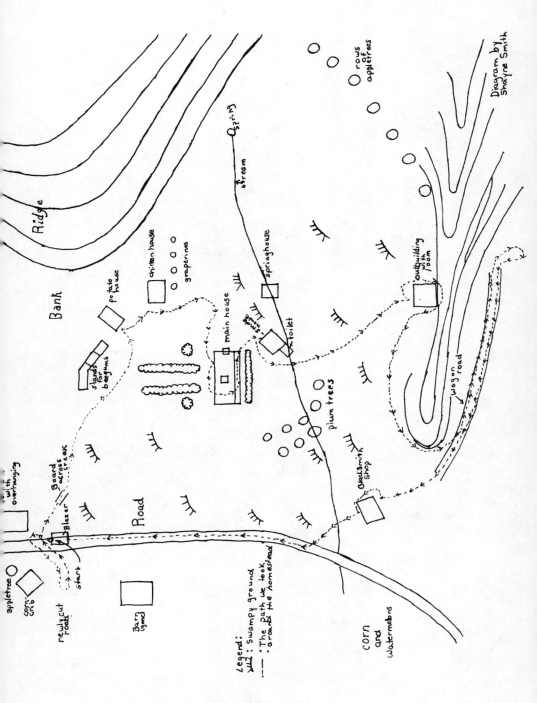

Diagram by Shayne Smith

Ridge

Bank

rows of apple trees

spring

stream

chicken house

grape vines

potato house

springhouse

main house

toilet

stands for beegums

outbuilding with room

plum trees

wagon road

Board across creek

Blazer

Road

blacksmith shop

with overhanging

start

newly cut road

corn crib

apple tree

Barn (yard)

corn and watermelons

Legend:
𝖜𝖜 : Swampy ground
--- : The path we took around the homestead

PLATE 445

PLATE 446

PLATE 448

PLATE 447

PLATE 449

seen it. They stole the organ, the guns, the sewing machine, a big cherry table, the beds, pictures, the clock, all the tools, *everything*. They stole it all."

We asked Hattie and Arthur if they would ride over to the farm someday and show us around, tell us about the buildings, what they had all been used for. So on a pretty Sunday afternoon, we all went up together and got these photographs and taped Hattie as she told us how the farm had once looked.

KIM WALL AND SHAYNE SMITH

The diagram (Plate 445) drawn by Shayne shows the path we took around the homestead, starting at our car and ending by walking up the road back to the car.

The pictures and text on the following pages are presented in sequence as Hattie took us from building to building, telling us about each area. We recorded her comments as she made her way around the once well-kept farm, remembering how it had looked in her parents' time and when Arthur, a bachelor, was in good health and lived there.

When we first got out of the Blazer, Hattie showed Kim the corn crib with the overhang (Plate 446).

"Now, across here from that post to this'un [the posts supporting the overhang, Plate 447] they had a heavy thick plank, and they made their tools on that plank, y'know, and they was put back up there [in the loft]. Tools of every kind [went in the loft]—hoes, rakes, shovels, things like that. And [they] used the back for a corn crib. Nobody didn't steal nothing then like they do now."

We asked if they kept a wagon under the overhang.

"No, they used that to throw wood and to work on their things they was a'making. Pa made a wagon under there and put it up [in the barn]. They was a big barn right here [just across the road]."

We spotted a freshly dug road and asked Hattie about it.

"Well, I'm a'gonna ask Art. Now that's all happened since we was up here, by granny.

"Art, where are you at? They're making a road here right in the middle of your field! Come here and look! (He see'd something he wants. I'm afraid he'll fall.)

"My son owns some land back in there—about twenty-one acres. Maybe they've gone over on him. Arthur! Look'a here. They're making a road in your field! (Lord, no, I've hoed corn and picked beans

and everything else many, many times there, and I want you to
look at the poplar trees. Lots can happen in twenty-five years.)

"Art, they went up there and they come right back down there.
I don't know what they're doing. They're makin' a road, it looks
like. Now come and look'a here what a one. I guess they done that
when that fire was out, man."

Art says, "That road goes on."

Hattie: "They's another one down here. I guess they done that
when that fire was out to keep it away from these buildings. That's
what I guess they done this for. They's another'n right out there.
That's what it's for. To stop that fire."

Art: "It don't amount to nothin', I don't think."

Hattie: "Now that was a corn crib [Plate 448]. They wasn't [a
loft] in the top. They wasn't even no top in it. That's a Royal red
apple tree [to the right of the crib] that my daddy set out just a
day or two before he died.

[Arthur has a roll of wire he found in the crib.] "I don't know
what he's got. Something he wants. You didn't see nothing of a
piece of chain up there [in that crib], Arthur? I'd love to have a
chain to put me a lock on that house out there down home. It'd
take a piece almost that long [about a foot]. We used to have all
kinds of log chains and trace chains that went to hook up the horses
or the steers. Had to have chains, you know."

Kim asked Hattie and Arthur if they wanted to walk to the house.

Hattie: "Well, we have to if we see anything about it. I hate to
go through this mess [the path has grown up in weeds, Plate 449].
You could see a pin in the road [they used to keep it so clean].
We kept it dug out. They great! . . . I can't get over that mud, I
don't believe . . . I'll try it [she makes it]. We had a foot log here.
We had this in cultivation right along in here [to the right of the
path].

We asked Hattie if this was the potato house [Plate 450].

"Yep. And the fruit cans were stored in it, too. Well, it's fell in.
That was once a tight place. You see, the cans went on that side
and the potatoes there. [Someone] took the door off from there, I
reckon. It's gone.

"I'd love to know what this is out here [Plate 451]. I think that
must have been the chicken house. Now, that's where we kept the
chickens.

"These old shoes have lasted, but now I can't hardly walk in
'em.

Hattie "There was some of the best grapes ever I ate [from these

PLATE 450

PLATE 451

vines beside the chicken house]. They come plumb on out here [out away from the house].

"We made potatoes in here [a nearby bottom].

"Well, you might have turned me out here and I wouldn't a'knowed it was home."

[Plate 452: A view of the main house on the left and the spring-house on the right, arrow.]

"Over there's the apple trees rotten and fell down—the first ones. Don't seem possible that that could be that big field of apples.

"Now, that's where we kept the milk and butter [that's the springhouse]. Right up yonder's the head of the spring and it came down through there, and then we had a trough that we'd catch the water in to take to the house to use. Right there at that old willow tree. And [the yard] used to be full of roses but I see they've all died. Looks to me like a wild grape vine's in it now.

"That's the apple trees. One of 'em was a horse apple and th' other one was a buff. This'un down here was a . . . now, let me see . . . I'll think of it directly.

"[There were apple trees] away up on that mountain there [Plate

PLATE 452

PLATE 453

453]. That's growed up there since we left. That field was away up yonder. You see where the old fence row went around there? Well now—it was away up there. Them trees has growed there since I left here. Yeah, they was a row of apple trees. There was a yellow apple tree, had brown spots on 'em, was the best things. And then they was two rows of apple trees went plumb across and four above them up in there.

"[The fence] went plumb around the field and down and back. All of it. No—down that way. You can't see near all of it unless you was on top of that hill there. There's where the most of the land is.

"My shoes are so slick I can't stand up. I've had one broke hip and I'd better be careful.

"I might find me a piece of chain here. There's one bench still standing there. They was two—one on each side. And this was . . . now somebody had to tear that out! I wouldn't care if that road was in Jerusalem!

PLATE 454

PLATE 455

"There's a little toilet that goes on the back. But that's the smoke-house where we kept our meat and apples [Plate 453].

"Pa set out [these flowers] just for a show. They smell good. I'll take that'un to the house. My parents set out these bushes [Plate 454]. One set one thing out and the other'n another. My dad set that out. He brought it from Georgia. But it never bore in his lifetime. It was just a little bit of a thing.

"[That blown-over evergreen] was one of them big trees. They wasn't that high [six feet] when I left here. I'll take that [sprig from the tree] home and set it out. Just put it down in the ground. That's the way he done that.

"Are we going on in? No, there's too many briars thataway. I'm just scared of slipping on these old shoes. They're slick.

"Now, boy, let me tell you, that's good to be as old as it is! [She points to the kitchen end of the house.] That was here when [our parents] moved here. And my older sister's done a hundred years old—she's dead, though—and all the rest of 'em was born here. Now, they was logs went plumb out across here and we'd set on them and this was just as pretty as it could be.

"Well, what in the name of God you reckon they done with the plank they took off from here? They've even come and got the table legs, and the [pie] safe, and the stove. Well . . . John Brown!

"This was our kitchen. You see how big it was? They've got the safe. They's an old cupboard in there but they took the glass safe and the stove.

"Looking at this thing and the way it used to be is. something else. What about them logs! [they're still in good shape, Plate 455]. Oh yeah, they keep coming and wanting to buy 'em but [Arthur] won't sell 'em."

Hattie comments to us as she looks into the living-room area,

"Now, on the other side is where the [sewing] machine was and Hyman Carpenter and Pa and Tom McDaniel built that chimney, and Pa and what little help he could get built the house. He done the fix n' of the logs.

"Now, then—when I was here before, somebody had come and broke [the bushes] all down to see it and they was just bare and look at 'em now. They're boxwoods—that's what they're called.

"And there's the big pear tree.

"I want you to look and see if you can find a little piece of chain. You know, like trace chains and such as that."

Art: "No, no—I've been all over it now, and upstairs and all."

Hattie: "The heavens and the earth! This was a beautiful floor. And there was a chimney. That's the biggest hearth rock ever I saw in my life. It'd get hot of a night and boy, it'd keep the whole house warm all night. Tore the mantelpiece down . . . um-m-m.

"Now, there's where the sewing machine was. In there. See, you can put several things in there. You know, that chimney's a'bending that way, ain't it?

"They was four beds [in the living room] and two in the kitchen. They was plenty of beds.

"Well, there's them big planks that [have] stayed there so long [Plate 456]. Somebody's cut a piece offa them. Here's where we had the coffee mill. You turned it like this to grind your green coffee after you parched it."

We asked why the coffee mill was on the porch.

"Well, we always kept it out there. [That board] was to hold the

PLATE 456   PLATE 457

mill steady. It come out here and turned thataway. Up here went a little round thing about like a teacup. Enough to pour coffee in to make a gallon. Well, then you parched it and poured it in there and then you turned the handle this way to grind it. Then you poured it in that little kettle and in a few minutes you had coffee. Parched it on slow coals in a oven. I've parched a'many, a'many panful.

"And that's the shop over there.

"Lord, have mercy! That loft's still good, ain't it? Yep. They took the beds, the springs, the quilts, the pillows, everything else. And took the top offa that dresser. It had a big glass in it."

Hattie and Kim walked through the swampy bottomland to one of the outbuildings.

"Well, you've got all the buildings now, have you?"

We told her we were still missing two.

"Well, couldn't you get 'em without me a'going over there?"

We assured her we could. We pointed out a building across the field that she didn't see.

"Straight across *where*? I don't see nary a one. You mean they's a house over there? I wanta go see it! Well, I'll go and see that. I can't remember nothing about that. How do we get over there? Scratch couldn't get through that! We're gonna cross a branch here somewhere. [Let's go] right through here. Now, there's a ditch here somewhere.

"You reckon you can cross it? Well, you cross and gimme your hand and I'll go, too! I didn't think I could jump it, but I did!"

Kim says, "Oh yeah, I knowed you could! I had faith in you!" He shows Hattie the little trail.

"I remember it now [Plate 457]. We put the potatoes back there. There's the dirt that covered them. And the loom's up there.

"They put that in there after I left here, for it was over at the

PLATE 458   PLATE 459

house up in that chicken house. There's part of it. There's a treadle. Somebody's pulled it all out. Wonder where the beam is? It was a big round thing.

"Lord, what a destruction! Destruction. Let's go on out. If I had all the cloth that'd ever been wound around on that, I wouldn't need nothing else."

We asked her if she wanted to take the loom back.

"No, I don't. It's all rotten. What could I do with that thing without the rest of it? And most of it's rotten. Let's go out here to the top of the hill and look over in the field.

"[Downstairs in this building] they kept Irish potatoes. That's all. They just called it the little outhouse."

Kim asked her why most of the buildings were built so low.

"I don't know why. I reckon they just wanted 'em that way.

"This used to be a wagon road [Plate 458]. Yeah. It ain't growed up, is it? Let's go on out there where the grape vines were. Cornfield. Find the stakes that the vines was up on. There was a long row of 'em. Right across there. That's what they call the oats—used to plant oats in it. And then down here—down in yonder—was a pasture and this here was where we made the sweet 'taters. Right along in there. And I want you to look at the trees!

"I'm gonna get me a black-gum toothbrush [Plate 459]. Birch don't chew good and soft like black gum. We used to come out over here a'toothbrush huntin' when the young'uns was asleep.

"I dropped one of them things, but one's enough.

"[Our land] ran plumb across the top of the hill out there. Wood-land. The pasture was right down in there.

"How come the road didn't grow up? Everything else did. I went up there one time—had an old broke-nose steer—to get a load of wood and he fell down—we couldn't get him up. I said to my sister, 'What'll we do with him?' He [had a pile of] wood on behind, you know.

"She said, 'Well, I don't know.' Finally we kept hollering and hollering and he got up, and we brought our kindlin' on to the house.

"If I hadn't come see'd it myself, nobody could've ever made me believe that this was the pasture. [Kim finds the fence.] Yeah, what about that?

"Right off down in there, there's two big apple trees that was the best things when they got ripe that ever was—right at the foot of this little hill.

"Law, when we was young'uns, right down in there is where we went to play. Go to Sunday school of a morning down here in a little log cabin. Come back and go down in there and play. And all of 'em's dead and gone but us that we played with. Had two horses down in there we usually rode.

"What about that! There goes the fence! It goes down yonder and back over to the road, and used to come up the road but the [new] highway tore it down.

"I remembered that little old house after we got up there to it. But I don't know who moved that loom over there. Allen, maybe. He lived there a lot after Ma and Pa died. There wasn't no electricity.

"That was the little bottom we made corn in, all the way up to where the fence went across [out from the blacksmith shop]. [Inside the blacksmith shop: Pa looked after the buildings when he was alive.] None of 'em started to fall that he didn't fix.

"They ain't a piece of chain or nothing *nowhere*. [That container was used] to drop the nails and the pieces of stuff that they were using in. And the anvil sit right there. But it's off down at town."

We asked Hattie if her father put his grape vines on a trellis.

"Oh yeah. He *tended* to his stuff. [From the grapes] we made juice and jelly and sometimes he'd make some wine. They was a sweet grape but they was red."

Hattie noticed a path.

"Wonder what they've been a'goin' out through there for? I'd love to know.

"Them plum trees is still there! Now we had fence about four feet high—palin's, they called 'em, garden palin's—a railing across

PLATE 460

PLATE 461

PLATE 463

PLATE 462

the bottom and one up here. You nailed one at the bottom and one up there—and somebody's took them all down and left—all the way around it till the chickens couldn't get in. We had chickens, guineas, ducks, geese, hogs, sheep, and cattle. And generally, one horse. Is that where we crossed the branch?

"We tended that in corn, too [between the shop and the house]. That was the garden, nothing but just vegetables. And the grape vines went all the way around the bottom there. There's some plum trees now.

"[The other side of the road] was tended in corn. And watermelons—we made watermelons up there every year.

"And I had a Irish potato patch right there. Pa was bad to move his Irish potato patch but the sweet potato patch stayed in the same place—way over yonder where we went right below the road there.

"We had plums, yeah. And they would be the best things. Now, Ma'd make all kinds of stuff out of them—preserves and jelly. Pa brought them plum trees from Georgia—*little* bitsey things.

"Makes a body feel bad to come back and look at such a mess as it's in."

We drove Hattie and Arthur back over to their house. A double-ox yoke hangs over a beam on the front porch [Plate 460], and from a tool shed behind the house, Arthur got a single-ox yoke to show us [Plate 461]. Arthur also showed us a kettle they still have that is over a hundred years old [Plate 462], and Hattie spread out a quilt she had made [Plate 463].

"WE MOVED AWAY TO . . . LICKSKILLET . . ."

Betty Crane is my grandmother. Of course I am prejudiced, but she is no ordinary grandmother. At eighty-three years of age, she lives alone, chops her own wood, and feeds wild birds chopped nuts from her hand.

While we were interviewing her about her life, she told us about the old log house she lived in when she was young. This house got my curiosity up, so my father and I went searching for it. We found it and although it was falling down, we have included accounts of it and pictures and a diagram as my grandmother remembered it. Betty Crane is a special woman and I hope you enjoy reading about her.

JOHN CRANE

Interviews and text by John Crane

My mother came from North Carolina. She was Maggie Vinson, and she married Ab Burrell. He was from Georgia. They run away and got married down at the Russell Bridge when they was young. The bridge was in South Carolina, and they crossed the bridge and got married. Mr. Russell was the justice of the peace. He was from down around Pine Mountain.

I was born in Highlands on May 19, 1895, and then we moved away to what they call Lickskillet, down under the mountain. I had ten brothers and sisters, including myself.

Poppy worked at Toxaway when they was building that dam, and then he worked at Wagner's mine if you ever knew where that was at. They mined garnets. Blue Valley. He worked them mines. I used to go down there with 'em and in them tunnels. He had his pick, and his hat with a candle holder, I guess it was, that hung on his cap. And they had a shop where they kept their picks and things. They had bellows that they pumped up there to heat their things on, and an anvil to beat them on. They made their own charcoal. They got their fire to burning and then they got dirt and covered it up and smoldered it and made coal. All them things I can remember better than I can something today. [They didn't have to have huge dirt mounds for the charcoal.] They didn't need that much. It was like a 'tater hill only bigger.

He was a dynamiter in the mines. They drilled by hand. One [would] turn the drill and the other hit it. I'd be afraid to do that, wouldn't you? I'd be afraid I'd miss! It was rough work, and every time he did a lot of blasting, he'd have a sick headache. He'd have to stay over there until the weekends, and then he'd come home. They had sheds [to stay in] and cooks to cook for them.

We didn't have no wagon at all when we lived at Lickskillet. We just had a horse that we'd ride sometimes. Go to the mill or something like that, you know. [When Poppy came home on weekends] they must have come in wagonloads from out at Toxaway to Highlands, and then he'd walk from Highlands on home. Then go back on Sunday evening.

With him gone most of the time, we had to work. We ain't like children now. Children now don't have to work like when I was growin' up. Soon as you was big enough to hold a hoe handle in your hand, you'd have to go after it. And, Lord, I've plowed many a day. Had a yoke of oxen and a turning plow after we moved to lower Tessentee. I'd plow all day with a turning plow. Used a single plow first, but after they got a turning plow, we used that—did

PLATE 465   Betty chopping
stove wood.

PLATE 464

PLATE 466   Creek near the old house where the Crane family got their water.

most of it with a mule or oxen. I used two oxen. They'd just creep along slow. I knowed how to do it. I had a whip. I didn't whip 'em much, but they was afraid I might. I had reins. Pulled 'em whichever way you wanted 'em to go. Then you would just plow one [steer] when you was cultivating with a single plow. Then they got later on they had those sweeps you could use. That would get the whole balk at once. What we called a balk was the space between the rows—just the ground. Have to run three times with a single plow.

But I was a boy when I was growing up. Didn't know much about housekeeping. Still don't know too much. I liked the outside. I still get out here every day and split the wood 'cause I just can't stand it without splitting it.

We raised tobacco. Poppy always had to have a tobacco patch where we'd have to catch the worms off the tobacco sometimes, and keep the tobacco suckered. They don't sucker it anymore like they used to. They used to take the suckers off and there was all big leaves, but they don't do that anymore. Now they don't even top tobacco anymore. We used to top it.

To put the tobacco up, Poppy'd cut it down and split the stalks down the middle into pieces and straddle them over poles, you know, and hang them up in the barn to dry. Then on damp days we had to twist the tobacco. Some used to put honey in it sometimes, but I don't think he did.

We had bees. We didn't have many gums, but we could get honey from anybody. Nearly everybody had bees back then. Hollowed-out logs [were what] you made your gums out of. Put sticks in them crosswise [for them] to build their honey on.

And we raised beans, onions, potatoes, lettuce, mustard, turnip greens, whatever we could get. We had to save our onion seed, and we'd have onions that'd make buttons on the top. Then we'd plant them and they'd make onions. Saved *all* our seed. We never knew what it was to buy them. We'd dry them and keep them in a rag of some sort—hang 'em up. [And the mice never got them.] We had cats and dogs. We never bothered about mice much.

We planted by signs. And they'd kill the hogs on a certain time of the moon. The meat'd be puffy if it was a certain time, and at other times it'd be greasy. And they say your stakes won't stay in the ground a certain time, but I've forgot just what that was. And they'd cut our hair at home and always used to put it under a rock, but I don't know why. Keep the evil spirits away, I reckon.

There were all kinds of things we believed. If a rooster crowed in the middle of the day, it was going to be falling weather. And my daddy, if a hen crowed, why, he went right out and caught her and wrung her neck quick as he could. Bad luck, he said. Bring you bad luck if you didn't kill her.

[Sometimes they told ghost stories.] Lord, it scared me to death for people to tell them. I'd be so scared I wouldn't sleep a wink. My sister, she wasn't afraid of nothing. I was afraid of the dark. She'd get me outdoors after dark and then she'd run off and leave me and just scare me to death nearly.

And I don't know if they really did or not, but there was one old lady lived down here on Gold Mine. They said she could witch anybody's cow and make her go dry, or die, or all things like that, but I never did believe it. She's dead now and I'd rather not say much about it, but didn't too many people like her.

There were peach trees all around the house. We had to clear all our land—fence it with split rails. We'd carry rails. Poppy'd split 'em. It tickles me to see people making a fence now. They don't know a thing about it. They don't put a stake in the corner—a post in the corner. What they do is put it in the wrong side. It just tickles me to see people trying. Our fences were ten rails high, and there were stakes in the corners [on the inside] to keep them from getting pushed over. We'd fence in [the gardens].

[For milking] you'd have to go and hunt [the cows]. We'd keep the milk and butter right in the spring—no springhouse. Sometimes have to go for miles hunting for the cow or the calves. Have to go maybe two or three miles to find the cow, but we had bells on them. Never lost one.

And we had chickens all over the place. Had a little barn with a loft in it to keep the feed, and little old stalls to keep the calves in. One or two stalls.

And we had our own hogs. The hogs run out, then, you know, in the forest and we had plenty of hogs. Our mark was a smooth crop and an undercrop on the left and a crop under the right. Poppy'd just get out and kill us a hog.

To cure meat—we'd put it out on the table and get it salted down and hang it up and let it dry. We'd do it in the house 'cause there wasn't no other building to do it in. And no can house. We never had any kind of cans to can. We'd put the jams in crocks and put beeswax on top. Didn't have no paraffin then. Used beeswax and a cloth towel tied on top.

Then we made leather britches beans and sauerkraut and pickled beans and things like that, you know. We made about everything we knowed how to.

And Poppy hunted. He was good at that. Turkey hunted. We used to eat coons, and I can't eat a bite of one now to save my life. We used to eat 'em when I was growing up. Stewed 'em. Seasoned 'em with a little hog meat. Sometimes Momma would put 'em in the oven after she stewed them. They was good then, but I can't eat a bite now. He took his dogs with him and he'd shoot 'em out of the trees. [He had a gun] where you had to put packing in it and your bullet and powder, and it had a hammer on it, and you had to have a cap on that hammer. When he pulled back the trigger, it made a loud bang. He had to make his own bullets. Had a thing to make 'em in, you know. He'd melt his lead and pour it in that thing [bullet mold], and as soon as it cooled, you could let [the bullet] out. He bought slabs of lead at the store, I reckon, for that. I never knowed him to kill a deer in all his life—he just didn't want to—but he'd kill hogs and coons, possums, anything thataway. Saved the hides and sold 'em. Stretched them on a board.

We ate possum then, but I don't know how we done it. Momma cooked it and I don't know how. And we had lots of squirrels. Used to be the woods was full of squirrels, but you don't see them no more. Back then you didn't have seasons, and you could hunt any time you wanted to.

A man came around once in a while and [would] buy and ship the hides. My Uncle George Vinson [was one who did it], and my Uncle Arl Snyder used to buy hides. He'd take 'em to South Carolina and sell 'em. Raccoon hide would be about seventy-five cents, and possum would be twenty-five. Poppy did trap some for minks, and he got a good price for them. He used store-bought traps.

Now our home place—listen, I hate to tell you, but it was home. It was a one-room house with no loft. Just one room. The snow would blow through sometimes and there would be three or four of us kids together sleeping on a bed, you know. Mommy'd get up of a night and there'd be snow over the top of our quilts and she'd take 'em off and shake the snow off and put 'em back on.

There wasn't any glass in the windows. Just two shutters. They opened from outside. And the door was white pine boards. He had nails for that [driven into strips that went across the boards to hold the door together]. There was a latch with a string. You just pull it if you wanted to go out or come in.

He hewed the chestnut oak logs to build it with, and Poppy made or built the house. He made the boards that covered the top. And he split boards to line the cracks of the house and he daubed them with mud, you know. And the floor was what people used to call

PLATE 467 The remains of the old house.

PLATE 469 Note the triangular pieces of wood logs that form part of the chinking.

PLATE 468 One of two wooden hooks on the outside of the old house.

PLATE 470 John looking around the fireplace of the old house.

PLATE 471 John with an old puncheon (floor piece) in interior of house.

puncheons. You know what puncheons is? They're split out of poplar in big slabs, you know, and then hewed smooth, and they're fitted onto the sills of the house and they're pretty as they can be. When you would scrub 'em with sand and lye soap, they'd just be as pretty and white.

We had to make our own brooms and scrub brushes, and sometimes we made shuck brushes, you know—have a board with holes bored in it and then you pull them shucks through there and make a shuck mop. [And for brooms] we'd go to old fields and bring broomsage in to make our brooms to sweep with. Just sage. Gather it together and put a loop in our string and pull it tight and then wrap it around to the top and then you pull the string through the stalk up there and then it'd hold. I got some down in Franklin one time and made me one that lasted for years. That's since I've been here. [Finally] wore it out.

And we had the two beds in the back end of the house, and then we had the table in the middle of the house—the eating table—and Poppy made shelves that we had the dishes on and the pots and pans. And we just cooked on the fireplace. We didn't have a stove till I was about ten years old. We cooked on the fireplace all the time. Every meal. The chimney was made out of rock daubed with mud.

[The fireplace] was in the middle of the upper end of the house. [And he put the shelves] in the corners by the fireplace. He made pegs and drove 'em in the logs for us to hang up our pots and pans with.

Then there was a split board as the fireboard. It wasn't too thick,

BETTY CRANE'S
HOME AS SHE
REMEMBERS IT.

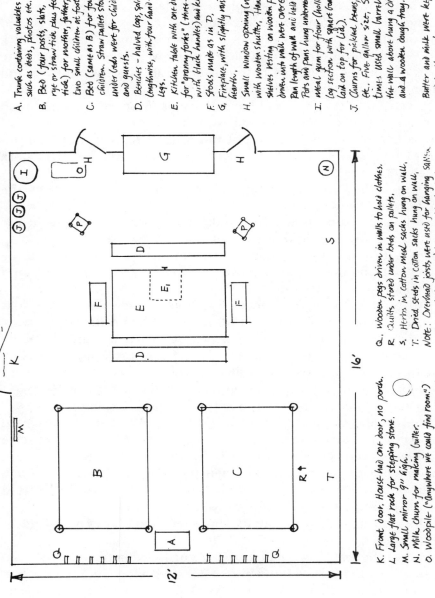

A. Trunk containing valuables such as deeds, photos etc.

B. Bed (four posts, slats, rye or straw tick plus feather tick) for mother, father, and two small children at foot.

C. Bed (same as B) for four children. Straw pallets stored under (beds were for children and guests.

D. Benches - halved logs, split lengthwise, with four hand-hewed legs.

E. Kitchen table with one drawer (E,) for "granny forks" (three-pronged with black handles) and knives.

F. Stools, made as in D.

G. Fireplace, with slightly raised hearth.

H. Small window opening (no glass) with wooden shutter. Hand split shelves resting on wooden pegs driven into wall were overhead. Pan length of wall and held dishes. Pots and pans hung underneath.

I. Meal gum for flour (hollow log section with square board laid on top for lid).

J. Churns for pickled beans, kraut, etc. Five-gallon size. Some - times used small barrels. On the wall above hung a dishpan and a wooden dough tray.

Butter and milk were kept cold in the spring.

K. Front door. House had one door, no porch.

L. Large flat rock for stepping stone.

M. Small mirror 9" high.

N. Milk churn for making butter.

O. Woodpile ("Anywhere we could find room.")

P. Ladder-back chairs with white oak split seat.

Q. Wooden pegs driven in walls to hold clothes.

R. Quilts stored under beds on pallets.

S. Herbs in cotton meal sacks hung on wall.

T. Dried seeds in cotton sacks hung on wall.

NOTE: Overhead joists were used for hanging sausage, meat, dried beans, dried pumpkin, etc. in bags.

12'   16'

PLATE 472   Betty Crane's home as she remembers it.

and he hewed it down with an adze. He got it down smooth. If he didn't like it, he'd whittle it down more. [It was held up with a peg in the wall on either side of the fireplace.]

And we didn't have no crane hung in the fireplace. We placed our wood in a way we could set our pot right on it and lay a stick around it, you know, so it couldn't turn over. And we pulled the coals out on the hearth to bake our bread in the [Dutch] oven and had a lid that went on it that you put the coals on top of the lid— and it had legs so you could have the coals under it. Cooked bread and baked sweet potatoes and Irish potatoes. Had two or three of them. And then we'd cook a pot full of leather britches and a pot full of beans, and 'taters on top of the beans, and a slab of pork in it.

Then we had a wooden tray that we made bread in [mix up the dough and knead it in the tray and then put it in the Dutch oven]. If you was cooking flour, you could make biscuits and put in the oven, or if you was baking corn bread . . . they used to get it up and put it [in oblong slabs or pones] and make maybe two or three pones out of it and put in the oven, you know. And then you could use whatever amount you wanted of it.

[At the table] we had benches that Poppy made out of logs split in half. The legs were made out of poles. We had some stools made like that, too—about eighteen inches or two feet. And the table was homemade. It had square legs, and I guess Poppy hewed it out of logs. It had what we called a knife drawer, where we kept our knives and forks and things in. It just had one drawer. He might have made some of the carving knives—I don't remember.

We had the dishpans [to wash dishes in]. We had a iron kettle that we boiled our water in for washing dishes. And we didn't have but one dishpan but we *needed* two. So we'd have to wash 'em and set 'em out on the table, and then put 'em back in the dishpan when we throwed the water out and scald 'em, you know. We used the table for a cook table and an eating table too.

The dishes was store-bought—most of them. They was kind of delft. What do you call it? Delft? Heavy.

To get the water, we had a gourd out there, and we would dip it up [from the spring] and put it in a wooden bucket. We had wooden buckets then, you know. And we'd carry it to the house. Wasn't any running water in the house. Poppy had a spring all rocked up pretty.

To wash the clothes, we had a battling bench, and we battled it on a block and then we boiled our clothes in a washpot until they was clean. After they was rinsed good, we'd hang 'em out. We just

toted 'em to the creek and rinsed them after we got them washed.
[The order was] wash 'em first, battle 'em good, and then put them
in with some soap and boil them for about thirty minutes after they
got boiling good. They was all sterilized good then. Then you take
'em out and battled on that block and then rinse them with that
rinse water.

I've helped make lye soap many a time. Sassafras stick a'stirring
it. Make it get to the right consistency. We'd drip it off our sassafras
stick to see if it was thick enough or not. Then we would put it
out in a lid or something and test it. You put grease in it to make
it, and if it don't eat up all the grease, you know it's not too strong.
I don't know why they always used sassafras. Add a little flavor.
We didn't have nothing to put in it [to give it a smell or anything,
except that]. They do now. And when they make it, they make it
where they have a [store-bought] lye now, and I don't know how
to make that. But we'd keep ours in an old jar or jug or something.
We didn't have much that got hard like they do with [store-bought
lye now]. They can make it in squares or thin. But we always had
a jug with lye soap. We didn't have no fancy soap then. We'd wash
the clothes with it, and we'd wash the dishes with it.

And we had one or two chairs. No rug. We never knew what a
rug was.

[There was no footmat outside the cabin.] Nothing but a high,
flat rock—steppingstone. No porch.

And on the puncheon floor here, there was marks cut on it to
tell the time of day when the sun shines. It done pretty good. We
could tell it when it was twelve. Like you can if you're standing
on your own shadow—you know it's twelve o'clock. Move on an
hour and it'd be a little bit farther. On a rainy day we just wouldn't
look. I think those marks were made with charcoal, and you'd mark
'em on again after you scrubbed the floor. There was dents in there
where they went.

For light, we had a kerosene lamp and a lantern. That was all
unless we happened to find some pine knots, and then we'd have
pine knots in the fire and read by the light of the fireplace. Read
schoolbooks, and maybe somebody'd give us [another]. I was awful
bad to read if I could get ahold of anything. I'd go places where
people had their house pasted with newspapers and catalogs and
I'd read everything on the walls. We just had boards on [the inside
of our walls, horizontally over the spaces between the logs], split
out about three or four feet long out of spruce pine. And then
mud in the cracks [between the logs]. Just plain mud. Some days
we'd have to sling mud all day. Then the bumblebees would plow

a hole in it and we'd have to daub that up. Where it'd come out, we'd fill it. Some of it would last for years and years.

And [Momma] had the wall covered with all kinds of medicines, you know, that you gathered out of the woods and all. Boneset, catnip, ground ivy, pennyroyal—I don't know what in all. Had them for everything. She washed them and put 'em up in bags—flour sacks [we didn't get many brown bags]—and hung 'em up on the wall. Wash 'em and let that drip dry and then put it up in cotton meal sacks and hang it up when it dries dry. They weren't labeled— she knew everything by looking at it, and she dried every plant that she knew of.

Boneset would break up flu or pneumonia either, and peppermint mixed together and make a tea out of it. It was terrible to drink, but it'd sure break up a cold or flu. She'd use the leaves and stems. Sometimes they'd put a little syrup in it. We didn't have much sugar then. We had syrup, or honey, mostly. Homemade molasses. We used to make our own syrup after we moved farther down on Tessentee later on.

But it was a mile to the nearest house from Lickskillet. [If someone needed help] they'd send some of us children to the neighbors, and they always come rushing as soon as anything went wrong. Sometimes you'd almost have pneumonia or something; and sometimes a baby'd come along and have to have a midwife and her help. Things like that. No one had doctors back then. It was all midwives.

Mama taught us our abc's on the mantel rock. We already knew the figures when we started to school. She taught us on the arch rock. [She would write on that] with a piece of charcoal.

We had to hike to school, and school took up at eight o'clock and let out at four. And in the wintertime, we had to take our lantern with us to the top of the mountain and hide it in an old burnt stump until we came back from school, and then we'd get it. We didn't have but two months' school then, and later on we had three. Mr. John Arnold was our first teacher, and he was a good one. He was from down around Franklin. School was just in the wintertime. I went through six [grades], I guess.

We used slates and slate pencils back then, you know. We had spelling matches and such as that. They did have Sunday school in this schoolhouse, too. It was up on Broadway is what they called it then. There's no building there now. It's gone. Had a little bell they rung to come in to books or come in from recess. It was a frame building the best I remember. We had a wood heater. We

PLATE 473   Wig looking in an old mica mine near the house.

PLATE 474   A waterfall near the old house.

brought our lunch in a syrup pail. We had beans or whatever we could get for dinner. Corn bread.

I was in intermediate arithmetic, language, history, and geography. I guess there was around nineteen or twenty students. It was a one-room school and one teacher. Our grades usually set in one place graded like that, and [when the teacher would call on us to recite] we'd all have to go up front. We had to write stories every once in a while for our English—things like that. We had books then, and we got to keep our books. I think they ought to get to keep them [now]. I think they like to review them. The state furnished them, and later on you had to buy them.

I had to walk about four miles [to school]. We come up from the head of Tessentee across Fork Mountain and down to the lower end of Fork Mountain—you know, where Broadway is. Now that's where we come to school. Had a springhouse down below the house. And we had playhouses built that we played in when we wasn't playing ball. We made our playhouses, us little girls did, with moss and whatever we could find. We played tag and ball. We had our bats, you know, and we batted the ball, and whoever caught it got to bat. We had to make our own balls out of wool or yarn. We never knowed what a bought ball was back then. Hewed the bats out of a piece of wood. The smaller ones would have flatter bats, and the grown-ups would have round bats.

I just had one dress that I wore to school all week, and right when I got home, I had to pull it off to keep from getting it dirty. We got the cloth from people that wove—paid for it in trade and Mother made the clothes. Money was scarce back then. Our other clothes were homemade hand-me-downs. The Thad Carpenters lived on the top of the mountain. They had a nice house. Had it painted white. But they was awful good neighbors, and all their let-down clothes come to us. They used to make britches. You'd have to make your own britches if you had any. And if you didn't, you'd do without. Mama used to call 'em jeans—or jeans cloth—and she made Poppy's britches. She was a good seamstress, but she sewed by hand for years before she got her sewing machine. It was homemade woven cloth—mostly cotton. We had to buy the cotton threads and then they wove it. And some people raised sheep and got wool.

The first shoes I ever had on, John Teague made them. They called 'em brogans then and they called the women's shoes "pokers." Poppy had us shoes made as soon as we was able to go to school. We didn't have no shoes till then. John Teague made 'em, and he made them with pegs—the soles put on with pegs, and [scallops cut around the] top of the girls' shoes and he left the boys' shoes straight. People usually brought him the leather and he made them for you, any size that you wanted.

Finally, later, Poppy bought a place down there at Tessentee and we moved down there. That's where he died. And it was a bigger house. It had a upstairs and a living room and bedroom. Big bedroom But me and my sister, we boxed in the porch and made a kitchen out of it, and then we got us a little cookstove. One of them little number seven's. It wasn't bigger'n nothing, you know.

After that, I got married. We couldn't hardly date, though. No dances. We had to sing if we made music. Momma didn't make music nor did Poppy. He didn't have any musical instruments at all. Poppy wouldn't let us sing nothing but gospel songs if he heard us. We had to slip if we sang any love songs or anything like that. They had ballads. People would write and give them to you and you'd learn from that.

But we couldn't go to dances or parties. [They'd have house raisings], but they'd have to go with us if we got to go, and then we couldn't dance. He didn't believe in dancing. He was very religious. Momma too. They'd let us go to any revivals or anything like that, [but that was our social life]. If I wanted to see a boy, they had to see him, too. They'd let him come to the house, but sometimes they wouldn't like him. I couldn't go with him no more if they didn't like him.

We didn't get to church every Sunday. [When we did go], we went to Tessentee or out to Broadway. They did have church in the schoolhouse sometimes. And they'd let us go to festival or something like that. But I guess that's the reason me and all of 'em married as early as we did—to get away! They was so strict on us. I guess not *too* strict, but we thought they was then.

We married at home, and then we moved to Georgia and stayed there a while and then moved back up here and stayed a while and moved to Dillard and stayed a while on Betty's Creek. There was a sawmill there when we lived there, and they had little cabins built for people to stay in. Then we moved from there back down to the Darnell place. It was over in the field where Bry Darnell had his house. We lived over there a while, and then we moved from there back this way. He'd try farming one year, and next year, sawmilling or something. We always come back to Highlands once in a while. Always renting. Never did build a house. My son owns this house.

I had six children—two girls and four boys. John's father is my baby.

HARVEY J. MILLER OF PIGEON ROOST

Nearly every community that has a weekly newspaper also has neighborhood correspondents whose job it is to report the neighborhood news through their weekly columns. Most of these columns are pretty dismal affairs that confine themselves to a roll call of visitors, illnesses, births, and deaths.

Occasionally, however, a columnist here and there goes light-years beyond that tired formula and fills the columns with sunlight. Harvey J. Miller, who was born in a log home in Pigeon Roost, North Carolina, and who only went through the sixth grade, is one such person. His first offering appeared over sixty years ago, when he was twelve, and he has been writing a column regularly ever since (now for the *Tri-county News* out of Spruce Pine, North Carolina).

And what a column! Every edition is filled with odd events, stories he has heard during the previous week, pieces of his own philosophy, and observations made by a mind intensely curious about, and awed by, all he sees around him. A sampling of past headlines hints at the richness of the work: "Ravenous Coon Stages Midnight Henhouse Raid on Pate Creek," "Sabbath Gnat Storm Plagues Pigeon Roost," "Helicopter Scares Cattle; Train Kills Three Head," and " 'Falling' Racer Snake Misses Preacher: Fox Chases Dog out of Woods."

And the stories are even better. This one is from November 14, 1963: "Rev. Harrison Street of the Pate Creek section of Pigeon Roost told me this one: He said the other day he cut down a maple tree on his farm and the tree was very knotty, and when he was trimming one of the large knots off the tree with an ax, he cut into a hollow place of the knot and out rolled a black snake like a ball. But as the snake went down the hill, it stretched out by degrees and then crawled away.

"He said that he didn't know how long the snake had been embedded under the knot—there had been a hole in the knot but it had completely growed over on the outside with a new piece of bark.

"It is believed that the snake had went into the rotten knothole to hibernate for the winter and the knothole on the outside had growed up. But it does not seem possible that it could do that in one winter's time. So the snake had a permanent home; in fact, it was in prison, as there was no other way for the snake to get under the knot but by only through the growed-up knothole."

Or this memory, one of hundreds parceled out over the weeks: "Away back 'yander' ever mother had certain ways to kill the first louse found on their children's head. The way the first louse was cracked could shape her kid's destiny. Crack it on a songbook and he would become a singer. On a Bible, he would be a preacher; or on a tin cup and he would become a great professor." (March 9, 1967).

We found out about Harvey through one of our subscribers, went to meet him, and were so impressed with his work that the Winter 1974 issue of *Foxfire* was turned into a book devoted to excerpts from the columns he wrote between 1950 and 1973.

During subsequent visits we have tape-recorded him, and the following section is a compilation of stories from those tapes.

Article and photographs by Ray McBride, Kim Wall, and William Brown

That writing, I enjoy that. The first typewriter I ever owned, I dug this spignet root. It was a good price, you know. I sold it and ordered me a typewriter. I done my stories by hand till I dug them roots. I just peck. I've got a bad hand. Fell in the fire when I was a baby and hurt them fingers there. Crooked. If it hadn't been for that, I could have done better.

I took this writing up when I was twelve years old and been at it ever since. The first piece was about my dog. I called him Mack. Me and my daddy was out clearing new ground one fall and he went up a holler chestnut [after a squirrel] and come out a limb way up—it was thirty, thirty-five feet high out there. And I told my daddy, I said, "What we gonna do?"

I called to him, and he come down just twisting, you know, over and over. When he struck the ground, struck on his feet.

And I studied about that, and I hadn't never read no papers much; and my sister, she lived in Erwin and she brought me a daily paper from Johnson City, Tennessee. I wrote to them. I was studying about that dog, and I sent the story and they printed it on the front page in block letters. And they wrote me a letter and wanted me to send the [community] news then. So I did that a long time. They just told me to write all the news. And then I wrote these special stories, and that got people interested in my writing. These personal items don't amount to much. People like the other stories better.

Now I write every week for the *Tri-county News*. I write about mother nature and the mountains and news. I use three typed sheets a week in my column. I'm known all over everywheres. They read my column. I've run my picture in my column and people I've never seen come up and say, "This here, ain't this Harvey Miller?" Say, "I knowed you by seein' your picture in the paper!" Ain't many people does this country correspondence anymore. [But you have to be careful.] If you bring something out in the papers, some people living might get hurt. "Oh you told a lot of things not true." I got a lot of stuff wrote and laid back because that is embarrassing when you bring something like that out. They say, "Oh that's my people!"

I've had some difficulty. One time somebody told a lot of stuff that wasn't even in [my column]. One man I saw in church, and he told me—he hadn't spoke to me in a long time—and he told me what was the matter. A man [had] told him [that I had written] a slanderous talk [about him], and he wouldn't speak to me for a long time. And I met up with him over here at the top of the hill at the church and he come to me, told me, "Harvey," said, "I've been hurt at you a long time."

And I said, "Yeah, I noticed you wouldn't speak to me."

And he said, "No." He said, "What you wrote in part of the paper . . ." and he wouldn't tell me what it was.

I said, "Did you read it?"

He said, "No." Said, "A man told me *he* did."

And I said, "That's a mistake."

He said, "I studied it all over the other day and I *thought* you wouldn't be allowed to put that in the paper just that way."

I said, "No. That'd be a'slandering you. I didn't do it."

He begged me to forgive him.

I said, "Well, you wouldn't say anything. You wouldn't speak so I didn't say anything to you."

PLATE 475 Harvey collects much of the community news for his column by visiting with his neighbors. Here Harvey (right) gathers material from Harvey Garland.

He said, "I feel better."

I said, "I do, too."

Lot of people *can't* read and [other] people tell them, "I seen it in the paper."

"Well," they say, "that's bound to be Harvey Miller. He's the only one writes." I tell them to get it out of the paper and come with it and then anything I have put in the paper, I can't deny it then. But it's just now and then. I get letters from everywhere telling me to keep on writing. Now I'm connected up with it. Keep on it. I quit it one time, not hardly a year. I was sick, you know. But I got back and been at it ever since. I like it. Seems like I get down and out and get to studying and writing and it picks me up.

Sometimes back then, them daily papers would edit my columns. Sometimes I wouldn't hardly know I'd wrote it. I didn't like that. That's about the reason I almost quit. A whole lot of people said, "Somebody's helping you." Said, "You're losing your style." So I got hooked up a long time ago with the *Tri-county News,* and that lady down there, she told them not to do a thing. That my writing was too good to fool with!

Do you know how I learned to write? With my finger thataway [making letters with his finger in the air]. I never could do no good with a chalk on account of that hand or something. I never could do no good, and I got out and got interested in writing doing that. My folks all thought I was going crazy. They kept watching me. My mother said, "Harvey, what are you doing out there," said, "with your finger?"

I said, "I'm a'writing."

Said, "You are?"

It wasn't long till I had learnt me how to do a good handwriting. That's right.

G. D. Barnett, merchant of Pigeon Roost, who has long held the title of champion snake killer of the entire immediate area, so far has found this season to be the most favorable of his entire career.

After killing three more snakes last week, he reached the mark of 111 to beat the record of 36 more than he has slain in any other previous year.

He said he had decided now not to quit at that, but to keep on killing them as long as he could find them.

Barnett has hunted for the snakes in a radius of about a mile along the Pigeon Roost Creek banks. He has them thinned down so scarce on his beat that he may take in a larger territory if he can get the allotted time.

He said good weather conditions aid in the search for snakes. When the sun shines bright just after a summer shower is the best time to look for them. He said they would come from their dens and be sunning on the rocks or climb up in small bushes.

He never counts a snake dead until he is quite sure it is. He generally blows off their heads with a single shot. He said he had shot 200 times at snakes and probably several more of the snakes escaped to their dens and died.

He kills the snakes only as a hobby and can't imagine how many he has ever killed. He believes that he has killed every kind of snake that inhabits this area.

Gene Bennett, son of Mr. and Mrs. Sidney Bennett, was stung so bad Sunday by honey bees that he had to receive emergency treatment at Memorial Hospital in Johnson City.

Mr. and Mrs. Duessel Jack Barnett and son, Larry, and daughter, Wilma Lee, of Jasper, Michigan, started back to their home Thursday after visiting relatives for two weeks here. While here, they received word that their garden crop had been destroyed in a hailstorm, and a terrific windstorm had blown away their car garage.

A representative of the French Broad Electric Corporation, which serves this area, visited all the homes of their customers here last week. He was traveling in a Jeep truck and found some of the side roads too rough for a Jeep to travel. In fact, the Jeep traveled to places a motor vehicle had never been before. Up in "School House Hollow" the Jeep got stuck in the mud and some men worked five hours getting it out.

PLATE 476   8/9/56

My parents wanted me to go to school, but I was sick a lot and couldn't go much. [I did get to go some, though.] We had one teacher, paid from fifty cents a day to sometimes thirty dollars a month. If they went through school and had four months of training, they was allowed to teach. We'd go from eight to four, and they'd be about twenty-eight to thirty of us in the whole school. The teachers was hired by committees [the equivalent of our community school boards today]. If they liked them pretty good, then they'd keep them. I've known them to stay three years. Most of the time they lived in Spruce Pine and walked. One lived across the river. She rode a little old pony from where she boarded. Come evening, you know, get on that pony and ride home.

One time, they was a woman [teacher] lived over here on Brummet's Creek. Her parents or somebody'd come after her every Friday evening, and bring her dog along. She would go home for the weekend. One [Friday] her dog got there and come in. That dog come running in the [schoolhouse]. It scared that teacher, and she thought something had happened to her mother. She told some of them to watch the children, and she said she was going down the road and look. She was gone a few minutes and they come. That dog was just ahead of them. But her mother was coming so they could walk back across the mountain [together].

Then there was one, he lived down on the creek. I'd come up in the morning and holler for him and I'd walk to school with him. Wasn't no riding to that!

They didn't have too many grades. They had a primer, a first grade, a second; then they had a speller, and on the last they had what they call geography and history and health. The last I went to school, I had a load of books. Books didn't cost much. We'd [buy them] in Huntdale. We had to buy them. And now like if you wanted to go every year in the same book, why, they would take you in. When I went to school, there was men and women there who were twenty-two years old.

We'd have a spelling match every Friday. I was just a little feller. You know how these spelling matches work. Two groups. They'll all pick on one to be a leader. They was one teacher, and his sister was a lot older than I was, and I got up beside of her and in a few minutes I had her spelled down. That teacher, boy, he shamed his sister. Said, "I'd be ashamed. That little Harvey Miller turned you down." Me and my cousin, when we got up there, we stayed there a long time spelling. She would be on the other side. I'd dread when she'd get up. She was hard.

Then on the blackboard we done our problems. We'd stand up there and do them. And slates. We had slates. Never done much on the writing paper.

And then we had a country doctor that'd come around once a year. Examine your tonsils. Boy, them children was skittish. He'd come in and sit down—have an old stool and look down your throat. Examine you. I was pretty big then, and that teacher come in and she said, "Harvey, you lead the way. You start off." Said, "Go on up."

I'd go up and he set down and looked at me. "You all right."

One time they got a dentist. That was a long time after I quit, though. They got to filling teeth. He come on horseback.

We took our dinner in a little syrup bucket. I'd take milk and corn bread. That was good eating. That was it. When my sister went, why, we would take enough for the both of us. When corn got full enough, now, that was big eating. They'd boil that corn, take roasting ears. That was good.

THE HOMEPLACE   457

Then during recess our biggest game was dog and fox. We had somebody appoint somebody to be the fox. The rest of us was dogs. See, we was right in the woods. Get up there in them woods. Sometimes we would get way back in the mountains there and making so much noise barking like dogs, you know, that we couldn't hear that bell ring and we'd come in late. But the dogs would have to catch the fox and bring him in. When they caught him, they'd have like a dog fight. You could hear them. Somebody would catch him, you could *tell*. You could hear them, and go see what was taking place.

When we started a new term, the new teacher didn't know the children. They would send a certain boy to go out to cut them a switch. Them boys got to wringing them [before they brought them in] so [the teacher] would give a strike and it'd fly all into pieces. That teacher, she come to me one day and asked if I'd go and cut her some ironwood switches. She said, "Now, I don't believe you'll do what *they* been a'doing." I went and found some good ones and brought them in, and talk about some boys getting it, they did.

But the teachers didn't keep order much. It was pretty noisy in there. That hurts about studying. They didn't keep much order. *Some* did, but about all of them was women teachers and them old big boys, you know, wouldn't mind.

About the biggest thing [we got punished for] was writing letters. Like a boy would write a girl a letter. One time me and a boy was sitting together. We oughtn't to have done it but we did. And we didn't like a certain boy. We wrote a love letter. That boy [I was sitting with] said, "You write it. Write a good love letter and when we are out, I'll slip in and put it in a girl's book."

I wrote it, and when we come back in, we kept watching, and we seen her read and read, and she took it up there and give it to the teacher. She read it and looked everywhere. And when we had another recess, she told that boy, said, "I want you to stay in here."

He stayed, you know, and she shut the door. Boy, that boy told me that he was gonna get it now. He come out and he said, "Boy, somebody played a trick on me." He said, "I never wrote her no letter. Somebody played a trick." He said, "She beat me to death about it. I couldn't tell her." He said, "She don't like me nohow." She had had trouble with him. He was pretty rowdy.

I told that boy [I was sitting with] that we done wrong there. He said, "Don't ever tell that boy or we will have a fight with him." I never would pull a trick like that again.

One day we got a new sheriff back in there, and he went to making raids on them moonshine stills. They'd get men in there to go a'still hunting. One day they come down, they had an old still and some of them drunk, you know. Me and the boys were settin' at the window and we went and poked our heads out to look and see, and, oh they come slapping their hats, you know. Teacher said, "What they doing?"

I hollered over [and] said, "They out here at this window slapping us with their hats!" Had them old high seats, and we'd poke our heads out. They were hollering, "Poke your heads back in there." One day I disturbed the whole class. We was sitting around that old long wood stove. It was one of them pot bellies. It was three or four feet long. We was all setting around there and a boy got that poker hot there at the front of it—got it red hot and he poked my leg through [a hole] in my overalls. Lord, talk about—see, I didn't know. I was studying. I didn't know what had taken place. Law, I screamed and jumped up. Now that teacher, talk about him with a limb. He hit him with a hickory switch.

I seen a man teacher one day strike a boy. He struck him; he jumped plumb across the seat. Big high seat, now. He went right over the top. The teacher went around to him and kept on beating him. That evening his folks come in. He did beat him up, you know. The teacher come told me, he said, "Harvey, you and me are friends. Now you stay with me." They didn't come in and he wouldn't go out. 'Fraid they'd come in and beat up on him. He said, "Stay with me if they come in." But they didn't come in, though, I have went many a day, just be me and the teacher. Students didn't like him. And back then, they didn't have any law. If you didn't go, then they didn't do nothing about it. No law. Parents wouldn't make them go.

We had two schools at the last on Pigeon Roost. Sometimes the teacher would get hurt or something and [the students] would walk and come [to the other one]. And had committees. Them committees had to sign them vouchers so the teachers could get their pay every month. This teacher I was telling you about where everybody got mad at him, he went and called on one of the committees and they wouldn't sign that voucher. Said he wasn't no good. Nobody wouldn't go [to his school]. He come back and told me that if I talked good to [the committee], he believed they would sign it. Said, "I'll give you a dollar."

I went over there and told them he was down sick with the rheumatism.

Said, "Well, he hasn't done nobody no good."

And I said, "He done *me* some good." Said, "He was good to

me." I said, "Sign it. This is the last of school. He won't bother no more no how."

I kept on begging and they said, "Bring it around here." Said, "I'll sign it."

I took and give it to him. He lived way over across the mountain. And he promised me a dollar, but I never did get a dime. But that committee told me, "If it wasn't for you, we wouldn't have signed it."

There was one teacher, they said he was the best teacher. He had taught for four or five years. He often begged me to come to him. He said, "Harv, now I'll *learn* you something. You going to them up there," said, "you won't learn nothing." Said, "Now if you'll come, I'll really learn you something."

But I never did go. It was a mile further, and I didn't want to take that extra mile. But they said he was one that tried to learn you something. Some of them, you had a lesson today—"Well, I ain't got no time. We'll wait till tomorrow [to go over it]." A lot of them teachers just set. But this one never did. He'd come to you to see what help you wanted. Where I first went to school, teacher set up there and if you needed help, you had to go up to her and ask. But that other one, he'd go to you.

There was one teacher, we had the answers in the back of our arithmetic. I would go up there and tell that teacher that I couldn't get the answer. She said, "Right there is a problem that I never could get the answer to." See, didn't get no help there. In arithmetic, I never did do no good. But in spelling and pronouncing words, that was my biggest.

Now that one schoolteacher I was telling you about, they found him dead out in the mountains in the snow. He had nineteen steel traps in his clothes and stuff. He had been killed, but it was all in kinfolks. All the kinfolks was on the jury. Everybody was kin to this boy they said done it, and the man who was dead was this boy's uncle. It was all mixed up. They didn't want to charge him. Found where he'd been choked to death. The jury said that he froze to death.

I wrote stories on that. I was sitting right there. When they had the main trial [I was there]. They locked the jury up in a room. This man that was in there, I walked up the road with him [afterward]. I said, "What did you find out?"

He said, "We know he was killed, but we didn't tell." Kinfolks, you know. Didn't want to get everybody into it. They said he had got bad to drink and they said he was mean to fight. So they killed him.

There was another man, a schoolteacher, over here at Rock Creek that they found him dead. They never could find out nothing, or they didn't, you know. Back then, if they didn't crack the case, they just let it off by mysteries. Mystery to it.

We had a place on the head of Pigeon Roost where there was bootleggers, and they said they was getting a lot of men killed in there. They is a place back in there; they call it Dead Man's Hollow. They was a man come out of college, and his people was rich people. Said he was going to Africa. Wanted him to go to the mountains of North Carolina and stay and train [for the trip]. He was found there at Cherry Gap Mountain. That was it. They said he was killed in there. They know he got to Cherry Gap Mountain. He was swallowed up there.

That moonshine whiskey. They would bring it out in wagonloads. They was bad men [connected with that]. One, they claim he had so many notches on his gun, he'd pull a smoking gun! He was the one they claimed killed so many people. A long time after they come down off Pigeon Roost, a man come down with a bunch of clothes. He said he found them back there, all bloody, you know. And then somebody found some bones one time and brought them out. It was a bad place.

Very few people ever save their own garden seed anymore. It seems everyone even arranges everything differently to grow in the garden from what they once did.

People once made 'tater hills for all kinds of root and vine crops to grow in. In fact, the hills were bedded with fresh barn stock manure; now the gardeners only make ridges and fertilizer in them, which they call plant food.

Even the sweet-potato plants are now set down in a furrow. I suppose they are harder to dig when planted that way, but they claim that a bigger crop is always produced and is never hurt very bad by dry weather conditions. They even say moles can't bother them as bad when they are not growing in big loose potato hills.

Pea patches were once planted so they would trail around the garden; now you always see them growing in about the middle of the garden patch and a pole rack rigged up for them to trail on.

Once we all grew shallot potato onions. Everybody around here has run out of seed. E. E. Seaton of Jonesboro, Tennessee, heard about this and he had about a quart of sets left and he sent them to me to swap for gourd seeds. The shallot sets arrived too late to plant, but we hope to have luck with them next spring.

Pieplant (rhubarb) is still a favorite here for most everybody. I didn't discover until this week that there are two varieties of it, the big and the little kinds.

Tansy and sage still grow in many people's gardens. Tansy is used for a medical tea and can be sold on the herb market. Sage is used for a sausage seasoning and flavoring purpose for meats and hogshead hash and hog jaw.

Just a few gooseberry bushes still exist in the gardens in this area. Years ago, a crew of workers paid by the government searched the forests over, destroying the wild gooseberry bushes as well as many of the kind that grow in gardens.

When people first began to grow head lettuce just a few years ago, they thought that was the worst thing ever to happen.

Very few people ever grow gourds anymore. I remember that my mother once owned a gourd that held exactly a measured bushel. She used the gourd to put feathers in when she was picking ducks and geese.

Some people grow broom corn in the gardens. Yes, people make homemade brooms on the style of the old round kind.

The women, it appears, no longer make kraut and sour green beans like they once did. Now sauerkraut is made in small vessels like half-gallon fruit jars instead of maybe fifty-gallon wooden tubs.

We have heard several old-timers grumble about the difference in taste of pickle beans now and like they used to taste. We believe there are people now who can prepare and fix beans to sour as good as anybody used to could, but people don't have the same kind of beans. We still have the same name for many of our beans as they did, yet that does not make them the same kind of beans as they once were. Most of the varieties of beans, like a lot of other things, have been changed and improved.

I have heard of folks planting what was called the white bunch beans and when they were grown and matured, they turned out to be just plain tough soup beans.

PLATE 477 6/5/58

My grandfather came in here from Cherokee, near Tennessee. He was part Indian. He took up land here. Homesteading. They built a big two-room log house.

I was born and raised on Pigeon Roost Creek. When I was born on July 10, 1909, I was premature. I only weighed a couple of pounds and they didn't think I was going to live. Aunt Ellen Miller was the midwife, and she told my daddy, "You ain't got a crying baby yet, just a baby doll." Said, "All I'll charge you for my service is a peck of onions." Said, "When you take your onions up, just give me a peck of sets to plant next year."

News spread out fast, and folks came out of the hills and hollers for miles about to see the tiny baby. A common-size teacup would fit on my head. Preacher James Chapman seen me and said he'd never seen or even heard of such a small baby, but he believed

PLATE 478 The Reverend Spencer Barnett, Harvey's grandfather.

PLATE 479 Hannah Hunnicutt Barnett, Harvey's grandmother.

PLATE 480 The log house where Harvey was raised.

I'd live. He thought I was put here by Providence for some purpose. He wanted me to carry his name, but my mother had already dreamed my name, so I was called Harvey, but she added his name, James, as my middle name.

That midwife said that when I went to crying, they could be more certain that I'd make it. That was before nursing bottles come about, and so they made me sugar teats out of brown sugar and butter. I know they done the best they could. They kept a fire going in the chimney night and day all summer long to keep a warm heat going in the room, and in about six weeks, I began to cry. Before then I was quiet as a mouse.

I was raised in a log cabin. My parents farmed. You know, I was sick till I was about thirty years old. Never did work on a public job. All I done was farm.

There was a bunch of us kids, but by the time they was gone, I was still at home. I didn't marry until [my mother] died. I stayed there with her. That's one reason I know so much of this old stuff. I lived with it so long. [At this point, Harvey described the house and the farm. As he talked, and with his help, we drew two diagrams, (Plates 482 and 483). The numbers in the following text correspond to the numbers on the plates.]

1. Upstairs in the house was a loft that we used for storage. We went up through a scuttle hole on the inside to go up into the loft. We didn't never put no beds or nothing in it.

PLATE 482

Note: circled numbers on diagram refer to numbers in text.

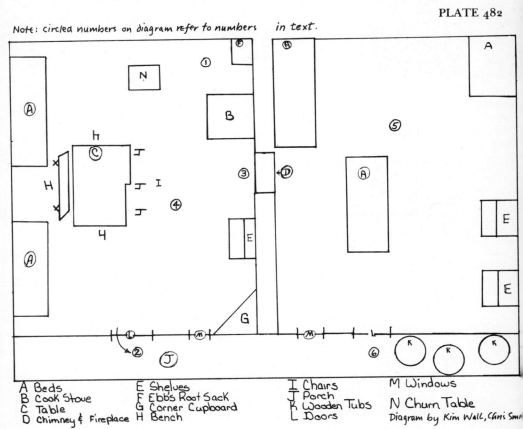

A Beds	E Shelves	I Chairs	M Windows
B Cook Stove	F Ebb's Root Sack	J Porch	N Churn Table
C Table	G Corner Cupboard	K Wooden Tubs	
D Chimney & Fireplace	H Bench	L Doors	Diagram by Kim Wall, Chris Smith

2.   You had to go out on the porch to go in the back room. Sometimes that snow would blow on the porch and you'd wade through that snow to go to the back room.

3.   There was a chimney corner there. The chimney was in the middle, see, and had that chimney corner there. That back room was bought and added to the [original one-room log house]. It was bought and hauled for over a mile. That fireplace is the only way

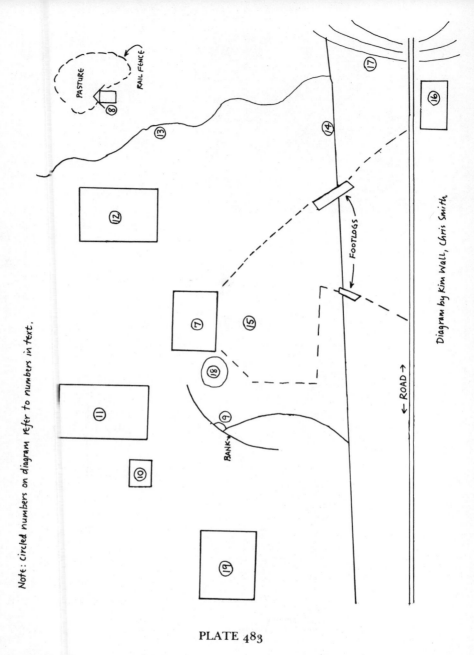

Note: circled numbers on diagram refer to numbers in text.

PASTURE

RAIL FENCE

⑧

⑬

⑰

⑯

⑫

⑭

⑦

⑮

⑧

FOOTLOGS

⑪

⑨

BANK

⑩

← ROAD →

⑲

Diagram by Kim Wall, Chris Smith

PLATE 483

we had to heat, and my mother done a lot of cooking there. Had a piece of iron across inside there to hang the kettles on. When that kettle was cooking, it'd go like an automobile. That was interesting. When I was little, I'd sit there and listen at that little kettle. Had a lid that fit tight on it.

4. This is where we lived. Had our wood cookstove in here. Had a table and two beds and some shelves and a big old corner cupboard

set in the corner. Had kitchen utensils on the shelves and silverware and old wooden bowls in the corner cupboard. And we had about six of them old-time chairs and one big bench here at the table— big table. And had one window. It was pretty dark in them old houses. And had a little table where we kept the churn, and had dishpans hung on the wall to wash the dishes in. No sink. And we dug roots and herbs in the fall of the year and my mother had a little sack hung here on the wall. When anybody got sick, she'd go to that little sack on the wall and get out herbs and roots: catnip, boneset, mayapple, lobelia, skullcap. That boneset would break a fever but it was bitter. People had an expression back then: bitter as boneset!

5.   We had three corded beds in this back room. There was a chimney there but we never did use it in this back room. Then we had some shelves for our clothes. No closet, just shelves. And no chairs. When you'd go in there, you'd sit on the beds. They had straw ticks, and every bed had a big old feather bed—put them over top of you and keep warm under them feather beds!

6.   We kept lots of things out here on the porch. That's where we kept pickled beans in a big old wooden tub. And hung dried beans on the porch and in the house, and pumpkins. And the kraut was out there in a tub. Had boards over those tubs so nothing couldn't get in.

7.   There was eight children and our parents living in the house. It was up on kind of a ridge. In the morning we'd hear that rooster crow when it'd go to peepin' daylight and we'd know to get up. When we got up we'd eat breakfast early and go out and go to working on the farm. The house had big cracks in the floor, and the porch—we didn't have it underpinned and that wind would come right up in there. I don't see how we made it, but, see, anybody that didn't know no better . . . Now I believe they'd take the pneumonia fever, but back then people got along pretty good about taking diseases. And didn't have a toilet or outhouse. Go to the barn or over here to the chicken house. And the woods was close. Never had an outside toilet until WPA workers went to building them for low-income folks in the early thirties.

8.   The barn was out here on kind of a flat. There was a little ridge you'd come down to go out here to the barn. This barn served as a schoolhouse and meetinghouse—church house—and we bought it. It stood over across the creek and we moved it and used that for a barn. Kept cattle, and hay up in the loft. Had stalls to put the cattle in. At one time we had, I think, thirteen head—young

PLATE 484   The Dave Miller family. Harvey, age three, is in his father's lap.

cattle and old cattle. My mother done all the milking and had two-gallon crocks to put that milk in. Take a teacup and dip that out at meals after she'd skimmed the cream off for butter. We used a lot of milk when we was all there—probably five gallons a day with churning and all. Had a barn lot and a pasture behind it. Had an old rail fence. Used that manure on the garden. Back then they didn't buy no fertilizer. Clean this barn. That was hard work. Had an old steer and a sled and we'd load that manure onto that sled out of the barn and haul it to the garden.

9.   We didn't have a springhouse. Had a box fixed at the spring, and put the milk in there in the summertime. She'd put that night's milk in there and we'd drink it the next day. Have that cold. The spring was way down in there, dug out and walled up. Down deep in the ground. Then the water ran on down to the creek. Had a ditch dug and that took care of that water. Stray dogs would come by every once in a while and rob milk from that springbox.

10.   Had chickens and ducks. They'd run around the yard. Then this here big floor, ducks set under that floor [of the main house]. One day my mother lost her thimble through a crack in the floor, and after then, why, down near the duck pond we found that. A duck had swallowed that there thimble! It had fell down under the floor and a duck had eat that. Shaw, she was glad to get her thimble back. They was hard to get ahold of!

11.   Had a garden up above the house here. Back then, now, we really growed a garden. And saved our own seed. Swapped seeds.

Nobody bought any garden seed. My mother was named Cindy, and this woman had some beans she had got from my mother, and after my mother died, this woman said, "Would you like to have some of your mother's beans?" And I called 'em Cindy beans. Had corn and mustard and turnips and tomatoes and cucumbers and all kinds of crops in here. Made soup beans and took them to the store—get so much for them there dried soup beans. We'd make enough stuff to do us and lived on that.

12. Here we had a regular 'tater patch. We'd grow a big 'tater patch.

13. There was a branch come down through here. Had to cross a branch to go to the barn.

14. There was a big creek went down here below the house plumb down the road. Had a path to lead to the house. Had to cross the creek on a little footlog. My daddy was a sick man, you know, and his head swimmed, and one time the creek was up and he pitched in and pulled me in and we both liked to drowned. He was leading me and he went in and pulled me in. Mother never would let me go with him no more!

15. Had a yard here and had it paled in. That's where my own dog liked to killed me one night. He was one-eyed and was the illest dog I ever seen. I opened the gate and that gate screaked, you know, and that dog was there and he didn't know me, and if I hadn't got my old hat off and fought and hollered and called his name, he'd a'killed me. Poppin' at my throat, you know. Them old-time gates, you'd open them and they'd screak like everything!

16. Over here across the creek is where we kept our hogs. Had a little flat over there and had a hog lot. And there was a mountain up here and they'd get out and go up in them mountains. They weren't fenced in. We just had a lot back then and let 'em run out. They'd get fat in the mountains on that chestnut mast, and in the fall of the year we'd go hunt our hogs up and bring 'em in and kill 'em. That was virgin forest. That forest never had been cut.

Me and my daddy went one time and found a sow that had nine pigs. We tracked her, you know. Went to a rock clift. Had her bed made out of leaves she'd carried. She was layin' in there. He said, "My little gelt sow had a lot of pigs." Nine pigs!

17. One time me and my brother went hog hunting up here on this mountain and found a still. Law, it scared us! Back then they claimed them blockaders would shoot you, and we run off. But we saw a hog in that beer barrel with its head stuck up! And it was

PLATE 485   Harvey as a teen-ager on his pony, June.

squealing—couldn't get out of there—and another one was running around. And we got gone and went to the house and was telling Mother and Daddy about finding that still over across the hill. My mother never understood, and she said, "Yonder comes a hog now down the hill and it's scalded!" It had that white beer on it. Them men that was there at that still had hid behind the trees when we come, and after we got gone, they pulled that pig out. Daddy went over there and put it up. And then a man a day or two after that— an old man that lived up above us came down and said, "Dave," said, "you can turn your hogs out now." Said, "That still's been fenced." Said, "They can't get in."

They said that made the best whiskey they ever run!

18.   We holed our potatoes up. Below the house here we had a 'tater hole. Covered that with boards and threw dirt over it. You could go there and had a place you could pull a board out and get your 'taters.

19.   And we'd make a cane crop. Make 'lasses. Now, that was something fine in the wintertime. Had our cane patch down here below the spring.

A red cow belonging to H. J. Miller of Pigeon Roost, who earned the title to her name early last fall as a 'tater-diggin' cow, has again proved herself useful by doing a job most needful.

The name of 'tater-diggin' was bestowed upon the cow after it was learned that she could take her front foot and pull 'taters out of the ground faster than old man Miller could himself.

However, it was later learned there was a drawback to her 'tater-diggin' career. She did it to her advantage. She would crawl through a fence and slip into the 'tater patch — dig 'taters as fast as she could, in seven or eight hills; then she would light in and try to eat ever last one of 'em.

Now here comes another story about the cow — that is, of making roads in the deep snow here and there around the home of Miller. That was good to take the job away from him as he was too poor in health to do it himself.

Miller reports the cow made several trips trudging through the twelve inches of snow, first going from her place at the barn to the house; then when this snow trail was completed, she made a similar road from spring to house, which would be the roads most traveled.

But when she started to fix another road from the house to the highway, Miller must have thought it was too long a pilgrimage in the snow, for he went a nearer way — headed her off and flagged her down with a little bucket of 16 per cent dairy feed. Understand this, though — this was after she had made the necessary snow trails and he had already thought of the new names — the suggested new names of 'tater-diggin' and snow-trampin' cow. She always earns her names the hard way. Miller said he was going to keep his fingers crossed from now on as to what jobs on his farm the cow could perform to keep her name in the news, as there is no doubt she will never earn a famous name as a milk champion.

PLATE 486   2/25/60

You know, old people back then paid attention to things [that people today don't bother with]. Like sweep with a broom under your feet, why, you'll never get married. Now you boys better not let nobody sweep under your feet! And now if you sleep under a new quilt, why, the one you dream of, you'll marry her. People back then—well, it worked out, they said.

Like when you get a new dog? Cut the hair off the end of his tail and put that hair under the doorstep and the dog won't leave. Stay right with you. Then you've got you a dog there.

And I know you've heared of this one: Never start a job on Wednesday that you can't finish the same day. Sometimes bad luck'll happen. Now my mother, you know, she'd never let us start on a big field of corn on Wednesday. Little ones [was okay] 'cause she knowed we could get it done. . . .

And if you get your hair cut, don't never throw it out outside. A bird'll get it and put it in a nest and you'll 'bout die with a headache. Now, I used to cut hair, you know, and an *old* man come and he had a little poke, and he'd get all that hair up when I'd get his hair cut and put it in his pocket. And I said, "What's that for?"

And he said, "I'm not gonna let you throw my hair out here on the outside and let the birds get it and," said, "me with a headache." Said, "I don't never have a headache." And I got checking on that, and, you know, all them old people believed that.

He'd take and turn a rock up. I'd see him and watch him, you know, go down the road. He'd come to a flat rock and put that hair under there and put dirt over it and go on.

I had a lot of those things wrote down here in this notebook. Yeah, here now. You ever hear about cattle having a holler tail? My remedy is slit their tail and put turpentine in it. Let that sink in. And cattle, when they got a bloat—you know, eat something that bloats them up? Put turpentine to her navel. Pour that turpentine—put it in a little pan or something, or jar cap, and hold it up there and it'll soak in there in a minute. I've tried that. That *helps* the cow.

Now, to keep your nose from bleeding, get lead from a bullet that killed a hog, beat it out round, and put you a hole in it and put a common red string to it and wear it around your neck. Keep that around your neck all the time. Has to be where it killed a hog. We had one here. [My daughter, Ethel,] lost her'n one time in the third grade and her nose went to bleeding, and we got it replaced with another [bullet].

I guess you've heared of this: If anybody springs their foot or arm—gets a sprain—why, make a poultice out of apple pummies [squashed apple pulp]. When they grind apples to make cider, you know, to make vinegar, they'd have pummies left. Get that out. You know, with a sprain, you take a fever in that, and [those pummies] are cool. Vinegar and salt poultice is good, too. You can use those pummies to make apple brandy, too.

And sometimes certain places you get milk sick or milk poison. There's a place back here on the head of Pigeon Roost they keep fenced in all the time because [what causes that] grows there. They call it white snakeweed, I think. And when you get it, it has a place it settles—might settle in the leg. They say that there apple brandy, if that don't cure it, nothing will.

My mother kept that little bag hanging on the wall, and when someone'd get sick, she'd know what to do, you know. My brother one night come in from the sawmill and coughing every breath, and oh, he was bad off. And she went in there and grabbed that little poke off the wall and went to getting out. She said, "He's got pneumonia fever." But next morning, she had that broke, but he's so weak he couldn't set up. Yeah, now, he had it. She used boneset tea for that.

She was a good doctor, but I saw her scared one time. Our daddy took the croup, and I reckon she was afraid she couldn't doctor anymore like she did before [since she was old then]. She got me and my brother out was at midnight [and sent us after my sister, who lived] way up on the mountain. Told us we had to go after

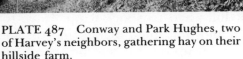
PLATE 487 Conway and Park Hughes, two of Harvey's neighbors, gathering hay on their hillside farm.

PLATE 488

her. Sick daddy, and she hadn't done a thing. He'd took the croup. He'd choke to death. Said, "You hurry and go get them."

We went and she hadn't done a thing. We lit the kerosene lantern. That's all the light we had. Oh it was way back on the mountain. It was, I guess, three miles we walked. But now we went up that mountain, and she told us, "Now, don't fool no time."

When we got back, why, he had got all right. I said, "What happened there?"

She said, "I doctored him at last." She said, "It cured him." She had him up when we went in. She had him up there at the old fireplace. She built a fire and had him baking his feet. I didn't ask her, but she greased his feet with something.

She told me the next day that she was nervous.

But back when I was young, it seemed like I never did see her get scared much. One night there was a storm and she was getting pretty old then. One night it come a heavy storm and rain, and we lived right up over the creek. We heard that creek. She come and called for us—wanted to take to the hills and I wouldn't let her.

It was a bad time, you know, the water around the door. Next day I told her, I said, "I never seen you do that way before."

She said, "I was scared." She said, "That was good; you begged us not to go to the hill."

I said, "There's no place there. No shelter."

Back then we didn't have any clocks, and they had sun marks to tell what time it was. My grandma and grandpa, where they lived, when it was light at the edge of the porch it was twelve o'clock. My uncle and aunt live there now and it still works. And when a shadow fell across a certain place on the back doorsill, it was six o'clock. The evening, six o'clock, was behind the house. And that worked out.

Where I lived [with my mother], there was a sun mark on the hill. It's there yet. We called it the Rye Field. This land was cleared up, this here wooded place. When [the sun would] get down there where the clearing started, it was six o'clock. We could see it way off the mountain [where we were working in the fields]. When the shadow of the mountain hit the edge of the clearing, we'd start off the mountain. We watched that. We'd say, "Oh it's six o'clock. Now let's go in." We called that Sun-mark Time.

We raised some feed on that hill—had to shock it up. Have to take and cut the top of the corn and pull them blades and tie the tops and blades together and shock it up till it dries and then haul it in and stack it up in them stacks. Big high stacks. There is somebody up on the stacks, and they throw it up to them. Bunch of men. It goes up fast. I've seen them take a piece of wood and [set it in the middle of the stack like a pole] and make them stacks higher. Go on up then. Then to get down, somebody would put a pitchfork in there to step on, or get on somebody's shoulders. One time I was stacking a stack of fodder way up high and they was a bullet, I heard that bullet a'singing in the air. It went like it was close to me. I was telling a man about it and he said, "Why, I guess it was a long ways off." Said, "You can hear them singing that way." But now I heard it go through! I never did hear the fire of the gun. I heard the bullet, though.

But we had to raise everything. No money. Didn't have much. Everybody in them old log houses papered the walls with catalogs and newspapers. Sometimes they would do it over and over and over, three times. They'd change that when it got yeller and aged. Redo that. Not long ago I seen that in a house. Put up with wheat paste. Then the rats would gnaw and eat that dough. Mother put bluestone in that, and that kept the rats away. It's a kind of poison. It's good to give dogs. Worm a dog, that bluestone.

Another thing we used them catalogs for was fly flaps. They would take and trim them. Back when I was a boy, somebody had to stand over the table all the time with a fly flap—keep the flies off. They was like a bee swarm. Everybody was that way here.

We have our own names for many birds and animals, especially us older folks.

We always call the chimney swift birds the chimney sweepers. The towhees, jorees; phoebe, pewees; turkey vultures, turkey buzzards; nighthawks, bullbats; and wood thrush, wood thrashers.

We call groundhogs whistle pigs. But all the wild animals is called varmints. The acorns and hickory nuts that grows in the mountains that many of the wild varmints live on is called mast.

As far back as anyone can remember here, the mail-order catalogs has been a favorite with the mountain people. Since the mountain communities no longer appear to be so backwards, the mail-order catalogs has lost some of its interest. The Charles William Store issued large catalogs like Sears, Roebuck and Montgomery Ward do today. The William Store went out of business 31 years ago.

Martha Jane Adams was another mail-order house that done big business here a long time ago.

Back in the early days, there was very few men who were Jacks-of-all-trades. Some men made split baskets out of white oak wood, while others made bedsteads. They had turning lathes that they made the tall post and spindle beds with. All of them was corded beds. Ropes used in the beds was made out of shucks or white-oak splits.

All the workmen done the furniture carving with knives. We have been informed that they were all slow in turning out the finished pieces of furniture in those days, but when they did get it made, it was done right.

Some of the finest red brick that I have ever seen was made right here on Pigeon Roost. Mr. Curby of Jonesboro made the brick on the I. L. Lewis farm to build three chimneys where Lewis was building a house. It is said Mr. Curby ground the mud in a machine sorter like a cane mill. The mill was also pulled by a horse. The brick was dried in a kiln that favored an apple-drying kiln. All the three brick chimneys stood erect after a fire destroyed the dwelling house.

PLATE 489   9/28/61

[To show you how poor people was, you know how we got our brass kettle?] My mother bought it. People would go broke and sell out. They would put the word out they were selling out. When people moved off, they'd sell things. So these people moved down in Crossville, Tennessee. Went on a train. They sold their things for what they could get for them. People didn't have much money. So that kettle didn't cost us over three or four dollars. We was offered forty dollars for it recently. Then another man said that he'd give me a hundred. I said, "I've been offered forty already, but I won't sell it." We still make apple butter in it. We take the apples and peel them the night before. For a quick run, you sugar them down the night before—twenty-five or thirty pounds for a twelve-gallon kettle. Depends on the thickness you want. Then the next morning you boil them off. Stir it with what they call an apple-butter stirrer. Boil it four to five hours if you want it thin. If you want it thick, you do it longer. Back then we sweetened it with molasses—keep stirring that in, and it would be way in the night before it was done. I've seen my mother take and slice it out, and it would be red apple butter. Now you put that sugar in and it's clear. Then she'd put it in crocks. It'd mold over the top of them crocks, but that wouldn't hurt it. They can it now. That's good eating.

We had big gardens—planted by the signs. Most people through here now still plant by the signs. Man yesterday told me not to sow my tobacco seed till next week. It wasn't a good time this week. He goes by the signs of the moon, you know. He said it wasn't a good time. Said to wait till next week. A lot of boys I know about even wait till a certain time to get their hair cut. One boy raised on Pigeon Roost, now, he'd fight anybody. 'Fore he'd have his hair cut, he'd wait till a certain time, you know [see *The Foxfire Book,* pp. 212–27]. My aunt always told me if I wanted my hair to grow to cut it on the new of the moon and then it would grow as the moon grows. Yeah. That made me think of it. When I was a boy, what would you say I made my hair tonic out of? Grape vines. These here wild grapes. Go and tap them and set you something under them. Get the juice out. That would help now. Make it grow better. Just cut [the vine] and set me a jar down and let it drip.

[Same way with] maples. That was where you got your maple sugar. We didn't make none ourselves, but there was people right around did. They done it mostly in the home there. They didn't go into it in a big way. But storekeepers would buy that [from you] in a store. It brought high.

That was good sweetening. And honey. Lots used that. People kept bees. Sometimes they'd swarm. Noon was when they come out. Some of them would go wild and go to the mountains. Have a tree cleaned out. They'd take off to the mountains. People'd hunt them bee trees and then cut them. [Or you can catch the swarms.] Beat on a plow point with a rock to make them settle. I've heard of men grabbing an old shotgun and shooting in them, but that there tears them up, they say. Gets them confused. Scattered. And some beat on dishpans with a spoon to make them settle. I've heard of that. The noise of that ring, I reckon, is what does it. You ever heard bees go over in the air? There is a noise, ain't they? Now, one time I was at the graveyard and they was having a decoration. Man lived right down in the holler below there had a lot of bee gums, and we seen a bee swarm a'coming. It looked like it was coming to that gathering on the little hilltop. Before it got there it turned. They was down low, you know. I don't know why [they turned]. Everybody said it scared them. If they'd got there to them people, somebody might have been hurt. But when they got there, they turned. Just rolled on over and over.

[But that maple sugar was one way of getting a little money.] And ginseng. Yeah, and that goldenseal. It brought a good price. It was scarcer than that ginseng was. Ginseng now is high. But that cultivated 'sang, it don't bring much. They can tell the difference by the fiber of that root. Now, they was an old man who is still living down here. He told me last summer about his boy. His boy bought a lot of 'sang [to resell to a dealer]. Said when he brought it to him, the old man said, "Son, you're ruint." Said, "That's culti- vated 'sang." He said, "You know what that brings?"

He said, "No." He said, "I know it isn't." But when he took it to sell it, it *was*. If he'd knowed, he said that he wouldn't have bought it. But he didn't know no better.

We gathered all kind of raw herbs. We'd pull pennyroyal and put it in a tub and take and run that off [just like making moonshine]. They bought that pennyroyal spirits at the store—so much a gallon. You get the root off and put the whole plant in there in water, put a little fire under that tub, and you have that straight pipe [com- ing out of the top of the sealed tub], and it runs out that pipe strong. And we used to get balsam. Take and get that. That was good kidney medicine. Spirits of balsam.

And now them bam buds [balm of Gilead buds]. You know about that, don't you? Boil them down and use that for a salve. They went one year for a dollar a pound. They're eighty-five cents now down here at North Wilkesboro. And there's a man that took a load of hides down there Monday. [That was another way to make money.] He took eighty-five. He called them rat hides. Muskrat hides. He said hides this year, it just ain't been cold enough so their fur's not thick. He said they was bringing a good price, though. He made money by taking them down there. He just called them rat hides.

Now, we got one pair of shoes a year, and we went barefoot except for on Sunday. Mother would make soup beans. Back then soup beans brought a good price. You've heard talk of that they call brogans? Buy those. Sell them soup beans. Take a big sackful— a bushel. Go and buy shoes and other things. Fall of the year. They would thrash those beans out. Set them a cloth on the porch—or a bedsheet or something—and thrash them out when they got dry. Took them and beat them out with a frail [flail]. They didn't bring the price they bring now. Now two pounds of beans are $1.40!

[Some people made their own shoes, since there wasn't much money. We didn't, but we made our own cloth.] Mother had a little spinning wheel. My sister took it off. Now, where we lived—you've heard talk of flax breaks, ain't you? In that old log house there was holes in there on the outside, and that was for flax breaks. And then she'd dye that. She used walnut hulls. And she used poke- berries. They called it pokeberry red. Put them in a pot and pour in a little water to cook it, you know. Dipped that in there. And she used egg shells. That give a kind of yellow color. Then make coverlets to go on them big old corded beds. And then have trundle beds under them—pull them out and somebody sleep in them, and in the morning push them back under them big old high beds. They was a pretty little old thing.

Then we kept geese to pluck for pillows and bed ticks. My mother would take ahold of them by their feet and turn them over there and pull that down off. Talk about squalling and letting on like it was a'hurting—losing them feathers. But it wouldn't take long till that growed back. Grow back prettier than it ever was. You know, one would turn off a whole lot of feathers. She had her a big old gourd. It would hold over half a bushel. Had the neck cut off. She called that her feather gourd. Put feathers down in there. That was the dandiest thing. [We didn't have to clean that down.] The geese kept clean in the branch.

One time Mother had three geese gone and we hunted for them everywhere and couldn't find them. Some of them heard an old man talking. His son-in-law lived way up in the holler from us, and he said there was three geese come over and come there. Mother said for me to come with her and we would go up and see if that is my geese. We went up there, and that man, he said, "Yeah, them geese come here," and he didn't know where from.

She said, "Them is my geese," my mother told that man.

He said, "How do you know?"

She said, she told me to catch one of them, and "I'll show him." I grabbed one and handed it to her and she had that toenail cut off. Said, "Right here." She said, "I cut that off there."

He said, "Is the others that way?"

She said, "Sure." I caught them and she said, "See there!"

He said, "Huh," he said, "them *is* yours. You *know*." Said, "Take them on."

Nelse Whitson, who is 85 years old and resides in the Raccoon Branch at Tipton Hill, reported to the writer that he carried the mail 70 years.

Whitson said his mail route started in the Tipton Hill section, where Tom Garland was postmaster and the post office was in his home, located at the farm where Orville Woodby now lives.

Whitson went from Tipton Hill to Red Hill, where another Tom Garland was postmaster and where Whitson turned back and went from there to Hollow Popular Creek, where John N. Peterson was postmaster.

Whitson walked and carried the mail with two mail pouches swung across his shoulders and was paid 33 1/3 cents a day or 2 dollars a week. It was about a 30-mile trip. He said there was several fences or drawbars across the road in the Bailey Settlement.

He said that he bought jeans cloth with some of his money that he earned carrying the mail and had his first jeans clothes homemade.

Whitson said that the schools were so few and far apart that he never had the privilege to attend school and never did learn to read and write, but he learned enough to be very good at counting figures in his mind and was good enough to operate a grocery store at Tipton Hill for 12 years.

He bought beef cattle and also swapped and traded on horses and cows in this area for many years. Whitson said he is good in figures yet, and that when he goes to the store and buys several items, by the time the merchant counts up the total amount on the adding machine, he already has it counted up in his mind.

Harrison Phillips of Brummetts Creek section is using an egg basket, which he has owned for 45 years, to carry eggs to the store. Mr. Phillips brought the basket made out of white-oak splits to Frank Griffith's store at Tipton Hill Wednesday and the basket was filled full of eggs, and Mr. Griffith told him that he would pay him a whole lot more for the basket than he would for all the eggs, as he deals in antique articles and has a large collection of Indian arrowheads on display at his store.

A local citizen reported that he was afraid of only two kinds of snakes — the big ones and the little ones.

Harvey Miller of Relief (not the writer) has recently purchased his first car.

PLATE 490   7/22/65

I had my geese fenced in. Had a rail pen. That kept them from bothering people's crops. I'd go to school in the morning and cut up apples and take stuff and feed them [on the way]. I went one morning—I had acid wood piled up there right down below where they was. I heard something or other. They had been telling bear tales and I heard something a'growling and I took off. You know, it scared me. I was pretty small. I heard something growl. I went out and got way up toward the house, and why, a man poked his head up over that acid woodpile. He went to laughing. He was a one-armed man. He said he was afraid I'd get gone [and get somebody] and afraid he might get shot!

Be sorta like that old woman I wrote about in one of my columns—but she was a witch. She'd turn into a turkey hen. There's a place called Turkey Cove, where wild turkeys would stay. One of my kinfolks would go in there early of a morning, and he got to going in there, and an old turkey hen was picking around. He got to shooting at it. He couldn't kill it. He hit all around. He'd shoot that old hog rifle—load that, pull down. Somebody told him, "You're shooting at an old turkey witch. Get you a silver bullet and shoot. You'll kill the witch, or 'bout kill it."

He did, you know, melt him a silver bullet, and one morning went in there at the same place and here come that old turkey hen

PLATE 491 Harvey with two of the chairs he saved from the log house in which he was raised. Note the witch mark over the door above his head.

PLATE 492

walking around, and he pulled down hard and shot. And it fell over, you know, flopped, rolled down hard. Gone. Disappearing. And it never come back that time. He went on home and somebody told him that that old lady was down with rheumatism and couldn't get out of bed. In a few days, she was out of bed and limped, always limped. He changed back to his old kind of bullets and never was bothered with a turkey witch no more. That was a true story. He died in Georgia. He was some of my kinfolks. My dad and mother tell me that was facts.

Them witches—we put witch marks over the door. Keep them away. They'll come and ask [to borrow] different things. You let them have a certain thing—something sharp like a knife or something—and that breaks the spell. If you refuse to give them what they ask for, some kind of bad luck will strike you. Everybody had a witch mark on their door. That was drawn on with fire coals. Let me show you a witch mark [he draws a star]. I used that a whole lot when I was young.

If the witches got too bad, you could go to them witch doctors and get them to help you. I had an uncle that was said to be a witch doctor. My daddy had a heifer. They found her rolled in a ditch. They rolled her out and she'd roll back in there. She couldn't stand up and they couldn't find nothing wrong with her. She hadn't hurt herself. And they sent for my uncle. He come, and he went and looked at her and examined her. He said, "She's bewitched." And he told Daddy, said, "Do you want me to doctor her?"

And Daddy said, "Law, yeah, drive that witch off."

He built him up a little fire and took his pocketknife and cut the ends of her ears a little off [and threw them in the fire and said some kind of words]. When that burnt up, she jumped up and run off.

He offered me that he'd teach me how to be a witch doctor when I was young. And I told my mother about it and she said, "I don't want you to get into that." I thought a whole lot about it, and I'd get out with my uncle and he'd tell me things and I got interested in it, but she said, "No, don't you get into that."

Back then, now, the witch doctors had a whole lot of work to do! Them witches now, they was local. We had them in our community. Local people.

One time a man saw a cow and she was pouring milk. [He asked to borrow some and they wouldn't give him none.] He got mad at them and come down. This old lady was milking the cow. He said, "You getting a lot of milk?"

She said, "Getting a peck bucket full."

He looked and looked at that cow and walked around and went on down the road, and the next morning that cow was dry. Never did give. And she went to nothing. I remember that. That old lady said that man put a spell—he bewitched her, you know. Put a spell on her. That used to happen. And they wasn't much they could do. My mother always stood a horseshoe up in the back of the fireplace behind the backstick to ward off the witches. Whenever I'd clean out the fireplace, she'd always say, "Harvey, put that horseshoe back."

I believe we've got them yet. Now, I seen an old woman not too long ago. She lived in the holler below me. And I had an old cow went crazy. I went down there and told her about that, and told that woman about the way that cow would do. She said, "Harvey, I'll go up there and doctor her."

She went up and she done what I told you my uncle done—had her knife and cut a little dab off the ear and she put that in a poke and took it to the house and we had a fire in the cookstove and she burned it in there. That evening we went back and that old cow was all right. She said, "Don't you talk about it. Don't tell nobody nothing." Said, "Somebody's going to be a'hurting." She claims she's a witch doctor. That ain't been too long ago. 'Bout eight, ten years ago.

Now, there's a place on Pigeon Roost called Hatterock Hill. An old man come there making fur hats and caps—that's the reason it's called Hatterock Hill—and somebody said he was a wanted man. Come a big bunch of men. You know, back then if a hundred men wanted to take a man out of jail, the law couldn't do nothing. A hundred men ruled the law. So a bunch of men came there to where that man was living under that rock cliff and got that old man and hanged him to a tree. After that, that place was hainted.

This man and me went up there one day. And he told me to climb up on that rock and, "I'll take your picture." Said, "I don't reckon there are any ghosts around." I'd been telling him that ghost story coming up the road. Well, when he got the picture back, he said, "Harvey, I got your picture back took on the Hatterock Hill and it looks like there's something—a shadow or something—up over you."

I said, "That's that ghost."

They say these here ghosts was the meanest people they is [when they were alive]. They don't believe in God or nothing. Certain people can drive them away. Drive a spike, a nail, in a tree. You can kill them ghosts—drive them away.

Now, they say if you see somebody coming . . . I heard of a woman that lives back in the holler and she seen her brother coming up the holler, and she went back in the house, went to doing other things, and waited a while. She went back and looked and never did see him no more. He never did get there, and he lived a way off. She was anxious to see him. In a few days she got word he was dead. Now, they say if you see them a'coming and [they] don't get there, that's a bad-luck sign.

Or a hen a'crowing. Now, this place where I'm wanting to go today, that old lady? I said, "You'ns got any chickens?"

She said, "I ain't got a chicken." Said, "We had one old hen and she went to crowing one day. And I told _____—he was out there with his little gun—to shoot her. You know, he had to shoot seven times before he killed that old hen. Throwed it down the hill. Throwed it away."

That man with me, he said, "What was that?"

I said, "That was a bad-luck sign for her, for a hen to go crowing like a rooster."

Yeah, now some people, they'll kill them there old roosters if they crow at night. One time when I was young, I went to Erwin [in Tennessee] and heared a rooster crowing all night down there and I thought that was something awful! When a rooster crowed of a night, he got his head cut off. People'd say some kind of bad luck was going to happen. Sometimes when they'd first go to roost they might crow two or three times, and people said there was gonna be bad weather in that many days. If he crowed three times, it would be bad weather in three days. But now if he crowed way in the night, he got his head cut off. They'd cook him and make chicken dumplings! If they didn't have nary another rooster, they'd kill the last rooster they had and get 'em another one from somebody else.

My mother believed a lot of them superstitions. One night she heared one crowing at eleven o'clock, and the next day we had that old rooster in the pot! A crowing hen was treated the same way.

And if a rooster comes to the steps and crows, that's a sign company's coming. Yeah, comes up on the steps and crows. However many times he crows, it'll be that many people coming. People bank on it. They look to that. A lot of that's fading out, though. But now like me, raised up with a lot of that, it'll still be in; but the children, they believe in some of that and some they don't. It's fading out.

Like, let's see. There's something about a frog. I forget now. There's some way you can bewitch by a frog. I've heard of girls, they claim, putting spells on boys. Take a frog, put it in a box and let it die in there, and then there's a certain bone pulled out of that frog and hooked to that boy and not let him know, and [it's] said he'll go crazy as a lunatic about that girl. Now, that's a story I've heard. Certain bone from that frog hooked up there on his shirt. You'll fall now! Some girl will hook you now!

Another thing I want to get across to you, about horseshoes. You've seen horseshoes tacked up around. Back when I was young, hawks were awful bad to catch chickens. Put that horseshoe up there. That warned the hawks off from catching little chickens. Put the horseshoes anywhere around where the chickens were.

You know, I had me a little old bantam hen setting in that cold weather the other day. She hatched out seven pretty little banty chickens. I kept putting them back in the nest every night for a couple of nights—afraid they'd get cold. Kept them in a box where that good nest was. Went out there and something or 'nother had killed every one of them. We thought it was a black rat, but couldn't see no sign. But they say, though, them old big black rats—that's what's bloodthirsty. A cat can't handle them. They say if one of them bites you, that's it. Them old black ones—poison.

And them black snakes. I've heard of them milking cows. They'll do that. There's a story about that. A man had a fine cow. She didn't give any milk and her tits, when she came in, were wet. And he didn't know what was wrong. He said he kept watching that old cow. She'd go to a stump and stand at that stump. Seed that old big black snake come out—come out there and get her milk. She'd let him do it. She'd go to that old stump. She'd know where that was.

A snake can charm anybody. And you know a cat can charm a snake? And birds. Now, we have a cat here'll bring in a lot of snakes.

Cats eat certain kinds of snakes. They can charm a bird. That tail a'going. They keep coming on up. That's the way snakes do a young'un. Mean! That's boogerman, them snakes is. They say it'll get around your neck and that's it. But there's people that will let a snake wrap around their arm. This here Florida boy come over here. He found a big old black snake up over there and he wasn't a bit more afraid of that—got it wrapped around his arm going up there. Oh, that looks scary getting toward his neck. He wasn't afraid.

Now, you know them snakes get in the woods where people is riding—you know, people riding in the woods? They'll come right down and get around anybody's neck. Fall there. Drop off the branch. They know when to do it—time to do it. One day I was going up the road here, going along. Heard something thud—come down. Looked at my feet. I stopped. There was a snake fell out of a bush. Fell right at my feet. It was an old racer.

But now people got pet snakes. I'm afraid of a snake. After we moved over here, we rented some land from an old man over on the mountain over here, and he had a pet snake and it stayed in an apple tree—hollow place in the apple tree—and he said, "If you see my pet snake around here, don't you'ns hurt it. I wouldn't take nothing for it. That's a pet." Said, "It won't bother you."

Now, my wife, we was there one day sitting under there. It poked its head out. My wife, she got her a rock and I told her, "Don't throw it. That's a pet snake." Well, she throwed that rock and it liked to come out of there, but it went back in, hurt bad. We looked for that snake every day. We never did see it no more.

That old man told us, "My pet snake is gone. I didn't want that snake killed." We didn't tell him. He said, "I ain't seen it." Said, "It's gone." We never did see it no more.

Garther Barnett's killed more than anybody. He'd kill every snake he seen. Had a rifle. He lives over there on a creekbank. He'd see a snake out on a limb—ker-bang! He'd know when he'd get one. That'd be it. The others, you know, they'd run a race with him. Keep a record. I lived over there and he run a store. He said, "I've got 140 snakes this year so far." Yeah, he went up to 300 snakes. He cleaned them out over there. You never see no more snakes. He had so far he patrolled. His wife would tend the store. He'd go up the road. You'd hear him shoot. Come back—put it on the record. He'd put down, "Killed so many snakes." Champion snake killer of Pigeon Roost.

But the old people on Pigeon Roost believed a lot of that stuff I was telling you. That was way back in the mountains [no cars,

PLATE 493 Harvey at the Barnett Cemetery on Grove Byrd's farm. Harvey's grandparents are buried there.

PLATE 494 Harvey with his neighbor, Aspie McCourry. The log building below is the house Aspie built when he and his wife first started housekeeping.

telephones, radios]. But now back then they was a lot of people on the road. [The road going up Pigeon Roost Creek] was the road that led to Tennessee. There was a lot of different people come through there traveling on horseback and walking. There'd be families. Some of them didn't have any money, and my brother—that was back before I can remember, but he remembered—he said one night they was a family of eleven. The man had lost his wife and he was moving them in to Tennessee somewheres. He had a big family, and he told my daddy, he said, "I tried all the way up the creek. It's getting late and I can't get nowhere to stay all night." He told my daddy he was a widower.

And my daddy told them, "Well, we'll have to try to keep you some way. Might fare a little." We just had two rooms and, see, they was a big family of us. But mother made beds on the floor. She had some extra bed ticks, you know. And they said they fared all right. Bedded 'em all down.

That man said he didn't have no money at all. The next morning, why, they went on up across the mountain walking. They had some things with them a'carrying them.

There was one old man come down across from Tennessee. It was a pretty cold time and he built him a fire in an old tree, and that tree stood there for years. People would say, "There is where the old man set the tree on fire." Burnt the inside out, you know. He stayed out on the ground around that.

But they was all moving. Like what we call today transient. They was changing places. I remember about one time I was up on the hill and I could see way up the road a half a mile, and seen what looked like three old women coming, and I went and told my mother. And it was up in the evening about two o'clock and she said, "Yeah, they'll come on through here."

And we kept watching for them, and we seen them coming. They was going to Huntdale. They went on down the creek, them old women. They didn't stop and talk. They just went on through like they was in a hurry.

Some went in wagons but most walked. I can't remember, but they said there was a boy went through. He was a kind of a queer boy. Said he had a big old dog right with him, and he went through, oh in a hurry. And the next day they was some people come through a'hunting for him; you know, a'tracing after him. Said there was something wrong with him. He wasn't right. We told them we seen him go up the road. Had a dog. Said, "Yeah." Said, "He left with a big dog." Went on. We never heard. See, like that, you never would hear no more.

And there was peddlers on the road. We called them Irish peddlers. They carried it on their back, you know. Sorta like a five-and-ten, little things. Tablecloths and all kinds of little things. Needles and stuff like that. What you used at home. Anybody could buy some good stuff from them. Ribbons.

Them peddlers, the way they worked that, they had a house below me. The people in the house kept boarders. They would be two or three of them Irish peddlers and they'd go in different directions. Like one would go across Bean Creek, and one to Cherry Gap. Come Saturday, they'd stay there over the weekend. You'd see them sitting out under shade trees. They knew where to come to. On Monday morning, they would take off a different way.

You had to pay money to them peddlers mostly. I know about one, one time, come to our home. My sister, we was out in the field and he come about dinnertime. He was a new one, you know. He got her to get dinner for him. He didn't pay no money, but he give her things to pay for the dinner. Said, "I'll give you this and give you that for my dinner."

And back then we had what we called a wheel store. Did you ever hear talk of a wheel store? They would come and have like a certain time on like Monday morning. Everybody [in the community] would gather up to a certain place and wait for the wheel store. Now they done good trading too. It was a big old truck and what we call now a trailer. He had his stuff in there like a store. You go in there and get what you wanted. He come from back in Yancey County. He would buy roots and herbs, too.

There was a man down one time. He wouldn't get up there where

I lived, up over Hatterock Hill. He would come down there as far
as the mail come. Mail come down there on the creek where Ike
Lewis lived, and people would meet out there and wait for him.
He'd be on horseback.

But one morning, I guess they was twenty people there. We seen
the old man what run that store [which was in competition with
the wheel store most of them dealt with]. And he come up there
where people had roots and herbs and eggs and everything [ready
to] sell to that wheel store, and he said, "What do you get for
this stuff?"

And we wouldn't tell him, you know.

And he said, "Take it down to *my* store, and I'll give you more
money than that." Said, "I want your people's trade up here."

And some of them went and talked with him. Were going down
there. And come to me and asked me, and I said, "No." I had a
bunch of stuff, you know. Eggs and chickens. And I said, "No, I'm
not going."

They said, "Why?"

I said, "Well, you've got a special day [on prices from this new
man]." I said, "If we all go, this [regular] man maybe won't come
back here no more if he sees us going down there." I said, "We'd
better keep [our regular man] here." I said, "[This new man is]
going to give us a special day, but next week he might not give us
as much as our [regular] man does." I said, "We better hold to
it."

Some of them said, "You're right about that." You know, he had
a list. He handed it around. Had a list of what he'd give. He went
on back. Said, "Come on down." He went on back. They's *some*
went. Just a few went.

That Hatterock Hill is fixed now. Back then it was rough. Had
more trouble there than anyplace on Pigeon Roost Road. When
we got our road fixed there, why, that mail come right past home.
And that held up for years. That there was WPA work. Fixed it
and we got our mail through. People ordered more stuff again than
they do now. There was a dozen big mail-order houses. When he
went on horseback, he'd have that horse loaded down with packages
tied, swinging.

After I married, me and my wife had three children—two girls
and a boy. After we had the first two, we moved down off Pigeon
Roost on account of them going to school. [It was too hard for
them to get there from our old home.] They all went through high
school. That's their graduation pictures over there. They got a lot
more of an education than I got.

INDEX OF PEOPLE

THE KIDS

Lynette Williams
Jay Yeary
Tommy York
Tim Young

THE CONTACTS

Ben Bar
Carol Bates
Pearl Bates
Florence and Lawton Brooks
Mrs. E. H. Brown
Marinda Brown
Dr. Rexel Brown
Dr. John Browne
Iola Cannon
Mr. and Mrs. Buster (Buck) Carver
Oscar Cook
Ethel Corn
Betty Crane
Lloyd Crumley
Carrie Cummings
Arthur Davis
Hazel DeMent

Mack Dickerson
Arthur Dills
Bertha Dockins
Happy Dowdle
Rex Duvall
Harriet Echols
Mr. and Mrs. Ernest Franklin
Sue Gainous
Lelia Gibson
Jack Grist
Blanche Harkins
Etta Hartley
Babe Henson
Henry Hicks
Stanley Hicks
Ernest Hodges
Roy and Milton Hodges
Edd Hodgins
Hershel House
John Rice Irwin
Bell Jones
Nora Jones
Daisy Justice
Helen Justice
Betty Justus

Ada Kelly
Hattie Kenny
Mr. and Mrs. Isaac Lovell
Mrs. Guy McCall
Mrs. Tom MacDowell
Veler Marcus
Oscar Martin
Ethel Meadows
E. O. and Marie Mellinger
Harvey J. Miller
Noel Moore
Phil Nichols
Richard Norton
Mrs. Geraldine Owens
Margaret Owens
Delma Patterson
John and Burma Patterson
Jucy Payne
Bill Phillips
Dave Pickett
Esco Pitts

Jake Plott
Fred Potter
Jean Ramey
Ernest Riddle
Hayes Rogers
Vaughn Rogers, Sr.
Clyde Runion
Kenny Runion
Nannie Ann Sanders
Mrs. Rae Shook
Jullia Smith
Mrs. M. C. Speed
Harley Thomas
Willie Underwood
Jake and Bertha Waldroop
Wayne Wall
Clay Ward
Ray Ward
Willard Watson
Leonard Webb
M. S. York

INDEX

Italic numerals *4*, *5*, and *6* refer to
Foxfire 4, *Foxfire 5*, and *Foxfire 6*, respectively.